Ill-Starred General

GEN. BRADDOCK.

Ill-Starred General

---◆---

BRADDOCK
OF THE COLDSTREAM GUARDS

by
LEE McCARDELL

. . . as the human tale unfolds its chapters of confusion and misfortune, so all proportions and relations fade and change.
— Winston Churchill

UNIVERSITY OF PITTSBURGH PRESS

Published by the University of Pittsburgh Press, Pittsburgh, Pa., 15260
Copyright © 1958, University of Pittsburgh Press
All rights reserved
Feffer and Simons, Inc., London
Manufactured in the United States of America

Paperback reprint 1962 (abridged), 1986 (unabridged)

Library of Congress Cataloging-in-Publication Data

McCardell, Lee.
  Ill-starred general

  Bibliography: p. 315
  Includes index.
    1. Braddock, Edward, 1695?–1755. 2. Great Britain. Army—Biography. 3.
Generals—Great Britain—Biography. 4. Great Britain—History, Military—18th
century. 5. Braddock's Campaign, 1755. 6. United States—History—French
and Indian War, 1755–1763—Campaigns. I. Title.
[DA67.1.B7M35 1986]   973.2′6   86-7015
ISBN 0-8229-5903-8 (pbk.)

CONTENTS

AUTHOR'S ACKNOWLEDGMENT

The author wishes to acknowledge, with sincere appreciation, the help of many friends and institutions in the collection and organization of material for this book. Without their assistance the book could not have been written. He wishes particularly to express his indebtedness to the late Henry Fickus, director of research at the Peabody Library, Baltimore; to Lloyd A. Brown, former librarian of the Peabody, now director of the Chicago Historical Society, and to all the members of the Peabody Library staff. In a large measure this is *their* book.

Others to whom he owes a special debt of gratitude include Francis C. Haber, editor of the Maryland Historical Magazine; Mrs. Ruth H. Martin, director of the Fort Necessity Museum at Farmington, Pennsylvania; Charles F. Wemyss Brown, of Glasgow, Scotland; Edmund Nicholls, of London, England; General Sir Gordon Holmes Alexander MacMillan, former governor and commander-in-chief at Gibraltar; William G. Renwick, of Weston, Massachusetts; Colonel Ian Wm. Gore-Langton M.B.E., commander of the Coldstream Guards; and Major Bobbie Phillips, Coldstream regimental adjutant.

He wishes to thank the Earl of Ilchester for permission to quote from his Lordship's *Lord Hervey and His Times* that portion of Hervey's letter relative to Fanny Braddock which appears in

Chapter IV; the American Historical Association for permission to quote excerpts from *Military Affairs in North America* by Stanley Pargellis; and the Clement Library, at the University of Michigan, Ann Arbor, for permission to quote from the Albemarle-Robinson correspondence contained in the Shelburne Papers.

The author is further indebted to the British Museum, the Principal Probate Registry, the Public Records Office, the Royal United Service Institution, the Lord Chamberlain of St. James's Palace, the College of Arms, the Guildhall Librarian, the Goldsmith's Company, and the Company of Gunsmiths in London; the Scots Ancestry Research Society and the Registrar General's Office in Edinburgh; the Bodleian Library at Oxford; the Victoria Art Gallery and Municipal Libraries, of Bath; the Royal Archives, of Windsor Castle; the Henry E. Huntington Library and Art Gallery, of San Marino, California; the Newberry Library, of Chicago; the New York Public Library; the Congressional Library at Washington, D. C.; the Enoch Pratt Free Library of Baltimore; the Pennsylvania Historical Society; the Maryland Historical Society; the Virginia Historical Society; and the State Historical Society of Wisconsin.

Finally, he wishes to thank Mrs. Agnes Starrett, director of the University of Pittsburgh Press, for her patience and painstaking in editing his manuscript; Mrs. Janetta Somerset Ridgely, of the Baltimore *Sun*, for many helpful suggestions in the preparation of the manuscript; and Miss Agnes Gosnell, of *The Sun*, for the tedious task of typing both manuscript and notes. He is indebted to his wife, Nancy Arnold McCardell, for tireless hours of research in Baltimore, New York, and London—and most of all, for encouragement to carry the project to completion.

January, 1958   LEE MCCARDELL

Ill-Starred General

BRADDOCK
OF THE COLDSTREAM GUARDS

BRADDOCK'S ROAD

BRADDOCK'S ROAD ········

Bedford

US 220

Cumberland

Pennsylvania
Maryland

US 30

PA 31

Ligonier

Youghiogheny River Lake

Greensburg

Mt. Pleasant

Connellsville

Ohiopyle

Murrysville

US 22

Youghiogheny R.

US 119

Fort Necessity

Allegheny R.

Brownsville

Uniontown

Ohio R.

Pittsburgh

PA 19

PA 136

US 40

Monongahela R.

Washington

Niles Anderson/Historical Society of Western Pennsylvania

I

END OF THE ROAD

1694–1755

E VERY SUMMER the bulldozers take another kink, another grade out of Braddock's road. U. S. Route 40, they call it now. So many changes have been made during the past 200 years that you have to leave the paved highway and search the woods and fields on either side to find the scars that mark the path it used to follow.

The original path was an Indian trail that crossed the Allegheny Mountains from the headwaters of the Potomac at Wills Creek, to the forks of the Ohio, now Pittsburgh. English traders blazed the trail early in the eighteenth century and drove their packhorses over it single file. Young Washington used it in 1753 on his mission to the French. Not until the hot, dry summer of 1755 did it become a full fledged road. That was the summer Major General Edward Braddock, marching a British army against the French at Fort Duquesne, widened and graded the trail for wagons and gun carriages.

Seven or eight miles from the forks of the Ohio, on the river hillside of a Pittsburgh suburb which bears his name, Braddock's army was routed in a battle with French and Indians. General Braddock himself was wounded mortally. By cart, litter, and horseback he retreated with his disorganized troops over the road he had built through the mountain wilderness.

A squat granite monument in a clump of pine trees, about a mile west of Fort Necessity, is presumed to mark Braddock's grave. No one knows exactly where he died, but the end came at an overnight camp somewhere in this general neighborhood, perhaps in a thicket of crabapple trees down in a hollow along a little stream which the old road followed behind the pines.

For two hundred years historians have denounced Edward Braddock as an adventurer, a sycophant, a bully brutal in his dealings with both soldiers and civilians. They have pictured him as a proud and pompous redcoat, a martinet who scorned the advice of a prescient young colonel of Virginia militia and who died of his own pigheaded stupidity in an Indian massacre which might have been avoided.

In truth, however, there is not much disinterested testimony to support all the calumny heaped upon Braddock.

Here is his story. It begins before he was born.

II

ANCESTRY AND EDUCATION
OF A GUARDSMAN

1660–1710

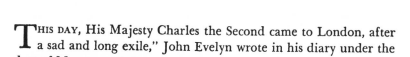

"THIS DAY, His Majesty Charles the Second came to London, after a sad and long exile," John Evelyn wrote in his diary under the date of May 29, 1660.[1]

Oliver Cromwell, arch-rebel and Lord Protector, had been dead nearly two years. His Puritan Commonwealth had collapsed. The exiled King's father, Charles I, condemned to death as a tyrant and a traitor, had become a martyr.[2] Every living Londoner knew the story, how the King had stepped through a window of the Whitehall palace Banqueting Hall onto a scaffold where the executioner waited leaning on his ax, a cold, sunny January day, eleven years before.[3] One blow of the ax had cut off the King's head.[4]

And now in 1660 that King's exiled son landing at Dover, May 23, from The Hague, had ridden up to London in a stately coach and entered the city on his thirtieth birthday.[5] Twenty thousand soldiers marched and rode into London with him. A mounted troop, pushing through the crowded streets at the head of the procession, brandished their swords and shouted:

"God save King Charles the Second!"

Church bells pealed. Horns blew. Kettledrums thumped. Butchers banged their knives together. Girls in crimson petticoats screamed: "God bless King Charles!"

John Evelyn, the diarist, stood in the Strand and watched the King drive past. Later he watched the girls in the crimson petticoats dance around the maypole. Bonfires were lighted after dark. Beeves were barbecued. Drunken soldiers staggered around the streets, pinching women, smashing Puritans' windows, stumbling to their knees in the taverns to drink the new King's health and bawl:

"Go' bless King Charles . . . a full and a free Parl'ment!" [6]

*   *   *

The free Parliament, meeting in September, passed an act for the "speedy disbanding of the army and garrisons of this country." [7] England was sick of soldiers. Five years of civil war had been followed by thirteen of military dictatorship under Cromwell.[8] But King Charles II contrived to keep, for the security of his person and his royal household, three troops of life guards, a regiment of horse, and two of footguards.[9] One of the regiments of foot was the Coldstream, organized in 1650 and commanded by "Honest George" Monck. The regiment had its name from a little town on the north bank of the river Tweed from where Monck had set out to meet the King at Dover and see him safely into London.[10]

The only regiment of Cromwell's New Model to survive the Stuart Restoration, the Coldstream, became the Coldstream Regiment of Foot Guards.[11] It adopted *Nulli Secundus* as its motto. To repay its commander for his services in the Restoration, the King created Monck a baron, Earl of Torrington, Duke of Albemarle, a gentleman of the bedchamber (salary £1,000 a year), knight of the garter, privy counselor, master of the horse, and captain general (pension, £7,000 a year).[12] When Monck died in 1669 he was succeeded as commander of the Coldstream by the Right Honorable William Earl of Craven, eldest son of a former Lord Mayor of London and a veteran of the Thirty Years' War, in which he had served under the great Gustavus Adolphus.[13]

The primary function of the Coldstream was ceremonial. It performed guard duty at St. James's Palace, an old Tudor castle of faded red brick in St. James's Park, the official residence of the King's younger brother, James Duke of York. Sometimes the Coldstream garrisoned the "Tower" or relieved other foot guards on duty at the royal palace at Whitehall where the King lived. A field officer of the foot guards was always in waiting upon the King; a detachment of foot guards followed him whenever he travelled.[14]

At Windsor Castle, on June 17, 1682, King Charles II signed a commission constituting one Edward Braddock, a lieutenant in Captain William Wakelin's company of the Coldstream. He became the father of the subject of this book. The commission was one of three authorized that day by the King, presumably to fill vacancies.[15]

Edward Braddock, sire, appears to have been a member of a highly respectable but undistinguished Staffordshire family whose arms—*argent a greyhound courant within a bordure engrailed sable* —had been recorded by the College of Heralds in 1663.[16] The arms and pedigree of another Braddock family had been recorded in Norfolk in 1563.[17] Under such variations as Bridock, Bradock, Bredock, Bredocke, Braddocke, Brideoak and Briddocke the name also appeared occasionally in the court records and parish registers of London and the home and midland counties. These Braddocks included a mariner, a ferryman, a saddler, a clerk, a factor, a debtor imprisoned at Newgate, and a Dublin alderman; all obscure and unimportant.[18]

The Staffordshire Bradocks (as William Dugdale, Esquire, Norry King-at-arms spelled the family name)[19] came from the small, remote parish of Adbaston, a crossroads hamlet in the farming country between the town of Eccleshall—known for its castle, an old episcopal palace that retained the ancient bridges over its moat— and the Shropshire border. Edmund Bradock, the head of the family, was a remote ancestor of our Braddock. John Bradock, eldest of five sons of Edmund Bradock, appears to have been sent to St. Peter's College, Westminster, and elected to Trinity College, Cambridge, in 1579.[20] At least three of Edmund's seven daughters married neighborhood squires.[21] The younger sons probably were apprenticed to the trades, as was customary in the families of the smaller gentry, and some of these sons, no doubt, went up to London. Edmund's fourth son had been christened Edward.[22]

EDWARD BRADDOCK, GRANDSIRE

Three years after the Restoration, an Edward Braddock, a twenty-one-year old wax chandler of St. Martin's-in-the-Fields, was granted a license to marry Elizabeth Cooke, spinster daughter of Richard Cooke, a farrier in the neighboring parish of St. Giles-in-the-

Fields.[23] The bridegroom was no ordinary tradesman. He played the harpsicon and sang so well that when he was 18 he had been sworn a Gentleman of the Chapel Royal, one of twenty choristers paid £70 a year to sing in the King's chapel at Whitehall.[24] These were the grandparents of the man whose story unravels in this book.

Services and prayers were read in the Chapel Royal three times a day. The Princesses Anne and Mary, daughters of the King's brother, the Duke of York, by his first wife, had been confirmed there. On holy days the King attended Chapel Royal services with the principal nobility. The most distinguished ecclesiastics preached. On Sundays and holy days the organ and choir were augmented by the sackbuts, cornets, and twenty-four violins of the King's band. Gentlemen and children (boys) of the Chapel Royal—the boys in Tudor gold and scarlet—sang the favorite hymns of the royal family.[25]

In an age when advancement was largely by royal favor, the position of a Gentleman of the Chapel Royal was no mean connection for a London wax chandler. Access to the King, or at least to his court, was a long step toward worldly success. Elizabeth Cooke's father must have been satisfied that she was making a good match. She was married with his consent to Edward Braddock at St. Magdalen in Old Fish street.[26] The year after their marriage, while still a Gentleman of the Chapel Royal, Braddock also became a member of the Westminster Abbey choir. Six years later he was appointed master of the Abbey children,[27] a position which made him responsible for their moral and Christian education as well as their musical education.

He and his wife had at least two children of their own, a son named Edward, and a daughter Elizabeth.[28]

At an early age Elizabeth married John Blow, a talented Chapel Royal boy soprano until his voice began to crack, then organist at Westminster Abbey and master of the Chapel Royal children, to whom he taught music, religion, reading, writing, arithmetic, geography, history, and the rudiments of Latin.[29] In 1677 Blow was named organist of the Chapel Royal, and from Archbishop Sancroft received the Lambeth degree of doctor of music. Thereafter he was known as "Dr. Blow," and although his forte was church music, he wrote a charming little masque, *Venus and Adonis,* for Mary Davis, a mistress of the King.[30]

EDWARD BRADDOCK, FATHER

But to the ears of Edward Braddock II, perhaps watching the King's red-coated foot guards parade at Whitehall and St. James's, no music seems to have been so stirring as that of a drum. The purchase of a commission was the established method of launching young gentlemen upon military careers.[31] An ode which his brother-in-law, Dr. Blow, had composed in honor of the King for New Year's Day 1681, may have helped win him royal approval. At any rate, young Braddock's connections were good enough to obtain him a lieutenancy in the elite Coldstream, a regiment generously officered by sons of the aristocracy.[32] Thus the father of our General led the way into the career his son, Edward III, was to follow unto death.

As a lieutenant of the Coldstream, Edward Braddock received £73 per year, subject to systematic deductions stemming from an arrangement under which the King farmed out the payment of his army to a contractor who received a commission of one shilling in every pound.[33] All army officers were gentlemen and £73 per annum were not necessarily enough to sustain the cultivated tastes of a gentleman in wine, women, horses, and periwigs. It was assumed, however, that a gentleman would have other sources of income and regard his pay as an honorarium. Those who did not were looked down upon as soldiers of fortune.[34]

If the low rate of pay and the purchase system combined to exclude from the army nearly all but men of independent means, it was a combination which met with general approval. The propertied classes, the only people whose opinions counted in Parliament, distrusted a standing army as a standing threat to English liberty. They had no wish to see it commanded by either mercenaries or courtiers dependent upon the pleasure of the crown.[35]

The colonel of a regiment was its proprietor in all but name. He contracted with the government to provide his men with clothing and equipment. By sharp practice on both accounts he was expected to clear £600 a year over and above his pay. Bribery for promotions, a common practice, also was profitable. Captains drew pay for all soldiers whose names appeared on their company rolls, and in spite of periodic musters to verify written returns, rolls were padded. This fraud and the manipulation of other reckonings too often enabled the average captain to rob the government of about £200 a year.[36]

The pay of a common soldier was 8 pence a day in a regiment of the line, 10 pence a day in the Guards. Normal peacetime enlistment was for life-long service. There were no age limits, no fixed standards of physical fitness. Beggars, vagrants, rogues, jailbirds filled the ranks. Desertion was frequent, discipline difficult, and punishment barbarous. Sometimes the disobedient soldier sat on the ground, one firelock under his hams and another over his neck being brought together forcibly by tightening a couple of cartouche box straps. Another form of correction was "riding the horse," a sharp wooden beam which the culprit straddled, his legs dragged down by a 60-pound weight on each foot. And the lash was used without mercy.[37]

The only army barracks were a few improvised at Somerset House, formerly the cold and draughty, though elegant resident of the King's mother, Queen Henrietta Maria, on the left bank of the Thames below Whitehall; at the Savoy, a vast stone building used as a hospital, a little farther up the river; and at the King's Mews, the royal stables at Whitehall. A few troops were stationed at the Tower. But most of the rank and file were put up in livery stables, cheap taverns, and ale houses. Officers found lodgings wherever they could, preferably in Westminster, near the old royal palace of Whitehall.[38]

Whitehall was a rambling jumble of gables, dormers, and Tudor chimneys hitched to a palladian building of Portland stone called the Banqueting Hall, scene of the first Charles' execution. A double-towered gateway of ornamental brick, studded with terra cotta busts and statues, opened on a maze of cobbled courtyards, a formal garden, a tennis court, and a bowling green. The royal apartments looked out upon the river, a privy stairway leading from the King's lodgings to a landing stage where the royal barge put in.[39]

Every morning the gay, cynical King, nicknamed "Old Rowley," walked in St. James's Park, behind Whitehall, to romp with the pet spaniels that made a stench of his bedroom. He was a great walker, striding along at a rapid pace. Hearing that Lieut. Braddock's company commander, Captain Wakelin, had wagered he could walk around St. James's Park five time in two hours, the King showed up one morning with his brother, the Duke of York, to watch the captain try it and to bet on the outcome. Wakelin won. He did five laps in an hour and forty-three minutes.[40]

But the park had another attraction for the King. Its gravel paths skirted the terrace garden walls of several houses facing Pall Mall. In one of these houses lived Nell Gwynn, whom the King was reported to have carried off from the Theatre Royal, Drury Lane, to become one of his many mistresses.[41]

Lieut. Braddock would soon discover that mere proximity to the court was no guarantee of advancement. Regardless of his qualifications as a soldier he could never hope to rise in the world as rapidly as favorites like John Churchill, thirty-two-year-old colonel of the Royal Regiment of Dragoons. John was the son of Sir Winston Churchill, a clerk comptroller of the Green Cloth, a department of the royal household concerned mainly with the commissariat. John Churchill had been commissioned an ensign in the First Foot Guards in 1666. He had served in Tangiers and Flanders. More rewarding than his military record was the fact that his sister, Arabella, was a mistress of the Duke of York, and that his wife, Sarah Jennings, was a court beauty and the confidante of the Duke's younger daughter, Princess Anne. It followed that Churchill himself was on an intimate footing with the Duke. Churchill had another advantage. He was a handsome, green eyed charmer whose second glance set aflutter every saucy maid of honor at the court. They whispered that he had been caught in bed with the Duchess of Cleveland, one of the royal mistresses, who had welcomed Charles to Whitehall on the night of his restoration.[42]

The King had no legitimate children. Gossips thought the Duke of Monmouth, his favorite bastard, might be made legitimate.[43] Otherwise the crown would pass to the King's brother, James Duke of York, a Roman Catholic convert. Following the death of his first wife in 1671, James had married the Catholic Princess Mary of Modena.[44] Two years later he had ceased attending Anglican services in the Chapel Royal. His younger daughter by his first marriage, the Princess Anne, often sat alone in the King's closet at the chapel receiving the bows and ceremonies normally directed toward the royal family. In 1684 Anne married the Protestant Prince George of Denmark, a man of few words and those in bad French. Anne's older sister, Mary, was the wife of William Prince of Orange, hereditary chief of the Protestants on the continent.[45]

Many English Protestants feared a Popish plot to restore the Catholic Church to English power. Thomas Otway's play, *Venice Preserved,* put these fears on the stage of the Theatre Royal in

Drury Lane the year Lieut. Braddock joined the Coldstream.[46] Openly accused of conspiring against the King, the Earl of Shaftesbury fled to Holland. The Duke of Monmouth, named a co-conspirator, followed him.[47] William Lord Russell was clapped into the Tower of London, charged with having plotted to waylay the royal coach and murder the King and his brother. In Lincoln's Inn Fields, a residential square where the Coldstream sometimes paraded, the foot guards helped keep the crowd back from a scaffold where Russell was beheaded.[48]

On Monday morning, February 2, 1685, the King had an apoplectic fit.[49] He lingered four days, amid the coming and going of doctors, bishops, bastards, mistresses, and, muffled in a cloak and using the back stairway, a Benedictine monk who was reported to have finally confessed him. Charles died shortly before noon, Friday. At 3 o'clock the Guards paraded at Whitehall gate to hear heralds proclaim James Duke of York, King James II. The new King promptly renewed the commissions of all Coldstream officers, including Braddock. To ingratiate himself, he granted the additional rank of lieutenant-colonel to all captains of his foot guards.[50]

For the coronation of the new King, on St. George's Day, Lieut. Braddock turned out in a brand new fold-faced scarlet coat, gold-fringed sash, polished steel corselet studded with gold nails, red broadcloth breeches, black turned-up hat with gold lace and a tour of white feathers. His regiment was posted around Westminster Abbey.[51] The Coldstream's aging commander, Lord Craven, followed the new King and his pale, dark-eyed Queen into the Abbey. The Queen's purple velvet train stretched out seven yards behind her on the blue carpet laid to the west door. Dr. Blow had resigned as the Abbey organist but he sang with the basses of the choir that day. As a peer of the realm, Lord Craven stood by when the Archbishop of Canterbury placed the crown on the new King's head. The crown was too big. It slipped down over the upper part of James's face.[52]

A Protestant uprising to put the exiled Duke of Monmouth on the throne had been anticipated, and nobody was surprised, early one morning in June, when word reached London that the Duke had landed from a Dutch ship at Lyme Regis, a small port on the Devonshire coast. Monmouth had declared war in a wordy proclamation denouncing King James as a "popish usurper of the Crown." [53] Seven companies of the Coldstream marched from London to help put down Monmouth's rebellion. After a rout of the Duke's army, at the battle of Sedgemoor, they helped take rebel prisoners to Salisbury, returning in mid-July to London where Monmouth was beheaded on Tower Hill.[54]

James used the rebellion as an excuse to increase the size of his standing army. Thirteen thousand troops, including the Coldstream Guards, were encamped at Hounslow Heath on the outskirts of London.[55] Roman Catholic recruits, the first since the Restoration, were enlisted from Ireland. Protestant officers who objected were cashiered. In a declaration of indulgence, proclaiming religious toleration, the King abolished religious tests for public office.[56] Four Roman Catholic peers were sworn in as members of the Privy Council. A Catholic was appointed to the deanery of Christ Church at Oxford University. The Papal Nuncio was received in state at Windsor. Catholic schools and chapels, closed since the Commonwealth, were reopened.[57]

Mass was celebrated publicly in the Chapel Royal, and the King was so pleased by the performance of an anthem composed by an Italian that he asked Dr. Blow if he could produce anything so good. Blow, who had been made a member of the royal band by the new King and appointed composer in ordinary to His Majesty, had just completed a new anthem, "I behold and Lo!" It was sung the following Sunday in the Chapel Royal, Edward Braddock I presumably in the choir.

At the close of the service the King sent his Jesuit confessor, Father Edward Petre, to express his approval to the Doctor. In his own opinion, the priest added:

"The anthem was too long."

"That's the opinion of one fool—I heed it not," snapped the Doctor.[58]

From Holland, where he had hoped to enlist the aid of England in a Grand Alliance against France, William of Orange watched his father-in-law anxiously. James was 52 years old. All five of his children by his second wife, Mary of Modena, had died soon after birth, and she was believed beyond having any more now. That William's Protestant wife, Mary, James's older daughter by his first marriage, would succeed her father, was a prospect generally taken for granted until the incredulous news broke—at first in the coffee houses, where all such choice morsels fell—that James's Catholic Queen was going to have another baby.[59]

It was a boy, born June 10, 1688. Protestant pamphleteers suggested the baby was either a bastard, or a base-born imposter slipped into the Queen's bed in a warming pan, probably with the contrivance of all forty people who were reported to have crowded into her bedroom and its anteroom to watch the royal delivery. Even Princess Anne, who still lived at Whitehall, was skeptical of the baby's parentage. But Braddock's regimental commander, Lord Craven, a member of the Privy Council, was one of those who signed the infant's birth certificate. The child was christened James Francis Edward.[60]

Only a few key conspirators knew that a letter, signed in cipher by seven Protestant peers, had been sent secretly to Mary's husband, William of Orange, inviting him to invade England. But every tavern soon heard rumors of troop concentration on the Dutch coast. Mail from Holland had been halted. Pacquet boats stopped sailing. Londoners hummed the words of a new popular song:

> The English confusion to Popery drink
> Lillibulero Bullen a la . . .[61]

And late on a Saturday night, November 3, a horseman galloped into Whitehall with the long awaited alarm. A Dutch fleet of six hundred vessels, bound west, had sailed through the straits of Dover that afternoon.[62] Three days later another jack-booted courier arrived from the south coast: William of Orange and his army had landed at Torbay, in Devon. Next came word that William, riding into Exeter on a white horse, had been greeted by white-surpliced choristers singing a Te Deum in the Exeter Cathedral. At Honiton, a few miles east of Exeter, a young English viscount-colonel of dragoons and men from the King's cavalry regiments had deserted to join William.[63]

King James called a meeting of all ranking officers still in London. One was General John Churchill. Another was the Duke of Grafton, a bastard of the late King Charles, who had succeeded Churchill as colonel of the First Regiment of Foot Guards. A third was Lieutenant Braddock's colonel, eighty-year-old Lord Craven of the Coldstream. If any of his officers had any scruples about fighting for him, said the King, he would be willing to take back their commissions. But as officers and gentlemen he hoped they would not repeat the shameful performance of the colonel of dragoons at Honiton. There was no question of Craven's loyalty.

Churchill, who already had made secret overtures to William, brazenly declared that he would fight to the last drop of his blood for the King. The Duke of Grafton was equally emphatic in his protestation of loyalty.[64]

James set out by coach for Salisbury. Churchill and Grafton followed him. Within a week, both of them, along with Princess Anne's husband, Prince George of Denmark, had sneaked away in the night to join William. At Whitehall, where Braddock was on duty with the Coldstream, sentinels were doubled over General Monck's old house, a dwelling in the palace yard where Anne lived with Churchill's wife, Sarah. But a morning came when both women were gone. Lord Craven himself questioned the sentries. He was told that in the middle of the night the Princess and the General's wife had slipped down a back stairway and left by a side door.[65]

"God help me," groaned the King when he got back from Salisbury. "My own children have forsaken me!" [66]

"The great favorites at court, priests and Jesuits, fly or abscond," Evelyn wrote in his diary for December 3. "Everything, till now concealed, flies abroad in the public prints, or is carried in the streets. . . . It looks like a revolution." [67]

London rowdies barricaded streets, brandishing sticks tied with orange ribbon and shouting:

"No Popery! A free Parliament! The Protestant religion." [68]

The palace gates at Whitehall were closed. A cavalry troop kept its horses saddled. The Chapel Royal plate taken to the home of the Spanish Ambassador near Lincoln's Inn Fields was stolen when a mob broke into the embassy, sacked the house, and set it afire.[69]

On the night of December 10 the Queen and the infant Prince of Wales left Whitehall. Half a dozen sentries saw them go, about 2 o'clock in the morning—two men, two nurses, the Queen, and the baby Prince. They went out through a little garden, using a master key. A carriage was waiting for them.[70]

Next night the King himself left, by a secret door in his bedroom and a private stairway. Wearing a short black periwig, an old camlet cloak, and a pair of shabby boots, he passed himself off on the Coldstream sentries as a servant of Sir Edward Hales, a Catholic who commanded the Fourteenth Regiment of Foot. The King's flight was revealed at breakfast time by the Duke of Northumberland, another royal bastard who commanded a troop of Life Guards.

The Duke was a Lord of the Bedchamber. In the absence of the Queen he had slept on a pallet in the King's room. He said the King had got up and left about 3 A.M., giving him strict orders not to open the door of the bed-chamber until the usual hour.[71]

All the higher army officers in London met later that day in Whitehall. Presumably on the advice of Lord Craven they decided to submit to William's authority; but they agreed, until they knew more about his intentions, to keep their men together and help civil authorities maintain order.[72]

On the following Sunday afternoon, much to everybody's surprise, the King came riding back to Whitehall in his coach with a mounted escort of Life Guards. He had expected to make his getaway on a Custom House hoy moored on the Thames below the city, but a party of Kentish fishermen had upset his plan by robbing him and bringing him ashore without, at first, recognizing him.[73]

His flight interrupted, James wrote a letter to the Prince of Orange, now at Windsor, asking him to come to London for a conference and telling him that St. James's Palace would be placed at his disposal. But the King had scarcely settled himself at Whitehall that Sunday afternoon when a Dutch officer, Count Zulestein, and two Dutch trumpeters cantered up to the palace gate under a flag of truce, with William's reply.

"Since I am here I hope he will come to St. James's," the King told the Count.

"I must plainly tell Your Majesty," replied Zulestein, "that His Highness the Prince will not come to London while there are any troops here which are not under his orders."

Zulestein rode away and the King went to bed. The Coldstream mounted guard as usual.[74]

Country people coming into London for market early next morning said blue-coated Dutch soldiers had occupied the suburban villages of Chelsea and Kensington, west of the city. All that day the guards at Whitehall and St. James's kept looking westward, expecting to see the Dutch. None had appeared when night fell, but a little after 10 o'clock a Coldstream sentry at St. James's challenged several horsemen riding down the mall in the park.

"Stand!" cried the sentry. "For whom are you?"

"The Prince of Orange."

One of the horsemen was Count de Solmes, an officer of William's staff. He asked to be taken to Lord Craven. He told the old Earl that three battalions of Dutch infantry and cavalry were coming down the avenue behind him, that the Coldstream Guards must be withdrawn from Whitehall. Drums were beating now across the Park. Lighted matches of Dutch musketeers glowed in the darkness. Craven went to the King's apartment. James was undressing for bed. He said there must be some mistake. Craven called in de Solmes who showed the King a written order to occupy Whitehall.

The old Earl reminded the King that he still held his commission, that as an officer and a gentleman he was perfectly willing to stand and fight, that not withstanding his age he would rather be cut to pieces than surrender. But the King said resistance was useless. He told Craven to comply with William's order and withdraw his men. At 11 o'clock that night, a week before Christmas, the Coldstream marched out of Whitehall, down the Strand, through narrow Fleet street and up Ludgate Hill, past St. Paul's. The bells of St. Paul's began to ring. It started to rain.[75]

Next morning the regiment was drawn up near the Tower of London to receive orders to march on to Rochester.[76] It was still raining. The ranks were "not well pleased," Evelyn noted in his diary.[77] Several dropped out of line, flung away their matchlocks, unslung their accoutrements, and walked off. But the remainder of the regiment, including Lieutenant Braddock, obeyed orders. At Rochester they overtook the King. He had come down the river from Whitehall in the royal barge. Three officers of the Coldstream called upon him and verbally surrendered their commissions.[78] Others, Edward Braddock among them, marched on down into Kent with their dejected companies to find winter quarters, some in Maidstone, some in Sitting Bourne, some in Dover.[79] The weather turned exceedingly cold, with long frosts and deep snow.[80]

A fishing smack took King James to France. His Queen and the baby prince had been sent ahead. The Most Catholic King of France, Louis le Grand, compassionately installed all three royal refugees at the Palace of St. Germain, near Paris.[81] In London, James was declared to have abdicated. On Wednesday, February 12, 1689, the kettle drums rolled and the trumpets pealed anew under the gateway at Whitehall. Heralds proclaimed William and Mary, King and Queen of England. William's brigade of blue-coated Dutch guards went on duty at Whitehall. Dutch officers took over the coffee houses in the old palace tilt yard, formerly monopolized by British guardsmen, lighted up their long clay pipes, and boasted of having driven out the Redcoats.[82]

Trusting no Englishman too far and suspecting the Coldstream to be thoroughly disaffected, William had no intention of bringing Braddock's regiment back to London. On the days fixed for the election of a new Parliament, the new King even ordered the Redcoats marched out of the towns in which they were quartered.[83] King James had increased the Coldstream in strength from twelve to seventeen companies. William reduced it to fourteen.[84] He took the regiment away from old Lord Craven and gave it to Col. Thomas Talmach, a former Coldstream captain who had got into trouble during the reign of Charles II by fighting a duel with a Jacobite officer.[85]

A few weeks later, when France declared war on Holland, William took advantage of a newly signed Anglo-Dutch treaty of alliance to order both battalions of the Coldstream to Flanders as part of a brigade under the turncoat Churchill, repaid for his treachery to James with the earldom of Marlborough.[86] On the arrival of the Coldstream at Helvoetsluys, a small, fortified island town in the dreary sand dunes of southern Holland, Lieutenant Braddock was advanced to the rank of Captain. This was a promotion which raised his pay, when he got it, with allowances for three servants, to £302.2.6 a year. The military establishment in London, where courtiers handled army funds, was undergoing a change of favorites. For months both officers and men were paid irregularly. Some of the officers were obliged to sell their horses.[87]

In all probability Captain Braddock spent the next five years in Flanders with his regiment. During this time he may have been married, perhaps for a second time, because in 1685 an Edward Braddock had been married to a Dorothy Lambert at St. Mary-le-Bone in London.[88] Dorothy seems to have disappeared from subsequent church records, lending conjecture to her death, possibly in Ghent, where Coldstream officers sometimes were joined by their wives after the regiment had gone into winter quarters. As a rule only a few favorites, recalled out of preferment, and those officers who were members of Parliament returned home to England for the winter.[89]

The Captain's mother, Elizabeth Cooke, died during his first year in Flanders. She was a lady of sufficient importance to be buried in the north cloister of the Abbey where her daughter, Elizabeth Blow, Dr. Blow's wife, had been buried in 1683.[90] The Captain's father, Edward Braddock I, was now clerk of the cheque of the Chapel Royal, a position which had increased his salary to £76 a year. It was the clerk's duty to keep an attendance record of the other gentlemen and priests of the Chapel Royal, and to provide the chapel candles. He received the residue of the candles as part of his fee, and as a wax-chandler by trade, he must have known how to make the most of that arrangement.[91]

The fighting in Flanders, a war of summer maneuvers among the windmills, never reached any sharp, decisive climax. For Captain Braddock it began with a battle at the little town of Walcourt, below Namur, on an August afternoon in 1690.[92] With long siege trains of slow-footed Dutch allies, the Coldstream marched and countermarched across watery meadows, from one walled town to another. A new campaign began each spring with the arrival of King William from England, and closed on his return to London in the fall.[93] At the end of three years only the lieutenants of Braddock's regiment had anything to show for their service. Each had been given the rank of captain-lieutenant to establish his foot guard precedency over lieutenants of ordinary regiments of the line.[94]

In January, 1692, the King dismissed Churchill, now becoming better known as Marlborough. London heard the Earl was in disgrace either for taking bribes or extortion from inferior officers.[95] In Flanders, where he had made no secret of his criticism of the King's Dutch favorites, it was assumed that he was being punished for his anti-Dutch attitude.[96] The truth was, the King had been told that Marlborough was carrying on a secret correspondence with the deposed James. Queen Mary's sister, Princess Anne, and Anne's husband, Prince George of Denmark, were dismissed from court because of their close friendship with Marlborough and his wife. In May the Earl was sent to the Tower, charged with treason, but was released for lack of evidence to sustain the charge.[97]

Late that summer, in the hedgerows of the Flemish village of Steinkirk, five British regiments were cut to pieces in a bloody defeat which British officers blamed on the King's arrogant Dutch favorite—Count Solmes—the same de Solmes who had led William's Dutch guards down the mall in St. James's Park and told Lord Craven the Coldstream must withdraw from Whitehall.[98] Steinkirk was refought the following winter in Parliament, where four or five British colonels who had been in the battle joined a debate, denouncing Solmes and other Dutch officers.

"Let English soldiers be commanded by none but English generals!" the colonel argued.[99]

Talmach of the Coldstream commanded them the next summer, 1693, when they suffered another disastrous defeat in another hedgerow battle near the village of Landon. Dead and wounded, many from the Coldstream were piled waist deep. The following year Talmach himself was mortally wounded and died in a British descent on Brest. Command of the Coldstream passed to a Cambridge-educated dare-devil, John Lord Cutts, a chesty young major general of thirty-four, who had been wounded at Limerick, Steinkirk, and Brest.[100]

At the end of October, 1694, Captain Braddock and five other officers of the Coldstream were granted home leave.[101] The Captain's wife, Mary, was pregnant. About the time he reached London a smallpox epidemic broke out. Deaths increased to more than 500 a day. Queen Mary was stricken and died three days after Christmas.[102] So began another winter of almost continuous snow, with freezing temperatures that covered the Thames with ice.[103] In the midst of this bitter weather, Mary Braddock's baby was born, a boy. The Abbey was still hung in black for the Queen's funeral when the child was christened at St. Margaret's, the church beside the Abbey.[104] In the big leather-bound baptismal register, the vestry clerk wrote:

Edward Bradocks to Capt Edw by Mary [105]

The Queen's funeral was held a month to the day after baby Edward's baptism. His grandfather, old Edward Braddock, I, marched with other gentlemen of the Chapel Royal near the head of the funeral procession to the Abbey, singing all the way.[106] An elegy on the death of the Queen, a black-bordered folio pamphlet written by a young lifeguardsman named Dick Steele, was dedicated to Captain Braddock's colonel, Cutts. Cutts, who occasionally wrote poetry himself, was so flattered that he gave Steele an ensign's commission in the Coldstream and made him his secretary.[107]

Being neither a member of Parliament, nor a court favorite, Captain Braddock was under orders to rejoin his command early in the spring.[108] Passes to Holland were issued at Whitehall on March 20 for the Captain and two servants, John Smith and Joan Price.[109]

The three of them probably went aboard ship near the Tower with a party of recruits early in April.[110] That summer King William captured Namur. The Coldstream was in the thick of this fight, losing 53 men killed and 112 wounded. Braddock's role was inconspicuous, but Cutts, the Coldstream's colonel, acquired his fourth battle scar, a cut across his head.[111]

On his return to London in October the King received an unusually warm welcome. But Cutts, who came back with him, became the hero of Namur. Cutts had never been troubled with modesty. The whole town soon heard how he had led the crucial charge of the grenadiers. His own glowing accounts of his charmed life under fire led Marlborough to nickname him "the Salamander." [112] Braddock also came home that fall, but on October 10 a detail of 180 Coldstream guardsmen, commanded by Captain Braddock, was ordered from London to Newmarket, England's horse-racing center and the first of half a dozen towns the King planned to visit before Christmas.[113]

The King set out on October 17. The footguards, two days ahead of him, took up quarters at Newmarket in the home of Richard Girling. There must have been some hitch about paying for the use of Girling's house, because Captain Braddock later signed the following warrant:

Guard House Newmarket.

These are to certify that the house of Mr. Richard Girling at Newmarket with four rooms in the ground floor and two rooms one pair of stairs was wholy taken up and made use of for a guard house for the officers and soldiers of the foot guards during his majesty's stay in these parts in October last and therefore I humbly recommend him for such allowance for the same as may be thought reasonable. Given under my hand this 2nd Dec 1695.

E. Braddock [114]

King William's wars dragged on without serious fighting through the summer of 1697. They ended with a treaty of peace, signed at the village of Ryswick, near the Hague.[115] Dr. Blow celebrated the peace by composing a new anthem, "Praise the Lord, Oh My Soul," which his father-in-law, old Edward Braddock I, sang with the Chapel Royal at a Whitehall thanksgiving service.[116]

Captain Braddock was home to stay for a while. His old battalion of the Coldstream was billeted in the Tower hamlets, in London's East End,[117] but his father, who now was choir master, lay clerk,

and copyist at the Abbey, lived in the Great Sanctuary at Westminster, in a house owned by Dr. Blow; [118] and it is more than
likely that the Captain's wife and little son, Edward, lived nearby,
perhaps in one of the neighboring parishes with which the family
was associated. More children were born to the Captain's wife.
Eventually there were six, three boys and three girls.[119] The girls
appear later in our story.

EDUCATION OF EDWARD BRADDOCK III

Had his father been an officer of higher rank, or his grandfather a
gentleman of more exalted station, young Edward Braddock might
have attended Westminster school, but there is no record of his having been enrolled.[120] His father may well have shared an opinion
held by many army officers of his generation that the study of Latin
and Greek was a loss of time, that public schools encouraged bad
company, and that universities produced pedants. The Rev. Dr.
Jonathan Swift had heard this theory expounded so clearly and
forcefully on one occasion by an officer in a coffee house that he
could still repeat it word by word:

> Damn me, Doctor, say what you will, the army is the only school for
> gentlemen. Do you think my Lord Marlborough beat the French
> with Greek and Latin? Damn me, a scholar, when he comes into good
> company, what is he but an ass? Damn me, I would be glad, by God,
> to see any of your scholars with his nouns and verbs and his philoso-
> phy and his trigonometry, what a figure he would make at a siege or
> a blockade or reconnoitering, damn me! [121]

At least two competent schoolmasters, his grandfather and Dr.
Blow, were close at hand, and young Edward may have received
his early education along with the choir boys they taught. At the
same time he lived in the sterner world of wars and rumors of wars,
of political upheaval and threatened ruin. No doubt, he saw as
many reminders and heard as many yarns about King William's
Wars as young Laurence Sterne, the son of another officer who had
served in Flanders. The Braddock household, like that of Sterne's
Tristram Shandy, must have had its Uncle Toby and Corporal
Trim in repeated attacks on the counterscarp at Namur.[122] And
certainly those stories influenced his wish to be a soldier. But where
Sterne's father had been a lieutenant in a regiment of the line, disbanded after the war,[123] Braddock's still held a captain's commis-

sion in the elite Coldstream and generally was addressed as "Colonel," his line rank. An effigy of the Coldstream's first colonel, Monck, in armor, was one of the sights people went to see in the Abbey.[124] And for all his conceit, the Coldstream's incumbent colonel, Cutts, was reputed to know more about storming parties than any other officer in the British army.[125]

But at the moment the army was not too popular. During his wars William had increased its strength to 87,000 men. Debts, taxes, and the number of drunken grenadiers in the streets of London had increased, too. Once a peace treaty had been signed, noisy demagogues in the House of Commons denounced all soldiers as thieves, seducers, a national plague, the scum of the earth. Hot tempered veterans of Flanders threatened to cane their detractors. Some of the members of the House carried pistols for protection. The King ordered all army officers to remain in their quarters.[126]

Pamphleteers joined the outcry against the army, contending that the defense of the realm might be entrusted safely to a stay-at-home militia trained a few weeks each year and officered by justices of the peace. One militia-minded Tory, Robert Harley, stood up in the House and moved that the military establishments be reduced to a force of not more than 10,000 men. The House confirmed Harley's proposal. It further resolved that every soldier in the British army should be either a natural-born or a naturalized Englishman,[127] that none but English troops should do guard duty at the royal palace of Whitehall.[128] This meant the return to Holland of William's brigade of Dutch blue guards. The King had hoped to keep at least òne battalion. His blues were ordered into red uniforms. William pleaded that they be permitted to remain.[129] While his appeal was before the Commons a Dutch laundress at Whitehall hung her wash too close to a charcoal fire (some said she put hot ashes in a closet) and set the royal palace ablaze. Captain Braddock's guards were called out to help fight the fire. They managed to save the Banqueting Hall, but the rest of the old palace was destroyed.[130] With it was destroyed any remaining public affection for William's Dutch retainers. The departure of his blue guards was delayed for a year, but at the end of March 1699 they marched out of London and took ship for Holland.[131]

Whitehall never was rebuilt. London's riverside dampness aggravated King William's asthma. He preferred Kensington, Hampton Court, and Windsor.[132] St. James's Palace in London was fitted

FAMILY TREE

EDWARD BRADDOCK

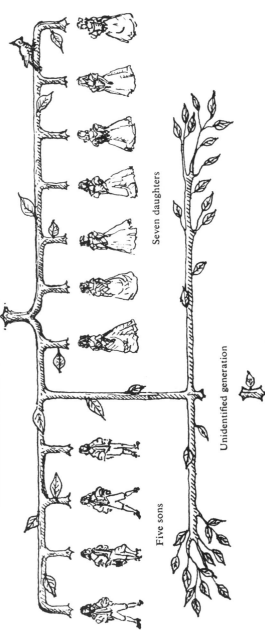

Edmund Bradock of Adbaston, Staffordshire, (*circa* 1571-1643); wife or wives (?)

Seven daughters

Five sons

Unidentified generation

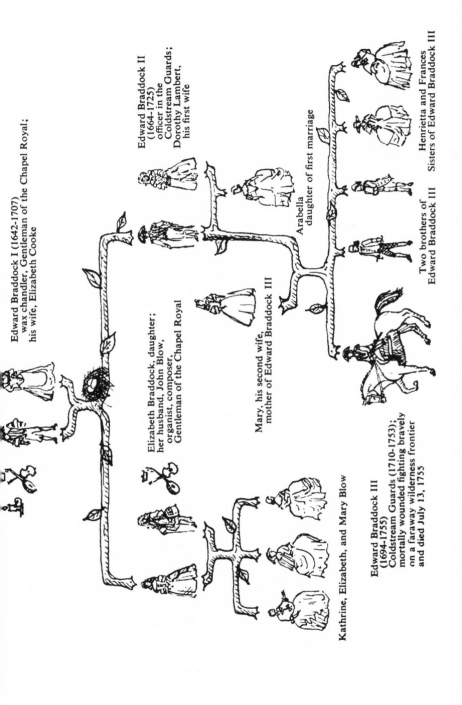

Edward Braddock I (1642-1707) wax chandler, Gentleman of the Chapel Royal; his wife, Elizabeth Cooke

Edward Braddock II (1664-1725) officer in the Coldstream Guards; Dorothy Lambert, his first wife

Elizabeth Braddock, daughter; her husband, John Blow, organist, composer, Gentleman of the Chapel Royal

Mary, his second wife, mother of Edward Braddock III

Arabella daughter of first marriage

Kathrine, Elizabeth, and Mary Blow

Edward Braddock III (1694-1755) Coldstream Guards (1710-1753); mortally wounded fighting bravely on a faraway wilderness frontier and died July 13, 1755

Two brothers of Edward Braddock III

Henrietta and Frances Sisters of Edward Braddock III

up as a residence for Princess Anne and her husband, reconciled to the childless King since the death of Queen Mary.[133] Newly uniformed Coldstream guardsmen went on duty at new sentry boxes in St. James's Park. Other details of foot guards attended the King, wherever he happened to be. But St. James's was the most popular post. Every day, when the Coldstream was on duty there, its drummers and hautboys played in the palace courtyard for the changing of the guard. Every Monday night the Princess gave a ball.[134] Sunday service in the chapel at St. James's became so fashionable that Bishop Burnett complained to the Princess about the ogling and sighing.[135]

"My house," Anne called her red-brick Tudor palace with its double-towered Gothic gateway into St. James's street. Its neat sash windows, crimson draped, looked out across the green park doing double duty as a children's playground and a promenade for fops and hussies.[136] Evelyn noted regretfully in his diary that Anne herself, a sweet but pasty-faced invalid on the fat and dowdy side of 35, "made so little figure" for an heir presumptive.[137] She had gone through seventeen pregnancies and only one of her children, the little Duke of Gloucester, lived long enough to play in the park. His death, at the age of 11, in the summer of 1700, led Parliament to pass an act of succession which provided, in the absence of any direct heirs of the heir presumptive, that the crown should pass to the House of Hanover, the German Protestant line of King James I, whose daughter Elizabeth had married the Elector Palatine.[138]

Although the expulsion of William's Dutch guards restored lost prestige of the Coldstream and other household troops, the reduction of the army's strength froze promotion. That the service now consisted entirely of officers was a poor joke to Captain Braddock who saw his profession slipping deeper and deeper into disrepute.[139] Many officers of disbanded regiments ceased to be "gentlemen." St. James's Park filled with idle veterans in threadbare coats and tarnished braid. Even their recently instituted half-pay fell into arrears. Parliament was deluged with claims and complaints. Discharged soldiers of the rank and file took the darker streets and more remote highways as robbers and thieves. Postboys, mail and stage coaches were held up. Cavalry and footguards were ordered out to patrol the roads.[140]

On routine guard duty at the Tower, Ensign Dick Steele of the Coldstream found time to write a solemn little book, *The Chris-*

tian Hero: An Argument Proving that No Principles but those of Religion are sufficient to Make a Great Man, deploring the irregularity of the military character.[141] Brother officers set him down as a disagreeable fellow, and teased him into fighting a duel. Partly in self-defense, Steele tried his hand at a comedy, "The Funeral, or Grief-a-la-Mode," produced in the spring of 1701 at Drury Lane. In his play Steele took another slap at the army by suggesting it was officered by indolent, arrogant younger sons whose only hope of success in times of peace lay in marrying a fortune.[142]

By that time most officers of the Coldstream were engrossed in more serious drama. The exiled James II died, September 15, 1701, at St. Germain. The day after his death a herald-at-arms appeared before the palace gate of St. Germain and proclaimed his son King James III of England, Scotland, and Ireland. In violation of the treaty of Ryswick, which had pledged him to abandon the Stuart cause and recognize the Protestant William, His Most Christian Majesty Louis XIV of France had promised the dying Roman Catholic James to "acknowledge and treat the Prince your son as King of England." [143]

To William this proclamation amounted to a declaration of war. Reports that he was signing new commissions at the rate of 200 a day heartened veterans who had been told for the past three years that their faces were a plague to the nation.[144] Cutts procured Ensign Steele one of the King's new commissions, a captaincy in Lord Lucas' regiment of fusiliers.[145] Steele's departure from the Coldstream, like his debut as a dramatist, was overshadowed by events of greater importance. King William's horse stumbled on a mole hill at Hampton Court, throwing his rider. The King's collar bone was broken by his fall. Fever developed. Within a fortnight he was dead and the Princess Anne was proclaimed Queen of England.[146]

On St. George's Day, April 23, 1702, eight-year-old Edward Braddock had an opportunity to see his father parade with the Coldstream for the coronation of the last of the Stuarts to occupy the throne of England. Too sick to use a coach, Anne was carried in a sedan chair packed with pillows from St. James's to Westminster Hall, and from Westminster to the Abbey.[147] Within a week after her succession Anne had named Marlborough captain-general of her armies. Her husband, Prince George of Denmark, became nominal head of the admiralty, but in practice it was controlled by Marlborough's brother, Admiral George Churchill. Marlborough's wife, Sarah, Anne's confidante since childhood, became mistress of the robes and keeper of the privy purse. The Marlborough regime had come into power.[148]

War against France was proclaimed by a herald in front of St. James's Palace gate on May 15.[149] Salamander Cutts joined Marlborough in Flanders.[150] On May 16, Captain Braddock, as senior company commander of the Coldstream, received orders to form a battalion of foot guards for an expedition being organized under the Duke of Ormonde. Six companies of the Coldstream rendezvoused with other troops on the Isle of Wight and sailed for Spain in July. It made a good story for the Braddock children when the Captain got home. Ormonde's expedition had swooped down on a Spanish treasure fleet in Vigo Bay. Fifty-six Spanish vessels had been sunk, burned, or captured. Five of those taken were loaded with bullion, vanilla, snuff, and cochineal. But the Coldstream's share of the prize money realized from the sale of this loot, divided one-ninth to general officers and eight-ninths to the regiments employed, amounted to less than £600.[151]

In Flanders, Marlborough had crossed the Meuse, reducing one fortress after another, with Cutts leading the storm troops at the taking of Liege. As a reward, Marlborough was raised to a Duke's estate with a pension of £5,000 a year.[152] But the Queen did not overlook Ormonde's adventure. Brigadier William Mathew, a Coldstream major who had commanded the battalion in Spain, was promoted to lieutenant-colonel. Braddock was made major of the Coldstream.[153] A £48 respite on his pay in that rank later became the subject of a petition to the Treasury and he received only £21.12 of the amount he claimed as due because there had been a misunderstanding about the actual date of his promotion.[154]

Cutts evidently had a good opinion of Braddock, for a year later he wrote Marlborough a letter recommending the promotion of Braddock and Captain Edmund Rivett of the Coldstream grenadier company. Marlborough must have shared Cutts' good opinion. In his reply the Duke wrote:

St. James 23, November 1703.

. . . Lieut. Col. Rivet delivered me this morning your Lordship's letter in his own and Col. Braddock's behalf, and I shall be very glad when Col. Mathews thinks of quitting the guards, that the vacancies may be supplied to your Lordship's satisfaction, being very sensible of the gentlemen's merits.[155]

The British army was not yet up to strength, having recruited less than half of the total of 18,000 men authorized by Parliament. Criminals, debtors, and paupers were drafted into the ranks. Magistrates were instructed to hand over to recruiting parties, then beating their drums at all the fairs and markets, any vagrants or unemployed persons who could show no means of support.[156] George Farquhar, an Irish dramatist who had served briefly with the army as a lieutenant in Ireland, used *The Recruiting Officer* as the title of a new comedy that popularized the song:

> *Here's forty shillings on the drum*
> *For all that volunteers do come,*
> *With shirts and clothes and present pay*
> *When over the hills and far away.*[157]

In February, Gibraltar was captured. A battalion of 400 Coldstream guards was shipped to help hold the Rock; but Major Braddock remained in London.[158] Cutts was abroad again with Marlborough, and Mathew had been knighted and appointed governor of the Leeward Islands.[159] Marlborough made good his promise. Braddock became lieutenant-colonel of the Coldstream.[160]

But the Duke had other things on his mind. That was the summer of his spectacular march to the Danube, where he won the battle of Blenheim over a combined French and Bavarian army. London went wild. Escorted by beefeaters, horse and foot, the Queen rode to Wrenn's still unfinished St. Paul's to give thanks for the Duke's victory. Braddock's footguards made a lane for the Queen to the big west door. She was carried in a chair from her coach.[161] Another spectacle for young Edward Braddock to remember.

Horse grenadiers, kettle drums, and trumpets welcomed the Queen's captain-general on his return to St. James's a few days before Christmas.[162] The 128 flags he had captured at Blenheim were paraded by Coldstream pikemen through the park to Westminster.[163] Steele's friend, Joseph Addison, commissioned to write an ode commemorating Blenheim, compared Marlborough to an angel that "rides the whirlwind and directs the storm." [164] The Queen presented the Duke with a 15,000 acre manor near Oxford, ordered a £250,000 palace built upon it at public expense, and put him down on her civil list for an annual grant of £5,000. Bounties totalling £42,000 were distributed among the officers who had served under him at Blenheim.[165] The whole country was caught up in an almost hysterical desire to share a little in the fame and glory enshrining the name of Marlborough. Fathers bought commissions for their sons as soon as they were old enough to strut. "The Grenadiers March," played at the Theatre Royal as an overture for *The Recruiting Officer,* almost became a national anthem.[166]

Lieut.-Col. Braddock seemed to be anchored in London. Somebody had to carry on the unrewarding garrison duties of the regiment's home station, and it was left to him to oversee accounts for mending the grates, for sweeping and emptying the "houses of office" at the Coldstream barracks. He sent off three hundred recruits to the only battalion of the Coldstream then in combat—not in Flanders, where the legend of the invincible Duke, unbeatable in battle, was taking root, but in Spain with the Earl of Peterborough.[167] A few months later Peterborough's army, including the Coldstream battalion, was defeated at Almanza by a Franco-Spanish force under the Duke of Berwick, Arabella Churchill's bastard son by James II. First reports of the battle received in London exaggerated British losses. Only 14 private soldiers and three officers of the Coldstream battalion were said to have survived. In Flanders, fortune again favored Arabella's brother, the Duke of Marlborough. His smashing victory over the French at Ramillies called for another thanksgiving at St. Paul's.[168]

On the Queen's new year list for 1707 Braddock was named a brigadier.[169] As lieutenant-colonel of the Coldstream, Braddock remained in active command of the regiment. Cutts had been made a lord chief justice of the Kingdom of Ireland and commander-in-chief of Her Majesty's forces there. But when Cutts died in Dublin at the end of January, Braddock was passed over. General Charles Churchill, a younger brother of Marlborough, who himself was still colonel of the First Foot Guards, succeeded the Salamander as colonel of the Coldstream and took command of the Guards' brigade in Flanders.[170] Early in March of the following year General Churchill was seized with an apoplectic fit. He retired to his Dorsetshire estate, "Great Mintern," presumably for the remainder of his life, but retained the colonelcy of the Coldstream.[171] A few weeks later, when four companies of the regiment were ordered to embark for Flanders, Braddock applied indirectly to the Duke himself for permission to go with them. In reply to his request came this letter:

Whitehall, 17 May 1708.

Sir—

I am sorry to be the author of such unwelcome news to you, because of the respect I have to you; I am to acquaint you, in the absence of the Secretary of War, with his grace the Duke of Marlborough's pleasure, signified by Mr. Cardonnel, that no officer of the guards older in commission than Col. Gorsuch is to embark for Ostend with the battalion of Guards. Your service therefore is not expected on the other side of the water, where they have already more brigadiers than brigades of foot.

> I am ever, with great sincerety, sir
> Yours &c.,
> James Taylor.[172]

Mr. Cardonnel was Adam Cardonnel, the Duke's confidential secretary. Col. Gorsuch—Charles Gorsuch—had been commissioned an ensign in the First Foot Guards in 1684, two years after Braddock got his commission as a lieutenant in the Coldstream. In other words, Braddock was senior to Gorsuch, who had commanded the first battalion of the First Foot Guards and its Coldstream replacements in Flanders for the last four years. But the guards were attached to Marlborough's headquarters. Marlborough did not wish that either Braddock or any other officer senior to Gorsuch should be sent out. The Flanders-bound Coldstream battalion accordingly was placed under the command of Lieut.-Col. Andrew Wheeler of the First Foot Guards, a junior to Gorsuch.[173] Gorsuch was wounded at Ghent on Christmas eve and died a short time later, if that was a matter of any satisfaction to the disappointed brigadier.[174]

His father, the choir master; his brother-in-law, Dr. Blow; and the Prince of Denmark also died that year. All were buried in the Abbey, his father in the north cloister near his mother.[175] The old choir master's genteel will, headed with an enormous and flourishing inscription,

IN THE NAME OF GOD AMEN, ... I, Edward Braddock, of the Parish of St. Margaret, Westminster, in the county of Middlesex, Gentleman, being in perfect health of sound and perfect mind and memory, thanks be given unto God therefore; calling to mind the Mortality of my Flesh and knowing that it is appointed for all Men once to Die, do make and Ordain this my last Will and Testament (that is to say) First and principally I give and Recommend my Soul into the hands of God who gave it hoping that I shall be saved through the Merritts of my Saviour Christ Jesue, and as for my Body it being the Mass of Substance of the Earth, to the Earth I committ to be decently buried att the Abbey or Cloysters of St. Peter Church of Westminster, or where else my executor hereinafter mentioned shall think fit. . . .

To his granddaughters, Katherine, Elizabeth, and Mary Blow, whom he prayed God to bless, he left a hundred pounds each. Katherine and Elizabeth were each to receive a silver salver, and Mary a porringer and two silver spoons. A large damask sheet was willed to Elizabeth, and the chest of drawers in his bedchamber to Mary. Another granddaughter, Arabella Braddock, was to have the harpsicon in the parlor. All his wearing clothes and forty shillings in silver were left to his servant, Elizabeth Longman. The residue of his estate he bequeathed to his loving son, Edward II, whom he named his sole executor.[176]

Another of Braddock's brother officers, Edmund Rivett, was killed in Flanders the next year at Malplaquet, a Marlborough triumph that cost 20,000 men, including 200 of the Coldstream battalion.[177] Perhaps, in the end, Braddock was lucky to have remained in London. On New Year's Day, 1710, he was one of twenty-four officers promoted to be major-generals.[178] This was almost as high as an undistinguished commoner of his station could hope to rise. He still held his commission as lieutenant-colonel of the Coldstream. And his next consideration seems to have been for his son Edward, now fifteen, an age when youngsters often entered the army.

EDWARD BRADDOCK III

The war, which had been going on for almost as long as Edward Braddock III could remember, and which was followed so closely in his home, must have widened the boy's world; but it was still a world that came into sharp focus only in London. And there the bitterness of politics and the fight for preferment presented another part of the young man's education. The conflict of English party politics within that world in the spring of 1710 raged around the Rev. Dr. Henry Sacheverel, a choleric high churchman who preached against the Queen's Whig ministry. The Whigs were the war party, the party of Marlborough. So violent were Sacheverel's anti-Whig sermons that he was impeached for seditious libel, tried before the Lords in crowded Westminster Hall, found guilty, and enjoined not to preach for two years. During the trial General Braddock's footguards were posted around Westminster Hall. Riots broke out. One man was killed. Nearly a hundred were arrested.[179]

Another vista of the world opened up to Edward Braddock, III, that spring, with the arrival in London of four North American "Indian Kings." The "Kings," sachems from the Mohawk Valley, had been brought over by four Colonial officers in an effort to impress the Queen and her ministers with the urgency of Indian affairs in a proposed expedition against the French in Canada and, at the same time, to impress the Indians with the power and wealth of England.[180]

Young Edward certainly knew what all boys knew about Indian warfare, how they massacred women and children and pared the skin and hair from the crown of a slain enemy's head. He can hardly have missed seeing the four sachems. Quartered at an upholsterer's in King street, Covent Garden, they were the subject of ballads, handbills, and newspaper advertisements. They visited Greenwich Hospital, the Woolwich dockyard, Hampton Court, Windsor Castle, and the Duke of Ormonde's country seat near Richmond. They attended service at St. James's. They sat for their portraits. At a Haymarket Theatre performance of *Macbeth* they were seated on the stage so that the audience might see them better. They drove through the streets in two royal carriages on their way to visit the Queen.[181]

At their audience they told her, through an interpreter, of their disappointment the previous summer, how they had hung up their kettles and taken up their hatchets to join her subjects against the French. They were fearful now, they said, "lest the French, who hitherto have dreaded us, should now think us unable to make war against them." Without her assistance, they told Queen Anne, they might be obliged to leave their country and seek new homes. They had often been importuned by the French to join them. They assured her they had no inclination to do so, and in token of their sincerity they presented her with belts of wampum.[182]

It was suggested that the Indians cross over to Flanders and watch the British army in action. They never got that far. But before they sailed for home in May, their luggage heavy with gift looking-glasses, scissors, glass beads, razors, combs, jews harps, Bibles, and books of Common Prayer, they did attend a review of horse guards in Hyde Park. Against the green of an English spring the Queen's jackbooted cavalry in breast plates, mounted on fat bob-tailed chargers, were the most impressive troops in the British army.[183]

But the horse guards were not for Edward Braddock, III. He was booked for the Coldstream as soon as his father could buy him an ensign's "pair of colors," then selling for £450.[184]

Queen Anne did not approve the promiscuous sale of commissions. When an advertisement appeared in the *Post Boy* stating that anyone interested in buying a commission could find out about it by inquiring of Mr. Pyne at Pyne's coffee house under the Scotland Yard gate, a Whitehall neighborhood in which many young officers of the guards lived, the *Gazette* came back with this announcement:

> Whereas, a scandalous advertisement has been twice published in the *Post Boy* "that whoever has a mind to treat about the purchasing of commissions in the army, either in our regiments or others, might apply to Mr. Pyne at his coffee house under Scotland Yard Gate near Whitehall, and they should be further informed of it," which is directly contrary to Her Majesty's expressed will and pleasure, sometime since declared and signified, as well at home as to her generals abroad, against the sale of commissions upon any account whatsoever; it is thought fit to give public notice to prevent any abuses or impositions that might happen therefrom; and whoever shall discover to her Majesty's Secretary of War, at his office in Whitehall, the authors of the said advertisement, shall have due protection and encouragement.[185]

But the General's negotiations were completed. He obtained his son an ensign's commission in Lieut.-Col. Cornelius Swan's company of the Coldstream. The transaction must have met with the approval of the Queen because she signed the commission for Edward Braddock, Junior, on the tenth of October, 1710.[186]

III

MORE EDUCATION AND A WAY OF LIFE

1710–1727

THERE WAS a story about "the major crying for his parrich," a witticism based upon the practice of granting commissions in the army to infants still of nursery age.[1] It was an old story about an old practice instituted in the days of Queen Anne's father, to provide support for the widows and children of officers who had died in the service. To correct abuses of the practice Anne had issued an order redefining the purpose of commissions for children and limiting their number to not more than two in any one regiment at one time.[2]

The commission which the Queen signed for sixteen-year-old Edward Braddock, Junior, was a man's commission. Edward Junior was not a large youth for his age, but he was no longer a child, and he was an army officer's son.[3] And an army officer's son, according to Dr. Swift, was "in every article, as fully accomplished at eight years old, as at eight and twenty, age holding only to the growth of his person and his vice; so that if you should look at him in his boyhood through the magnifying end of a perspective, and in his manhood through the other, it would be impossible to spy any difference; the same airs, the same strut, the same cock of his hat, and posture of his sword, (as far as the change of fashions will allow) the same understanding, the same compass of knowledge, with the very same absurdity, impudence and impertinence of tongue." [4]

[31]

Tall, dark, bush-browed Dr. Swift had left a country parish near Dublin and come to London to press the claim of the Irish clergy for Queen Anne's bounty, a royal revenue grant then enjoyed only by the English cloth. The Doctor had taken lodgings near St. James's and got his mail at the *Cockpit,* at the office of his friend, Captain Richard Steele, formerly of the Coldstream.[5] After Steele had quit the army he had become the government gazetteer at a salary of £300 a year. He was also writing a penny paper of his own, *The Tatler,* published three times a week.[6]

Steele knew in what directions the political winds were blowing. After the Sacheverel trial, in the spring of 1710, parliament had been prorogued. During the summer the Queen had begun to dismiss her Whig ministers, replacing them with Tories.[7] In August the militia-minded Tory Harley, three-time speaker of the house, had been made chancellor of the exchequer and virtual prime minister. Parliament had been dissolved and new elections ordered for October 5.[8] In his *Tatler* for July 4, Steele had printed a letter satirizing Harley and the new ministry. Now, he told Swift, he was waiting for the lightning to strike. He expected to be sacked any day.[9]

"Everything is turning upside down," Swift wrote to his friend Esther Johnson (Stella) in Ireland. "Every Whig in great office will, to a man, be infallibly put out: and we shall have such a winter as hath not been seen in England." [10]

On Friday, October 5, 1710, election day, riots and drunken brawls broke out all over the country. No. 235 of Captain Steele's *Tatler* for Tuesday, October 10, the day young Braddock's commission was signed, contained a noncontroversial essay on parental favoritism.[11] Election returns from the rural districts were still coming in. First reports of a 6-to-1 Tory triumph proved to be an exaggeration, but 270 members of the old parliament lost their seats. The Whigs were going out of power.[12]

A few days later Captain Steele lost his job as gazetteer.[13] Three of Marlborough's general officers, Thomas Meredyth, George McCartney, and Philip Honeywood, were ordered to sell their commissions for drinking "destruction" to the new Tory ministry in camp in Flanders. Their story, as it came back to London, said they had dressed up a hat on a stick, calling it Harley, and discharged a pistol at the thing, glasses in hand.[14]

Backstairs buzz and bumble at St. James's Palace had seeded the party upset. As young Braddock must have learned, if he had not already heard in his own home, the high and mighty Sarah, Duchess of Marlborough, was fighting a formerly indigent cousin, Mrs. Abigail Masham, for the Queen's favor.[15] The Duchess and her husband were allied with the Whigs. Mrs. Masham was a Tory. Immediately at stake in their squabble were the fortunes of two brigadier generals, both former officers of the Coldstream. One was Mrs. Masham's husband, Sam, and the other was her brother, Jack Hill. Neither was much of a soldier but both had been luckier, or more astute, than Braddock's father at winning the patronage of the Queen.[16]

Mrs. Masham, a hatchet-faced woman with a red nose, was a cousin of the Duchess of Marlborough on her mother's side. The Duchess had brought her to court and procured her a place as one of the Queen's bedchamber women—not a *lady* of the bedchamber, but a sort of royal waiting maid who, kneeling, handed the Queen's shift to the lady who helped her Majesty dress. The bedchamber woman poured water from a ewer on the Queen's hands when she washed, drew on the Queen's gloves when her Majesty could not put them on herself. She smoothed the Queen's pillows, emptied the slops, fetched her nightly cup of frothed chocolate, played the harpsichord when her Majesty was melancholy. At night she slept on the floor, across the Queen's door.[17]

Anne had grown attached to Mrs. Masham who, it turned out, was a cousin of her new prime minister, Harley, as well as a cousin of the Duchess. For many years the Duchess had been the Queen's most intimate friend, and Anne had been guided almost exclusively by the Marlboroughs ever since joining them in the conspiracy against her deposed father, the former King James. Over those years Sarah had turned arrogant, petulant, presumptuous. Mrs. Masham was more amiable, less demanding. Her influence with the Queen increased. Jealous hatred of Mrs. Masham became an obsession with the Duchess. As groom of the stole and mistress of the robes, entrusted with management of the privy purse, the Duchess still occupied apartments at St. James's, but she had not spoken to the Queen for the last six months.[18]

Mrs. Masham's husband, Sam, eighth son of a baronet, was a soft-spoken, good-natured, insignificant fellow who had been page, equerry, and groom of the bedchamber to the Queen's husband, the late Prince George of Denmark. In 1697 Masham had been

made an ensign of the Coldstream, and in seven years time became
a captain. Later he obtained the colonelcy of a regiment of horse,
but being strictly a nonfighting soldier he spent most of his time
around St. James's, bowing low, skipping to open the door for his
superiors, and occasionally playing cards with the Queen and his
wife.[19]

Jack Hill, Mrs. Masham's tall, unkempt, four-bottle brother, was
a nephew of Brig.-Gen. James Stanhope, now in command in Spain.
Through his Marlborough connections Hill had become a page
to Anne when she was a princess and, in 1703, had been commissioned a captain in the Coldstream. Two years later he had succeeded Stanhope as commander of the Eleventh Foot, and with
that regiment had followed Stanhope to the Peninsula. At the battle of Almanza, where he commanded a brigade, Hill had been
captured and his regiment almost destroyed. Returning to England he had reorganized the Eleventh Foot and had taken it to
Flanders, where he served briefly as an aide to Marlborough.[20]
The Queen asked Marlborough to give Hill the colonelcy of the
Fourth Dragoons, a select regiment whose commander, Lord Essex,
had died. The Duke refused.

"Good for nothing," was his opinion of Jack Hill.[21] Hill's preferment over the heads of other men of greater merit and longer service would "set up a standard of disaffection to rally all the mal-
content officers in the army," the Duke told the Queen.[22]

But she was determined to do something for Mrs. Masham's
brother, and when Marlborough failed to include his name in a
list of colonels submitted to her for promotion to the rank of
brigadier general, the Queen refused to sign any of the commissions until the list had been extended to take in Hill. As a result,
thirty colonels had been promoted on New Year's Day 1710–the
day the elder Braddock became a major-general and ten months
before the younger Braddock's first commission–both Hill and
Mrs. Masham's husband, Sam, being swept along in the flood.[23]

The party battle between the Whig and Tory covered a wider
front. Harley, as head of a new Tory ministry, hoped to discredit
Marlborough and end the war by concluding a popular peace.[24]
As a secretary of state, to deal particularly with the French he
chose Henry St. John, a Jacobite Tory whom Dr. Swift thought
"the greatest young man I ever knew." The Doctor ticked off St.
John's gifts: "Wit, capacity, beauty, quickness of apprehension,

good learning and an excellent taste: the greatest orator in the House of Commons, admirable conversation, good nature and good manners, generous and a despiser of money." [25]

St. John also set a pace for London's most notorious rakes, and when the news of his appointment at a salary of £6000 a year reached one of the establishments he patronized, its madame was said to have exclaimed to the frail sisterhood she handled: "Six thousand a year, girls, and all for us!" [26]

Guardsmen on duty at St. James's soon came to recognize most of the characters who were now the talk of the town: Harley, St. John, the Duchess of Marlborough, Mrs. Masham, Mrs. Masham's husband, and her brother. Of the lot, the Duchess was the most striking in manner and appearance. She was still a beauty, slender, erect, fair hair shining, tongue needle sharp. But of all who came and went at the old red brick palace, young Braddock was given to understand, Mrs. Masham was the most powerful.[27] "She could make the Queen stand on her head if she chose," [28] was the opinion of many.

Dr. Swift took over *The Examiner,* a Tory weekly started by St. John. Every Thursday the paper turned out a scorcher on the Marlboroughs.[29] In its issue for November 16 the Doctor dropped a hint that the Duke might be plotting counter revolution or treason. The next Thursday he drew up a balance sheet estimating that the Duke and Duchess of Marlborough had received from England, in lands, grants, pictures, jewels, and jobs the equivalent of £540,000. The Doctor compared this with the triumphal car, the arch, the statue, and the laurel wreaths, calculated to have a total value of £994 11s 10d, received from ancient Rome by one of its successful generals. He further accused the Duchess of appropriating £22,000 from the privy purse. In his December 14 number Swift took up the defense of "an innocent lady," obviously Mrs. Masham, and by implication charged the Duchess of Marlborough with insolence, bribery, and nepotism. The Thursday after Christmas *The Examiner* drew a parallel between Marlborough and Cromwell.

The Duke's private life, his unfaithfulness to James II, his sister's shame as the King's mistress, his own early amours with the faded Duchess of Cleveland were dragged out and published in a book, *Secret Memoirs and Manner of Several Persons of Quality.* Stories of Marlborough's avarice were told and retold: The Duke padded his muster rolls. He drew large allowances in the field under pretense of maintaining a public table at his headquarters while he dined at the messes of subordinate officers. He blew out his candles quickly to save wax. When in London he walked home at night rather than pay the hire of a chairman.[30]

Three days after Christmas, 1710, Marlborough returned to London from Flanders. On the outskirts of the city people cheered him from their doors and windows, pressing in around his carriage. To avoid further uproar he changed to a hackney coach. But drums, trumpets, rigid ranks of guardsmen received him in the palace courtyard. He looked older, heavier than when young Braddock had seen him last. His polished breastplate corseted a threatening paunch. That evening he waited on the Queen and according to reports, got a cool reception.[31]

On January 17 he again went to St. James's. An account of his humiliation became the talk of barber shops. The Queen had asked him to return the golden key which the Duchess carried to the royal wardrobe. He had pleaded on his knees that his wife be permitted to keep it. The Queen was firm. The Duchess of Somerset was to replace the Duchess of Marlborough as groom of the stole. Mrs. Masham was to become the keeper of the privy purse.[32]

Not until the end of January was the army assured that the Duke would again be commander-in-chief in Flanders.[33] Seven hundred men had been ordered picked from the two regiments of footguards for service abroad but only 120 were drawn from the Coldstream, fifteen from each of the eight companies in London. They sailed for Holland with the Duke on February 21.[34] General Braddock remained in London, senior officer of the footguards there, and his son, the Ensign, seems to have remained with him. On March 1, Mrs. Masham's brother, General Hill, was named commander-in-chief of an expedition to be sent against the French in North America. Five of Marlborough's battalions were ordered home from Flanders to join the expedition.[35]

A new daily paper, *The Spectator,* written by Captain Steele and his friend Joseph Addison, came out the day of Hill's appointment. General Braddock may well have read its second issue with more than ordinary interest. He may even have recommended it to his son. Steele, introducing a fictitious character called Captain Sentry, "a gentleman of great courage, good understanding, but invincible modesty," remarked that the military profession was "a way of life in which no man can rise suitably to his own merit, who is not something of a courtier as well as a soldier." [36]

Nine war vessels and forty transports carrying seven or eight regiments of foot and half a battalion of marines sailed under Hill's command for the conquest of Quebec.[37] The elder Braddock may have envied Hill his opportunity, but the departure of the Canadian expedition probably was a matter of complete indifference to his son. It had never been suggested that Hill's force should include footguards. Colonial service was not popular with the army. In years past officers had been broken rather than go to the West Indies. Far more attractive was the prospect of plunder and good living in France.[38]

Late spring rains puddled the country roads around London. Farmers and their wives made hay and picked strawberries.[39] In the first warm days of June the Queen told Mrs. Masham to pack up for their summer visit to Windsor.[40] One of the few favors General Braddock could bestow upon his son would have been to include him in a detachment of 200 from the Coldstream and First Regiment of Footguards, with officers proportionable, ordered to march to Windsor and attend the Queen during her stay.[41] They were still there when the news arrived that eight of Hill's transports had gone down on the rocks in the St. Lawrence. Nearly eight hundred soldiers had been drowned. The expedition had turned back without having come within sight of Quebec. Hill himself appeared at Windsor a few days later to make the best of a bad report to the Queen, blaming stormy weather and untrustworthy pilots.[42]

Semi-secret negotiations with France were under way but the two parties were still divided when Parliament met in December. Harley, who had escaped an attempted assassination by a disgruntled French marquis serving in the British army, had been created Earl of Oxford and made Lord High Treasurer.[43] The Tories, led by Harley and St. John, favored a peace conference. Marlborough and the Whigs opposed it.[44] Parliament adjourned for the Christmas holidays. During the recess a report of the commissioners of public accounts, circulated privately among its members, charged the Duke with having received £6,000 a year from Sir Solomon Medina, the army's bread and wagon contractor, and 2½ per cent of the pay of foreign troops in the British service. The total involved was between £170,000 and £250,000. Robert Walpole, a truculent

Whig and former secretary at war, was accused of having approved the payment of £1,000 to a friend on a forage contract.[45]

On New Year's Eve, 1711, the Queen broke her supreme commander. She told him, in a letter, that she had no further use of his services.[46] Public announcement of his dismisal, printed in the *Gazette* for New Year's Day, shocked every man in the army.[47] Command of the First Foot Guards was then transferred from Marlborough to the Duke of Ormonde. Ormonde also was made general of the Queen's land forces. Marlborough's quartermaster, William Cadogan, was removed as Lieutenant of the Tower and replaced by Hill.[48] There is no record of either of the Braddocks having gone to Flanders that spring with a detachment of 200 men from the First and the Coldstream regiments, the usual replacements for guards brigade on foreign service. If they went they saw no combat. Ormonde was under orders to keep his troops in camp.[49]

The Tory-controlled House of Commons found Marlborough's acceptance of money from a contractor "unwarrantable and illegal." The Duke went into voluntary exile in Holland. Walpole, voted guilty of bribery, was sent to the Tower.[50] General Braddock went down to Portsmouth and then to Plymouth to disband a regiment of foot and one of horse for which there was no longer any need.[51] St. John, now Viscount Bolingbroke, in reward for his services to Harley and Mrs. Masham, set out for Paris to hasten the peace negotiations which were concluded at Utrecht on the last day of March, 1713.[52]

The six Coldstream companies which had been in Flanders came home to crowded barracks at Hampton Court and the Savoy with a peace-time grumble: better billets were available on the town at sixpence per week.[53] Listening to the tall, interminable tales of older, bolder guardsmen back from the wars, Ensign Braddock helped draw up warrants for the purchase of brooms and mops. He told off detachments on occasion to transport officers' baggage to Windsor.[54] His father, the General, who had seen so many removed suddenly or pushed ahead at whim, could only counsel patience. The invalid Queen was failing. She chewed her fan. More than ever before she needed a tot of brandy in her tea.[55]

Both Oxford and Bolingbroke were reported to be in touch with agents of the Pretender, who would if crowned be James III. Should the Pretender turn Protestant, many Jacobites thought, it might be a simple matter to repeal the Act of Settlement which fixed succession on the German House of Hanover.

Anne's crypto-Jacobite Ministers apparently had set out to purge the army of Whigs.[56] Lieut.-Col. Thomas Coote of the First Foot Guards, who had been very active in some rejoicings at the *Three Tons Tavern* on the anniversary of King William's birthday, and who was reported to have drunk publicly the health of the Elector of Hanover, was called on to sell his company. Two other lieutenant-colonels, told to sell out, were replaced by Roman Catholic officers. Three captains of the regiment were dismissed summarily. Seventeen other officers were listed to go if they refused to resign. Wholesale dismissals could not be made without the Queen's permission. Apparently that was all that delayed a purge.[57]

At *Jenny Man's* coffee house in the Tilt Yard, sometimes called the "Hanover Club" because of the absence of outspoken Jacobites among the officers who gathered there, it was expected that the Coldstream would be the next regiment to receive special treatment. A long list of generals, colonels, and captains was said to have orders to sell out unless willing to "serve the Queen without asking questions." [58]

> *God Bless Queen Anne, the nation's great defender.*
> *Keep out the French, the Pope and the Pretender* [59]

children had sung when young Braddock was growing up. Now they were singing it again. Fanatical Protestants, arguing the perils of Popery against what they feared was a threatening Jacobite resurgence, fell back on an old watchword: "No wooden Shoes!"[60]

The usual detachment of General Braddock's foot guards to attend the Queen on her summer retirement to Hampton Court and Windsor was ordered out on July 7, 1714.[61] But the Queen, obviously unwell, remained at Kensington. On Friday morning, July 30, 1714, while she was having her hair combed, she had an apoplectic stroke. Six doctors were called. The Privy Council assembled.[62] Rumors multiplied by the hour: the Pretender would land in Scotland with 12,000 to 14,000 French troops. . . . Two Irish officers were enlisting men in London and Westminster for the Pretender. . . . Three drummers of the First Foot Guards had been arrested for leading a demonstration for the House of Hanover. . . . The Bishop of Rochester offered to head a troop of Life Guards in his lawn sleeves and declare for James III, the Queen's brother. . . .

The Queen favored her brother—although a proclamation issued in her name offered a reward of £5,000 for his apprehension should he land or attempt to land in Great Britain or Ireland.[63]

On orders from the council, General Braddock doubled all guards and increased the garrison at the Tower. Four regiments billeted in the country around London marched into the city.[64] Heralds and life guards kept their horses saddled in the Kensington palace courtyard, ready to ride and proclaim the new king as soon as the doctors said the Queen was dead. They said she was dead at half past 7 Sunday morning, August 1, 1714.[65]

The heralds and life guards mounted up and clattered off to St. James's, where the foot guards presented arms and the courtiers stood with bared heads while a special herald proclaimed, to the roll of drums and the peal of trumpets: ". . . the high and mighty Prince George, Elector of Brunswick Lunenburg, is now, by the death of our late sovereign of happy memory, become our only lawful and rightful liege Lord, George, by the Grace of God, King of Great Britain. . . ."

Cannon at the Tower thundered. "God save the King!" [66]

The King arrived from Hanover on Saturday, September 18, 1714. On the ship with him came one of his mistresses, his son, sixty-three courtiers, clerks, cooks, and other attendants, all speaking German. The Duke of Marlborough, who returned from exile the day after Anne died, met the new king at Greenwich with a grenadier battalion of guards including two companies of Braddock's Coldstream.[67]

A million and a half people crowded the streets of London to welcome the new king when he entered the city. His coach, last in a train of two hundred loaded with English nobility and gentry, was an enormous model of the carriage maker's art, glazed and varnished, a-glitter with gilt, emblazoned with the royal arms, and drawn by eight horses with postillions. Detachments of artillery, city marshals on horseback, the King's kettle drummers, mounted trumpeters, sheriff's officers marched at the head of the procession. More foot guards lined the street, up to the gateway of St. James's.[68]

Days passed before some of the old palace retainers got a good look at the new King, a pompous, methodical German of middle-age and medium height, with a big nose, a dipper mouth, and empty eyes. As a rule he wore a shabby brown suit sprinkled with snuff and made use of only two rooms in St. James's Palace, eating and sleeping in one and giving audiences in the other. His short, fidgety, blue-eyed son, George Augustus, was on bad terms with the King and afraid of him. Young George's pretty wife, the Princess Caroline, was the most attractive and intelligent member of the new royal family. Her bust, reputed to be the finest in Europe, aroused the admiration of every Englishman. She spoke English perfectly and was not awed in the slightest by her stuffy father-in-law, who hated her.[69]

The gilded state coach, harnessed to six satiny bays, took the new King and the Prince and Princess of Wales from St. James's to Westminster for the coronation, exactly one month after the King's arrival. Foot guards lined a platform raised between Westminster Palace and the Abbey. The square swarmed with drummers, trumpeters, choirboys, aldermen, privy councilors, bishops, barons, viscounts, marquises, and dukes—the peers in crimson velvet robes with their coronets in their hands. Packed crowds watched, and remarked that there was no queen. The ladies of the court did not walk in the procession.[70]

Sophia Dorothea, the King's consort, was still alive. Twelve years after her marriage to the Elector of Hanover she had had an affair with a soldier of fortune. The lady was whisked away to the Castle of Ahlden, twenty miles north of Hanover, where she remained in seclusion.[71] Conjugal infidelity was exclusively a male privilege at the court of Hanover.

Marlborough was reappointed captain general of the army and colonel of the First Foot Guards,[72] but there was still feeling against him. At a dinner shortly after his reinstatement, Captain George Chudleigh of the First Foot Guards made a speech expressing his admiration for the Duke and his confidence in him. Two days later, at the first court held by the new King at St. James's, a Mr. Alworth, a member of Parliament for Windsor, remarked that the Captain would have done better to keep his mouth shut. The Captain's brother, Capt. John Chudleigh of the Coldstream, heard what Alworth said and challenged him. In spite of efforts by another Coldstream officer, Col. Andrew Bissett, to prevent their meeting, the Captain killed Alworth in a duel in Marylebone field.[73]

Marlborough's superannuated brother, Gen. Charles Churchill, given to understand that he was no longer wanted, resigned his commission as colonel of the Coldstream. But once again the elder Braddock was passed over. The Duke's old quartermaster, Cadogan,

was given command of the regiment. Braddock stayed on as its lieutenant-colonel.[74] His commission and that of his ensign son were
renewed by the King on January 11, 1715. With all other officers
remaining in the service they took a new oath of fidelity:

> I swear to be true to our sovereign Lord King George and to serve
> him honestly and faithfully in defense of his person, crown, and dig-
> nity against all his enemies and oppressors and to observe and obey
> His Majesty's orders and the orders of the generals and officers set over
> me by his Majesty. So help me God.[75]

The Hills and the Mashams disappeared. Ormonde and Bolingbroke fled to France, joining up with the Pretender, sometimes
called the Chevalier St. George.[76] New elections returned a Whig
majority to the House of Commons, and Robert Walpole, released
from the Tower and made paymaster of the forces, became chairman of a House committee which took the lead in proceedings
that impeached Oxford (Harley), Bolingbroke, and Ormonde for
high treason.[77] Ormonde nevertheless remained popular with
Tories and Jacobites, while the German King George I was slow
to endear himself to any of his new subjects, least of all to his
household troops. He wanted them dressed as cheaply as possible,
and grudgingly conformed to the English court custom of giving
new clothes to his regiments of guards on his birthday, March 28.
The new red coats and white shirts were cut from coarser and
cheaper materials than those to which the soldiers were accustomed.[78] "Hanover shirts," some sneered at their new issue of
linen. They snipped samples of the cloths used in both their new
shirts and coats and handed them around in the taverns as
"Hanover cloth." One detachment, marching to the Tower, pulled
out their shirt tails and showed them to shopkeepers along the
way. "These are Hanover shirts," repeated the guardsmen. That
night some of the soldiers threw their new shirts over the King's
garden wall at St. James's.[79] Others flung theirs into a bonfire at
Whitehall. "Ormonde for ever!" someone shouted, half in jest and
half in protest.[80]

On May 29, the anniversary of the Restoration, people gathered
around the statue of Queen Anne in front of St. Paul's. "Down
with the House of Hanover!" they yelled. "God bless King James
the third!" [81]

And on June 10, the birthday of the Pretender, the Lord Mayor
of London called out the militia. Braddock's guardsmen were

posted in the streets to prevent persons from wearing white roses, the Jacobite badge.[82]

Jacobite demonstrations broke out in Lancashire. In the Scottish highlands a shifty Jacobite nobleman, "Bobbing John" Erskine, the Earl of Mar, stirred up the clans, and early in September raised the standard of the Pretender at a mountain village in the Grampions. The Duke of Argyll, named commander-in-chief in Scotland, hurried north to put down the revolt.[83]

Marlborough was no longer fit for duty. General direction of military operations was left to his friend General Stanhope, now a secretary of state. Three of Stanhope's old lieutenants in Spain, Gen. Wade, Wills, and Carpenter, all received commands.[84] Once again the elder Braddock found himself garrison-bound in London with the Coldstream, encamped in Hyde Park to recruit four new companies. This was a little too much after thirty-three years of service. On September 28, 1715, he resigned his commission.[85]

His lieutenant-colonelcy of the Coldstream, with a fixed market value of £5,000, was sold to Lieut.-Col. Richard Holmes.[86] Under new service regulations promulgated by George I, Braddock may have continued to draw half-pay as a retired major general.[87] Whatever his means, he had had enough of the army. He intended to retire to Bath with his wife and their two unmarried daughters, Henrietta and Frances. Two of his sons had taken care of themselves, one settling in Norfolk.[88]

His third son, Edward, remained with the Coldstream, encamped in Hyde Park until they went into winter quarters, twelve companies in the Tower hamlets and six in Finsbury.[89] Young Edward read about the Scottish rising in the newspapers. Three days before Christmas, James Edward Stewart stepped ashore in Scotland, at Peterhead. But his insurrection had been crushed. In February he returned to France, a price of £100,000 on his head. King George made the end of the rebellion official in April when, in a translated speech read by the Lord Chancellor, he told Parliament the Pretender had fled.[90]

Homesick for Hanover, the King was impatient to get away from England. He was tired of St. James's where, people said, he sat around in the evening drinking beer seasoned with tobacco and kicking the toes of his boots against Queen Anne's wainscoting. He wanted to do a little hunting in a country where people spoke his language. He wanted to see a mistress left in Hanover because she

was a Catholic.[91] On the morning of July 18, 1716, the guard at
St. James's was turned out to see the King drive off with the Prince
of Wales to the Tower, where they took a boat for Gravesend.
There the Prince left his father aboard the royal yacht and returned to St. James's, Guardian of the Realm during his father's
absence.[92]

On the first day of August, 1716, Ensign Edward Braddock was
promoted to lieutenant in the Coldstream grenadier company, commanded by Captain Henry Pulteney, a younger brother of William
Pulteney, secretary at war.[93] The price of a Coldstream lieutenancy
was £900. But Braddock must have been a capable young officer,
and ready for advancement. The grenadiers were picked men, the
privates the tallest in the regiment, chosen for size because they
were expected to throw a hand grenade farther than an ordinary
soldier. They wore high, peaked mitre-like caps which made them
look even taller than they were. In column they occupied the front
ranks. In line they stood on the right. Storm troops, they were
expected to take the lead in all hazardous operations. They suffered battle losses in proportion.[94]

For the time being all military service was humdrum and routine.
But the standard of the recruit had fallen to its lowest level since
the accession of George I. Every week deserters were brought into
Hyde Park, tied up to halberts or to a tree, and flogged with cats,
rods, cloak straps, and stirrup leathers.[95] In October the Coldstream
struck its tents, fourteen per company, and returned to the Tower
hamlets and Finsbury for the winter. The next summer the regiment returned to the park, hats well cocked, hair tucked up, drummers and hautboys festooned with £16 to £25 worth of gold lace.
When the King was in town, officers of the Coldstream mounted
all guards in regimentals and gaiters.[96]

That November, 1717, the Princess of Wales gave birth to a son,
the first prince of Hanoverian blood to be born on British soil.[97]
The christening of this infant led to an open quarrel between the
King and the Prince of Wales. The Prince wanted to name his son
Louis. The King held out for *George William,* and had his way.
The King also insisted that the Duke of Newcastle, one of the
richest men in England, stand as one of the child's godfathers. The
Prince hated the Duke. As soon as the King had left the Princess's
bedroom, where the baby was baptized, the Prince walked over to

Newcastle, shook his fist and shouted, in heavy German accent: "You are von rascal—I shall find you!" [98] The king thought he said "fight," which he regarded this as an insult. He ordered both the Prince and the Princess of Wales to move out of St. James's Palace— but to leave their infant son and three daughters there. The Princess was permitted to return to visit her children, but the baby prince died before the year was out.[99] His death did not constitute a dynastic catastrophe. Caroline had another son, Frederick Louis, now 10 years old, who had been left behind in Hanover by his grandfather's orders, presumably to secure the family claim on the old electorate in case anything went wrong with the new kingdom.[100]

Banished from St. James's, Caroline and her husband set up their own establishment at Leicester House, a straggling old two-story mansion with a Dutch garden facing Leicester Fields, half a mile from St. James's. People called Leicester House "the Prince's pouting place." Notice was published in the *Gazette* that anyone attending audiences there would not be received at court. But all the pretty maids of honor had followed the Princess to Leicester House. After a decent period of mourning its spinet tinkled and minuets and masquerades kept its windows yellow with candle light long after those at St. James's were dark.[101]

Braving the King's displeasure by calling at Leicester House were Alexander Pope, who was translating the *Illiad;* John Gay, who had collaborated with Pope on a new comedy, *Three Hours After Marriage;* Philip Lord Stanhope, the future Earl of Chesterfield, whose wit already had impressed the House of Commons; John Lord Hervey, son of the Earl of Bristol, somewhat effeminate but in demand as a beau; Richard Lumley, Earl of Scarborough, an amiable card-loving colonel of horse grenadiers who would be Braddock's next regimental commander; and the younger Charles Churchill, son of the old general and a former Coldstream captain now enjoying notoriety as the lover of Anne Oldfield, the reigning actress at Drury Lane.[102]

Army officers had other things than a royal family quarrel to talk about. In the House of Commons a parliamentary Jacobite, William Shippen, had argued that the British army was too large for peace time. Shippen also said that a speech which the King had delivered on the subject of army strength "seemed rather calculated for the meridian of Germany than Great Britain," and that "the King is a stranger to our language and our constitution." The reaction of the Commons had been a vote, 175 to 81, that Shippen's remarks were "highly dishonorable to, and unjustly reflecting on His Majesty's person and government." The House also ordered Shippen to the Tower. He was released at the end of the session but never silenced. Once a year, for the next twenty-three, he stood up in the House to move that the strength of the standing army be reduced.[103]

In May, 1718, when the Coldstream again pitched tents for its summer encampment in Hyde Park, Lieut. Braddock fought a duel with sword and pistol with Col. John Waller. Waller appears to have been the grandson of an Irish regicide and a former cavalry officer who represented Castletown in the House of Commons.[104] As regards the cause of the duel, the record is blank, but apparently honor was satisfied and the lieutenant was not injured. In August he acquired a fifteen-year old superior officer: William Anne Keppel, second son of the Earl of Albemarle, was commissioned a captain and lieutenant-colonel of grenadiers with the Coldstream.[105]

Winter brought the threat of another Jacobite revolt. The Pretender was received in Madrid, acknowledged King of England by the Spanish Court. The renegade Duke of Ormonde sailed from Cadiz for Scotland to press the Pretender's claim.[106] British troops were assembled in the west of England, one battalion of the Coldstream at Chippenham. But a storm scattered Ormonde's fleet. Only two frigates reached Scotland. They landed about three hundred Spanish soldiers who surrendered after a half-hearted fight at Glenshiel.[107]

By way of reprisal, a secret British expedition including seven companies of the Coldstream and commanded by Viscount Cobham sailed from the Isle of Wight for Spain, early in September, 1719. They landed in Vigo Bay at the end of the month. Lieut. Braddock's company may have been among the grenadiers who were the first to hit the beach. They found the countryside so well supplied with wine that their officers had difficulty organizing them for an attack, but the Spaniards surrendered the citadel of Vigo on October 4, after eight guardsmen had taken possession of the gate.[108]

By mid-November all the guardsmen were back in England to resume normal garrison duties, attending the King on his return from another visit to Hanover (the officers being warned to take care that the men detailed for this had good breeches); guarding the Royal Princesses Amelia, Caroline, and Louisa at Hampton and Windsor (three highwaymen had robbed a maid of honor in the hindermost coach of their parents' retinue between Kensington and Richmond the previous May when the Prince and Princess of Wales were paying the children a visit) and at Kensington (where the soldiers would observe such orders as might be received from the Countess Dowager of Portland, governess to their Royal Highnesses); putting down a weavers riot in Spitalfields Market (using only their swords). The guards also stood by during the financial panic of 1720.[109]

Cannon fire and a peal of bells on April 15, 1721 marked the birth of another son to the Princess Caroline at Leicester House.[110] The din was followed by the most astonishing order ever issued to the Coldstream Guards: they were to let their whiskers grow. Frederick William I, King of Prussia, father-in-law of King George's daughter, Sophia Dorothea, had been named one of the child's godfathers and invited to attend the baptismal ceremony on May 2. The King of Prussia admired bearded soldiers. The men of the Coldstream were a shaggy lot until word reached London that the King of Prussia would not be there for the baptism. The new member of the royal family was christened William Augustus.[111]

"An honest blockhead" was Lady Mary Wortley Montagu's estimate of William Augustus' grandfather. Lady Mary, a society leader often at court and in favor with Princess Caroline, was the witty wife of a former ambassador to Turkey. She lived at Twickenham, in a cottage near Pope. But who was the "superfine Mr. Braddocks" who danced attention on Lady Mary's friend, Elizabeth, the 45-year old Countess of Bristol? Could it have been one of Lieut. Braddock's three brothers? [112]

Lady Mary never identified him completely. But she wrote to her sister, the exiled Countess of Mar, in Paris, that the eccentric and vivacious Elizabeth, a lover of pleasure and play, "has left off the dull occupation of hazard and basset, and is grown young, blooming, coquet and gallant; and to show she is fully sensible to the errors of her past, and resolved to make up for time misspent, she has two lovers at a time and is equally wickedly talked of for the gentle Colonel Cotton and the superfine Mr. Braddocks." [113]

On June 22, 1727, the honest blockhead was in his carriage at the Dutch frontier town of Osnabruck. On his way back to Hanover for one of his frequent visits he had topped off a heavy German meal with a dessert of watermelons, strawberries, and oranges. The load was too much for his 67-year old digestive system. Stricken with a paralyzing cramp, King George I died.[114]

Capt.-Gen. Marlborough also was dead when the Coldstream paraded in October for the coronation of George II and Queen Caroline. Cadogan had been named to succeed the Duke as the colonel of the First Foot Guards, and Scarborough had succeeded Cadogan as colonel of the Coldstream.[115] The venerable Sarah, dowager Duchess of Marlborough, now almost 70, attended the ceremonies with a five-foot train of silk and ermine on her heavy crimson robes of state. When the procession halted on its way to the abbey, she took a drum from the guardsman and sat upon it in full view of the crowd which laughed and cheered her. This was the fifth coronation she had seen.[116]

Walpole had become Sir Robert Walpole, Prime Minister. One of his first suggestions to the new king was that he send immediately for his elder son, Frederick Louis, still in Hanover, so that Frederick Louis might take his rightful position at Court as the new Prince of Wales. Around St. James's hung a belief that both the King and Queen would have been glad to exclude him from the throne in favor of his chubby little brother, William Augustus, Duke of Cumberland, a grave and solemn child of seven who liked to ride, hunt, and watch soldiers drill.[117]

Prince Frederick Louis arrived by packetboat from Helvoetsluys on a rough December day. Landing at Whitechapel, about seven in the evening, he took a hackney coach to St. James's, alighted at the Friary, and walked down to the Queen's backstairs. To the officers of the Coldstream, taking his measure in the dimly lighted colonnade of the old palace, the new Prince of Wales was not imposing. Somebody said he played the fiddle, a silly instrument in the opinion of soldiers who had heard drums thundering and fifes squealing "Malbrook" when the great Duke, home from the wars, took his salute with a flourish in the palace courtyard.[118]

IV

SCANDAL AT BATH

1715–1732

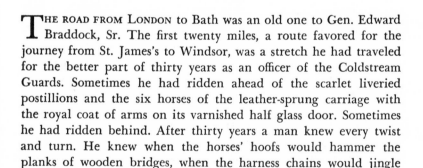

THE ROAD FROM LONDON to Bath was an old one to Gen. Edward Braddock, Sr. The first twenty miles, a route favored for the journey from St. James's to Windsor, was a stretch he had traveled for the better part of thirty years as an officer of the Coldstream Guards. Sometimes he had ridden ahead of the scarlet liveried postillions and the six horses of the leather-sprung carriage with the royal coat of arms on its varnished half glass door. Sometimes he had ridden behind. After thirty years a man knew every twist and turn. He knew when the horses' hoofs would hammer the planks of wooden bridges, when the harness chains would jingle on slack traces. He knew when Windsor Castle would come into view, the way Milton saw it, high-bosomed in tufted trees across the fields.[1]

Familiar landmarks along the road began with Chiswick churchyard, just outside of London, where the Duchess of Cleveland was buried, poor lady. General Braddock was old enough to remember her as a slightly faded mistress of Charles II.[2] Then the road crossed Hounslow Heath, where King James had assembled the Coldstream and other troops while London waited for the Protestant wind that would bring William and Mary—Mary who ran through the old royal palace at Whitehall before her fugitive father's breath was out of the place, peeking in the closets and turning up the quilts on the beds.[3]

The road to Bath ran past the wrought-iron gates of old ducal seats, the villas and brick walled gardens of dead-and-gone dandies, past cottages beetlebrowed with thatch and dooryards bursting with wallflowers. Summer treated the road's travellers to the cidery whiff of orchards, the sedgy freshness of river banks, the odor of stale, sticky tavern beer, sweet after the dust and the smell of horses and sweat and saddle leather. Winter offered the warmth of sea-coal fires, glowing red in tavern grates. And there was no lack of taverns along the road to Bath. One after another their swinging signboards hung out their names, The Coach and Horses, The White Horse, The White Hart, The Red Cow, The Seven Stars, The King's Head, The King's Arms, The Crown, The Castle.[4]

Gen. Braddock, retired and travelling by coach to Bath, 106 miles west of London, saw rural England in its prime. Never again would hedgerow, box, English oak and beech, cattle-dappled meadow and shepherding vale show themselves so green and tidy. Never again, as in the receding age of the Good Queen Anne, would half-timbered and overhanging houses, bow windows, and squat church towers blend so neatly into the vista of narrow village streets—narrow, that is, except a few places like Marlborough whose broad High Street was wide enough to hold a market in its lap.[5]

It took the Bath coach a day and a half to reach Marlborough, the town for which the great Duke had taken his title, seventy-four miles west of London.[6] The Duke had been a lucky one, starting out in the foot guards like the elder Braddock, a boy with a squeaky voice, but out-stripping him at every turn to become England's richest man and most famous general—"Malbrook," the Old Corporal who never lost a battle.[7] The younger Braddock would be as proud as his father had been to serve under the Old Corporal. The great Duke understood, better than any one else in his day, the blast of disciplined infantry fire. It took thirty-seven words of command to put his foot soldiers through the exercise of loading and discharging their firelocks. But they fired by platoons instead of by ranks. No army in Europe could match British infantry fire power.[8]

And so to Bath went General Braddock, to *The* Bath as it was called, where fashion flocked as soon as June closed the London season. Mild year-round climate and old Roman hot springs supposedly beneficial for palsy, rheumatism, gout, neuralgia, sciatica, vapours, and diseases of the liver, originally had made Bath a resort for both real and imaginary sufferers. Visits by the late Queen Anne and her husband in later years had raised the stock of the town as a place of fashion, filling it with people whose principal purpose in life was to eat, drink, and gamble. Its floating population ran into the thousands. Free and easy introductions made it the match-making center of the country, a strategically favorable last stand for retired major generals with unmarried daughters.[9]

A small, magnificent Gothic abbey rose above the rooftops of Bath's yellow stone and stucco houses, ranged on the slopes and terraces of a natural ampitheatre in the elbow of a quiet little river, the Avon. A peal of the Abbey's ten bells customarily welcomed distinguished strangers to Bath. His party settled, the head of the family was expected to pay the bell ringers half a guinea for their trouble. He subscribed two guineas toward music and entertainment, a fee which entitled him to three tickets for the balls held each Tuesday and Friday night at the Assembly Room. Another guinea or a half went to the bookseller for reading material. Another subscription was expected at the coffee house to pay for pens, ink, and writing paper—the visitor must tell his friends where he was and whom he was seeing.[10]

The General and his family probably found Bath agreeable after London. Those who used the hot springs took an early morning dip, anytime between 6 and 9 o'clock. Ladies, carried from their lodgings to the baths in sedan chairs, wore chip hats and voluminous bathing clothes of yellow canvas or brown linen. Pants and shirt of the same material were the proper bathing costume for gentlemen. The water was piping hot, varying from 115 to 120 degrees, and snuff boxes were neglected while the bathers wiped the sweat from their faces.

If he followed custom, the General breakfasted in a coffee house where he could read the London papers. Later he might meet his wife, and sometimes their daughters, in the Pump Room, a pavilion overlooking the baths, where most visitors congregated for three glasses of hot mineral water drawn by waiters from cocks encased in marble behind a balustrade. An orchestra played in the pump room. From there visitors strolled over to the abbey for morning services.[11] The abbey was actually a cathedral whose fan vaulting was surpassed only by the roof of King's College Chapel at Cambridge.[12]

After church people walked in the sunshine, in the flagged and gravelled squares. They rode, played cards until dinner time, 2 or 3 o'clock, then went back to the pump room, stopping in the Abbey for evening services before tea. Balls began at 6 o'clock with a minuet. On nights when there was no ball, there were concerts, lectures, theatricals—not too well patronized—cards and dice.[13] Richard (Beau) Nash, a gamester generally accepted in the newspapers as Britain's *arbiter elegantarium* had been appointed master of all public ceremonies. Nash managed the balls, the promenades, the card and dice tables and the chairmen of the town. He also fixed the lodging rates.[14]

John Wesley, a young preacher from Oxford and the son of one of Marlborough's chaplains, thought Bath a den of vice, but generally speaking its worst sins were idleness and frivolity.[15]

"How d'ye do?" is all one hears in the morning and "What's trumps?" in the afternoon, Lady Mary Wortley Montagu once complained.[16]

The Braddocks found no shortage of agreeable company. The Duchess of Marlborough, who had brought the failing Duke to Bath, returned after his death with her favorite granddaughter, Diana Spencer, whom she hoped to marry to the new Prince of Wales—the one who played the fiddle.[17] Lord Peterborough, a garrulous veteran of the war in Spain, had settled in Bath and could be counted upon to talk about the Coldstream battalion at the battle of Almanza.[18] Lieut-Gen. Edward Wolfe and his wife who, like the Braddocks, had a son in the army, spent several weeks in Bath each year.[19] The Braddock's elder daughter, a pretty girl called Fanny, made friends easily. She was introduced to Lord Hervey, the new Queen's confidant, a gentleman of the bedchamber and the husband of Mollie Lepell, a favorite St. James's wit and beauty.[20]

Lord Hervey, sickly and effeminate, suffered from gallstones, was losing his teeth, and was on a diet. He had come to Bath on the advice of his physician, Dr. George Cheyne, a trustee of Bath's proposed Mineral Water Hospital and an authority on the healing qualities of the spring.[21] Hervey took a liking to Fanny Braddock, but was not always kindly in his feelings toward those who came to Bath in search of health or happiness in their old age and affliction. He wrote to Lady Mary Wortley Montagu:

I came to this place yesterday, from which you may imagine I am not yet sufficiently qualified to execute the commission you gave me, which was to send you a list of the sojourners and inmates of this place; but there is so universal an affinity and resemblance among the individuals that a small paragraph will amply serve to illustrate what you have to depend on. The Duchess of Marlborough, Congreve, and Lady Rich are the only people whose faces I know, the rest are a swarm of wretched beings, some with half their limbs, some with none, the ingredients of Pandora's box personified, who stalk about, half remnants of mortality, and by calling themselves human, ridicule the species more than Swift's yahoos.[22]

Hervey's wife, who had come to Bath with her husband, found the place and its people amusing. In a letter to Mrs. Henrietta Howard, a former maid of honor and now the King's new mistress up in London, she said: [23]

Lord Peterborough has been here for some time, though by his dress one would believe he had not designed to make any stay, for he wears boots all day, and as I hear, must do so, having brought no shoes with him. It is a comical sight to see him with his blue ribbon and star and a cabbage under each arm, or a chicken in his hand, which, after he himself has purchased at market, he carries home for his dinner.[24]

The bumptious Peterborough, an admirer of Mrs. Howard, could be a bore, with his interminable stories of beautiful Spanish women, how he had once turned a cannon on a convent to force one pretty woman to come out—a frightened woman whose face and figure had almost escaped him when she ran into the convent for refuge. "The Spanish ladies, of all other," he insisted, "have the most noble and reasonable sentiment of love. . . ." [25]

"I think Bath a more agreeable place to be in than London," Mrs. Howard told Dr. Swift after visiting the spa. "All the entertainments of the place lie in a small compass, and you are at liberty to partake of them or let them alone, just as it suits your humour." [26]

The Braddocks soon settled down as residents rather than visitors. The General bought one of eighteen new houses on Trim street, a new development just outside the old city wall.[27] Later the Wolfes took the house at No. 5 Trim street, a two and a half story residence with a classic façade designed by John Wood, an architect who was lifting Bath's face with a new city plan in the palladian manner.[28]

Late in October, 1724, General Braddock's wife, Mary, died. She

was buried in the Bath abbey church.[29] Something may have told
him that his own days were numbered, for two weeks after his
wife's funeral he made his will.[30] Evidently he was concerned for
the future of his two unmarried daughters, Henrietta and Frances.
He divided equally between them his entire estate—South Sea stock,
South Sea annuities, the Trim street house, its furnishings, his
jewelry, plate, and all other personal possessions, valued at a total
of at least £6,000.

". . . only paying to my son Edward Braddock the sum of One
Hundred Pounds of lawful money of England to buy his mourning," said the General's will.[31] Of his other two sons, if either was
still living, there was no mention.

The General died the following April, 1725. He was buried beside his wife in the abbey church.[32] His two daughters, named sole
executrices, probably took his will up to London (where it was
probated) to show it to their brother, Edward.[33] The only personal
possession of the General which seems to have passed into Edward's
hands—and young Braddock may have received that before his
father died—was an officer's sash woven of red silk, twelve feet long
and thirty inches wide, with long tassels at each end. Embroidered
into the open mesh at each end, above a row of standing human
Figures, was the date "1709," the year (old style) the General received his commission from Queen Anne as a major-general.[34]

Fanny Braddock had had so many beaux since her nineteenth
birthday that she had been in no haste to marry. Now she fell in
love with an adventurer, "the celebrated S———, who at that time
went by the name of *the good-natured man*," according to Oliver
Goldsmith.[35] The character of *Honeywood* in Goldsmith's comedy,
The Good Natured Man, may have been modeled after "the celebrated S———," but the full name of Fanny's lover appears to have
been lost.[36]

John Wood, the Bath architect who knew Fanny, said "she was
naturally of a gay temper, exceedingly generous, good natured in
the highest degree, affable, pleasant in conversation, and so full of
wit and humour that some of her letters and other writings, as
well in verse as in prose, with proper explanations would have
done honor to her memory. . . ."[37] Withal apparently she was
naïve. When S——— was arrested and imprisoned in London for
debt, she announced her intention of paying off his creditors.[38]

Beau Nash, who knew Fanny and probably had known her father, was in London when she came up from Bath to do what she could to bring about the release of S———. Evidently she had ignored everybody's advice, including that of her brother and sister, to leave the fellow alone. They appealed to Nash, one of the greatest living experts on coxcombs, to try to dissuade her. He talked to Fanny as plainly as a gentleman could speak to a lady in the stilted language of the day. He told her that what she was doing would ruin both herself and the man with whom she was infatuated.

> So warm a concern for the interests of Mr. S—— would, in the first place quite impair her fortune in the eyes of his sex, and, what is worse, lessen her reputation in the eyes of her own [said Nash (according to Goldsmith)].
> Thus bringing Mr. S—— from prison, would be only a temporary relief; a mind so generous as his would become bankrupt upon the load of gratitude; and instead of improving in friendship or affection, he would only study to avoid a creditor he could never repay. Though small favors make good will, great ones destroy friendship.

Fanny rejected the Beau's advice, as she had declined that of others. She paid S———'s debts and set him free. And as wiser people had warned her, he never came back. Goldsmith says he died in jail. And her loyalty to the man she loved won her no corresponding sympathy in Bath. Her friends fell away. She ceased to be a belle. Her sister Henrietta died in 1729,[39] leaving Fanny alone in the world, as far as anyone in Bath knew, except for her one brother, Lt. Edward of the Coldstream, in London.

Only Nash seems to have taken pity on Fanny. He watched her closely. After Henrietta's death, when Fanny began to appear more and more frequently at the Bath card and dice tables, he tried to help her, reproving her whenever she deviated from a professional gambler's rules of caution. She lost heavily. She lost everything she owned, including Henrietta's share of her father's estate which she had inherited, but she took her bad luck bravely.

"No one should ever be sensible of her losses, were they at the last extremity," she had been heard to say.[40]

Her money gone, she fell into the hands of Dame Lindsey, a broken-down opera singer, who used her as a decoy for a gambling table in one of Bath's assembly rooms, an association which gave Fanny the name of a loose woman. Nash rescued her from this infamy and got her a position as a governess in the Wood home.[41]

Wood, the architect, his wife, and their three children lived at

No. 24 Queen Square, the center house in an imposing block of three done in his best palladian manner. In the summer of 1730 Fanny rented part of Wood's house and maintained her own apartment there. Wood found her a perfect lady, with friends of the best character. But she had become psychopathic.

"For about six months before her death she lost no opportunity of viewing the moon with my telescopes; nor of talking with me about the beauties of that luminary and what pleasures souls departed from this earth must have, should the Almighty destine them for that planet," Wood recalled later.

She asked a surgeon, a friend of Wood, what means of suicide was the easiest, attended by the least pain. She had difficulty sleeping. She tried to tire herself by long walks up and down the vales of the Avon valley with a genteel servant woman whom she had playfully nicknamed "Nash." When she went to bed Fanny tied a handkerchief over her eyes and left her candle burning, in case she awakened. Sometimes she would pace her room until exhausted. Her servant woman locked her in her bedroom every night, slipping the key back under the door to assure her mistress she would not be disturbed until she awakened normally, usually about 7 o'clock each morning, when she rang a hand bell to call "Nash." [42]

Some word of his sister's misfortune surely reached Lieut. Edward Braddock in London. He may have been embittered by reports that she had gambled away every remaining penny of the £6,000 inheritance which their father had managed to lay up in a lifetime for his daughters' security. But gambling was a common vice. Young Braddock had seen plenty of it in the army. Ordinary soldiers in the footguards supplemented their meager pay when off duty by working as porters in gambling houses where their officers played at cards and dice night after night.[43] A more likely explanation of the Lieutenant's lack of sympathy may well have been Fanny's infatuation with S———, and her refusal to accept any advice on that affair.

In the summer of 1731 young Braddock's regiment encamped, as usual, in Hyde Park with the other footguards. They were reviewed and exercised before their Majesties, the King and Queen and the Prince of Wales, firing eighteen volleys. According to the newspapers the troops made a fine appearance [44]—which was more than could be said for the Prince. Even when mounted on a white charger, with gold-plated harness and bearskin saddle holsters, Frederick looked small and insignificant.[45]

Down in Bath, Fanny was still living with the Woods, but presumably without paying any rent. In August, Wood and his wife went up to London, leaving Fanny with their three children. One of Wood's workmen agreed to sleep in the house at night while the architect was away.[46]

Wood had planned to be back by September 8, but he was delayed two days. The night he was expected home, Fanny hanged herself. Full details awaited Wood on his return, two nights later.

On the dining room window of her apartment, the afternoon before she killed herself, she had scratched with a diamond ring left by her father:

> *Oh Death! thou pleasing end to human Woe;*
> *Thou Cure for Life, thou greatest Good below!*
> *Still may'st thou fly the Coward and the Slave,*
> *And thy soft Slumbers only bless the brave.*

She had had supper that night in Wood's study, playing cheerfully with his two older children until bedtime, dandling them on her knee; and on the way to her own bedroom she had looked into the nursery on another child, asleep in its cradle. "Nash" had left Fanny alone, locking her bedroom door as usual and slipping the key underneath. It was the first time, as far as "Nash" could remember, that Fanny had ever wished her a goodnight.

About half-past two in the morning, Wood's workman, sleeping downstairs, was awakened by a thump on the floor. He listened, heard Fanny moving about her room, as was her habit, assumed all was well, and went back to sleep. But no bell rang for "Nash" at 7 o'clock next morning. None rang at noon. The servant woman grew alarmed. The door of Fanny's room was still locked and the key inside.

At 2 o'clock "Nash" called for help. A workman raised a ladder to the window of Fanny's bedroom, climbed up, lifted the sash, pushed back the shutters, and saw what had happened. Fanny had knotted two girdles over a closed closet door, stepped off a dressing stool, and strangled.

On a table set in front of her fireplace lay Sir John Harrington's translation of *Orlando Furioso*, opened at the story of Olympia who by ingratitude of a bosom friend was ruined and left to the mercy of the world. In the pocket of her white nightgown was another girdle knotted in a noose but broken, apparently in a first and unsuccessful attempt at suicide. Her head was bruised as if she had fallen. Evidently that was the noise which had awakened the workman downstairs.

A coroner's jury held an inquest, returned a verdict of suicide while *non compos mentis,* and Fanny was buried next night in the Abbey church with her parents and her sister.[47]

"Poor Fanny!" Braddock was reported to have said when word of his sister's death reached him in London. "I always thought she would play till she was forced to tuck herself up." [48]

He was not being quite as heartless as this may have sounded to some people. He was using an accepted slang expression of the day.

Bath was always good for a scandal in the newspapers, and the September issue of the sixpenny *Gentleman's Magazine* provided its readers with all the lurid particulars "of the unhappy self-murther of Miss Fanny Braddock at Bath."

> Mrs. Braddock went to bed, no ways disordered in her senses or behavior. . . . She got out of bed again, and, 'tis supposed, employed some time in reading because a book lay open on the table.
> She put on a white night gown, and pinned it over her breast; tied a gold and silver girdle together, and hanged herself to a closet door in this manner: At the end of the girdle she tied three knots, at about one inch asunder, that, if one slipped, another might hold, then opening the door, put the knotty end of the girdle over it and locked the door again, and making a noose at the other end, put it about her neck, by getting on a chair, and then dropping off it; she hung with her back against the door, and had hold of the key with one of her hands; she bit her tongue through, and had a bruise on her forehead which last might be occasioned by the breaking of a red girdle she'd tried first, which was found in her pocket with a noose on it, and there were two marks on the door. . . .
> She was buried in a decent manner in the Abbey church, in the grave of her honest, brave old father, a gentleman who had experienced some undeserved hardships in life; but who might be said to be thus far happy, that he lived not to see or hear of so tragical a catastrophe of his beloved daughter.

Fanny became a legend of the gambling tables. Her death inspired newspaper articles on the subject of suicide. She was "the celebrated Miss Fanny Brado-k" in the *Political State of Great Britain* for October.[49] Her death found its way into a cheap anonymous ("with key") anthology of "Modern Amours" published in London in 1733. Wood recounted the story in his *Essay towards a*

Description of Bath, a book published sixteen years later. Goldsmith picked it up and embellished it with the art of a professional
rewrite man for his biography of Beau Nash. Fanny's death was
responsible, to some extent, for the introduction of a bill in Parliament to prevent excessive and fraudulent gambling, and to sup-
press all private lotteries and the games of faro, basset, hazard, and
the ace of hearts.[50]

Lord Hervey was at Hampton Court when he heard of Fanny's
death.[51] To Stephen Fox, a friend who lived at Bruton, a market
town below Bath, he wrote:

> I am really jealous of her character on this occasion, and quite hurt
> by those impertinent and simple people who endeavor by such paltry
> comments to detract from it. I liked her living, and I honor her dying.
> I dare say if it could be known, Adrian, Anacreon, or Petronius did
> not die with more unconcern. Cato made much more bustle about it;
> though he makes a much better figure in Lucan and Addison, than
> she does in *Fog* and the *Craftsman.*
>
> Nor are these all the absurdities I fret at and grow lean under upon
> this occasion. There are full as many bad moralists who descant on
> this subject as ignorant anatomists; and I am forced to sit and hear
> things advanced by my brother-Courtiers which if they did not make
> me peevish would infallibly make me laugh. I dare make no answer to
> them, because I am sure, if I should dash their redundant stream of
> folly with one drop of common sense, these inexhaustible sluices, their
> mouths, would never be shut: and I should either be hooted through
> the Palace for an atheist, or at least run the gauntlet through staring
> eyes and pointing fingers wherever I went.[50]

When Hervey told Augustus Schutz, Master of the Robes and
Privy Purse, that he thought Fanny had "done mighty right,"
Schutz fairly foamed with an outburst against self murder, "flying
in Almighty God's face."

"You will easily imagine I did not enter in an argument," said
Hervey. "I should as soon think of reasoning with a kicking dog
or a biting horse." [52]

It is not likely that Braddock fared much better with his brother
officers than Hervey with his brother courtiers. Temporary notoriety as the brother of the celebrated Fanny Braddock, self mur-
derer, was not the sort of fame sought by a lieutenant of the Coldstream Guards. He had no wish to become involved and there was
nothing he could do now—except stay away from Bath.

Wood waited five months for some one to claim Fanny's personal
effects, then felt justified in having them sold at public auction to

satisfy a bill of £52.3.4 owed him when she died.[53] Beau Nash was at the sale, to run up the bids, and a morbid desire on the part of many to own something which had belonged to the unfortunate woman brought in more than Fanny owed. A small surplus was turned over to her brother.

"Though it ought to have gone to me," said Wood resentfully, "as a consideration towards the damages I sustained on the score of her untimely death." [54]

V

COVENT GARDEN INTERLUDE

1732–1738

RAIN WASHED the last lingering winter chill from London brick and flagstone. The gardeners at St. James's bent over their spades. Trees along the mall turned feathery green. Carters hauled fresh yellow gravel from a scow moored at the King's old Whitehall landing stage and spread it on the wet paths in the park. Spring was returning, with the smell of grass stained earth across untrimmed hawthorne hedges and half ploughed fields. Casement windows opened early in the morning to receive it.

Between 5 and 6 o'clock the bells of fifty churches tolled for early service. By 7 the barbershops were filled with bristly faces and uncurled wigs. But officers of the guards, off duty, slept until 9, when the fops got their breakfast and their mail at the Young Man's Coffee House, at Charing Cross. Older and lustier officers preferred *Jenny Man's,* in the Tilt Yard. At both places, hazy and rancid with tobacco smoke, breakfast usually began with a small beer or a draft of wine. Morning headaches were chronic.[1]

Drunkenness was no vice. Strong beer made Britons broad and brown. And ever since the days of King William, when the importation of French brandy was prohibited, the distilling trade had been encouraged by the government as a domestic market for home-grown grain and a source of painless tax revenues. Taverns, mug-houses, brandy and gin shops lined the narrow streets of London.

A night's entertainment invariably ended with the bottle. Early morning churchgoers would step over the drunks laid out on the pavement in front of the public houses—but never over an officer of the guards. An officer was a gentleman with a body servant who, if necessary, carried him home, but there was a record of two captains of the guard having been drunk on parade at Whitehall.[2]

At 10 o'clock the drums beat. A new palace guard assembled to relieve the old one, at half-past, in the courtyard of St. James's. From 12 until 2, if the weather were good, officers off duty joined promenaders in the park. Dinner might be anytime between 2 and 5, the later hours the more fashionable. Another drink at the coffee house settled the port wine served with dinner. Practically the whole of the guards' mess, from colonel to ensign, were reputed to spend the evening in what was known as "a certain notorious house in St. James's street." [3] Others headed for Covent Garden, to go to the theatre, drink in the cheaper taverns, or amuse themselves in the night houses there.

Covent Garden, a seedy square off Drury Lane behind the Strand, had been developed a century earlier on the grand Italian style as an elegant residential place. Now a smelly fruit and vegetable market was growing up in the original piazza, faced with solid rows of arcaded Inigo Jones mansions and a church that looked like a Tuscan temple. Actors at the theatres had lodgings in the neighborhood and people were beginning to call the church—St. Paul's Covent Garden—"the actors' church." [4]

Beggars, bullies, bawds, sots, pimps, prostitutes, pickpockets made a good thing of Covent Garden after dark. No timid gentleman went there alone and unarmed. It was easy enough to shake off some drab trying to sell faded violets she had picked from market refuse, but a thief with a knife, a belligerent drunk swishing a blade was another matter.[5] All this made Covent Garden a favorite rendezvous for rakehell bucks and bloods bent on drinking, gambling, wenching. They scoured the taverns, beat the rounds, toured the brothels—breaking furniture, smashing windows, and chucking waiters, porters, madames, dishes, and glassware into the street. Some of these rowdies organized themselves into clubs.[6] One of the lustiest, known as the Hell Fire Club, had a brilliant and eccentric Jacobite, Phillip Duke of Wharton, as its leader.[7]

There was a story that Fanny Braddock's brother, during a

drunken brawl with Wharton and his crew, heaved a bottle which put out one eye of Robert Lord Clancarty, elder son of a dissolute and debauched Jacobite.[8] Clancarty himself was a slovenly drunk who generally passed out during the evening. He had served as a Naval officer who was an intimate of Swift and Bolingbroke and, through family connections, had hopes of being named governor of Newfoundland. That he had lost one eye in a drinking bout was common knowledge. But there was some question as to who threw the bottle.[9]

William Hogarth, an artist who lived in Covent Garden, had just completed a series of six story-pictures, "A Harlot's Progress." [10] Theophilus Cibber, son of Colley Cibber, the actor, had made the story into a pantomime. Engravings of the pictures were reproduced on fanmounts, and on cups and saucers.[11] Hogarth's next series, "The Rake's Progress," was unadulterated Covent Garden. The scene of one plate was laid in the *Rose Tavern,* a night resort of low character, next door to the Royal Theatre, Drury Lane. For a pot of beer the porter of *The Rose,* known as Leathercoat, would lie down in the street and allow the wheels of a coach to pass over him.[12]

John Gay's smashing comedy, *The Beggar's Opera,* had touched on the sordid night life of Covent Garden. And when young Henry Fielding, a budding playwright and the son of one of Marlborough's old captains, sat down in the spring of 1732 to turn out something bright and novel for the summer season at Drury Lane, he could think of nothing better than a burlesque laid in the back parlor of a Covent Garden bawdy house. He wrote it hastily, in two short acts, and titled it *The Covent Garden Tragedy.*[13] We analyze it here because of its alleged relationship to Braddock.

Fielding's new play opened on Monday night, June 1, at the Drury Lane Theatre.[14] Its cast included Theophilus Cibber and Katherine Raftor, a jovial little red-haired Irish actress who was to become one of the immortal ladies of the Georgian stage under her married name, Kitty Clive.[15] The action of the play began with the arrival of the mighty *Captain Bilkum,* preceded by a porter named *Leathersides,* in the back parlor of one *Mother Punchbowl's* Covent Garden brothel. *Bilkum* was a bully and thoroughgoing rascal. He threatened to break the head of a chairman who complained *Bilkum* had paid only half his fare. Greeted by *Mother*

Punchbowl, who asked what he wished, *Bilkum* replied: "Get me a wench and lend me half a crown."

Mother Punchbowl pined for the good old days

> *When Colonels, Majors, Captains and Lieutenants,*
> *Here spent the issue of their glorious toils.*
> *These were the men, my Bilkum, that subdued*
> *The haughty foe, and paid for beauty here.*
> *Now we are sunk to a low race of beaus,*
> *Fellows unfit for women or for war. . . .*

Bilkum who apparently had just quit one mistress in a huff fumed:

> *Oh! Tis not in the power of punch to ease*
> *My grief-stung soul since Hecatissa's false,*
> *Since she could hide a poor half-guinea from me.*
> *Oh! had I searched her pockets ere I rose,*
> *I had not left a single shilling in them. . . .*

He still had no money with which to pay for the girl he wanted and one of *Mother Punchbowl's* brood refused to extend his credit because, she said, he had paid her on a previous occasion with counterfeit notes. The madame tried to persuade this wench to be less exacting, arguing that a bawdy house needed at least one bully, while *Bilkum* gloated aside over the prospect of getting what he wanted "once more, unpaid for." At the same time *Mother Punchbowl* counseled her girls:

> *Never give your easy mind to love;*
> *And poise the scales of your affection so*
> *That a bare sixpence added to the scale*
> *Might make the cit apprentice or the clerk*
> *Outweigh a flaming colonel of the guards.*
> *Oh! never give your mind to officers,*
> *Whose gold is on the outside of the pocket. . . .*

There was a duel, and the wench for whom *Bilkum* hoped was reported—erroneously, it turned out—to have hanged herself on the curtain rods of her bed. The play ended happily with the actors dancing to a fiddler's tune.

> *For such examples as this and that*
> *We are all taught to know I know not what.*

And Miss Raftor, who played one of *Mother Punchbowl's* bawds, spoke an epilogue concluding:

To be a mistress kept, the strumpet strives,
And all the modest virgins to be wives.
For prudes may cant of virtues and of vices,
But faith, we only differ in our prices.

Apparently Fielding had worked into his play a lot of personal neighborhood scandal familiar to his first night audience.[16] The bucks in the pit quickly recognized *Leathersides* as Leathercoat, the porter of *The Rose*. They laughed loudly, but their mirth was muffled in whistles and catcalls from others in the audience. Critics reported the performance dull and obscene. They said the play presented nothing that might not be observed any night at a notorious bawdy house to which several members of the audience paid a visit when the curtain came down.[17] The show was withdrawn from that summer's bill. But a printed version sold for a shilling on the bookstalls.[18]

The female characters in the play might have been drawn from a dozen women known around Covent Garden. One was a Mother Needham, who had stood in pillory not long before. Another was a Mrs. Haywood, described whimsically by Fielding as "a useful woman in the parish of Covent Garden." But somebody assumed that the *Hecatissa* to whom *Bilkum* referred was a Mrs. Upton with whom Lieut. Edward Braddock of the Coldstream Guards was reported to have been intimate. Braddock accordingly was identified by some with *Bilkum,* and from there it was but a short step to assume that the hanging episode referred to his sister Fanny.[19]

Mrs. Upton was said to have been keeping Braddock, and according to a vicious piece of gossip passed on by Sir Robert Walpole's son, Horace:

"He (Braddock) had gone to great lengths with her pin money, and was still craving. One day that he was very pressing, she pulled out her purse and showed him that she had only 12 or 14 shillings left. He twitched it from her, 'Let me see that.' Tied up in the other end he found five guineas. He took them, tossed the empty purse in her face, saying 'Did you mean to cheat me?' and never went near her more." [20]

Once it got into circulation, the purse story helped spread another scurrilous report concerning a duel Braddock was said to have fought with Col. Samuel Gumley, a former Coldstream officer who had transferred to the Royal Dragoons. Gumley was the son of John Gumley of Isleworth, a wealthy glass manufacturer and army contractor whose daughter had married William Pulteney. Pulteney, the brother of Braddock's captain and former secretary at war, had just settled some political differences of his own in a duel with Fanny Braddock's champion, Lord Hervey.[21]

Before they quarreled Braddock and the younger Gumley had been friends. Gumley was a good natured wit. And as they were about to step off and engage in combat, the story said, Gumley tossed his purse to Braddock and said: "Braddock, you are a poor dog. Here, take my purse; if you kill me you will be forced to run away, and then you will not have a shilling to support you."

Braddock threw it back, insisting they fight. In the duel Braddock was disarmed but was too proud to beg for his life. And the story ends that Gumley walked off and left him standing there.[22]

Braddock was no dullard.[23] One of his associates was Col. James O'Hara, Baron Tyrawley, a bright, irresponsible Irish wit who enjoyed the acquaintance of Pope, Chesterfield, and Theophilus Cibber's father, Colley, the actor-poet-laureate.[24] Like Braddock, Tyrawley was a general's son. Four years older than Braddock, he had served under Peterborough in Spain and with the Duke in Flanders. At the age of twenty-three he had succeeded his father as colonel of Royal Fusiliers. When in London Tyrawley spent most of his time at *White's*, a St. James's street coffee house noted for gaming, and enjoyed the society of some of the more complaisant ladies of the theatre. One of his former mistresses, a Mrs. Bellamy, an actress now playing in Dublin, had become his mistress when she was only 14 years old.[25] There is no reason to assume that Braddock's morals were any higher than Tyrawley's, but he bore no closer resemblance to *Captain Bilkum* than did Tyrawley. These were days when malicious gossip ruined many in public life, and Braddock did not escape.

He was thirty-seven now. During his twenty-two years in the Coldstream he had advanced only one grade. Many other officers had been in the service for twenty years without rising above a captain's rank.[26] It had been their misfortune to enter the army almost at the end of Queen Anne's war, the beginning of a long period of Walpole peace. With the exception of Tyrawley, who was in perpetual difficulties over the management of his own affairs, Braddock had no friends of any consequence to seek him special favor.

He must have known his sister Fanny's friend, Lord Hervey, the

Queen's confidant. Hervey lodged at the foot of the Queen's back stairway to gather gossip, fetch chairs, carry candles, and call coaches. But Hervey roughed his cheeks, tripped like a lady as often as he strutted like a lord, and did not endear himself to guardsmen at St. James's by speaking Latin whenever one came within earshot. Pope had nicknamed him "Lord Fanny," an association which Braddock must have found painful.[27]

Immaculate in white gaiters and scarlet regimentals, Braddock helped marshal strangers who came to St. James's with tickets permitting them to watch the royal family eat in a state room set aside for that exhibition. He inspected sentries at the sentry boxes either side of the St. James Street gate where men of fashion in gold laced coats and heavily powdered women in 9-yard hoops, paying court to the royal family, passed in and out by coach and sedan chair, attended by linkmen and liveried footmen. In the absence of a superior officer, he ordered out the drummers to beat a salute whenever a member of the royal family passed through the gate.[28] It was part of the King's routine, when at St. James's, to watch the changing of the guard from the palace windows. Once a year the King reviewed the Coldstream and the other household troops.[29] But in all probability he did not know that a lieutenant named Braddock existed.

The court Braddock now served was pitched upon a higher level than that of George I. But in many respects, as far as the royal family was concerned, it was as coarse and vulgar as that of Charles II. George II, who liked to regard himself as a ladykiller, slept with other women as frequently as he slept with his wife, and he rarely slept alone. The Queen's virtue was never questioned. Prime Minister Robert Walpole, whose conversational vocabulary drew heavily on the kennel and the stable, attributed the Queen's influence over the King primarily to their physical relationship, and in advising her how to handle her husband he often spoke the language of Mother Punchbowl. He shocked the Princesses.[30]

The King thought of himself as a soldier. He had been with Marlborough at Oudenarde in 1708, and hated to think of growing old without another battle.[31] Twice he had been disappointed. In the summer of 1731 Captain Robert Jenkins, master of the brig Rebecca, had sailed into London from Jamaica to report that Spanish coast guards had boarded his ship in the Caribbean, tied him up to a yardarm, cut off his ear, and bade him carry it back to his master, King George. The Captain had called at court, his dissevered ear in a small box packed with cotton, but Walpole had refused to regard mayhem as an act of war. Four years later, during his annual visit to Hanover, George had been offered the Rhine command of a proposed Austro-British army if he would bring England into a war Austria was waging against France and Spain. Walpole held fast to his peace policy.[32] "There are fifty thousand men slain in Europe this year and not one Englishman," he said quietly.[33]

Frederick Prince of Wales, was associated politically with Walpole's opposition.[34] His parents detested him, and two young army officers who were members of Parliament, William Pitt and John Fane, Earl of Westmoreland, had been broken because of their friendship for the prince. Frederick attended his father at troop reviews and was reported to have military ambitions which were not encouraged by the King. The Prince actually showed more interest in the theatre than in the army.[35]

Following the example of his father and his grandfather, Frederick had several mistresses, some of them not too nice. One night he slipped out of St. James's palace alone into the park to keep a rendezvous with a woman who robbed him of his watch and twenty-two guineas, and who was chased by a grenadier, possibly one of Braddock's. That seems to have been the lieutenant's nearest approach to a personal contact with the Prince.[36]

Frederick's younger brother, William Augustus, the chubby little Duke of Cumberland, was still a boy, a grave and solemn blue-eyed child who still liked to watch soldiers drill.[37] William Augustus had recruited his own company of miniature Coldstream guardsmen among the sons of his father's courtiers. Dressed as a corporal, he drilled them in the palace gardens. His parents doted on him as much as they despised his older brother whom the King called a puppy.[38] Braddock would come to know the Duke better.

Braddock had another opportunity to see a group of North American Indians in the summer of 1734. A chief, his wife, their son, and five warriors from Mr. Oglethorpe's colony visited London. The men refused to wear breeches, but the King received them, in their clouts and red and black war paint, in a room next to the guard room at St. James's. The Indians placed two skins in the King's hands and laid feathered sticks on the skins in token of entering into an alliance with the English. Ladies of the court thought the Indians hideous and terrifying. The gentlemen thought them slightly comic.[39]

On February 10, 1736, Braddock became a full-fledged captain of the guards with line rank of lieutenant-colonel. Now and then his guards did riot as well as sentry duty but all soldiers were still regarded by many Englishmen as instruments of oppression.[40] The long Walpole peace had not increased the army's popularity. In 1737 the Friendly Society of Military Members, an officers club of the guards brigade which met fortnightly at a tavern called *The Goat* in Fuller's Rents, was ordered to divide its box and disband. Who knew what an officers club might be plotting? [41]

Using the nom de plume *Frank Firelock,* an officer who claimed to have entered the army as an ensign under Marlborough and who now was attached to a regiment stationed outside London, wrote a letter to the paper *Common Sense* early in July, 1737, complaining that he and his brother officers were being shunned and slighted by the community in which they were quartered.[42]

"I am told that at court, and among people of fashion, a General Officer is still admitted; that is to say, when company is not engaged with some great man, such an Italian fiddler or singer," said *Firelock,* "but in the country it is much worse, for the better sort will not converse with us at all and inferior folk look upon us as their enemies."

Firelock also observed that officers who never had seen any service except "foolery at reviews" talked of promotion in terms of who could carry an election. To this the *Daily Gazeteer* replied that considering who presided at reviews—in London, the King—*Firelock's* remarks on that score could only be regarded as a glaring mark of disloyalty.[43]

Braddock's Coldstream and other foot guards were in summer camp in Hyde Park, preparing for their annual "foolery," outlined by this order:

At 6 o'clock tomorrow morning Colonel Pultney will exercise the seven battalions, by the wave of the colors as usual, when the King sees them. The officers to appear in their new regimental clothes, gaiters, square-toed shoes, gorgets, sashes, buff-colored gloves, regimental laced hats, cockades, the button worn on the left side, and twisted wigs, according to the pattern. The men to appear perfectly clean and shaved, square-toed shoes, their hats well-cocked, and worn so low as to cover their foreheads, and raised behind, with their hair tucked up well under and powdered, but none on their shoulders, the point of their hats pointing a little to the left, with cockades fixed under the loops as usual, their arms perfectly clean, the hilts of their swords and buckles of their accoutrements made as bright as possible.[44]

The King saw them but did not think they performed their exercises as well as they should. He said his troops in Hanover would have done better.[45]

He and the rest of the royal family, including the Prince and a new Princess of Wales, Augusta of Saxe-Gotha, had taken up their summer residence at Hampton Court. The Princess was in a family way, her confinement due in October. The Queen told Lord Hervey that she was not at all convinced that Frederick was responsible for his wife's pregnancy, and that she did not think her son above trying to palm off a suppositious child as his own legitimate heir. Frederick resented his mother's attitude so bitterly that when the Princess began to feel premature labor pains about 10 o'clock on a Sunday night, July 31, he carried her off in a coach back to St. James's where she gave birth to a daughter.[46]

This "extravagant and undutiful behavior in a matter of such great consequence as the birth of an heir to (the) crown" enraged both the King and the Queen. They commanded the Prince and his wife to leave St. James's as soon as the Princess could travel,[47] and the couple left, as they had arrived, in a coach without escort. The sentry on duty at the gate was ordered not to salute them. Posted in the Coldstream orderly room was a notice:

> It is His Majesty's command, that none of the three regiments of Foot Guards take any notice of the Prince or Princess of Wales, or any of their families, until further orders.[48]

The Prince took his wife first to a house he owned at Kew, then to Norfolk House in St. James's Square.[49]

"I hope to God I never see him again," said the Queen.[50]

She got her wish. Within two months she was on her deathbed. The King forbade Frederick to see her. But she saw her other children, including William Duke of Cumberland, who had moved into Frederick's old apartments at St. James's.[51]

Queen Caroline died Sunday morning, November 20, 1737.[52] In the Coldstream orderly room, appeared this

ORDER FOR MOURNING FOR HER LATE MAJESTY
Every officer is to have a scarlet coat, buttoned to the waist with a mourning button, and faced with black cloth, no buttons on the sleeves or pockets, black cloth waistcoats and breeches, plain hats, no less than

four inches in the brim, with crepe hat-bands, an end appearing at each corner of the buttoned side of the hat, mourning swords and buckles; and to get crepe for their sashes; to be all ready for Sunday Se'nnight, the 4th of December; and the following officers must not fail to have theirs ready on any account whatever: Lieut-Colonels Legge, Braddock, Needham; Captains Corbett, Milner, Williamson; Ensigns Stanhope, Gansell and Rudyard.[53]

By order of the Lord Chamberlain, all theatres were closed the day after the Queen's death.[54] When they reopened, on January 2, Tyrawley's former mistress, Mrs. Bellamy, had returned from Dublin and appeared at Covent Garden in the title role of *The Fair Quaker of Deal,* a popular Restoration comedy.[55] Here, for the first time in several years, Mrs. Bellamy saw an eight-year-old daughter she had borne Tyrawley. The child, named George Anne Bellamy, was brought to the theatre by a nurse who had seen Mrs. Bellamy's name on a playbill.

"My god!" exclaimed the mother, looking at the little girl. "What have you brought me here? This goggle-eyed, splatter-faced, gabbart-mouthed wretch is not my child! Take her away!" [56]

Tyrawley was not in town. He had been sent to Lisbon as British ambassador to Portugal.[57] The little girl went to live with a former domestic of Tyrawley, a peruke-maker, and his wife who kept a shop at St. James's street.[58] Braddock, who had known George Anne since infancy, became a second father to the child.

"Pop," he called her, an endearing nickname which her father also used.[59]

And George Anne returned Braddock's affection. She found him amiable, confiding, and benign. She said later in her memoirs that she could never understand why some thought him rude and coarse.[60]

VI

JENKINS'S EAR AND THE FORTY-FIVE

1738–1745

Even as Queen Caroline lay dying from what polite society described as "mortification of ye bowels," colonial rivalries were pushing royal family affairs into the background. Spain had challenged British maritime supremacy. London's West India merchants and ship owners had addressed an appeal to the King and carried a petition to the House of Commons protesting arbitrary search and seizure of their vessels by the Spaniards. Cargoes were said to have been condemned and crews inhumanly treated.[1] A House of Commons committee called in and questioned Captain Jenkins of the brig *Rebecca*—the same Jenkins who accused the Spaniards of having cut off one of his ears in 1731. Before the bar of the House of Commons he repeated his story, how the Spaniards slashed at his head with their cutlasses, almost but not quite cutting off his ear. Jenkins said they had torn it off bleeding and flung it in his face. He still carried the ear in a little box of cotton.[2]

"Jenkins's Ear" became a war cry. The newspapers took it up. Ballad writers worked it into songs for such popular tunes as "A Bawd Always Dies in Her Drink."[3] Pope referred to it in a new satire, "One Thousand Seven Hundred and Thirty-Eight." A hack by the name of Sam Johnson, who had been writing up the debates in Parliament for the *Gentleman's Magazine,* turned out a poem, *London,* that went through three editions on the strength of lamentations for Britain

. . . triumphant on the Main,
The Guard of Commerce and the Dread of Spain,
Ere Masquerades debauch'd, Excise Oppress'd,
Or English Honor grew a standing Jest. . . .[4]

Letters of marque and reprisal were issued against the ships, goods, and subjects of Spain. Vice Admiral Edward Vernon, boasting he needed only six ships to capture Porto Bello, where most Spanish raiders were fitted out, weighed anchor with a British squadron at Spithead and sailed westward.[5]

On the third Thursday in October, 1739, the heralds, in emblazoned tabards, mounted their horses in the stable yard at St. James's and rode to the palace gate to proclaim that His Majesty George II "relying on the help of Almighty God, who knows the uprightness of our intentions, have thought it fit to declare and do hereby declare war against the King of Spain." [6]

With horse guards to clear a way through exulting crowds, the heralds rode on to Temple Bar, drums pounding, trumpets ablare. All the church bells of London began to ring.[7]

"They may ring their bells now," muttered old Walpole bitterly. "They will be wringing their hands before long." [8]

Captain Edward Braddock was 45 years old when the bells rang, still a bachelor, inclined to stoutness and addicted to snuff. But his hair was still brown,[9] when he went without a powdered wig, and he must have shared the public enthusiasm which greeted the prospect of war to plunder Spain and her rich treasure ships from the West Indies. Recruits turned out in such numbers that for the first time in years army officers were able to pick and choose their men.[10]

Six new regiments of marines were authorized.[11] Five men were drafted from each company of footguards to provide sergeants and corporals to discipline the new regiments. Captain Anthony Lowther, a fifty-two-year-old Malplaquet veteran of the Coldstream, was commissioned a colonel to command one regiment.[12] The marines, it was assumed, would be the first troops overseas, the first to get their hands on the Spanish gold pieces and wedges of silver which every soldier imagined he saw on the sixpenny maps of the West Indies that were being sold in London as fast as they could be printed.[13]

On January 29, 1740, the Coldstream's colonel, the Earl of Scarborough, died suddenly. He had been reported to be suffering from an illness in the head—some said madness—and it was first given out that he had died of apoplexy. Later it was learned that he had shot himself with a pistol, in the mouth, the bullet lodging in his skull. Scarborough was a bachelor with bastard children by the Duchess of Kingston, but his death was believed to involve a scandal with the Duchess of Manchester. Gossips said he had given his word to marry her when her husband died. He had chosen death, they said, as an alternative.[14]

Under the command of regimental Lieut.-Col. John Folliott, an iron disciplinarian who threatened to break any sergeant or corporal showing up on parade with his men in soiled linen, the Coldstream encamped in Hyde Park the middle of March. Officers were directed to provide themselves with tents and full field equipment.[15] Other camps were to be established at Hounslow Heath and Black Heath, and orders were out to begin preparations for the movement of ten regiments to the continent.[16]

A few days later Lloyd's coffee house in Lombard street heard that Vernon had captured Porto Bello with only six ships, just as he had said he would. A Spanish army payroll of $10,000,000 had been seized and distributed among the members of his expedition. All London hailed Vernon a hero. Congratulatory addresses to the King from both houses of Parliament extolled the Admiral's victory. Medals were struck off bearing his likeness, with the catchphrase, "He took Porto Bello with Six Ships." Vernon's head became a favorite sign for public houses.[17]

The *Craftsman* for April 12 recorded public reaction to his exploit by publishing an imaginary tavern conversation between Mr. John Tar, mariner, just back from Porto Bello, and Mr. Thomas Lobster, a foot soldier in one of His Majesty's regiments of Guards.

"You must have had a vast fleet and a very great army to do all this," said Lobster after listening to Tar's account of the taking of the town.

"No, you fool," said Tar. "We did it with six men of war only, and a couple hundred of you landsmen whom the noble Governor of Jamaica was kind enough to lend us; for the Admiral had none sent with him from home."

"Surely, Jack, this can't be true. You must rodomontade a little."

"Ey, ey, that's just like all of you Fair-weather Sparks, who make a very pretty figure in Hyde Park, at a review, with your tucked-up hair and powdered shoulders. . . . Ah! Tom, I wish you had took my advice when you got Dolly the milkmaid with child and gone to sea with me instead of listing for a soldier, and loitering away your spare time at home."

"Look ye, Jack," retorted Tom Lobster, "don't grow scurrilous, and abuse your betters, for you can't be so ignorant as not to know that we have the title of gentlemen soldiers; whereas you are called nothing but Tarpaulins at best—why look ye here, Jack; does not this new red coat, laced hat and sword at my side look more genteel than your old pitched jacket and dirty'd trousers? If you have done your king and country more service than us, as you pretend, it's not our fault. We durst not fight without orders. . . ."

Lobster had not heard of the congratulatory addresses to the King, or of the freedom of the City being presented to Admiral Vernon. He said he and the other members of his regiment never read anything but pro-government newspapers like *Gazeteer* which, subsidized with public funds by the Walpole ministry, were sent free to their quarters. They would not dare read opposition papers, like the *Craftsman*.

"We would stand a fair chance of running the gauntlet or being tied neck and heels if we were caught reading them," he said, "for our Sergeant says they are filled with nothing but treason and sedition, and faction and Popery and blasphemy."

Tar found this hard to understand.

"What have you redcoats done to put'n out of humor?" he asked.

"Why nothing at all, Jack, that I know of."

"Flesh! Tom, I believe thou has nicked it; for I don't hear that you have done anything of late, besides playing the devil at your quarters and burthening the parishes with base children."

At Jack's suggestion they drowned their differences in rum, an unfamiliar spirit to Lobster. "We swam in it at Porto Bello and Jamaica," the sailor boasted.

His pockets were full of gold and silver Spanish coins. He slapped one down on the bar and called on Kate, the barmaid, for a good sneaker of rum punch for Lobster. "Put a biskit and some nutmeg in it—that's our way at sea." [18]

But the King's heart remained with his lobsters. He named his nineteen-year-old favorite son, William Augustus Duke of Cumberland, to succeed the late Earl of Scarborough as colonel of the Coldstream.[19] The Coldstream had moved from Hyde Park to Hounslow when it was joined by the Duke, whose chubby boyhood had developed into a massive physique. He made a good appearance in his white periwig, low three-cornered hat, scarlet coat and white breeches, with a finely wrought silver basket-hilted sword. He rode well. He was gracious. His affability and good sense won the esteem of every officer in the regiment.[20]

The Duke reviewed the Coldstream, watching its scarlet ranks wheel and mesh in patterns of pale blue lapels and flapping cuffs looped back with white braid.[21] Lieut.-Col. Folliott kept his red-coats on their square toes—buckles shining, musket barrels gleaming, long white gaiters spotless, powdered hair tucked up well under low cocked hats pointed at an angle. The Duke himself marked the hang of each black leather pouch on each right thigh, the hitch of each sword and bayonet in its double frog on the left. But he saw no action with the regiment. In October the Coldstream returned to winter quarters.[22]

Wednesday, November 12, was Admiral Vernon's birthday. London rang its bells for the hero and after dark lighted candles in its windows. Public dinners were held in the absent Admiral's honor. But a bigger war than that of Jenkins's Ear was in the making. The Holy Roman Emperor, Karl VI of Austria, had died in Vienna.[23] Early in his reign Karl had promulgated a pragmatic sanction decreeing that when he died his hereditary Habsburg domains should descend undivided to his daughter, Maria Theresa, Queen of Hungary. As a part of his peace policy, Walpole had agreed that England should become one of the guarantors of the Emperor's decree, along with France, Spain, Prussia, and other European powers.[24]

To most Englishmen "the pragmatic sanction" was as meaningless a phrase as "the balance of power." They felt no obligations toward the Queen of Hungary, not even when Parliament voted her a subsidy of £300,000 and authorized seven new regiments of foot and four of marines.[25] Col. William Hanmer of the Coldstream was selected to command one of the new regiments. Passing over more than 200 officers on half-pay, Walpole named four new colonels from among members of Parliament. In the House of Lords the choice of these four was blasted as political jobbery to buy Walpole votes in a parliamentary election to be held in the coming May, 1741.[26]

During the election a detachment of fifty footguards was called from St. James's Palace and the Savoy barracks to put down a riot in Covent Garden. An opposition mob stoned Lord Sundon's coach, and one of his lordship's footmen had his skull cracked with a brickbat.[27] Witnesses later told the Middlesex Grand Jury that the soldiers had intermeddled with civil liberties, and the jury, in its presentments, expressed alarm at "so daring a violation and insult on our freedom and liberties and the dangerous consequences of military power exercised in civil affairs." It recommended court "orders and directions for preventing and discouraging the like heinous offense in the future." [28]

None of this was permitted to interfere with the King's annual visit to Hanover. Early in May a twelve-oared barge had rowed him down the river to the royal yacht, anchored near London bridge. The Tower guns boomed as the barge glided by, its oars beating the dirty Thames silver in the May sunshine.[29] His Britannic Majesty's Hanover holiday was not so bright. Bavaria and France joined his nephew, Frederick William of Prussia, in repudiating pledges as pragmatic sanction guarantors.[30] A French army, moving eastward to attack Prague, headed for Osnabruck on the Hanover border. George II, returning to England, passed through Osnabruck shortly before the French marched in.[31]

In a belated effort to enlighten its readers on dynastic politics, the *Gentlemen's Magazine* published a map of Germany and an account of the pragmatic sanction.[32] Cynical young officers strutting in and out of the Tilt Yard coffee house joked about the proper way to salute a Frenchman—with open arms and a kiss on the right cheek.[33] Captain Braddock, well beyond the strutting age, knew from his father the proper way to salute a Frenchman—the Malbrook way, with fire by platoons!

The May election had returned Walpole with his majority in the Commons dangerously reduced.[34] Dissatisfaction with the slow progress of the War of Jenkins's Ear was increasing. Sir Robert was blamed for the failure of an attack by Vernon on the Spanish colonial stronghold at Cartagena. Vernon's champions contended that the fault lay with the troops of the expedition under Brig. Thomas Wentworth. The British army's best troops, it was argued, had been kept in England. The officers of these sent to Vernon had been either gentlemen whose quality and interest entitled them to preferment, or worthless adventurers—both groups equally unfit to command troops in battle. Officers of American troops which had joined the expedition were reported to have been worse—blacksmiths, shoemakers, tailors.[35]

A solemn man in clerical garb stopped in front of St. James's and called to a guardsman on duty at one of the sentry boxes either side of the gateway, under the palace clock:

"Did you ever see the Leviathan?"

The sentry looked at him blankly.

"No sir," he said.

"Well," said the man in the blackcoat, who looked like a parson, "he is as like Sir Robert Walpole as ever two devils were like one another!" [36]

Sir Robert's son, Horace, who had just returned from the grand tour to take a seat in the new parliament as one of two members representing the Cornish borough of Callington, was amused by what he called the mad parson story and passed it on in one of the first of a series of interminable letters to a friend, Horace Mann, the British charge d'affairs at Florence.[37]

Most of young Walpole's letters that fall and winter were stuffed with fashionable westend chitchat about balls, operas, and masquerades. Sir Thomas Robinson—a long, lean amateur architect, not to be confused with the short, fat British minister of the same name at Vienna [38]—had taken off the doors of his house to make room for two hundred guests at a ball. The plump, flaxen-haired Duke of Cumberland had been one of the guests, footing country dances like a bear. One of Braddock's former brother officers, Lieut. Charles Churchill of the Coldstream, the younger General Charles Churchill's bastard son by Anne Oldfield, had been there making eyes at his future wife, Sir Robert Walpole's bastard daughter, Mary. Supper was served at midnight. They danced until 4 in the morning.[39]

In February Sir Robert Walpole resigned as the King's prime minister. Control of foreign affairs passed to John Lord Carteret, who fully recognized the pragmatic sanction. The Earl of Stair, named field marshall and ambassador plenipotentiary to the Dutch, was sent to The Hague to discuss the dispatch of British troops to the continent to protect Hanover and the Netherlands from France and Prussia.[40] Three battalions of foot guards, part of the household cavalry, six regiments of dragoons, and twelve of the line were ordered to gather up their camp equipment and embark for Flanders.[41]

"We are now all military," Horace Walpole reported. "No parties but reviews. No officers but hope to go abroad—at least it is the fashion to say so." [42]

The Duke of Cumberland quit the Coldstream to succeed the late Sir Charles Wills, who had died on Christmas Day 1741, as colonel of the First Foot Guards.[43] Charles Spencer, 35-year-old Duke of Marlborough, a great-nephew of the Old Corporal, replaced Cumberland as commander of the Coldstream. Braddock's battalion of the regiment remained in London, but Spencer went to Flanders.[44] The King and the Duke were expected to join the army there any day. Their luggage, their linen, their saddle and sumpter horses were shipped from Gravesend to be ready for them when they arrived. But they stayed in England all that summer.[45] The Dutch, at peace with France, had no wish to offend her and were reluctant to become involved. Grudgingly they permitted the British troops to land in their country. The only fighting that occurred in Flanders that summer was a brawl between British soldiers and Dutch butchers in the market square at Ghent.[46]

Braddock's friend Tyrawley came home in the fall from Lisbon, at his own request, for military service. He was given command of a brigade of five regiments on the home establishment.[47] Tyrawley brought with him from Lisbon fourteen bars of gold—a gift from the King of Portugal—a Portugese mistress, and a brood of swarthy, illegitimate children who, according to George Anne Bellamy, gave his Stratton street residence more the appearance of a Turkish seraglio than the home of an English lord.[48]

George Anne was growing up. A bosomy, blue-eyed girl of twelve or thirteen who read poetry and drama, she was now acknowledged by her mother as a daughter. Mrs. Bellamy had never been entirely successful as an actress. She was a beauty with striking figure lacking animation [49] and playing only occasional engagements at Covent Garden. She saw possibilities in her daughter and arranged George Anne's first stage appearance in a benefit pantomime. Later in the spring of 1742, George Anne had played *Miss Prue* in Congreve's *All for Love,* a comedy not exactly suitable for well bred children.[50]

When Tyrawley returned to London she left the peruke maker's home and went to live with her father, his Portugese mistress, Donna Anna, and their children. Tyrawley avoided Mrs. Bellamy and gave George Anne strict instructions to stay away from her.[51] The new arrangement was not a happy one for George Anne. The Stratton street household consisted of three girls by different mothers, and assorted boys. All the boys except George Anne's full

brother, who usually was at sea with the Navy, eventually went off
to school, and when summer came Tyrawley took a box at Bushy
Park.[52] He spent much of his time attending the King at Richmond, but he took George Anne on at least one visit to his friend
Pope, the poet, who insulted the child by turning her over to a
housekeeper with instructions that the young lady be shown the
garden and given as much fruit to eat as she wished. Chesterfield,
who happened by during the visit, rode home in the Tyrawley carriage and soothed George Anne's wounded pride with adult flat-
tery.[53]

Tyrawley had not lost his eye for a pretty actress. In due time he
was on the trail of Peg Woffington, a bewitching Irish girl who
had played with Mrs. Bellamy in Dublin and at Covent Garden.[54]
Dressed in boy's clothes as *Sir Harry Wildair* in *The Constant
Couple,* a favorite Farquhar comedy repeated on ten successive
nights at the Garden, Peg sang a naughty song that charmed her
audience:

> *Thus Damon knocked at Celia's door,*
> *He sighed and begged and wept and swore:*
> *The sigh was so*
> *She answered 'no,*
> *No, no, no!'*
> *Again he sighed, again he prayed:*
> *'No, Damon, no, I am a maid;*
> *Consider, no, I am a maid,*
> *No, no, no!'*
> *At last his sighs and tears made way;*
> *She rose and softly turned the key:*
> *'Come in,' said she, 'but do not stay;*
> *I may conclude*
> *You will be rude:*
> *But, if you are, you may.'* [55]

"I have played this part so many times that half the town be-
lieves me to be a real man," she complained one night, coming off
the stage in *Sir Harry's* breeches.

"Madam the other half *knows* you to be a woman," was the
pointed reply of James Quin, a young Irish actor.[56]

The other half included one of Braddock's brother officers. Capt.-
Lt. Julius Caesar, of the Coldstream, with whom Peg lived as a
mistress.[57]

In a general promotion of officers in the spring of 1743 Tyrawley was made a major-general. The Duke of Cumberland and his friend the young Earl of Albemarle, Braddock's former 15-year-old grenadier captain now grown up and with a regiment of his own, also became major-generals. The young Duke of Marlborough was made a brigadier. Folliott, lieutenant-colonel of the Coldstream, was transferred to the First Foot Guards.[58] The Coldstream's first major, George Churchill, succeeded Folliott as regimental lieutenant-colonel, and the second major, William Douglas, became first major. This opened the way for Braddock's promotion to second major, an advancement which cost him £1,200, at the established rates, over and above £2,400 he could get for his captain's commission.[59]

He and Tyrawley were still in London that summer when an allied army of some 40,000 British, Austrian, Hanoverian, and Hessian troops, commanded by King George, marched up the river Main, then retreated and unexpectedly defeated a French force of 60,000 at the village of Dettingen, above Frankfurt. The Duke of Cumberland got a musket ball in the calf of his leg, but the brigade of guards, commanded by young Marlborough, came off without a single casualty. The brigade had been posted at the rear of the column to protect its elaborate headquarters train of 662 horses, 54 cars, 35 wagons and 13 berlins from an anticipated attack which never developed. Theoretically the Guards had held the post of honor. Actually it had been a place of safety.[60]

"The maiden heroes of the guards are in great warmth with General Ilton (a Hanoverian commander) who kept them out of Harm's way," Walpole wrote in another of his gossipy letters which, true or false, had power to ruin a reputation with a phrase.[61] "They call him 'the confectioner' because he says he *preserved* them."

Behind the dispatches telling London of the battle came reports of dissatisfaction of English officers with the King's partiality toward his Hanoverians. When rations ran short the English were said to have drawn only two days' subsistence while the Hanoverians received four. The King was quoted as having criticized his English troop for lack of discipline.[62] Lord Stair resigned as field marshal, offended by the King's preference for the advice of his Hanoverian generals. Marlborough resigned as a brigadier, rather than share his quarters with a Hanoverian general. He also resigned as colonel of the Coldstream.[63]

Old General Wade, a leaden soldier who played cards with the King and whose professional reputation rested largely upon a system of military roads he had constructed in the Scottish highlands, was expected to succeed Stair. Tyrawley knew Wade. He had no desire to serve under him; so when the King offered Tyrawley the post of ambassador to Russia, he accepted.[64]

Tyrawley's daughter, George Anne, took lodgings with the daughter of a Westminster apothecary, a genteel Mrs. Jones who with her husband kept a china and bijou shop near St. James's. Tyrawley allowed George Anne £100 a year for clothes and other incidental expenses but cautioned her against having anything to do with her mother.

Mrs. Bellamy had married again. Her second husband, a dissipated officer young enough to be her own child, went off to Gibraltar with his regiment, stripping her of every valuable she possessed. She appealed to her daughter, asking her to come and live with her. George Anne did what her mother asked, and her allowance was promptly cut off.[65]

During a visit to Mrs. Woffington at Teddington, in a house filled with theatrical people, George Anne met Thomas Sheridan, a Dublin manager; David Garrick, a young actor enamored of the beautiful Peg; Christopher Rich, the Covent Garden Theatre manager, and his daughters. The young people amused themselves with amateur theatricals. George Anne showed unusual talent. When she and her mother returned to London, making their home with friends of Mrs. Bellamy in Henrietta street, it was decided that George Anne should go on the stage.[66]

Mrs. Bellamy talked to Rich. He was willing to try George Anne in the role of *Nominia* in Otway's tragedy *The Orphan*. But Quin, his male star, balked at being cast with an unknown girl described on the bill as "a young gentlewoman, being her first appearance on any stage." Quin's protest was overruled. The play was put on with him in the lead. For three acts George Anne suffered from an acute stage fright that almost robbed her of voice and motion. In the fourth she found herelf. At the end of the play Quin took her in his arms.

"Thou art a divine creature," he cried, "and the true spirit is in thee!" [67]

She did *Lucia* in *Cato*, *Arsinoe* in *Marianne*, *Anne Bullen* in *Henry VIII*. She played a minor role with toothless old Colley

Cibber in *Papal Tyranny in the Reign of King John,* a hitherto
unstaged tragedy which Cibber hauled out in a fit of February
(1744) patriotism as a public warning against the Popish Pretender. John Gay's patron, the Duchess of Queensbury, and the
London diplomatic corps turned out to patronize the young actress,
daughter of the British ambassador to Russia. After the fashion of
the day George Anne also was pursued by a young Mr. Montgomery
and the fifth Lord Byron, a dissolute old rake.[68] Quin heard. He
called her into his dressing room one day after rehearsal.

"My dear girl, you are vastly followed, I hear," he told her. "Do
not let the love of finery, or any other inducement, prevail upon
you to commit an indiscretion. Men in general are rascals. You are
young and engaging, and therefore ought to be doubly cautious." [69]

She declared she would listen to no proposal but marriage—and
a coach! Mr. Montgomery was frank. He told her he could not
afford marriage. But old Lord Byron was not easily put off. He
hung around the theatre, back stage, and with the help of a friend
abducted George Anne and tried to seduce her. She was rescued by
her brother, the Naval officer. The scandal got into the newspapers.
Mrs. Bellamy refused to believe her daughter's plea of innocence.
The girl had a nervous breakdown. When Sheridan, the Irish
theatre manager she had met at Mrs. Woffington's, offered George
Anne an engagement in Dublin, mother and daughter welcomed
the opportunity to leave London without farewells.[70]

If Braddock, her second father, neglected George Anne in her
distress, it may well have been because of a sudden crisis in national
affairs. Bonnie Prince Charlie (Charles Edward Stuart, the Pretender) had slipped away from Rome two or three days before
Christmas, 1743.[71] In February he was seen at Dunkirk where the
French Marshal Saxe was reported to be assembling transports,
men-of-war, and 15,000 troops for a descent on England. A British
diplomatic messenger on his way to London from Paris, carrying
dispatches from the English ambassador, was arrested and searched
at Calais. His Britannic Majesty George II sent messages to both
houses of Parliament, warning them the country was in danger of
invasion.[72]

Overnight, Braddock's military duties ceased to be a matter of
garrison routine. *Habeus corpus* was suspended. Suspect Jacobites
were arrested. Guards were doubled at the Tower and at St.
James's. Three extraordinary councils were held in the palace with a

great coming and going of coaches and couriers. The Earl of Stair
and the young Duke of Marlborough waited upon the King, in
bed with rheumatism, to offer their services. The Earl was made
commander in chief of all troops in south Britain. Lt.-Col. George
Churchill of the Coldstream, was named one of nine new brigadiers
to help Stair organize home defenses.[73]

The threat was still from Dunkirk toward London, Kent, and the
South coast, along the channel patrolled by the French fleet, its
white sails in full view on a clear day.[74] On February 9, 1744, Braddock's second battalion marched to Rochester and Sittingbourne, a
route which took them down the old Roman road called Watling
street.[75] Winter was almost over. Fresh, damp ocean air blew over
the downs, sweet with the promise of early blossoms in the hop
gardens and the apple and cherry orchards either side of the
road. As English soldiers on their way to repel a foreign foe, the
redcoats were cheered in every village along the way. Whenever
they halted near a public house the tavern keeper and his barmaid waited, smiling, to fill their mugs, free.[76]

But they soon wore out their welcome. A storm smashed and
scattered the French transports at Dunkirk. Charles Edward dropped
his invasion plans.[77] Patriotic Kentishmen, keen to watch a channel naval battle from the white cliffs and green headlands of their
native shore, were disappointed.[78] Innkeepers began to complain
about drunken soldiers. Orders were issued that not more than six
should be quartered in any one house.[79] And on March 20, Braddock's battalion returned to London where drafts of twelve men
were taken from each company as replacements for the footguards
in Flanders.[80]

Louis XV signed his long expected declaration of war against
England. But the allied army in Flanders, left entirely to old General Wade, advanced, foraged, skirmished, and retreated, always a
safe distance from the French. Brigadier Churchill of the Coldstream commanded the guards brigade with Wade. Braddock remained in London.[81] The Coldstream colonelcy, vacant since the
resignation of young Marlborough, was given to the Earl of Albemarle, now a staff officer with Wade.[82] Early in October Wade's
health broke down. He applied for leave to return to England and
resigned his command.[83]

Stair declined to reconsider his resignation as field marshal. The
Duke of Cumberland was named captain-general, a title last held

by the great Marlborough, and invested with command of the entire allied army in Flanders. As much as he was attached to his son, William Augustus, the King hesitated to entrust so vast an operation to so inexperienced a young soldier; for he was in his early twenties. It was agreed, without public announcement that he would be advised in his military operations by older and more seasoned officers.[84]

Cumberland himself chose six British aides-de-camp, four of them from the footguards. From the Coldstream he picked Viscount Bury, Albemarle's son, and Lieut. Joseph Yorke, third son of the Earl of Hardwicke, one of Newcastle's confidants.[85] From his own regiment, the First Foot Guards, he chose Capt. William Henry Lord Ancrum, son of the third Marquis of Lothian, titular head of an old and distinguished Scottish border family, and Capt. Henry Seymour Conway, handsome supercillious younger brother of the Earl of Hertford, and an Eton schoolfellow and cousin of Horace Walpole who took credit for having called Conway to the Duke's attention.[86] The other two aides selected by the Duke were Charles Baron Cathcart, a professional soldier's son who had served in Flanders, and Capt. Robert Napier, an inconspicuous but competent infantryman from the Second Foot with experience in the quartermaster general department.[87]

A few days before Easter, 1745, the Duke left for Holland, a fair, fat, pop-eyed prince of twenty-three-going-on-twenty-four and gaining weight so rapidly that his neck was being squeezed out of sight between his small ears and his drooping shoulders.[88] Arriving in Brussels, he reviewed the allied army. His British troops paraded in new uniforms.[89] Fifty miles to the southwest the French army, commanded by Marshal Saxe, was investing Tournay, one of thirty-five walled towns in Flanders toward which military operations customarily were directed. The French king and the Dauphin were in the French camp to watch the progress of the siege. Saxe, carried in a wicker litter half dead from dropsy, watched Cumberland's allied forces creep toward him in short, cautious, methodical marches. At the village of Fontenoy on the river Scheldt, five miles southeast of Tournay, the two armies met.[90]

George II had left London and was on his way to Hanover for another holiday when the first blood curdling accounts of the battle took away Whitehall's breath. Nearly 10,000 British and Hanoverian soldiers were reported killed, wounded, and missing. Casualties in the Guards Brigade alone exceeded 700. Never before had so many British officers been lost in a single action.[91] Of the Guards alone thirty-three had been killed or wounded. Among the slain Coldstreamers were Lieut.-Col. Samuel Needham, regimental adjutant for twenty years, and Lord Cathcart's younger brother, Shaw, an ensign. Charles Churchill and Julius Caesar had been wounded.[92]

"The second regiment of the English guards (Coldstream) . . . must certainly have been almost entirely destroyed," said a Paris letter reprinted in London. "We took from them a pair of colors and two pieces of cannon. . . ."[93]

But the home battalions took disaster in their stride. Three days after the shocking news of Fontenoy replacements embarked for Flanders.[94] Three lieutenant-colonels—Braddock not among them—8 captains, 8 ensigns, 4 surgeons, 16 sergeants, 16 corporals, 8 drummers, and 540 private men made up the contingent which took its leave "in a very cheerful manner," *The Gentleman's Magazine* reported.[95]

Col. James Ingoldsby of the First Foot Guards, a Cumberland favorite and one of the scapegoats blamed for the defeat, was court martialed. Ordered to attack a French redoubt, Ingoldsby had procrastinated, pleading contradictory orders.[96] The Duke of Cumberland was the object of more pity than blame. Letters from Flanders, without exception, praised his bravery and consideration for his soldiers. He was a strict disciplinarian, insisting that officers and men wear proper uniform, that baggage be reduced to a minimum, that officers remain in the field with their commands, and that no officer below the rank of brigadier keep a coach, chariot, or chaise while on active service.[97] He also rewarded merit. Viscount Bury and Capt.-Lt. Julius Caesar became full captain-colonels of the Coldstream after Fontenoy. The Coldstream's first major, William Douglas, became colonel of the 32nd foot, and Braddock succeeded Douglas as first major of the Coldstream.[98]

On the night of July 4 an express from Ostend informed London that the French had seized Ghent and Bruges, cutting off a detachment of 4,000 men and surrounding the Duke's army. Next came a message that only 500 had been captured, that the army was safe, and that the Duke had won a victory, killing 15,000 of the enemy and taking 5,000 prisoners.[99] The King was still in Hanover. The Lords of the Regency knew neither what to believe nor what to do.[100] The truth was, Cumberland had retreated northward. A French army had marched toward Ghent, capital of the Austrian Netherlands and supply base for the allied Army. A Hanoverian general, Baron Moltke, sent by Cumberland to relief of Ghent with 4,000 horse and foot, had run into the French. Moltke's cavalry had cut its way through. His infantry had retreated. Ghent surrendered on July 6 but Moltke's cavalry escaped, riding on to Ostend.[101]

Ostend, a naval base, was of more importance to the allies than all the rest of Flanders. All ordnance stores were accumulated at Ostend.[102] Its garrison was down to about 1,200 men, not enough to man the enceinte of its dilapidated defenses.[103] Lord Stair asked the Lords of the Regency to give him two battalions of Foot Guards, undertaking to hold Ostend with that many reinforcements.[104] The Regency hesitated. Forces for home defense were down to 8,000. So ever-present were the fears of another Jacobite invasion, that the Lords of the Regency dared not reduce their slender home defense until they had firsthand information regarding the true state of affairs abroad—nor did they dare abandon Ostend, so vital to the English should a quick withdrawal of Cumberland's army become necessary.[105]

Casting about for a dependable man to send to Ostend, a military man upon whose observations and judgment they might depend, the Regency came up wih Col. Edward Braddock, first major of the Coldstream Guards. He was ordered to Ostend, to look over the situation and return as quickly as possible.[106] Cross channel sailing time, if the wind held, was 8 or 9 hours, 16 if the breeze were light.[107]

The summer had been rainy and the crossing probably was not too comfortable for a middle-aged officer of the foot guards.[108] He found Ostend harbor, a deep, narrow basin crowded with shipping, smelling of rope and fish and English coal smoke. Flemish speaking porters swarmed the quay where the packet tied up, grabbing for the passengers' luggage. Uniform houses of wind-and-weather beaten brick, with corbie-stepped gables, lined Ostend's exactly straight and narrow streets. If Braddock spent a night in Ostend, he must have put up at one of two English inns where the board floors were sanded, where the bread came in rings, and claret wine was the cheapest.[109]

To the town's weary garrison, who probably looked as if they slept in their clothes, Col. Braddock's well cocked hat and shining buckles may have seemed out of place. But the shape of a soldier's hat, like the dressing of his hair, was a matter of much thought at St. James's. The wig must come low on the sides of his face to hide his ears. The hat, edged with gold lace, must be cocked low. The pale blue lapels of Braddock's long scarlet coat were fastened back with twelve gold loops and twelve gold buttons. White lace cuffs dangled at his wrists. His skin-tight pale blue breeches barely showed between the bottom of his long scarlet waistcoat and the high tops of his spotless white gaiters, reaching well above his knees.[110]

At any rate Braddock could see that Ostend was not defenseless. On the north and west the town faced the sea, lying below high water level in the protection of a granite-faced seawall. A morass laced with ditches protected its landward side. The only dry-footed approach was over sand dunes to the south, along a strand submerged at flood tide when the town was almost completely encompassed by the sea. A double ditch filled with sea water lay around the ramparts, enough to discourage any storming party.[111]

Ostend's acting governor, General O'Conor, was a weak, worn-out old man, who at the first hint of a French attack, had ordered the sluice gates opened to flood the low country around Ostend. From Brussels the Austrian Minister to Flanders, Count Kaunitz, had countermanded this order. No one knew why.[112] The strength of Ostend's garrison, nearly 4,000 Austrian, Dutch, Hanoverian, and British troops, exceeded first reports. Moltke's hussars, creating a forage problem, would be more of a hindrance than a help in a siege.[113] It was generally agreed that the addition of three battalions of infantry and some artillery would put the place in a better state of defense. Ostend could be supplied indefinitely from the sea.[114]

Braddock returned to London with a report along these general lines, but only one battalion of troops was sent from London. This was a provisional battalion of foot guards. It consisted of drafts of 15 men from each of three guard battalions still in London. They were not the pick of the lot, but rather those judged good enough for garrison duty. Made ready for foreign service, they assembled on the parade at St. James's with the oldest and least efficient officers of the three battalions. Under command of Col. Rowland

Reynolds, of the Third Guards, they marched to Margate where fourteen transports were waiting.[115]

Reynolds's force reached Ostend on August 7.[116] A few days later French batteries of heavy ordnance, mounted on sand dunes along the beach, brought the entrance of Ostend Harbor under an enfilading fire that prevented further assistance from the sea. Cannon ball and bomb shells rained into the town. The besiegers' entrenchments drew closer, and after three days of steady bombardment Ostend surrendered on terms permitting its garrison to withdraw with honors of war. Artillery, ammunition, and provisions laid up in the town were lost.[117]

An official dispatch from Ostend's Austrian governor, General Chanclos, itemizing the terms of the capitulation, were waiting for King George II when he returned to London from Hanover. Offsetting the loss of Ostend was the capture of Louisburg, a French stronghold in North America, by an army of New England colonists. Tower and park guns were fired, government offices illuminated, bonfires lighted, and bells rung to celebrate this victory. But Louisburg was 3,000 miles away, on the island of Cape Breton, a place few Londoners had ever heard of.[118]

"Cape Breton? An Island? Wonderful!—show it to me on the map," exclaimed the Duke of Newcastle.

He ran his finger over the map, found Louisburg on Cape Breton.

"So it is, sure enough," he said, "I must go and tell the King that Cape Breton is an island." [119]

He could also tell the King that a letter from Inverness said, "The Young Chevalier [pretender] has certainly landed in the highlands."

For months Charles Edward Stuart had been reported to be planning a summer descent on Scotland. The British defeat at Fontenoy had made him confident of success.[120] On June 22 he had embarked at Nantes aboard an 18-gun brig *La Doutelle,* loaded with 1,000 stand of arms, 1,400 or 1,500 broadswords, and some small field pieces. At Belle Isle, in the Bay of Biscay, the brig was joined by a 66-gun ship, the *Elizabeth,* and the two proceeded in convoy. Four days at sea they were intercepted by a British man-of-war, the *Lion;* and after a nine-hour engagement at close range the *Elizabeth* was damaged so badly she turned back. *La Doutelle* ran away, made the Irish Channel, and on July 25 anchored in Lochnanuagh on the west coast of Scotland.[121]

So remote was the place of his landing that weeks passed before letters from Edinburgh removed all doubts that the young Pretender was in Scotland.[122] But the Lords of the Regency issued a proclamation offering £30,000 for his capture. The war office ordered all army officers in England and Scotland to repair immediately to their posts.[123] There was not a man to spare. The draft for the relief of Ostend had reduced the strength of the foot guards in London to a point where those normally on duty for 24 hours at a time were now standing 48.[124]

Privy Councillors and general officers of the Army met with the King at Kensington on Friday the thirteenth of August, 1745.[125] Letters to raise the militia were dispatched to the lord lieutenants of the counties of England and Wales. London and Westminster militia already had been ordered to hold itself in readiness.[126] Ten battalions, including the brigade of guards, had been ordered home from Flanders, and the old Anglo-Dutch treaty had been invoked for the movement of 3,000 Dutch troops from Holland to Scotland, where Sir John Cope commanded the King's scattered forces.[127]

From being an officer detached for special service, Braddock reverted to his regular duties as first major of the Coldstream. To bring the guard regiments up to full strength, a bounty of 16 shillings was offered every recruit who would join up before the 24th of the month, although a special order forbade the enlistment of Scotch, Irish, papists or vagabonds. Quarters must be provided for officers and men of the battalion returning from Ostend. Ground must be marked off in Hyde Park for the encampment of the other battalions ordered home from Flanders.[128]

Transports carrying the first of these troops reached Gravesend on Monday, September 23, 1745. Wherries brought the guards ashore at the Tower. The Coldstream battalion, assigned temporary quarters at the Tower, formed up by companies and marched in briskly, their white gaiters in cadence with drum beats, their sidearms clinking.[129] Not quite so smart were some of the returning line regiments which had been campaigning in quagmires off the paved roads of Flanders. Redcoats were wrinkled and rusty, spatter-dashes stained, hats uncocked and boots broken from long marches in the rain. Some were wounded. Some were lame. Many had lost their wagons and their baggage.[130]

The *Gazette* reported the Young Pretender and his army of

Scotch rebels as having left Perth and moving southward.[131] The news was late and incomplete. As a matter of fact the rebels had routed two green regiments of Sir John Cope's dragoons, defeated the remainder of Cope's army at Prestonpans, and entered Edinburgh.[132] An express brought Whitehall the news of Cope's defeat on Tuesday, September 24. It sounded incredible. A rabble of raggamuffins, loosie hillskippers from the Scottish highlands armed with claymores, Lochaber axes, and with no cannon heavier than one-pounders, scattering an army of the King's regulars in a ten-minute fight? [133] In the opinion of one anonymous officer who wrote a newspaper critique of Prestonpans:

"Rude troops breaking in upon an army by violence, is much the same as a mad unexperienced fellow running headlong on a fine fencer; he parries here, retreats there, plays with his adversary till he has spent his spirits, and then disarms or dispatches him. To suffer troops to be broke by a sudden shock, is a fatal error in the military science."

This expert urged army preferment of "men who rather attend to their professions, and shine there, than at courts and levees"; always concluding, that "he who neglects this business to wait on nods and smiles, is fitter to be a pimp in a bawdy house than to command fleets and armies." [134]

This attack on Sir John, and a pamphlet along the same line, entitled "An Enquiry into the Conduct of G----l C-e," were answered in the London *Evening Post* by another officer who declared the conduct of the King's officers at Prestonpans to have been above reproach.[135] One who had come off with honors was Peter Halkett of Pitfirrane, an M. P. for Inverkeithen. As a lieutenant-colonel of the 48th Foot, one of the six regiments raised in 1741, Halkett had kept five officers and fourteen men together and firing until the rebels offered them terms.[136] Braddock would hear of Halkett again.

Meanwhile the King ordered Marshal Wade, whom he had named commander in chief of all forces in Britain, northward toward the Scottish border with 8,000 horse and foot. Lord Tyrawley, back from Russia, went with Wade reluctantly as his second in command. The troops left much to be desired.[137] John Wesley, an Oxford don who was preaching a new Christian doctrine called "Methodism," encountered some of them at Doncaster, "drunken, cursing, swearing soldiers who surrounded us on every side."

"Can these wretches succeed in anything they undertake?" Wesley wondered.[138]

There were reports of a Paptist-Jacobite plot to burn London and massacre its inhabitants. Irish Catholics were suspected of setting a series of fires. An outbreak of cattle distemper, which made Londoners afraid to eat beef, butter, or milk, was blamed on Papists who were accused of poisoning country water supplies. Catholic priests and servants were arrested. A detachment of Braddock's footguards took possession of the Lincoln Fields playhouse for a guardroom, seventy remaining under arms day and night against emergencies. City gates, dockyards, and the Tower were locked after dark. Six regiments of London militia patrolled the streets.[139]

The militia was eager to show its strength to the King. On October 25 this order was read to the Coldstream, now encamped in Hyde Park:

"If the militia are reviewed tomorrow by His Majesty, the soldiers of the three regiments of guards are to behave civilly, and not to laugh or make game of them."

The militia marched next day, all six regiments passing in review before the King who stood on the terrace of the royal gardens at St. James's for three hours to watch them pass.[140]

The Young Pretender's army, estimated at 7,000 to 13,000 horse and foot, took Carlisle and moved down the west coast of England to avoid Marshal Wade.[141] The *Gazette* printed extraordinary twopenny editions to keep London informed of the rebels' progress. In contrast to the King's soldiers, seldom ready to move before 9 o'clock in the morning, the Highlanders were up and on the go at daybreak. Each man was armed with sword, target, musket, and dirk. For provision they drove cattle with them, and each man carried a bag of oatmeal. The grandson of James II, already a romantic figure in Jacobite eyes, was described as a melancholy young man in a gray wig, marching on foot in Highland plaid with a blue sash, a blue bonnet, and a white rose.[142]

The Duke of Cumberland, returning from Holland somewhat heavier than he went away, made a less appealing figure. But he brought with him five more troops of horse, a regiment of dragoons, and four regiments of foot.[143] On November 16 the King ordered most of these toward Lancaster. The Duke, who had established a temporary headquarters at St. James's, was sent to Litchfield, a little cathedral market town in Staffordshire, where more troops, including a brigade of foot guards, were to assemble.[144]

Three days before the first battalion of the Coldstream received orders to join the Duke, Braddock was commissioned lieutenant-colonel of the regiment.[145] He had been dickering for the promotion, which cost him £5,000, since the end of September when Lieutenant-Colonel Churchill was appointed colonel of a regiment of marines. The deal seems to have involved the sale of Braddock's majority to Captain Charles Russell of the First Foot Guards, for £3,600. As lieutenant-colonel of the Coldstream, Braddock became senior officer and acting brigadier of the guards brigade.[146]

The King held a military levee at St. James's for all the officers of his footguards before they marched to Litchfield. When they had gathered he told them, in his German accent:

> Gentlemen, you cannot be ignorant of the present precarious situation of our country, and though I have had so many recent instances of your exertions, the necessity of the times and the knowledge I have of your hearts induce me to demand your services again; so all of you that are willing to meet the rebels, hold up your right hands; all those who may, for particular reasons, find it inconvenient, hold up your left. . . .[147]

Every right hand in the room went up. The King tried to thank them but walked out, choked with tears.[148]

Litchfield was more than a hundred miles from London. Late autumn storms had been followed by colder weather, rain turning to snow, as the Coldstream paraded in Hyde Park the morning of November 25 to begin its march northward.[149] If and when they met the Pretender's army, the ranks growled, they would neither give nor take quarter.[150] They were expected to march at least ten miles a day, resting every fourth day. From London to Barnet, to St. Albans, to Dunstable, to Newport Pagnell Braddock's brigade used the same road, then the Coldstream battalion swung eastward, through Northampton, but rejoined the main column beyond Coventry.[151]

They made the march in eight days, over icy country roads in wind and snow, with a convoy of wagons for their tents and baggage. The first of the three battalions arrived in Litchfield on November 30 without loss of a single man from accident or sickness. The Duke rode out of town nearly two miles to meet the Coldstream, which closed the column when it marched in two days later.

It was bitterly cold now. Straw and fires were ordered for sol-
ders who could not be quartered in the public houses. As an
added discomfort the bread supply ran out and had to be supplemented with biscuit.[152] Litchfield, a town of only about a thousand
people, did what it could for the troops, the first to occupy it since
Civil War Royalists and Parliamentarians had fought around its
three-spired red sandstone cathedral.[153]

London had not forgotten the Duke's army. The Common Council had subscribed £1,000 for the purchase of knit woolen gloves,
woolen stockings, flannel waistcoats, watch coats, spatterdashes, and
blankets. A three-night benefit of the *Beggar's Opera* at Drury
Lane, with Mrs. Cibber playing Polly and the tallow chandlers
providing free candles, enriched the soldiers' relief fund by £600.
Quakers, clothmakers, skinners, drapers, fishmongers, goldsmiths,
coopers, stationers chipped in, bringing the total to £5,000.[154]

The Young Pretender occupied Manchester. His army took the
road to Macclesfield, coming straight toward the Duke. Braddock's
foot guards moved forward, two battalions to Stafford and one to
Rugeley.[155] At 11 o'clock on the night of December 2, Cumberland advanced with Braddock's brigade and other troops to the
cross-roads town of Stone, 25 miles directly south of Macclesfield.
By 4 in the morning they were in position to dispute any further
advance by the rebels in that direction.[156] The Pretender's cavalry
made a feint toward the Duke, but the main column of the rebel
army took a road forking left to Derby. Cumberland fell back to
Litchfield.[157]

December 6, 1745 went down in history as Black Friday.[158] That
day London learned the rebels had side-slipped the Duke's army
and occupied Derby. The road south from Derby lay open and un-
defended. London closed its shops. A run on the Bank of England
was forestalled by the old device of paying off in sixpence. The
Archbishop of Canterbury made up a special prayer to be said in
all the churches. King George was reported to have ordered his
yacht anchored at the Tower stairs, ready for a quick getaway.
The Duke of Newcastle was said to have shut himself up in his
apartments, debating whether the time had come to transfer his
allegiance to the House of Stuart.[159] Any day now, as the Jacobites
sang, might be

. . . the time we see,
That the King shall enjoy his own again! [160]

The grenadier companies of the footguards, which had been left in London, and all other unassigned regular troops and artillery were ordered to Finchley, a northern suburb of the city. William Hogarth, the artist, watching the confusion of soldiers, sutlers, wagons, and camp followers pouring out along Tottenham Court turnpike between *The King's Head* and *Adam and Eve,* two popular taverns either side of the road, drew what he saw in a comic picture which he called "The March to Finchley." [161]

December 6, 1745, also was a black Friday for Charles Edward Stuart. People had flocked along the road to see him and his kilted Highlanders, to hear his squealing pipers, but he had failed to incite them to revolution. Since leaving Carlisle he had been joined by hardly two hundred men. In all Lancashire, where Catholics and Tories abounded, only one squire had taken up arms for his cause.[162] His force was down to about 4,500. On the same day London trembled, Charles Edward Stuart and his army marched out of Derby, by the same route they had entered, withdrawing toward Lancashire.[163]

Cumberland waited at Litchfield. This time he wanted to be sure which way the rebels were going. He had posted Braddock's foot guards around his headquarters, the home of J. Inges, Esq., a justice of the peace, with orders to draw up in the street, facing away from the house, in case of an alarm.[164] On December 9, the Duke started in pursuit of the retreating Pretender with two regiments of dragoons and a thousand infantry volunteers, including 400 foot guards mounted on horses lent by Whigs who lived in the neighboring countryside.[165]

In response to urgent dispatches from Newcastle, the greater part of the Duke's army marched south, through London, bound for Kent and Sussex. There was still fear of a French invasion on the south coast.[166] Braddock's brigade, minus the 400 volunteers with Cumberland, returned to London. Their wagons, carrying sick and lame on top of tents and baggage, did not arrive until the day after Christmas. The half frozen Coldstream guardsmen went into winter quarters in Finsbury and Southwark taverns and at the Tower.[167]

A nobleman in waiting at St. James's showed the King a print of Hogarth's "March to Finchley," dedicated to his Majesty. George II examined it suspiciously. He studied the picture's central figure, a doleful grenadier beset by two pregnant women. Behind the grenadier an officer grabbed a milkmaid rudely and kissed her. Most of the other soldiers in Hogarth's print appeared to be drunk and disorderly. Indignantly the King drew back.

"Pray, who is this Hogarth?" he asked.

"A painter, my liege."

". . . Does this fellow mean to laugh at my guards?"

"The picture, an please your Majesty, must undoubtedly be considered a burlesque."

"What! A painter burlesque a soldier? He deserves to be picketed for his insolence. Take his trumpery out of my sight!" [168]

VII

FLANDERS

1746–1753

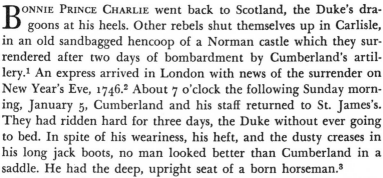

BONNIE PRINCE CHARLIE went back to Scotland, the Duke's dragoons at his heels. Other rebels shut themselves up in Carlisle, in an old sandbagged hencoop of a Norman castle which they surrendered after two days of bombardment by Cumberland's artillery.[1] An express arrived in London with news of the surrender on New Year's Eve, 1746.[2] About 7 o'clock the following Sunday morning, January 5, Cumberland and his staff returned to St. James's. They had ridden hard for three days, the Duke without ever going to bed. In spite of his weariness, his heft, and the dusty creases in his long jack boots, no man looked better than Cumberland in a saddle. He had the deep, upright seat of a born horseman.[3]

People stood in the street and cheered when he rode out of St. James's later, rested and refreshed, in a blue coat with bright red facing, a brass-buttoned waistcoat, his three-cornered hat at a rakish angle. He was the conqueror of Carlisle.[4] His cynical brother, the Prince of Wales, who was entertaining at dinner, ordered a sugar city from his confectioner as a centerpiece for the table and tried to amuse his guests by pelting it with sugar plums. Frederick would never be a soldier-prince.[5]

On Cumberland's recommendation Lieutenant-General Henry Hawley had been named commander-in-chief in Scotland, taking over the incompetent Wade's army to press pursuit of the Young

Pretender northward from Carlisle. Hawley was a hard-handed old cavalryman who had been second in command of the horse at Fontenoy.[6] But the same dragoons who had run away for Johnnie Cope at Prestonpans ran away for Hawley at Falkirk, below Sterling, where Charles Edward's Highlanders won an unexpected victory.[7]

"My heart is broke," wrote Hawley to the Duke in a personal letter. "Such scandalous cowardice I never saw before." [8]

Thirty-one dragoons were hanged for desertion. Thirty-two foot were shot for cowardice. Hawley became known as "Hawley the hangman." [9]

No additional troops were sent north, but on his father's orders the Duke set out for Scotland with two of his aides, Bury and Conway.[10] Braddock presently heard that Conway had been given command of the 48th foot, a regiment which Braddock would come to know only too well in the years ahead.[11]

Early in February—the Young Pretender was again in retreat but snow had delayed his pursuit by the Duke now commanding [12] Hawley's reorganized army—four wagons and a coach load of prisoners taken at Carlisle arrived in London under guard.[13] They were the first of many rebels whose custody, as they gradually filled the city's jails, provided a new responsibility for Braddock's foot guards. That same month two transports out of Ostend, carrying a French regiment to Scotland, were captured off the coast by a British man-of-war. Twenty-nine deserters from the British army in Flanders,[14] some of them foot guards, were found in the rank and file of those aboard. Court-martialed at Whitehall, all twenty-nine were sentenced to death. Only five—any five—were ordered executed. The twenty-nine threw dice on a drumhead for their lives. Five from the foot guards lost. They were shot in Hyde Park on a Wednesday morning, April 23.[15]

That same day an express from Edinburgh brought Whitehall word that the Duke of Cumberland had routed Charles Edward's army at Culloden House, near Inverness.[16] Riding hard behind the express came Lord Bury with an official dispatch.[17] Of the Duke's 5,000 soldiers, only 50 had been killed and about 250 wounded.[18] But the rebel losses were never counted. Scattered in flight and retreat, many had been ridden down and sabred by Cumberland's cavalry far from the battlefield. Before the battle began the Duke had recommended the bayonet, and when it was over, one regiment of foot—Barrell's—boasted that every one of its bayonets was blood-ied or bent.[19] Injured and dying Scots on Culloden field had their brains bashed out with musket stocks. One lot of helplessly wounded was said to have been burned alive in a farm shed where they had taken refuge. Others, robbed and stripped of their cloth-ing, lay in agony for two days among the uncollected dead on the rainsodden moor. The Pretender escaped, dressed like a woman, to France.[20]

More prisoners arrived in London from Scotland, along with loads of captured claymores, iron-stocked pistols, and long barreled highland muskets. Five alleged ringleaders of the rebellion, the Earls of Cromartie and Kilmarnock, Lords Lovat and Balmerino, and the Marquis of Tullibardine, were lodged in the Tower. Other leaders were sent to Newgate. Rebel army officers were taken to Marshalsea prison, and common soldiers to New Gaol, in South-wark, and Tilbury fort. Military guards had to be provided for all these places, as well as for several inns where rebels who had turned King's evidence were confined. A temporary barracks was built at New Gaol for the fifty guards on duty there.[21]

In the ballrooms of Westminster, hooped petticoats billowed and swirled in a new romp, "the Culloden reel." "Culloden" was the title of a new ballet at Sadler's Wells.[22] But lurid tales of the Duke's cruelty, wild yarns about vanquished Scots having been fed poisoned bread and stuffed into the holds of prison ships on stone ballast, persisted even after his return to London. Pillage by his soldiers had got out of hand. Houses had been burned, crops de-stroyed, cattle driven off, and women insulted. To Jacobites and Tories the Duke became "Billie the Butcher." [23]

The foot guards provided a detail at the execution of the first nine rebels to be condemned. They were hanged on Kennington Common. Each of the nine was cut down at the end of five min-utes, before he was dead, and disemboweled. His entrails were thrown into a pile of blazing fagots and the head was chopped off. Two traitors' heads were impaled at Temple Bar. The guards also provided a detachment for the old palace yard, at Westminster Hall, where Cromartie, Kilmarnock, and Balmerino were found guilty of treason and sentenced to death. Cromartie was pardoned. Tullibardine died in the Tower. Old Lord Lovat was still awaiting trial.[24]

At 6 o'clock Monday morning, August 18, 1746, one thousand of

Braddock footguards, 15 from each company, marched through the
city from the parade at St. James's to Tower Hill. The hill, the
roofs of the houses around it, the masts of ships in the river were
covered with people, waiting to see the execution of two of the
rebel lords. At the direction of a colonel of the guards, possibly
Braddock, the black cloth over the rail of the executioner's platform was tucked up, so the crowd could see everything. One
stroke of the axe cut off Kilmarnock's head. It took three to behead
Balmerino.[25]

The scaffold used in the executions was still standing nearly a
month later when Braddock assembled the first battalion of the
Coldstream on Tower Hill to embark on a secret expedition against
the French. His battalion was to be part of a body of 8,000 picked
troops rendezvousing at Plymouth under the joint command of
Admiral Richard Lestock and General James Sinclair.[26] The
guardsmen marched to King's Stairs of Tower wharf where lighters
waited to carry them down the river to transports lying at Gravesend. Standing on the wharf to watch the guards embark was the
Duke of Cumberland.[27]

He "spoke to every man as they passed him with the greatest
freedom," bidding them do their duty against the French, "and
generously ordered two shillings to each man," the newspapers reported later.[28]

Colonel Russell, now Braddock's second major, made no protest
when one soldier's wife broke through the ranks to take a farewell
kiss of her husband. And the Duke, in spite of his reputation as a
stern disciplinarian, seemed to be amused.

" 'Tis like you!" he called good naturedly to Russell.[29]

Officers and men climbed into the boats and shoved off in high
spirits, the soldiers huzzaing:

"Long live King George and the Duke of Cumberland!" [30]

But the weather turned bad, the winds were wrong, and Lestock's
fleet sailed before the transports carrying the foot guards came
within sight of Plymouth Hoe.[31] Both battalions landed and encamped, reembarked a fortnight later and sailed for the Bay of
Biscay, then put about abruptly and headed home.[32] Sinclair's force,
furnished with only such maps as it had been able to buy in the
shops of Plymouth, had landed near Quimperle, plundered a few
convents and villages, smashed the altars of several Catholic
churches, marched to Port L'Orient and broke into the magazines

of the French East Indian Company. From Port L'Orient they had attacked Port Louis, apparently without plan or purpose. On the morning of October 19 the entire expedition returned to Plymouth, Braddock's foot guards without having set foot on enemy soil.[33]

Off Dungeness the guards' homeward-bound transports ran into a gale that swept away knapsacks, water flasks, camp kettles, and other field equipment stowed topside.[34] On October 24 they reached the Downs, and three days later disembarked at Deptford and the Tower, the sick going ashore in covered barges.[35] Baggage was carried back to Whitehall to storerooms in the Tower, and the troops marched to assigned winter quarters in Holborn, Finsbury, and the East End.[36]

"The guards are come back too, who never went," Walpole told Mann in a bantering letter that ridiculed the operation from start to finish.[37] "In one single day they received four several different orders!"

All Braddock had to show for the past six weeks, largely a campaign of brandy and lemons against seasickness on a rolling transport, was a contingent bill for £42.12.6, covering barge, hoy, horse and wagon hire, and the making and mending of barrels for powder and ball put into cartridges at Plymouth, and then taken out again when the cartridges were opened up to save the powder. His quartermaster also turned in a statement for £153.16.4. for the repair of arms damages in the Dungeness storm and the loss of equipment washed overboard.[38]

Early in the spring of 1747 Cumberland opened a new campaign against the French in the low countries. Great exertions were made to land a preponderant force in Flanders so as to terminate the war without further delay.[39] But in the middle of April a French column of 25,000 men under Count Lowendahl penetrated the Dutch province of East Flanders. The French took the towns of Hulst, Sluys, and Sas-van-Ghent, the port of Ghent. They occupied the island of Cadsand at the mouth of the West Scheldt. The Dutch were thrown into panic.[40]

On Thursday, May 9, the second battalion of the Coldstream, under Braddock's command, was ordered to occupy Flushing (the British for Vlissingen), a fortified seaport opposite French-occupied Cadsand at the mouth of the Scheldt.[41] The battalion moved out in the usual manner—by barge to Gravesend where tubby transports lay at anchor.[42] The soldiers climbed the gangway ladders and the ships wound down London river with the tide, past flat green pasture lands where the May morning mist veiled grazing cattle. Beyond the docks of Sheerness, where the Thames spread four miles wide to meet the sea, a waiting escort of sloops and men-of-war shook out their brown sails. The transports, rolling with a heavy wallow, were not built for speed and it was the Wednesday after the movement had been ordered before they sighted Walcheren Island.[43]

Dikes twenty-five feet high hid Flushing from the sea.[44] Only the windmills, the church steeples, and the red tile roofs of the town's higher buildings were visible to the troops aboard the transports tacking into the Scheldt. The French held the lower bank of the river. Every Dutch post over there had been taken. Fighting had ceased. Three British regiments sent earlier to the aid of Hulst had been ferried back across the Scheldt by small craft to South Beveland, the next island up the river from Walcheren.[45]

Braddock landed his battalion at Flushing and reported to Major-General John (Daddy) Huske, a former Coldstreamer who had been named commander-in-chief of all British troops in the Dutch province of Zealand.[46] The French were reported to have collected flat-bottomed boats for a descent on Zealand.[47] The Prince of Orange had toured the province to arouse its inhabitants to self-defense. But British officers who had seen the Dutch in battle did not anticipate much resistance should the French attempt a river crossing.[48]

Farther to the east, Saxe and the Duke of Cumberland took their times at grand maneuvers. The two armies finally clashed on July 2 at the village of Lauffeld, near Maestricht. Again Cumberland was defeated. Saxe followed up his victory by sending Lowendahl to besiege the town of Bergen-op-Zoom, thirty miles east of Flushing on the Dutch mainland and reputedly the strongest fortress on the continent.[49] The French bombarded the town with red-hot cannon balls, setting fire to its largest church and destroying nearly 400 of its 1,300 houses.[50]

Braddock's Coldstream battalion stood fast at Flushing where the thick, damp air of the Zealand summer caused an almost continuous fog.[51] The little seaport boasted none of the blandishments of a garrison town. The French beans, salted fish, Dutch butter and cheese of Walcheren island never ran out. But there was a limit to red-coat endurance of water-filled ditches and tarred piles, of red-armed Dutch girls in neat white caps, forever scouring immaculate woodwork and polishing spotless window panes. There was trouble, too, over the clipped ducats with which the soldiers were paid. Sutlers would change them only for men who spent a shilling or more for liquor.[52]

Unaccustomed to persistent fog and humidity, the battalion swept with ague and fever. The more seriously ill were carted off to the allied army hospital at Otterhout (Ostrout) near Breda. A physician, sent to Flushing to make an inspection, was told that strangers always had been subject to sickness there in the summer time.[53] An order from Henry Fox, the secretary at war, directed Braddock to transport his entire battalion to Breda.[54] The Prince of Orange was understood to be in charge of this operation and to be assembling a force which included Braddock's battalion, but the details were far from clear. Braddock's next immediate superior, Brigadier-General William Douglas, had died of fever in Beveland.[55]

Applying to Dutch officials for boats in which to move his men to Breda, Braddock was told that none could be provided without an order from the Prince of Orange. The harassed battalion commander immediately dispatched an officer, Lieut.-Col. John Parsons, to obtain the necessary order from the Prince, believed to be in the neighborhood of Bergen. At the same time he sent an express to the Duke of Cumberland to inform him of the death of Douglas.[56]

At 4 A.M. on the morning of September 16 (New Style), the sixty-fifth day of its siege, Bergen-op-Zoom fell. It was taken by a combination of treachery and surprise, according to reports reaching Braddock.[57] One account said a party of twelve French grenadiers had slipped through a small breach in a ravelin, frightening away its Dutch defenders and opening the way for a storming party of 500 who reached the center of the town before the alarm bells could be rung. Sleepy Dutch officers, awaking to find French troops in the marketplace outside their windows, ran away in their nightgowns.[58]

Three days later Braddock was still without any word from either the Prince or the Duke, still without transport, unable to comply with the orders he had received from the secretary at war. No doubt he also was under pressure by Zealanders, frightened by the fall of Bergen, to remain where he was. In desperation he wrote to Chesterfield, a secretary of state:

My Lord:

I take the liberty to address myself to you in relation to the regiments that are in this province. The sickness increases daily and some men that were sent to the grand hospital at Otterhout and sent back yesterday as cured are already relapsed. I have sent enclosed the opinion of the Physician whom His Majesty was pleased to order hither. I send you this because I cannot as yet put in execution the order I received from the Secretary at War to transport the troops in this island to Breda, the States of Zealand having absolutely refused to furnish any boats till they have an order from the Prince of Orange to whom I have dispatched an officer who is not yet returned.

I sent a fortnight ago an express to His Royal Highness the Duke upon the death of Brigadier Douglas who is not yet returned and am in great distress regarding the regiments in South Beveland. The States of Zealand have sent to me to direct 'em to obey the orders of the Dutch Major General there, the commanding officer there having received the same order from the Secretary at War as I have here.

We were very much surprised here at the loss of Bergen but I believe not so much as you were in England. I am afraid when the truth comes out it will appear a very black story.

I have this moment received a letter from the States of Zealand to desire we may not leave these islands till there is an order from the Prince of Orange or other troops to replace us. As I know very well even if we had had conveyance we could not have got into Breda till the Prince of Orange had given directions for our reception. I did directly send an officer to him to know his pleasure. I beg your Lordship's pardon for giving you this trouble and am

With all respect
My Lord
Your Lordship's
Most Obedient
Humble Servant
E. Braddock

P.S. It is very likely our communication will be cut off with Holland but by long sea in a very few days.
Flushing September 19th 1747 [59]

But Chesterfield had no intention of becoming involved. Writing from Whitehall a week later, he informed Col. Braddock:

Sir

I would not defer returning you my thanks for the favour of your letter of the 19th Inst N. W., tho' I have nothing to say to you upon the contents of it but to refer you to the orders, which you will receive from his Royal Highness the Duke, as to the future disposition of the troops in the islands of Zealand.

In the mean time the King is persuaded, that no care will be want-

ing on your part for their ease and conveniency in their present sickly
condition, and approves of your care hitherto.

I am Etc.,
Chesterfield [60]

Later in the fall Braddock's battalion was transported from
Flushing to Eyndhoven, a town about twenty miles south of Bar
le Duc, where it went into winter quarters with the rest of the allied army. A draft of 128 men arrived in Flanders from the home
battalions to replace losses in the guards brigade, including those
of the Coldstream who had died of fever.[61] The Duke of Cumberland, who was nearsighted in one eye and fearful that a fever he
had contracted in Holland would destroy the sight of the other,
issued an order that sergeants of the foot guards would leave off
wearing ruffles because he could not tell commissioned from non-
commissioned officers. He was no longer an easy man to get along
with.[62]

"There are prodigious discontents in the army: the town had got
a list of a hundred and fifty officers who desired at once to resign
but I believe this was exaggerated," Walpole said.[63] "*We* (the Duke)
are very great and very exact disciplinarians; our partialities are
very strong, particularly on the side of aversions, and none of the
articles tally exact with British tempers. Lord Robert Bertie received a reprimand the other day by an aide-de-camp, for blowing
his nose as he relieved the guard under a window (the Duke's);
where very exact notice is constantly taken of very small circumstances."

In May, 1748, Braddock's battalion assembled with the rest of the
Duke's army near Roermond, north of Maestricht, which was being
beseiged by Saxe. The two armies encamped within sight of each
other and the Duke watched the French from a churchsteeple, but
the fighting was over.[64] On March 11 a peace congress had met at
Aix-la-Chapelle, and by the end of April it had reached a preliminary armistice agreement. The opposing armies retired behind imaginary lines, that of the British extending across Brabant from
Steenberg to Roermond.[65] The definitive peace treaty, signed October 18, ended military operations.[66] The guards brigade, including
Braddock's battalion, marched to Wilhelmstadt from where it
sailed for home nine days before Christmas.[67] A winter gale scattered their transports. Cavalry horses aboard ship died by the score,
or had to be killed and thrown overboard.[68] Part of the Coldstream

landed at Yarmouth on December 20, and the rest of it at the Downs on January 29, 1749.[69]

Braddock's battalion had been assigned billets near the Tower and in the Parish of St. Luke's, Middlesex.[70] As fast as they returned to London all companies of the Coldstream were reduced in strength, from 60 to 48 men.[71] The haler of the older soldiers were transferred to an invalid corps for garrison duty at the forts around London, along the coast, and in Scotland. All told, nearly 1,300 men were discharged from the Guards brigade.[72] Once again the streets of London, its parks and taverns, were packed with idle, demobilized redcoats, a scene which carried Braddock back to the days of his childhood, at the end of King William's wars.[73] This time the government recognized its responsibilities. Cumberland and Lord Halifax, president of the Board of Trade, worked out a scheme to provide free land in Nova Scotia for all discharged soldiers and sailors willing to emigrate.[74]

For those who remained in the army there was no relaxation of discipline. A Sergeant Hartley of the Coldstream and Drummer John South of the First Footguards, found guilty of desertion to the French, were sentenced to be shot in Hyde Park. The judgment was carried out between 7 and 8 o'clock on a Monday morning, a detachment from every company of the three regiments of the guards brigade conducting the prisoners to the place of their execution. Drummer South fell dead after the first volley, but the Coldstream sergeant went down only wounded. He lay on his back, writhing and moaning:

"Lord have mercy on my soul! . . ."

A second file of guardsmen, held in reserve, fired another round to quiet him.[75]

To Walpole, unacquainted with the difficulties of eighteenth century military discipline, harsh military punishment was reprehensible. He blamed the code on Cumberland, whom he nicknamed "Nolkejumskoi." [76]

"His savage temper increases every day," Walpole told George Montagu.[77] "George Boscawen is in a scrape with him by a court martial, in which he is one; it was appointed on a young poor soldier, who to see his friends had counterfeited a furlough of leave only for a day. They ordered him two hundred lashes; but Nolkejumskoi, who loves blood like a leech, insisted it was not enough—has made them sit three times, though everyone adheres to the first

sentence, and swears they shall sit these six months till they increase the punishment."

Occasionally the guards were called out to quell riots. One occurred at a sailors' pay office in Block street, and another at a
bawdy house in the Strand. The Haymarket theatre was wrecked
by a mob. Covent Garden was another trouble spot. An officer and
65 men were stationed at Temple Bar. But except for minor
emergencies the Coldstream was back on its routine, providing es-
corts for civil prisoners between jail and court, keeping peace at
public executions, standing sentry at St. James's, furnishing detachments for Windsor, Kensington, Hampden Court, wherever the
King happened to be residing.[78]

Braddock himself presently took a London house in Arlington
street, off Picadilly, within easy walking distance of St. James's and
Whitehall—one of those typically narrow, vertical Georgian terrace
houses, two rooms deep, five stories high, with a modest fanlight
above its entrance.[79] It was built, probably, of the yellowish gray
brick then coming into favor and stood near the foot of the street.
Arlington street had been fashionable ever since the Duchess of
Cleveland lived there. Braddock's neighbors included Horace Walpole, who lived on the east side of the street, facing Lord Carteret,
the Earl of Bath, and the Duke of Richmond, who had larger
houses with imposing porticoes and courtyards.[80]

Practically the entire population of Georgian London, except
bachelor lawyers who lived in "chambers" and the city's slum
dwellers, occupied tall, narrow terrace houses, one floor for eating,
one for sleeping, a third for company, and a fourth for servants,
with a basement kitchen below street level.[81] Looking to Braddock's
personal needs was Thomas Bishop, a Coldstream guardsman who
had been with him in Flanders and was now employed as his body
servant.[82] Bishop could cook if necessary. But officers of the Guards
on duty at St. James's usually breakfasted at a tavern near the
palace and dined at Pontack's, an eating house in Abchurch street,
at White's, or some other club.[83]

Braddock's pet, George Anne Bellamy, had returned from Dublin and was living with her mother in a house on Tavistock street,
off Convent Garden.[84] "The Little Bellamy," as she was called, was
small and fair, but a full-blown beauty now, her bosom ample, her
cheek bones high, her blue eyes limpid and widely spaced. She had
a sweet, flexible voice, inexhaustible spirits, and her father's Irish

humour. She passed herself off for a sixteen-year old but was believed to be nearer twenty.[85] Back at the Covent Garden theatre, she was playing in *Venice Preserved* when the treaty of Aix-la-Chapelle was signed.[86] So demure was her manner off stage that many actors in the company thought her a prude.[87]

She had become reconciled to her father. On a visit to Dublin he had heard only the best of reports of her from his sister, a Mrs. O'Hara, who had introduced George Anne to Dublin society. His old friend Chesterfield, while lord-lieutenant of Ireland, had made the Dublin theatre fashionable by attending when George Anne's name was on the bill.[86] Tyrawley was proud to be pointed out as the father of a beautiful young actress. He was seeing more and more of Peg Woffington, but he promised to sup with his daughter three or four nights a week. He still refused to have anything to do with her mother.[88]

Mrs. Bellamy, retired from the stage, had been converted to Methodism and gave herself up to gloomy meditations on death.[89] Anxious to see her daughter securely married, she had picked out a husband for her, a middle-aged Irish linen merchant, a Mr. Crump. He was willing. Her mother pressed George Anne to accept him.[90]

"I wish, madam, you would marry himself," said the girl in exasperation. "I can have no objection to him as a father-in-law, but have a most insuperable one to him as a husband." [91]

Peace had been declared in February 1749 with the usual fanfare of heralds at St. James's Gate, Charing Cross, Temple Bar, Chancery Lane, Cheapside, and the Exchange. But it was not celebrated until £14,000 worth of pinwheels, flowerpots, and skyrockets had been set off in the Green Park at the end of April, killing two people. The fireworks were followed by a series of semipublic jubilees, masquerades, and garden parties lasting well into the dusty days of a warm May. George Anne was playing in *The Provoked Wife* at Covent Garden and carrying on an affair with an old admirer, George Metham, the irresponsible young heir of an unimportant Yorkshire baronet.[92] Suddenly one night her father walked into her room.

"Pop, I've got you a husband," he announced.[93]

"I hope then, my Lord, you have found out my choice," she said, thinking of Metham.

But her father had found Crump, the same Mr. Crump to whom

her mother had tried to marry her. Apparently Tyrawley had heard about Crump from his sister, Mrs. O'Hara. He had investigated the linen merchant and concluded he would make a suitable match. Everything had been settled for the marriage. George Anne was horrified. She had planned to marry Metham, whose mother had died, leaving him a fairly good estate. Moreover, George Anne was pregnant.

When she stepped out on the stage that night in the character of *Lady Fanciful* in *The Provoked Wife,* the first person she saw was Crump, seated in the front row of the pit.

Metham stood behind the scenes, pale and dejected. She had told him her father's choice. When the prompter's bell rang for the fifth act, Metham called George Anne into a hall backstage, gathered her up in his arms, costume and all, swept her through the door into a waiting coach, and made off with her. Her unexpected departure caused an uproar. Quin stepped out in front of the curtain to apologize for the sudden disappearance of his leading lady.

Metham set her up in a furnished house in Leicester street. Her father disowned her. Metham promised to marry her and later that summer took her to York, where a few days before Christmas, she gave birth to a son. By February 1750 she was back in London, a thoroughly notorious woman paragraphed in all the newspapers. Her reappearance on the stage of the Covent Garden theatre in *Venice Preserved* sold out the boxes. She and Metham took a large house beyond their means in King street, St. James's, an establishment which attracted all the cheaper fashion of town until Metham ran out of money, exhausted his credit, and had to go back to York where they had left their infant son with George Anne's mother.

Now a confirmed woman of the world, George Anne moved into a thinly furnished house on Frith street, Soho. She still kept two servants and a coach and four, and entertained at cards, sometimes at a profit. She made the acquaintance of Cumberland's friend, Fox, the secretary at war, and of Jack Calcraft, a tall, florid, red-headed, blue-eyed young clerk in the secretary's office. On the first visit to her house in Frith street, Fox discovered that George Anne was unable to pay her bills. When he had gone she found a £50 bank note under a Chelsea china figure on the mantel piece.[94]

Hiring a good man cook to prepare the *petit soupers* indispensable to the high night life of the Covent Garden district, she borrowed another £1,000 and set up a faro bank with two friends of her father, General Richard Wall, a good natured Irish adventurer who was the Spanish minister in London, and Compte Haflange, the Bavarian ambassador. She and the Marquis de Vernieul, a French nobleman she had met through Metham, always dealt the cards. The bank flourished. Her house became a demimonde rendezvous. Army officers and other members of the diplomatic corps dropped in.[95] Braddock must have felt at home there. He had acquired a reputation as a "joyous, rollicking soldier of the old fashioned type, rather popular in London as a good companion and good fellow, who loved his glass with a more than merely convivial enthusiasm." [96]

George Anne did not give up the theatre. Young, stylish, light-hearted, radiant in blonde beauty, she turned intensely serious on the stage, so serious that she was not at her best in comedy but excelled as *Desdemona*. Critics praised her expression of rapture, her tenderness, the amorous glow of her features in passages of conjugal affection. Her chief fault was a strong taint of the old fashioned *titumti* cadence in her voice. But William Rufus Chetwood, the bookseller-dramatist-critic, said she was improving and would cause no wonder if she soon reached the top of perfection.[97]

She finished that season at Covent Garden. In September—a fine, dry September with Kensington's horse chestnuts in second bloom—she joined the company at Drury Lane to play *Juliet* to Garrick's *Romeo* while Mrs. Cibber and the dashing Barry appeared in the same roles at Covent Garden. From September 28 until October 11 it was the only play in town, each theatre trying to outdraw the other and papering the house, if necessary, to fill it. Mrs. Cibber's *Juliet* was a modest girl lost in an ecstasy of love. The little Bellamy, radiating passion and adoration, played a slim, amorous, soft-voiced wench impatient for her lover's arms.[98]

Early in the new year, 1751, she was summoned to Leicester House. Their Royal Highnesses, the Prince and Princess of Wales, Thursday night habitues of the theatre, wished to do her the honor of a command performance on her coming benefit night, March 18. Their choice was John Hughes' five-act tragedy, *The Siege of Damascus*.[99] The week before George Anne's benefit, the Prince was taken ill. He went to bed, was blooded and blistered, seemed better, and was sitting up on the night of March 20 when a sudden fit of coughing seized him and he died.[100]

The Lord Chamberlain posted a notice fixing the period of deep mourning from Sunday, March 31, to Sunday, June 20. Theatres were ordered closed for two weeks. Out came the black hangings, the sconces for the candles at Westminster, black bombazine and tippets for the ladies at court, crepe hat bands and weepers for the gentlemen. Col. Braddock put on a black sash. His scarlet uniform coat was faced with black. For the Prince's funeral, on a cold and rainy Saturday night, April 15, guardsmen lined the way from the House of Lords to the southwest door of the Abbey, holding lighted torches in either hand.[101]

Some profane Jacobite circulated this epitaph:

> *Here lies poor Fred*
> *Who was alive and is dead:*
> *Had it been his father,*
> *I had much rather;*
> *Had it been his brother,*
> *Still better than another;*
> *Had it been his sister,*
> *No one would have missed her;*
> *Had it been the whole generation,*
> *Still better for the nation;*
> *But since 'tis only Fred*
> *Who was alive and is dead*
> *There's no more to be said.*[102]

Frederick's eldest son, George, was only thirteen years old. His mother, the Princess of Wales, was named regent with a council of fourteen, headed by the Duke of Cumberland.[103] But the Duke kept away from politics. He spent much of his time at the "Ranger's Lodge," a royal villa in Windsor Park, amusing himself with a private menagerie and four Barbary horses, the gift of Hungarian Marshal Bathyani, who had served with him in Flanders. Cumberland had lost none of his flesh. His weight now exceeded 250 pounds.[104]

His control over the army remained unimpaired. The King signed all promotions and general orders, and Fox, as secretary at war, countersigned them, but as captain general the Duke was still in command and his stern standards of discipline continued to prevail.[105] A foot soldier sentenced by a court martial to receive a thousand lashes on the parade at St. James's at three different times, may have been the poor fellow who was about to be punished one afternoon when George Anne was walking in the park with Braddock.

She asked Braddock to "beg off. the offender," and apparently he tried speaking to the officer in charge, Col. Alexander Drury, regimental lieutenant-colonel of the First Foot Guards. Drury's response was not even courteous. How long was it, he asked Braddock, since he had divested himself of brutality and the insolence of his manners?

"You never knew me insolent to my inferiors," replied Braddock. "It is only to such rude men as yourself that I behave with the spirit which I think they deserve." [106]

It was a bad year for George Anne. One of her best friends, a Miss St. Leger, niece of an Irish peer, had been married after a long courtship to Metham's most intimate friend, Major Ralph Burton of the 48th Foot. But Metham refused to marry George Anne. They had separated. The break had come after a January birthday dinner she had arranged for Metham. The dessert, ordered from Robinson, a bon ton confectioner, had been a little more sumptuous than she could afford. In front of their guests Metham had embarrassed her with rude criticism of her extravagance. In a burst of anger, which she later regretted, she vowed she would have nothing more to do with Metham.[107]

Jack Calcraft, the war office clerk, who had become friendly with Metham and was one of the guests at the birthday dinner, began to take an interest in George Anne. His jealousy aroused, Metham implored her forgiveness. At the depth of his romantic agony he threatened to kill her and commit suicide if she refused. She clung to her vow. Burton dissuaded him from suicide, but Metham challenged Calcraft to a duel. George Anne, on the verge of hysteria, took refuge at the Thames river country home of friends, a Mr. and Mrs. Gansell, whose son, William, was a captain in Braddock's regiment. Metham did not follow her, but Calcraft did, offering her a marriage contract in which he promised, under bond of £50,000, to make her his wife within six or seven years. He said he could not marry her immediately because he had promised his patron, Henry Fox, the secretary at war, "not to enter into a serious engagement with a woman in public life."

On the advice of old Mr. Gansell, George Anne accepted Calcraft's offer. Returning to London, where she resumed an engagement at Drury Lane, she went to live with Calcraft in Brewer street, above St. James's. Most people, Braddock and her father among them, assumed that she had married Calcraft. They thought him an ideal mate for an impulsive, improvident young woman, habitually in debt. "Honest Jack" Calcraft as some called him, was a practical fellow, the son of a Grantham town clerk, and so adept at figures that no one doubted he would make a fortune.[108]

Calcraft had been a paymaster and contractor for the King's troops during the last rebellion in Scotland, and had taken advantage of his clerkship in the office of the secretary at war to build up a lucrative private business of his own as an army agent. That is, he was an agent for army colonels who received and disbursed all money issued by the paymaster general for the pay, clothing, and subsistence of the regiments they commanded. The commercial transactions involved in this system made it convenient for the colonel to have a London business agent. For his services the agent customarily retained a commission of ten pence in the pound, or some £300 to £500 annually per regiment.[109]

To help Calcraft in his operations as an army agent, George Anne made the most of her acquaintance among military men. Both Braddock and her father could be useful here. She had already established a reputation as a hostess who set a good table, and as an actress she was a celebrity. Officers of the first rank were invited to dine at the house in Brewer Street. The secretary at war himself began to drop in for meals. His wife, Lady Caroline Fox, became the godmother of a daughter born to Calcraft and George Anne.[110]

"No war, no politics, no parties, no madness and no scandal," Walpole wrote from London to Mann at the beginning of 1753. "In the memory of England there never was so inanimate an age." [111]

The tranquility was deceptive. Nothing had been settled by the Treaty of Aix-la-Chapelle. Its twenty-four articles were more of an armistice than a peace. In North America, where no fixed boundaries had been drawn between British and French possessions, border incidents posed a constant threat of war. Two Englishmen, Governor William Shirley, of Massachusetts, and William Mildmay, Esq., had been named by King George to meet with two French commissaries in Paris to discuss the boundary question. For three years the four men toiled over maps, documents, arguments, and allegations. In 1753 Shirley left Paris in disgust, the issue still unsettled.[112]

The *London Magazine* printed an account of a battle in the Ohio valley where French and "French Indians" had destroyed a village of the Twigtree (Twightwee) Indians who were friendly toward the English. The Twigtree chief was boiled and eaten by his conquerors and, according to the magazine, the "French Indians" scalped a white man, took out his heart and ate it, cut off his fingers and sent them to Canada to collect a reward offered by the French for Englishmen. Here was a matter which, if true, should be taken up in Paris by the Earl of Albemarle, now British ambassador extraordinary and minister plenipotentiary to the French court.[113]

Albemarle, who was reported to have settled down in Paris with sixteen cooks and a new mistress, also had been appointed governor of Virginia.[114] He still held the colonelcy of the Coldstream, although Braddock, as lieutenant colonel, was in active command of the regiment.[117] As a commoner, Braddock could never hope to become the colonel of the Coldstream. Command of the household troops was still reserved to the nobility. Albemarle's successor would be chosen by the crown.[115]

"Between you and me, what do you think made our friend Lord Albemarle colonel of a regiment of the guards, Governor of Virginia, Groom of the Stole and Ambassador to Paris?" Lord Chesterfield was speaking.[116] "Was it his birth? No; a Dutch gentleman only. Was it his estate? No; he had none. Was it his learning, his parts, his political abilities and applications? You can answer these questions as easily and as soon as I can ask them. What was it then? Many people wondered, but I do not; for I know and will tell you. It was his air, his address, his manners, and his graces. He pleased, and by pleasing, he became a favorite. . . ."

But Braddock had made up his mind to have his own regiment. He had seen enough colonels sitting around in the clubs and coffee houses of St. James's, drawing fat profits of as much as £600 a year by merely clothing regiments they seldom saw. And while he was about it, he wanted a good regiment, one in which an ensign's commission would bring at least £250 or £300. His own commission as regimental lieutenant-colonel of the Coldstream had a fixed value of £5,000 whenever he chose to sell it.[117]

Before the first month of the new year of 1753 was out, the opportunity for which Braddock had been waiting presented itself. The Royal Horse Guards (the Blues), had been without a colonel since the death in 1750 of Charles Lennox, second Duke of Richmond, one of Braddock's former neighbors on the courtyard side of Arlington street.[118] On January 27, 1753, the King was pleased to give the Blues to Sir John Ligonier, until then colonel of the Second Dragoon Guards. The Honorable William Herbert, fifth son of the Earl of Pembroke and colonel of the Fourteenth Foot, succeeded Ligonier as colonel of the dragoon guards. Braddock applied for Herbert's foot and got it, selling his Coldstream lieutenant-colonelcy to the Coldstream's first major, Hedworth Lambton.[119]

George Anne saw another agency coming up for Calcraft. This one, she knew, would be easy. Some agents charged exhorbitant rates. Some, according to an old stage joke, required their colonel-clients to carry life insurance at the rate of 8 per cent. But Braddock had no qualms about Calcraft. He gave him the agency of the Fourteenth Foot without waiting for George Anne to ask. She figured it would bring them £300 a year.[120]

VIII

GIBRALTAR

1753–1754

THE FOURTEENTH, or the Buckinghamshire Regiment of Foot, had a history that went back to Monmouth's rebellion. Originally it had been Sir Edward Hales's regiment of foot, named for the Roman Catholic baronet who raised its first company of one hundred musketeers and pikemen and who later helped King James II in his first attempted flight to France.[1] The Fourteenth had fought in Flanders during King William's Wars, and in Scotland during the first Jacobite rebellion. Returning to England in 1742 from a fifteen-year tour of duty at Gibraltar, it had made another campaign in Flanders and fought another Pretender in Scotland, winning a measure of renown at Falkirk for holding its ground when other troops panicked. It had been in the first line at Culloden. Ordered back to Gibraltar in 1752, it was still there when Braddock became its colonel.[2]

All colonial and foreign garrison service was unpopular with the army's rank and file. An order to proceed to Gibraltar usually resulted in wholesale desertions. The only ones who looked forward to duty there were a few hardened, cunning old soldiers whose weakness for wine and women made them content with chronic insobriety and common law wives. "The Rock" was notorious for bad quarters, poor food, malaria, and smallpox. Five hundred soldiers had died there of fever in 1727. Among the troops a fear persisted that the secretary at war might forget how long their regiment had been on "The Rock." He seemed to have forgotten the Fourteenth Foot for fifteen years.[3] But for a commanding officer, Gibraltar offered certain compensations. In London it was assumed that he would make the most of opportunities to fleece everybody he could.[4] The governor of Gibraltar enjoyed emoluments reckoned at not less than £20,000 a year, including ground rents, permits, wharfage, and license anchorage fees.[5]

Maj. Gen. Humphrey Bland, one of the army's most able and experienced officers, had been sent to Gibraltar as its governor after the peace of Aix-la-Chapelle. Bland was a Yorkshireman, then in his sixties, who had begun his military career under Marlborough, serving in practically every campaign of the past half century. He was also the author of a textbook, *Treatise on Discipline,* which had become the Bible of the British army, and he lived up to its stated principles so rigorously that two of young James Wolfe's friends under Bland at Gibraltar complained of "too much duty." [6]

Bland had been called home in the summer of 1752 to become colonel of the King's dragoons and governor of Edinburgh Castle.[7] Lord George Beauclerk, colonel of the Nineteenth Foot, which was on duty at Gibraltar until relieved by Herbert's Fourteenth, and then Herbert himself, severally acted as commandants of the Fortress in the absence of a new Governor. Braddock's commission as colonel of the Fourteenth, announced in January, was not signed until February 17, 1753.[8] He booked passage to Gibraltar soon after, presumably to succeed Herbert as commandant and acting governor.[9]

Braddock had no ties in London, except his house in Arlington street and his attachment for George Anne Bellamy.[10]

At the end of a three-weeks' voyage [11] Braddock saw the slate gray limestone humps of Gibraltar rearing their barren crests a thousand feet above the dark green sea. From the deck of his ship the western slope of the Rock, overgrown with wild olives, looked almost tropical after a raw, cold winter in London. The sunshine was bright as broken glass. When Gibraltar lay in shadow, even dappled shadow, its dark green bay was a sublunary sea. Over the moorish castle and the town of blue-washed houses with red tile roofs, crowded between the anchorage and the steeply climbing mountainside, hung the faint familiar acrid odor of British sea coal. Gibraltar had a fuel problem. Not so many years ago a British garrison had ripped out and burned its quarters as winter fire-wood.[12]

Braddock went ashore. The guard had turned out. The drums beat a ruffle.[13] A group of officers waited on the mole to receive the new colonel and see him to his headquarters. The narrow rubble-paved streets, rising sharply from the seawall, were crowded with swarthy, pock-faced Moors, Spaniards, Genoese, and Jews.[14] The governor's residence, a converted Franciscan convent, looked down across a terraced garden of palms to the dark green sea. Spring was a pleasant season at Gibraltar, but the summer was sticky, ener-vating, oppressively sultry, and insufferably hot. Morning and eve-ning parade and Sunday church services became burdensome. The open cesspools of the town and the dead air in the lee of the moun-tain made the place a stinking hole.[15]

In addition to Braddock's own Fourteenth, the Gibraltar garri-son consisted of another regiment of foot, the Sixth, and a company of the royal regiment of artillery.[16] The Sixth, which had relieved the Thirty-Second after the Fourteenth relieved the Nineteenth,[17] was commanded by Lieut.-Gen. John Guise, a veteran of the First Foot Guards who had seen combat at Malplaquet and Carthagena.[18] In May the London *Gazette* announced that the King had ap-pointed Guise, governor of Berwick, thereby eliminating the pos-sibility of his out-ranking Braddock at Gibraltar. But any hopes which Braddock may have had of remaining the senior officer there were blasted when Maj. Gen. Thomas Fowke, a member of Cum-berland's staff in Flanders, was named governor of Gibraltar.[19]

Braddock's entire stay at Gibraltar seems to have been a tour of frustration. Neglected since the siege of 1727, the post had fallen into ruin and decay. So badly constructed was the foundation of one battery, near a new mole, that it sank until its parapet tum-bled down. Guns were dismounted. Rubbish choked the ditches on the land side of the works. Stores were depleted. Some of the musket balls in the magazines, almost empty, were too big for the calibre of the muskets Braddock's men carried. The soldiers' bar-racks in the old Moorish castle, a converted nunnery, and other old Spanish buildings of the town were rookeries.[20]

That winter a plague raged on the African coast. Special pre-cautions were taken with regard to incoming British ships which might have called at African ports. There was also some difficulty with the Alcaid of Tetuan, in Morocco, a principal source of supply of provisions for Gibraltar's garrison.[21]

Braddock seems to have consoled himself at Gibraltar with Mary Yorke, the wife of John Yorke, a lieutenant fireworker of the royal regiment of artillery on duty there.[22] Yorke had joined the regiment as a cadet gunner in the summer of 1746. On a lieutenant's pay of three shillings per day he cannot have been able to do much for a wife living with him in a foreign garrison.[23] Exactly what Mary Yorke's relations were to the bachelor colonel of the Fourteenth Foot is a matter of conjecture. They may have been the same as those of George Anne Bellamy. Braddock spoke of Mary simply as one of his "good friends." [24]

* * * * * *

All this while his destiny was shaping beyond the seas, in North America, where the Marquis of Duquesne, newly appointed French governor of Canada, had sent a force of a thousand or more men from Montreal by way of the St. Lawrence and the lakes to occupy the Ohio Valley.[25] This was the vast tract of virgin territory west of the Allegheny mountains which had attracted the attention of a group of wealthy and influential Virginians interested in land speculation. In 1747 they had formed a joint stock venture, the Ohio Company, to take up 500,000 acres of land beyond the mountains and establish trade with the Indians there.[26]

France claimed the Ohio country by right of discovery and exploration. The English colonies of Virginia and Pennsylvania claimed it as part of their royal grants. It had never been mapped and its boundaries were uncertain. English and Canadian backwoodsmen, who carried on a fur trade with the Indians, were the only whites who had ever seen the Ohio. Among the Englishmen there was a bad feeling as a result of rival claims on the Ohio lands; Pennsylvania traders, by far the more aggressive, had little use for the Virginians.[27]

Thomas Lee, a former acting-governor of Virginia and the president of the Virginia colonial council, was one of the founders of the Ohio Company, a closed corporation of fifteen to twenty partners, mostly Virginians, tied together by social, political, and family bonds.[28] The non-Virginians included John Hanbury of London, a wealthy Quaker merchant and British army contractor with whom colonial shippers and Virginia planters dealt, and Arthur

Dobbs. Robert Dinwiddie, lieutenant governor of Virginia, also was a partner. The Lee, Dobbs, and Dinwiddie interests gave the company a semi-official status.[29]

At the headwaters of the Potomac river, opposite the mouth of Wills Creek, the company built a two-story log storehouse. Thomas Cresap, a Maryland frontiersman who had settled nearby, was authorized by the company to begin clearing roads. Christopher Gist, a Virginia scout and surveyor, was commissioned by the company to cross the Allegheny mountains, explore the Ohio valley, and explain to the Indian's living there the plans and purposes of the Ohio Company. A trail was blazed across the mountains, from Wills Creek toward Redstone creek, on the Monongahela river, and a dozen families built log cabins beyond the mountains at a place called "Gist's plantation." [30]

French reaction to this was violence, beginning at the village of the Twightwees. English traders were robbed, killed, carried off into captivity, and held for ransom.[31] The French built a new fort near the west end of Lake Erie. A report that they intended to build three more on the Ohio raised the specter of a chain stretching across the back country from Canada to Louisiana.[32] Virginia's Lieutenant Governor Dinwiddie wrote a letter of protest to the commander of the new French fort, informing him that he was on British territory and directing him to withdraw. Maj. George Washington, adjutant of the southern district of Virginia and a brother of Lawrence Washington, first chairman or manager of the Ohio Company, delivered the letter on December 12, 1753 to the commander of a French post, Fort Le Boeuf, near Lake Erie. In the middle of January, Washington returned to Williamsburg, the Virginia colonial capital, with the Frenchman's reply: Dinwiddie's letter would be sent to the Marquis Duquesne but the commander of the French fort would remain where he was until he received orders to the contrary from his own general.[33]

Spring came to London, and with it, on March 6, 1754, death for the right honorable Henry Pelham, first lord of the Treasury and chancellor of the Exchequer. Henry Fox, secretary at war; William Pitt, paymaster of the forces; and Pelhalm's older brother, the Duke of Newcastle, bickered and bargained among themselves to succeed to the prime ministry. Newcastle won out after a week of political scuffling. The Duke offered Fox the place of secretary of state, with leadership of the House of Commons, but Fox preferred to remain secretary at war. Sir Thomas Robinson, former ambassador to Vienna, whose command of the German language and knowledge of continental protocol were held in high esteem by the King, accepted the offer Fox turned down.[34]

On April 2 the *Gazette* announced Braddock's promotion to the rank of major-general of His Majesty's forces.[35] At about the same time a dispatch from Virginia informed Whitehall that a messenger "sent to enquire whether the French had built forts at the back of our settlement" had returned with word that 1,500 French regulars had built three on lands for which several gentlement in London and Virginia held a grant from the King.

"If the French are not soon drove off and forts built by the English on the Mississippi they will have such strongholds that it will never be in our province to expel them," said a newspaper paragraph.[36]

But it was midsummer before Braddock, still at Gibraltar, could have read in the *Gentleman's Magazine:*

> *Account of a Journey from ˜Williamsburg to the* French *Fort, near Lake* Erie *in* Virginia.[37]

This was the first detailed report of Washington's trip from Williamsburg to the French fort and of his wintry return across the mountains. By the time Braddock read it, Washington, now the colonel of a regiment of Virginia volunteers, had led a force of about four hundred men back across the Alleghenies for the purpose of building an English fort at the forks of the Ohio. A party of backwoodsmen had reached the forks in April, in advance of Washington, and begun to build a stockade, when a swarm of bateaux and canoes brought a French force down the Allegheny River from the general direction of Lake Erie. The woodsmen retreated. The French demolished the stockade and began on its site a larger work which they named Fort Duquesne. Seizure of the English stockade was regarded in Virginia as an act of war.[38]

Washington, whose regiment was still advancing slowly toward the enemy, surprised and captured a small French scouting party. During the engagement Ensign Jumonville, brother of the French captain, Coulon de Villiers, was killed. But shortage of supplies and lack of reinforcements obliged the Virginians to fall back to a temporary defense which they called Fort Necessity. Here they were attacked on July 3 and after a nine-hour fight parlayed with the French and agreed to withdraw, abandoning nine swivels and most of their baggage. News of this disaster reached London in August.[39] The *London Magazine* for that month published a copy of a letter from Washington to his brother Jack after that first engagement with the French. "I heard the bullets whistle, and, believe me, there is something charming in the sound," the colonel wrote.

Older soldiers smiled when they read this. King George remarked "he would not say so, if he had been used to hear many." [40] Horace Walpole picked up Washington's letter and embellished it in one of his own giving Mann the news of Washington's defeat:

"The French have tied up the hands of an excellent farfaron, a major Washington, whom they took and engaged not to serve for a year. In this battle, he said, 'Believe me, as the cannon balls flew over my head, they made a delightful sound.' " [41]

"Braggart" was the word Walpole used in his memoirs to describe Washington at this time.[42]

Dinwiddie also was writing letters—letters to Newcastle, to Robinson, to Fox, and to Lord Albemarle, still titular governor of Virginia and British ambassador at Paris. In all these letters Dinwiddie urged that regular British troops be sent to Virginia to drive back the French.[43] As a soldier, Albemarle was inclined to agree with Dinwiddie. From Paris he wrote to the Duke of Newcastle:

> Washington and such may have courage and resolution but they have no knowledge or experience in our profession (of arms); consequently there can be no dependence on them. Officers, and good ones, must be sent to discipline the militia and to lead them on as this nation; we may then (and not before) drive the French back to their settlements and encroach upon them as they do at present upon us.[44]

In London, Newcastle talked things over with John Hanbury, the Ohio Company's London promoter. They called in a young army lieutenant, Horatio Gates, a godson of Horace Walpole. Gates had just returned home from Nova Scotia where he had served under Col. Edward Cornwallis, governor of that colony, but was too sensible to answer questions about the state of affairs in Virginia.[45] Newcastle also talked with Arthur Dobbs, an Irish gentleman, newly appointed governor of North Carolina, who was about to sail for America.[46] Dobbs departed a short time later aboard the man-of-war "Garland," carrying £10,000 in specie from the home government for Dinwiddie's use in the defense of the colony, a crown credit for a similar sum, and the assurance that two thousand stands of arms be shipped to America.[47] At Hanbury's suggestion Dobbs also took to Governor Horatio Sharpe of Maryland a crown commission as a lieutenant-colonel of foot and instructions from the King to assume command of all English forces raised in that part of the continent.[48]

There was no question of the direction in which Franco-British relations were drifting. In June the Toulon squadron had been sighted between Cape St. Vincent and the Western Island, standing for North America. Next came a report from Cadiz that ten French men-of-war, lately arrived there from Toulon, had sailed westward.[49] The newspapers published statements that 8,000 French troops, with their wives and children, had been sent to America in 1752, that a shipload of cannon and ammunition had been unloaded at the French fortress of Louisbourg, captured by the American colonists in the last war but returned to France after Aix-la-Chapelle.[50] Governor William Shirley of Massachusetts, who had conceived the capture of Louisbourg—the one noteworthy British victory of that war—had returned to Boston, after quitting the abortive boundary commission sessions in Paris, and organized a force of 1,100 men to reconnoitre the Kennebec river. He built two forts on the Kennebec to protect the northern British colonies against French encroachments from Quebec.[51]

Had Newcastle been a sensible man he would have lost no time discussing the North American situation with the Duke of Cumberland or other army chiefs. For months Cumberland had been convinced that the French were on the road to war. He was, in a sense, the unofficial head of a British war party. But Newcastle and his ministry had no wish for war. Besides, Cumberland had indicated through his friendship with Fox that he was opposed politically to Newcastle. Not until September did Newcastle seek professional military advice.[52]

Admiral Lord Anson, first Lord of the Admiralty, held the opinion that American regiments should be organized to fight the French.[53] The Captain General had considered sending sergeants and corporals of the guards brigade to instruct colonial militia and volunteers. But the King, who at first opposed sending any regulars to the colonies, rejected that proposal. The plan as finally agreed upon called for raising two regiments in America and sending over two regiments of British regulars with "a general officer of rank and capacity." [54]

The Duke mentioned Maj.-Gen. Braddock as an officer of rank and capacity suitable for the mission.[55] Perhaps his old Coldstream commander, Albemarle, had nominated Braddock. Perhaps George Anne Bellamy, who knew Albemarle's daughters and daily became more intimate with the secretary at war, helped advance the prospects of her second father. Perhaps Cumberland himself, remembering Braddock at Litchfield or at Flushing, needed no suggestions. There was some speculation that the officer chosen to command the expedition might later become a colonial governor. And so, any officer who had attained the rank of major general was regarded as being qualified to fill the post of governor, and Braddock had served as acting governor of Gibraltar.[56]

Toward the end of summer a 60-gun British warship, the "Deptford," had dropped anchor at Gibraltar to take on supplies of fresh water and provisions. The Right Honorable George Edgcumbe, a tough young naval officer with excellent St. James's connections, was captain of the "Deptford" and acting commodore of the British squadron in the Mediterranean.[57] Braddock's old friend, Tyrawley, had been made governor on Minorca.[58] The "Deptford" was to call at Minorca after leaving Gibraltar for Italy. . . . The prospect was too tempting to be resisted. Early in September the General boarded the warship for Italy.[59]

On Sunday, September 22, 1754, Sir Thomas Robinson wrote from Whitehall to the Duke of Newcastle, then down at Claremont, his country seat near Epsom: [60]

My Lord,
 I was honored with Your Grace's letter of yesterday before I called upon the Duke of Cumberland this morning. His Royal Highness had been with the King. He acquainted me that he had thought of Major General Braddock as the properest person to command the troops in North America. That the King had mentioned sending the Highland Regiment and the raising of independent highland companies; but his Royal Highness was of the opinion it would be better to send immediately 2 regiments upon the Irish establishment, and upon their present low footings, to be complemented in America, and that, not in Virginia only, but from the other colonies too who should furnish their quotas of men: that the sending Highlanders already regimented would be losing the *corps* were the men to remain in America and the raising new independent companies of Highlanders would be so much loss of time; whereas the officers of the 2 Irish regiments now proposed

would be sufficient with their men to discipline any new recruits to be made in America; and His Highness believed the King would consent to this: but His Highness said all this and everything else that may be thought of in a military way was of no effect until His Majesty's servants fix the bounds of the French in America—*How far they shall come and no farther,* which being once done and laid down as a government measure whether of war or of peace, the most express and distinct instructions should be drawn for the commander-in-chief that he may not be liable to further reproaches, from one or the other colony, or be sacrificed, one day or other, to the clamours of merchants at home, or their interested correspondent abroad:—otherwise it would not be dealing fairly with an officer of His Royal Highness's recommendation. His Highness imagined Governor Shirley has gone with 10,000 men to attack Crown Point. I explained the present operation up the Kennebeck: His Highness thinks the operation must be in several parts, particularly *Crown Point,* the regaining a footing on the Ohio and building forts there to cut the French chain from Quebec to the Misisipis, and still, more particularly the attacking of the French forts upon the neck of the Peninsula at the head of the bay of Fundi all which His Royal Highness thought we were authorized to do. . . . He thought with respect to the fixing of quotas of money, should more properly be left for the present commanding officer. . . .

I shall, in confining myself to a bare relation, only add at present that as your grace wishes H. R. H. would determine something this day, so your grace has a general officer and two regiments: which I should humbly think is a preliminary to your grace's satisfaction and a great foundation laid for the meetings on Tuesday and Wednesday next. . . .[61]

The two regiments chosen tentatively for the expedition were the Forty-Fourth and the Forty-Eighth foot. Then in Ireland, both had been raised in 1741 and both had seen pitched battle against the Scots in the second Jacobite rebellion. The Forty-Fourth was commanded by Sir Peter Halkett, who had been with five of its companies at Preston Pans. The Forty-Eighth, Conway's old regiment, had been at Culloden and now was commanded by Col. Thomas Dunbar, a former lieutenant colonel of Folliott's Eighteenth Foot.[62]

As the first instance in English history of any approximation of the military occupation of a colony, the proposed expedition posed new questions of policy regarding military colonial expenditure. The status of the troops would be the same as if they were in a foreign country. They would be in America at the expense of the mother country, but they would owe their allegiance not to the local representative of the crown, but to the general officer in command. The home government (and consequently the Commons) would hold only that measure of control which they exercised over troops on foreign service.[63]

The Ohio Company's Mr. Hanbury stood to make a neat profit on the expedition. Apparently he had advanced the £10,000 in specie, minus a commission of 2½ per cent, which Dobbs had taken to Dinwiddie, and for which Hanbury would be reimbursed by the Crown as soon as Parliament got around to army estimates.[64] It was also understood that Hanbury would provide additional funds for the deputy paymaster general who went with the troops.[65]

Sir Thomas handed the letter, summarizing his conference with Cumberland, to Lord Halifax, president of the Board of Trade.[66] Halifax was going down to Claremont and would take the letter directly to Newcastle. At the same time Sir Thomas made arrangements to wait upon the King next morning at Kensington Palace. Only one thing seems to have worried the pompous secretary of state, and that was Braddock's reputation as something of a rounder. Sir Thomas must take that up with the King. He did. And after seeing the King next day, he wrote Newcastle another letter:

My Lord,
Since seeing Lord Halifax, who I know is gone to your Grace extremely well satisfied with all that has passed with respect to America, I have been to Kensington. I had no occasion to make the King a report of what happened yesterday. Whether H. R. H. had spoken to the King *before* or *after* I had waited upon His Highness, His Majesty recapitulated to me all most all that the Duke had said to me, applauding in the highest manner his son's great scheme, assuring himself, upon His Royal Highness's words, of the sucecss of it, and showing his surprise, not without the great satisfaction, how H.R.H. could have made himself so entirely master of the subject. In a word, my Lord, I never saw the King so entirely pleased, and could I think discern no less satisfaction below stairs. I humbly hope that all doubts, if there are any, will be removed at or, rather, before the meeting. There would, I should humbly presume, be no difficulty in fixing secretly in one's own heart an ultimatum for both *operation* and *negotiation,* for *political* not *imaginary* boundaries, for *solid* not *charter* limits. Such a principle, once resolved upon and adhered to will surmount everything.
The King had ordered me to express His Majesty's approbation of the Earl of Albemarle's zeal. His Majesty has a good opinion of Mr. Braddock's sense and bravery and has heard he has become very stayed. His Majesty has likewise a good opinion of Col. Dunbar, who has been thought of, as proper, to go with his regiment in order to supply Mr. Braddock's place in case of accident. His Majesty is for

sparing all sorts of arms, furniture, ammunition, artillery and engineers. He looks upon the whole as the highest national service. . . .[67]

Final arrangements were approved on Thursday, September 26, when Newcastle, Anson, Halifax, Robinson, and Fox attended His Royal Highness, the captain general, at St. James's.[68] Halifax did not agree with the adopted plan of operations. He favored an attack upon Niagara and Crown Point, to cut the French line of communications before moving on the French fort at the forks of the Ohio. He thought the convoy of provisions and artillery through the woods a hazardous undertaking.[69] He discussed the advisability of setting up a common fund in the colonies to pay the cost of recruiting troops there, a fund to be available as needed to the commander in chief of the expedition. One of the two regiments of foot to be recruited in America would be commanded by Shirley and the other by Sir William Pepperell, commander of the 1745 Louisbourg expedition. Lower ranking officers of these two regiments would be drawn from the half-pay list. The war office published their names on October 7 and announced they would embark immediately.[70]

Sir Thomas wrote to Albemarle, outlining the plans for the expedition. And on October 9 the Earl, acknowledging Sir Thomas' letter and expressing hopes for success of the enterprise, replied from Paris:

> Having been told that General Braddock is in Italy, I have wrote him a circular letter, under cover of his Majesty's several ministers and consuls in those parts, to advise him to set out on his return to England, immediately upon the receipt of it, but without mentioning to him that the public service required it, but only business of the greatest consequence to himself, but thus if my letters should be inspected at the post offices, nothing uncommon might be concluded upon them.[71]

There was no need of secrecy. Everybody who read the London newspapers knew about the expedition. Orders had been issued by the Duke of Dorset, lord-lieutenant of Ireland, directing all officers of Dunbar's and Halkett's to repair immediately to their posts. The two regiments, making together 900 men, were ordered to embark at Cork as soon as transports could be ready to receive them. Wind and weather permitting, they should reach Virginia by the end of December. Acting Commodore Augustus Keppel, second son of the Earl of Albemarle, would command the squadron, which would include H.M.S. "Centurion" and three 20-gun ships. Warrants were issued to press sailors to man thirteen transports and three ordnance ships. The transport captains were called to the Navy office.[72]

A great number of hands was put to work, day and night, at Woolwich and the Tower, making up cartridges and ball, fitting arms, preparing carriages for cannon to be loaded at Chatham. Freight vessels were contracted. Drums, accoutrements, marquees, tents for 8,000 men were loaded aboard the ships "Isabella" and "Mary" for Virginia. A captain, four lieutenants, 60 bombardiers and mattrosses held themselves in readiness to embark at Woolwich. On October 7 the names of all officers selected for the two American regiments were published and it was announced that they would embark immediately at London. A Scottish baronet, Sir John St. Clair, lieutenant colonel of Offeralls Twenty-Second Foot, was appointed quartermaster general of the forces going to America with the rank of a full colonel. James Montresor, former chief engineer at Gibraltar, was appointed chief engineer of the expedition. James Richter, Esq., was made commissary of the musters. James Napier, master surgeon of the hospitals in Flanders, was named director of a hospital for the expedition. Additional surgeons and officers of the train received orders to embark the first of November.[73]

The *London Magazine* published an ode in imitation of Horace, dedicated "to a friend, on his embarking with other officers for a winter's campaign in North America." [74] And there was no question as to who would win the coming fight.

"A Frenchman who piddles on fricassee of frogs can no more encounter with an Englishman who feeds upon beef, than the frog in the fable can swell her body to the size of an ox," said a cocky newspaper writer in the London *Connoisseur*. It was a British army tradition that one Englishman could beat three to five Frenchmen.[75]

The West Indian war has thrown me into a new study: I read nothing but American voyages, and histories of plantations and settlements [Walpole wrote Bentley]. Among all the Indian nations I have contracted a particular intimacy with the Ontaouanoucs . . . they pride themselves upon speaking the purest dialect. . . . My only fear is, that if any of them are taken prisoner, General Braddock is not the kind of man to have proper attentions to so polite a people; I am even apprehensive that he could damn them, and order them to be scalped, in the very worst plantation accent.[76]

Walpole also had been making inquiries about the General, who lived on his street. "Braddock is a very Iroquois in disposition," he told Mann.[77] "However, with all his brutality, he had lately been governor of Gibraltar, where he made himself adored, and where scarce any governor has endured before."

In early October the noise of London's preparations for war reached Paris. At Fontainebleu the Duke of Mirepoix, French ambassador to London, gave his master, Louis XV, a full report. There was talk of a conference to settle Anglo-French difficulties. M. Rouille, the French foreign minister, questioned Albemarle sharply about Britain's intentions and was assured that the measures being taken in London were no different from those of France for many years: ships, men, and arms were being dispatched to the English settlements in America for their own protection.[78]

The postscript of a letter from Albemarle at Fontainebleu on October 23, written shortly before another meeting with Rouille, told Robinson: "I have just now received a letter from Marseilles, which informs me that Maj.-Gen. Braddock set out from thence for Paris the 17th instant, having been 40 days on board Commodore Edgcumbe in his passage from Gibraltar to that port." [79]

Braddock did not tarry in Paris. On Sunday morning, November 10, he returned to London,[80] probably with the happy satisfaction of every home-coming Englishman who once again feels the city's firm, flat paving under foot and sees the slender spires of Wren churches against the sky. He went directly to his house in Arlington street. Later that day he waited on the King and the Duke of Cumberland.[81] His appointment as general and commander of all British forces in North America, dated September 24, 1754, was waiting for him.[82] During the next three weeks he spent most of his time at the War Office, the rebuilt Horse Guards in Whitehall, where Cumberland's adjutant and secretary of military affairs, Col. Napier, and other army chiefs were at work on plans for the expedition. The Duke himself was there every day.[83]

Braddock had long and repeated interviews with the Duke. He talked with Fox and with Newcastle, who impressed upon him the importance of "moderation" in the "article of expense." Napier had accumulated a packet of letters, statistics, memoranda, sketches of regulations, suggested orders.[84] All these were being

worked into a plan of campaign which later would be written up
in the shape of formal and private instructions to the commander
of the expedition. On receipt of those instructions Braddock was
to proceed without further delay to America aboard one of His
Majesty's ships of war.[85]

Col. St. Clair, he was told, had gone ahead to establish magazines and a park for artillery, at Wills Creek in the province of
Maryland. There would also be a flying hospital at Wills Creek
and a general hospital at Hampton, in Virginia. Orders were being
sent by the Secretary of State to the colonial governors of the various colonies, directing them to provide victuals, quarters, and transportation for Braddock's army and to obey his orders for quarter-
ing troops, impressing carriage, and performing other services for
which the colonial governments would be expected to pay.[86]

Cumberland felt strongly about the French in America. He had
read that the lands of the Ohio, rich in iron ore and coal and convenient to water carriage, represented a greater acquisition to
France than all of Flanders. Rather than lose one foot of that
territory he said he himself would oppose the French in America.
In his talks with Braddock he emphasized the necessity of strict
discipline among the troops of his expedition. He cautioned him
against surprise and against panic which might be caused by the
Indian allies of the French.[87]

Parliament met on November 14. The King's speech made no
specific mention of the war in America. Fox, the secretary at war,
presented estimates which totaled nearly £50,000 for Braddock
and his staff, the hospital, and the train that would be sent from
England, and the two regiments to be raised in America. Braddock personally was to be allowed £10 per day, and the Fourteenth
Foot, still at Gibraltar, was to remain under his command. All the
estimates were approved. Mr. Hanbury would be taken care of
later.[88]

Both Covent Garden and Drury Lane revived *The Recruiting
Officer.* George Anne Bellamy, who earlier in the fall had appeared
at the Garden in *Volpone,* kept open house in Brewer street.[89] Fox,
the secretary at war, had asked George Anne to serve as his aman-
uensis—she wrote such an excellent hand! She and the secretary
were often alone together. He named George Anne's first son by
Calcraft, "Henry Fox Calcraft," and thereby set the tongues to
wagging. Because of her intimacy with Fox, many officers looked

upon her as "the captain's captain," an excellent person through whom to seek preferment with the war office, and she picked up agencies for her husband, one after another, from Sir John Mordaunt, Col. John Campbell (later Duke of Argyll), Col. Philip Honywood, and Col. Peregrine Lascelles.[90]

During the last days in London, Braddock made her house in Brewer street a headquarters. He must have been elated by his new command and its opportunity to achieve military distinction after so many years of unrewarded service. But he was apprehensive. He was sixty years old, and about to set off on a journey that would take him 4,000 miles from home.[91] He must have heard George Anne's bell-like laughter as she moved around the crowded card tables in her drawing room, a graceful figure who had outdone all the actresses in London with the quality and cut of her gowns and petticoats—although George II was said to have complained that her hoops were too large.[92] She was close to Braddock's heart. She might be a demi-rep but she was lovely, a quick-witted, fascinating little blue-eyed blonde of high, inexhaustible spirit.

"If you knew what that girl could do as well as say, you would not be surprised at anything relative to her," said Quin.[93]

Braddock also thought of Mary Yorke, beside Gibraltar's dark green bay—and called upon his solicitor to draw up a will that read:

IN THE NAME OF GOD AMEN. I, Edward Braddock Esqr., Major General of His Majesty's Forces and Commander in Chief of an Expedition now fitting out for America, Considering the Uncertainty of this life and being now in Perfect Mind, Memory and Understanding, Do make and Ordain this to be my last Will and Testament in manner and Form Following (That is to say) I give, Devise and Bequeath all my Ready Money, Securities for Money, Plate, Linen, Furniture and all my other Personal Estate and effects whatsoever which I am now Possessed of or Entitled to, or which I shall or may be Possessed of Entitled to at the time of my Decease. Unto my two good Friends, Mary Yorke the wife of John Yorke, a Lieutenant in the Royal Regiment of Artillery now on Duty at Gibraltar and John Calcraft of Brewer street in the Parish of St. James, Westminster, Esqr., and their heirs and Assignees forever to be equally divided between them Share and Share alike. I Do Hereby Also Give, Devise and Bequeath all and every Real Estate I may be now Entitled to, or which I may be in Possession of or Entitled to at the time of my Decease either by purchase or otherwise unto the said Mary Yorke and John Calcraft their Heirs and Assignees forever to be equaly (sic) Divided between them share and Share alike. And it is my Will and Pleasure and I do hereby De-

clare the same so to be that all Moneys and other Advantage whatsoever which may accrue to the said Mary Yorke from this my Will shall
not be subject or liable to the Debts or Controul of her said husband
John Yorke or any Future Husband but shall be to Her own separate
Use Benefit and Advantage. And I do hereby Give her full Power and
Authority to Join with the said John Calcraft in Giving Acquittances
or any other Necessary Discharges in her own Name and which shall
be good and Effectual Notwithstanding her Coverture as she cou'd or
might have done had she been Sole and Unmarried. And I do hereby
Nominate Constitute and Appoint the said Mary Yorke and the said
John Calcraft Joint Executrix and Executor of this My Will Hereby
Revoking all Former Wills by me at any time heretofore made. In
Witness whereof I have hereunto Set my Hand and Seal this Twenty-
fifth Day of November in the Year of Our Lord One Thousand Seven
Hundred and Fifty Four.[94]

The will may not have meant exactly what it said about John
Calcraft. There is good reason to suppose that Braddock intended
to leave half of his estate to George Anne Bellamy, not to his
agent. But just as he took precautions to protect Mary Yorke
against the debts of her husband, so he may have wished to protect
the improvident George Anne against her creditors. Calcraft, whom
Braddock presumed to be George Anne's husband, was the practical head of their household. No claimants would ever close in on
him. By conveying George Anne's portion to Calcraft, his heirs and
assignees forever, Braddock probably thought he was securing it
to her.[95]

It was a handsome document, that will, twelve by fifteen inches,
in flourishing script. In the presence of three witnesses, Thomas
Morgan, Joseph Eddy, and James Rubins, the General signed it
boldly: *E. Braddock.* And in a dab of red wax behind his name he
pressed the Staffordshire Braddock family seal, *argent a greyhound
courant with a bordure engrailed sable*—the same crest which appeared on his government plate supported with the royal lion and
unicorn.[96]

The very same day he signed his will, Braddock's formal orders
were drawn up at St. James's—eight long foolscap pages of detailed
instructions from the King "for our Well Beloved friend Edward
Braddock Esq., Major General of our Forces and whom we have
appointed General and Commander of our troops and forces that
are now in North America and that shall be sent or raised there,
to vindicate our just rights and Possessions in those parts." [97]

Braddock also received a set of private instructions, authorizing

him to draw on the paymaster of North America for levy money
for American recruits—the King hoped it would not exceed £3 per
month—and a set of secret instructions directing him to begin operations in the south as soon as weather would permit.[98]

There was a long letter from Napier, beginning:

> His Royal Highness the Duke, in the several audiences he has given
> you, entered into a particular explanation of every part of the service
> you are about to be employed in; and as a better rule for the execu-
> tion of His Majesty's instructions, he last Saturday communicated to
> you his own sentiments of this affair, and since you were desirous of
> forgetting no part thereof, he has ordered me to deliver them to you
> in writing. . . .[99]

The gist of all these instructions, formal, private, and secret, was
that Braddock should drive the French from Fort Duquesne and
garrison it, and then reduce the French forts at Niagara, Ontario,
Fort Champlain, Crown Point, and Beausejour on the Nova Scotia
isthmus. If unable to command personally these operations, he was
empowered to name subordinate commanders, and he was to use his
own British regiments wherever provincial troops were unavailable.
The Ohio operation was to come first. *Braddock had no choice in
overall strategy.*

"As to your design of making yourself master of Niagara, which
is of the greatest consequence, his Royal Highness recommends to
you to leave nothing to chance in the prosecution of that enterprise," Napier wrote.

That was the only attribution of any part of the plan to Braddock.[100]

Finally came a letter from the pompous Robinson, an after-
thought, informing Braddock that the King authorized him to
summon to council of war such officers of His Majesty's Fleet who
were of equal rank.[101]

On his last night in London, Braddock had supper at the Brewer
street house. Other guests included his aide de camp, Captain
Robert Orme, a young officer of the Coldstream Guards, and Major
Burton, of the Forty-Eight Foot, still mourning the loss of his
wife, Miss St. Leger.[102]

Before he said good night and good-bye, Braddock told George
Anne he would never see her again, that he was going with a hand-
ful of men to conquer whole nations. On a map of North America
he showed her where his troops would have to cut their way

through miles of woods, cross mountains, and ford rivers to reach the French forts. "Dear Pop," he said, "we are sent like lambs to the altar."

As he left her house that night he pressed some folded foolscap into George Anne's hand. She unfolded it and looked at it by candlelight when he had gone. It was his will.[103]

I X

COLONIAL PROBLEMS

November 1754–April 1755

H IS MAJESTY's SHIP "Norwich," a four-rater of 50 guns,[1] was anchored at Spithead in November when a courier came down from London with a letter for her commander, Captain Samuel Barrington.[2] The Captain broke the seal, opened the letter, and read:

By the Commissioners for
executing the office of
Lord High Admiral
of Great Britain & Ireland.

You are hereby required and directed to receive on board His Majesty's Ship under your command Major General Braddock, with his Attendants, Servants and baggage, and as soon as they are embarked, you are to make all possible dispatch in proceeding to Virginia, where you are to land them; Victualling the Major General, his Attendants and Servants as the Ship's Company while they continue on board.

You are to remain at Virginia till the arrival of the Hon. Augustus Keppel, commander-in-chief of His Majesty's ships and vessels employed and to be employed in North America; and then follow his directions for your farther proceedings.

Given under our hand the 19 November 1754.

Anson
Will Rowley
Chas. Townsend.

By Command of their Lordships,
J. Cleveland.[3]

It is not likely that Captain Barrington was elated. November nights were growing cold and raw. *The Star and Garter,* over on the point at Portsmouth within full view of his quarterdeck, provided a snug harbor with a good bottle and a glowing grate.

Braddock's baggage arrived at Portsmouth a week later and was put aboard the "Norwich." But the sailing was delayed. Barrington's instructions were changed. He was directed, in another message from the admiralty, to place himself under the command of Keppel immediately and await further orders from him.[4] Keppel had taken Braddock to Cork aboard his flagship, the "Centurion," another four-rater of 50 guns, to superintend and hasten the embarkation of the troops.[5]

The two regiments, far below normal strength, had been scattered from Limerick to Dublin when ordered to rendezvous at Cork. At first it had been proposed to embark only 340 men of each regiment with 700 stand of arms and recruit each to 700 in America. Later the British nucleus of each was increased to about 500 by drafts from other regiments—the Twentieth Foot at Exeter, the Eleventh at Salisbury, the Tenth and the Twenty-Eighth at Limerick, the Twenty-Sixth and the Royals at Galway. Sir Peter Halkett also picked up a few recruits in London.[6]

The British army had not changed much in Braddock's lifetime. Officers, as a group, were loose and profligate. The non-coms, as faithful as old family servants, looked down on the privates as scoundrels, and many were. Recruited from jails, slums, and gin shops, the majority of the privates in the regiments of the line were dirty, discontented, and debauched, insolent and insubordinate, drinking when off duty until blind drunk. The Forty-Fourth and the Forty-Eighth were two of the most worthless regiments in the army. And the drafts with which their depleted ranks were filled brought together all the least desirable soldiers of the six other regiments from which they were drawn. Such drafts always produced the dregs. Their colonels had no intention of losing their best men. And none was eager to go. They had heard that they might remain in Virginia for three years.[7]

The Twentieth, commanded by Lord Bury, had marched into Exeter to take up winter quarters at Rougemont Castle when called upon for a draft of 100. The draft marched off to Pill, the Bristol pilot station, where vessels lay to ferry them to Cork.[8] James Wolfe, who had just joined the Twentieth as its lieutenant-colonel, and who would make his name more illustrious than Braddock's in the coming war, was under no illusions about any soldiers in the British infantry.

"I have a very mean opinion of the infantry in courage," said Wolfe in a letter to his father at Bath, after Braddock's defeat, but citing early instances to back up his opinions. "I know their discipline to be bad and their valor precarious. They are easily put into disorder, hard to recover out of it. They frequently kill their officers through fear, and murder one another in their confusion." [9] And prophetically . . . "Our military education is by far the worst in Europe. . . . It will cost us very dear sometime hence. I hope the day is at a distance, but I am afraid it will come."

Braddock soon discovered that his journey to Cork had been unnecessary. There was no possibility of his speeding the embarkation. Sergeants, corporals, drummers, and private men drafted from the other regiments had been assembled for a fortnight. Twelve wagonloads of arms from Dublin Castle had reached the neighboring port of Kinsale but the chests were still on the docks. Some of the vessels under charter for the expedition, and due from Gravesend on November 1, had not yet reached Ireland. Bad weather was blamed for the delay.[10] Lieut.-Gen. Thomas Bligh was coming down from Dublin to superintend the embarkation; so Keppel put about for Spithead, arriving there December 20. He kept his broad pennant flying from the "Centurion" but transferred Braddock to the "Norwich." [11]

Three days before Christmas, 1754, the wind was right and the two ships sailed together for Virginia.[12] Aboard the *Norwich* with Braddock were his aide, Captain Orme; his secretary, William Shirley, Jr., son of the governor of Massachusetts; Braddock's body servant, Thomas Bishop, the old Coldstream guardsman who had attended him for years; and Francis Delboux, the General's cook.[13] Cold rain, fog, and a heavy swell awaited the two ships at the end of the English channel. Wise sea travelers always prepared themselves against a long voyage by laying in a supply of wine, cider, bottled beer, brandy, sugar, and lemons for punch.[14] But nothing could be done about the tempestuous North Atlantic weather which separated the two ships on the high seas.[15]

Most of the troops which were to follow them embarked in cold, clammy January rain that made the narrow streets of Cork and the green hills enfolding its harbor look more inviting than they had ever looked before.[16] The sulky redcoats hunched their shoulders against the chill. The most fortunate wore matchcoats and flannel waistcoats.[17] Barges lightered the soldiers to transports anchored in the River Lee. Alongside the transports the barges kept heaving and banging their fenders while the soldiers clambered up wet, slippery gangway ladders to decks wet and slippery under dripping rigging, then down other ladders into smokey between-deck stench where they stuffed their paillasses with rancid straw. The wardroom and cabins were reserved to officers.[18]

Underway in the same track of bad weather which the "Norwich" and "Centurion" had taken, the transports heeled heavily, ports on the lee under water. One man was lost from a yardarm.[19] Beer, biscuit, salt butter, salt beef, watered rum, and once a day "scaldings" of hot oatmeal in a wooden dish from the galley were the standard rations. Creaking gear and clanking pump chains kept the wretched soldiers awake all night. The weaker recovered from seasickness only to succumb to scurvy. They got no pity from the sailors who had a saying: "A messmate before a shipmate, a shipmate before a stranger, a stranger before a dog, a dog before a soldier." [20]

Both foremast and mainmast of the "Norwich" had been sprung by ocean gales when she sailed in through the Virginia Capes on the afternoon of Wednesday, February 19, 1755, to give Braddock his first glimpse of the New World.[21] The scene from the vessel's deck was that of a noble bay with a sandy beach, almost as flat as the mouth of the Schedlt, its rising landline flecked with patches of melting snow. But the air was sharp. In contrast to the green shadows of Gibraltar, the surface of this bay had a hard, cold glint.

The "Norwich" anchored a mile off shore. Barks, sloops, and smaller craft tumbled in the shelter of the capes, but there was no sign of the "Centurion's" lofty, reeling head—as those aboard the "Norwich" remembered seeing her last. In neither the broad vistas of the James River, stretched before them, nor the long wide face of ocean gray behind, was there another vessel large enough to have been a transport.[22]

It was too late to go ashore that day, but Braddock was rowed in next morning and landed at Hampton, a neat town of red brick, white wood, and plaster hip-roofed houses. Breakfast was served at the *Kings Arms,* which also set out a noble dinner of ham and turkey, a breast of veal with fat Chesapeake Bay oysters, Madeira wine, punch, and cider. Two months' confinement aboard ship gave the meal an extraordinary relish.[23]

Two letters awaited Braddock at Hampton from St. Clair, who had reached Virginia on January 7 with Lieut.-Col. Robert Ellison and James Mercer, two half-pay officers assigned to service with the two provincial regiments to be raised in America. St. Clair reported that he had made one journey to Wills Creek, returned to Williamsburg, and had set out on another to inspect troops and look for supplies.[24]

The deputy quartermaster general informed Braddock that he had selected for the army's proposed general hospital two small warehouses in Hampton, the only vacant buildings in the town, and had arranged lodgings for hospital officers and any overflow of patients up to a total of 150. Neither carpenters nor lumber had been available for a temporary emergency building of boards. And there were no spare beds in the town; so St. Clair had ordered a hundred wooden cradles to be built. He had named John Hunter of Hampton, resident agent of the expedition.[25]

On Saturday, February 22, Keppel's flagship arrived in the bay with a sprung foremast.[26] Next day the General, Commodore Keppel, Orme, and Shirley rode up to Williamsburg, the colonial capital.[27] By English standards the countryside was a desolate, barren overgrowth of pine woods. Night was coming on by the time they entered Williamsburg's broad, sandy Duke of Gloucester Street. Except for the wide Palace Green leading to the Governor's house, a steep-roofed mansion of red brick with a cupola, they might have been in almost any English country town.[28]

Negro servants came running from the gates of the Governor's Palace for their horses. Lieutenant Governor Dinwiddie himself came down the six front steps of the house to meet them. His first question must have been the inevitable: "What kind of a crossing did you have?"

"My own voyage was troublesome," said Braddock.[29] "A passage of seven weeks in which I had very bad weather . . . very fatiguing."

Under the drawing room candelabra the Lieutenant-Governor and the Major General could look each other over. Dinwiddie saw a shorter, stouter man than he had expected, but a smartly turned out British officer in red coat, crimson sash, and gold lace, exuding a faint odor of snuff. The General had a good face, regular features, and the unmistakable click and carriage of a guardsman. Braddock saw a blue-gray-eyed Scotsman of his own age, a little puffy from good living, possibly a little harassed, and maybe a little self-conscious of his embroidered buttonholes.[30]

Dinwiddie was a Glasgow merchant's son who had started out in the government service as a customs office clerk in Bermuda.[31] Standing before the General and the Honorable Keppel (a younger man with a big nose and receding chin,)[32] Dinwiddie may have felt himself in the presence of superior people. But Albemarle's lieutenant governor and his former lieutenant colonel were not too far apart. Dinwiddie represented the bureaucrat's inflexible devotion to royal authority; Braddock, the soldier's blind obedience to the King.

Dinwiddie introduced his wife and daughters, Elizabeth and Rebecca, who probably welcomed the handsome Orme and the younger Shirley as they had earlier welcomed St. Clair.[33] The Deputy Quartermaster General was not in town. He had set out for Winchester to inspect some recruits. An express was dispatched to overtake him and fetch him back to receive his chief.[34]

"A very good ingineer (sic)," said Dinwiddie of St. Clair. "A very diligent, good officer. . . . Sensible. . . . An amiable man, full of spirits, with discretion and good judgement."[35]

The deputy quartermaster claimed to have fought in Italy with Count Browne,[36] a celebrated general in the army of the Empress-Queen Maria Theresa, and had given the Governor's family the impression that he had been in most of the courts of Europe.

"And his observations on them are very judicious," said Dinwiddie.[37]

With horses and guides provided by the Governor, St. Clair's two travelling companions from London, Ellison and Mercer, had gone on to New England to join their regiments.[38] What about the two regiments of regulars coming from Ireland?

Braddock said they should arrive within a fortnight.[39]

Dinwiddie said he hoped they would get over the Alleghenies and be "doing business" by the beginning of April, that they would not tarry on their march.

"If they do," he said, "I fear that by that time the French will be greatly reinforced."[40]

He had received a letter for Braddock from Governor Sharpe of Maryland, acting commander of the English forces. Enclosed in the letter was a detailed sketch of Fort Duquesne and a note smuggled out of the fort by Capt. Robert Stobo, one of two hostages left with the French by Washington at Fort Necessity. Sharpe's letter also contained the journal of an English adventurer, one Thomas Forbes, who told a story of having deserted the French garrison at Duquesne the previous October. Both Forbes and Stobo reported the fort undermanned by a force of not more than 400.[41]

Braddock must have asked about the number of Indians with the French. How were the Indians disposed toward the English? How many might he expect to join his expedition?

Dinwiddie said he had a man out, a fellow named Gist, the Ohio Company's chief explorer, who knew all about the Indians and who probably would bring in about 120 Catawbas, the best fighters of all the tribes. Perhaps some Cherokees, too. Many of the Iroquois, the Indians of the Six Nations, had joined up with the French. But the Indians wanted to be on the winning side.[42]

"The dress of our regulars and the number of our forces will engage many of the Indians to join us, and many of the French to desert," said Dinwiddie. "If they should see our regulars appear with some cohorns. . . . I dare say many of the Indians will leave them." [43]

He expected the Catawbas to meet at Winchester at the end of March to confirm a peace between northern and southern tribes.

"And I hope for some warriors from them and the Cherokees to join our forces," he said.[44]

Braddock reminded Dinwiddie that Sir Thomas Robinson had written a circular letter to all the governors of the colonies, informing them that the King expected them to supply funds, recruits, and transporation for the expedition.[45]

Yes, the Governor had the letter and he had talked to Governor Dobbs on Dobbs' arrival from England in October. The Virginia assembly had granted £20,000, and since late in the fall he had been doing his utmost to accumulate enough beef, pork, dried codfish, salt, and flour to sustain a force of 3,000 men for eight months. He had signed contracts for 1,100 head of cattle to be delivered at Wills Creek between June and August. He had also advertised in the Virginia *Gazette* for recruits for the two regiments of regulars, offering one guinea bounty for enlistment.[46]

"I have listed near a thousand men," said Dinwiddie, reeling off his accomplishments. "If more are needed, I think they may soon be raised. I have ordered sixteen wagons to be built, but we shall want a hundred." [47]

Everything the army needed as it advanced beyond Wills Creek would have to be hauled over the mountains.

"Those better acquainted with these things than I am seem to make light of it," said the Governor.[48]

But the transportation of supplies had been one of Washington's gravest problems.[49] In tidewater states like Maryland and Virginia, where networks of rivers and creeks provided cheap and convenient transportation, there was a shortage of horses and wagons.[50] The price of a four-horse wagon at Wills Creek was £70. The freight rate was 12 shillings per hundred weight.[51]

Because tobacco, the principal farm product of Virginia, was the only crop raised in any quantity over and above domestic needs, Dinwiddie had been obliged to seek many of his supplies outside Virginia and there had been difficulties with some of the other colonies. Hearing that meat and flour which he might have purchased for the expedition were being sent by New York and Pennsylvania merchants to the French at Louisbourg, in exchange for rum, sugar, and molasses, Dinwiddie had issued a proclamation forbidding Virginians to trade with the enemy.[52]

Braddock had heard about that trade in London. In so far as it involved shipping it was a naval matter which had already been called to the attention of Commodore Keppel who planned to take any measure necessary. Braddock also had heard that the government of Pennsylvania, under the control of pacifist Quakers, had asked to be excused from furnishing any troops "as they are not a fighting people." [53]

Dinwiddie wagged his wig. He seems to have kept to himself on this occasion any feeling or opinion he may have had about the conflicting claims of Virginia and Pennsylvania for the Ohio country and their rivalry for its Indian trade.

"I want words," he said, "to express the obdurate and inconsistent behavior of our neighboring colonies, not as yet awakened from their lethargy, North Carolina, only excepted, who have voted £5,000 for the expedition. Maryland assembly is now sitting. Pennsylvania assembly adjourned without voting one farthing. . . . I am afraid it is downright obstinacy." [54]

Although the Governor would have been quite willing to have both the General and the Commodore as his guests, Braddock went to the *Raleigh Tavern,* down around the corner from the Palace Green on the Duke of Gloucester Street.[55] A large, rambling wooden building painted white, with a dormer-windowed second story and a leaden bust of Sir Walter Raleigh in a niche above its front door, the *Raleigh* had the reputation of being one of the best taverns in North America.[56] Its proprietor, Alexander Finnie, who planned to follow Braddock as a sutler, laid himself out to please his distinguished guest.[57]

"He is (I think) a very fine officer and a sensible, considerate gentleman," was the Governor's opinion of the General after their meeting.[58]

St. Clair, quite the young dashing officer in Hussar uniform, rode back into Williamsburg next day [59] while Braddock was dictating two short letters to Shirley, his secretary. One of the letters, which would let George Anne know of his safe arrival, was addressed to Fox, the Secretary at War. It began:

Sir,
After a passage of seven weeks, in which I had very bad weather, I arrived here where I found everything in great confusion, as I had expected. A great deal of money had already been spent here, though very little done. . . . Pennsylvania will do nothing, and furnisheth the French with everything they have occasion for . . .[60]

The other letter was to Col. Napier, the Duke's adjutant:

Sir,
After having passed through all the dangers of the sea, from which I escaped, I arrived here the 20th of this month. The Governor assures me that the people are likely to be more tractable and that they see the necessity of providing for me all the succor which they must be obliged to furnish in an enterprise that particularly regards themselves.
So little order has reigned among them hitherto that much has been spent in doing very little. Sir John St. Clair had arrived at this moment. This man is indefatigable. . . .[61]

St. Clair was quick tempered, too, inclined to find fault with those more patient than he was.[62] But in his first verbal report to his commander, he had some legitimate complaints. To begin with, there was a dearth of adequate maps. The country through which Braddock's expedition was to march had never been surveyed topographically,[63] and the only maps of the province of Pennsylvania which St. Clair had been able to obtain were extremely sketchy, not to say inaccurate, beyond the Susquehanna river. On January 14, one week after his arrival in Virginia, St. Clair had written to Governor Morris of Pennsylvania and asked him to send any maps or drawings he might have of that province. When a month had passed without any reply to his letter, St. Clair had written a second time, repeating his request. He was still waiting for an answer.[64]

What was called "the fort" at Wills Creek, which was to serve as an advance base of operations for the expedition, was a stockade enclosing a small piece of ground, St. Clair said. It was not even well located. He had seen it. He had gone to Wills Creek to inspect the post. He had met Governor Sharpe of Maryland at the so-called fort. Sharpe, who had made two trips to Wills Creek within the past two months, knew what was wrong with the place as a fort and had ordered another larger work constructed on higher ground. St. Clair had left directions for the palisading of a house near the fort for use as a powder magazine. He had considered building cabins for Braddock's troops but now realized that the season would be far enough advanced for the army to live in tents by the time it reached Wills Creek.[65] The problem of forage for the army horses still worried him.

"I am afraid we will not be able to cross the mountains till the grass begins to shoot," said the Quartermaster.[66]

The only road to Wills Creek was frightful, particularly the 85-mile stretch from Winchester.

"The worst road I ever traveied," said St. Clair.[67]

Thinking it might be possible to send artillery and supplies up the Potomac to Wills Creek by boat from Alexandria, he and Sharpe had come down the river by canoe, a five-day journey. Falls and rapids, St. Clair had seen, made the Potomac an impractical route even for canoes and batteaux between the mouth of the Shenandoah and Rock Creek.[68] The troops would have to march to Wills Creek. Forage and other supplies would have to be hauled most of the way by horse and wagon.

St. Clair had asked the Virginia governor to contract for horses and Dinwiddie said he had rounded up 120 and hoped to have 250 soon.[69] There was no immediate hurry about this, said St. Clair. "If we had more, how are they to be fed?"[70]

On his way down the Potomac[71] from Wills Creek, St. Clair had tried to make contracts for forage. The river valley was thickly wooded and thinly settled, but he had been told that many of the settlers at the foot of the mountains, back from the river, were Dutch farmers who would provide wagons to carry supplies to Wills Creek and he believed he could gather 200 wagons and 1,500 horses there by May 1.[72]

The country beyond Wills Creek was much the same as the Apennines, where he had served with Count Brown during the War of the Austrian Succession, said St. Clair.[73] He had gone two miles the other side of what he called the "South Branch" to look at the mountains.[74]

"The mouth of the Savage river is the place where we ought to cross," he told Braddock.[75]

Braddock certainly showed his quartermaster Stobo's sketch of Fort Dusquesne, a formidable looking bastioned fort surrounded by a 15-foot ditch and set in the forks of the Ohio in such a manner as to be open to land attack on only two sides.

"We shall be obliged to break ground at the fort," said St. Clair.[76]

That was a professional soldier's way of saying that trenches would have to be opened and siege operations conducted.

As to the provincial recruits needed to bring the two regiments of British regulars up to a strength of 700 men each—St. Clair had reviewed some of the men enlisted by Dinwiddie. Many, by the Governor's own admission, were idle, drunken fellows. At least 300 were not even of the proper size for a regiment of regulars. Some of the mutinous, unruly garrison of the so-called fort at Wills Creek, St. Clair told Braddock, were 60 to 70 years of age and so crippled that they had "neither the legs to get up on the heights nor to run through the valleys" if attacked. One good company of 80 men had been raised in Maryland, but the quartermaster had dismissed more than 40 of a New York company as invalids unfit the military service.[77]

"The latter seem to be drafted from Chelsea," said St. Clair.[78] (Chelsea was the royal hospital for old and disabled soldiers in London.)

St. Clair suggested that the provincial recruits least suitable for the two regiments of regulars be organized into companies of carpenters and rangers. Braddock approved that, fixing the organization at two companies of carpenters and four of rangers and adding a company of light horse.[79]

In anticipation of the arrival of the transports bringing his two regiments of regulars, Braddock issued his first order in Virginia:

No. 1

His Excellency General Braddock orders that the commanding officer of each ship upon their arrival at Hampton roads shall immediately send a return inclosed to Mr. Hunter, at Hampton, specifying
the number of sick, the time of their illness, and the nature of them.
And that every commanding officer shall with the utmost dispatch apply to Mr. Hunter for boats to carry the sick on shore which shall be
executed with all imaginable care and expedition, and that a subaltern
officer of each ship shall see their men safely conveyed to the place appointed for their reception, which Mr. Hunter will show them; and
that the surgeons or mates of the two regiments and the Train shall
attend the sick of our corps. Every commanding officer to take particular care that as soon as their sick are sent ashore, all the hatchways be
uncovered, scuttles opened and the platform thoroughly washed and
cleaned, no officer or soldier, except the sick, to lie ashore upon any
account. The hospital to continue on board until the General's further
orders.[80]

Many of Braddock's first days in Williamsburg were taken up
with correspondence. In accord with his instructions he had Shirley
write to all the colonial governors, advising them of his arrival in
America, reminding them of the earlier letters they had received
from Sir Thomas directing them to give his expedition any necessary assistance, including money, and asking them to meet him at
Annapolis at the beginning of April for a conference on the general plan of campaign against the French.[81]

Between the optimistic Dinwiddie and the gloomy St. Clair,
Braddock had little on which to base any concrete plan. No supplies had been warehoused. No common stock of money had been
raised. No transport had been organized. And as far as he could
see the prospects of obtaining much immediate help from the
other colonies were poor. New England would have her hands full
with Shirley and Pepperell. Neither Maryland nor the Carolinas
were wealthy. Rich German-Quaker Pennsylvania's refusal to become aroused against the French was underscored by a letter St.
Clair received from Governor Morris on February 28, six weeks
to the day after St. Clair's first request for Pennsylvania maps.
Morris wrote:

Such is the infatuation and obstinacy of the people I have to deal
with, or at least their representatives, that though their country is invaded, yet I could not persuade them to act with vigour at this junc-
ture, or even grant the supply expected by the Crown and recommended by the Secretary of State.[82]

"The behavior of the Quakers and the Germans is intolerable,"
said Dinwiddie.[83] "They have a great number of Germans among
whom there are many Roman Catholics, as also in Maryland." [84]

Braddock said he would answer Morris' letter. At his blunt dictation Shirley wrote:

> I cannot help expressing the greatest surprise to find such pusillani-
> mous and improper behavior in your assembly, and to hear of faction
> and opposition when liberty and property are invaded, and an abso-
> lute refusal to supply either men, money, or provision.[85]

Braddock warned Morris that when he billeted his troops for
the winter he might "regulate their quarters" in such a way as to
"repair by unpleasant methods" the damage done his expedition
by the action of the Pennsylvania assembly. In a softer tone he said:
"I hope you will not impute any part of this letter as being addressed or directed to you. I am perfectly satisfied of your good
intention. . . ."

This sharply worded message, sealed with red wax and inscribed
by Braddock

> *On His Majesty's Service—*
> *To the Honorable Robert Hunter Morris,*
> *Esquire, Lieutnt Governor of His Majesty's*
> *Province of Pennsylvania at*
> *Philadelphia*

moved at maximum speed. It went galloping out of Williamsburg
in the saddle bag of an express carrying an order from the General
to Governor Shirley, at Boston, to pick up Lieutenant Governor
DeLancey of New York and meet Braddock at Annapolis.[86]

Morris, meanwhile, had complied with St. Clair's request for
maps. Enclosed in another letter en route to Williamsburg was
"A Map of Pennsylvania, New Jersey, New York and three Delaware counties" made by Lewis Evans in 1749 and in process of
being revised for publication that summer as "A General Map of
the Middle British Colonies." The original map did not extend
much farther west than the Conococheague. It showed a wagon road
extending west from Philadelphia to the Potomac, but only a path
over the mountains beyond Shippensburg to a point called "Black
Log." [87] The revision would show a road from Shippensburg to
Ray's Town, and trace an Indian trail used by traders from the fort

at Wills Creek to Fort Duquesne, a distance of 106 miles.[88] This was the route which Braddock's army would follow, over the mountains and across the Castleman and Youghiogheny rivers to the forks of the Ohio.

St. Clair had sent a commissary to Pennsylvania to contract for 100 wagon loads of flour to be delivered at the Conochocheague by March 20. If wanted by the army to carry these stores farther, the wagons were to be taken into the service. St. Clair pointed out that his maps showed no direct road by which either troops or supplies from the northern provinces might reach Braddock's army on its march. Considerations of both security and supply called for better communications, he argued. He thought the road west from Philadelphia should be extended through Ray's Town as far as the headwaters of the Youghiogheny. Braddock agreed.[89]

Braddock began to think about the artillery in his train, en route to Virginia aboard the transports. He was to have four 12-pounders, six 6-pounders, four 8-inch howitzers, and fifteen cohorn mortars. If, as St. Clair anticipated, it should be necessary to lay siege to the French fort, he might need more heavy guns. Braddock discussed this with Keppel. The Commodore said he would give him four more 12-pounders and ordered Captain Barringer to remove four from the upper tier of the "Norwich" and turn them over to Mr. Hunter at Hampton, with 1,000 shot and 50 barrels of powder.[90]

But Keppel had his doubts about Braddock being able to get guns that heavy over the mountains. He recommended that the General buy up rope for luff tackles and, while he was about it, take along thirty stout, able-bodied seamen familiar with block-and-tackle.[91] Braddock knew, from what he had seen in Virginia, that his army would have to cross many streams without bridges. Floats would be needed to ferry the troops and the train over rivers too deep to be forded.[92] He gladly accepted Keppel's offer of a detachment of sailors. They were organized immediately under Lieut. Charles Spendlowe of the "Norwich" and ordered to hold themselves in readiness to join the troops when the transports arrived.[93]

A personal letter addressed to the General from George Washington of Mount Vernon, congratulating him upon his arrival in the colonies,[94] led Braddock to make inquiries: What had happened to Washington? Dinwiddie knew. The young man had resigned his commission when the Virginia regiment he had commanded at Fort Necessity was broken up into separate companies. A reorganization had been ordered because captains of independent companies holding commissions from the King had refused to take orders from a colonel of militia commissioned by a colonial government. Young Washington's pride had been hurt. He had resigned, although he had told friends his inclinations were "strongly bent to arms." [95]

Dinwiddie seemed to regret having entrusted the command of his Virginia troops to so inexperienced a militia officer. He had even suggested to Sir Thomas Robinson that he, Dinwiddie, be given command of all forces raised in the colony, but nothing had come of this.[96] At the end of the Fort Necessity campaign, what was left of the Virginia regiment had marched to Alexandria, badly in need of clothing and supplies. So many had deserted, spreading reports that the regiment had disbanded, that Washington had published a notice in the Maryland *Gazette* declaring all such rumours false and offering a reward of one pistole for any deserter taken up within two miles of quarters, two pistoles for any picked up at a greater distance.[97] Washington himself had retired to Mount Vernon, the Potomac river estate he had inherited on the death of his brother, Major Lawrence Washington, seven miles below Alexandria.[98]

At Braddock's direction, his aide, Captain Orme, wrote to Washington:

Sir,
   The General having been informed that you expressed some desire to make the campaign, but that you declined it upon the disagreeableness that you thought might arise from the regulation of command, has ordered me to acquaint you that he will be very glad of your company in his family by which all inconveniences of that sort will be obviated.
   I shall think myself very happy to form an acquaintance with a person so universally esteemed and shall use every opportunity of assuring you how much I am

                                        Sir
                                        Your Most Obedient Servant
                                        Robert Orme aid de camp [99]

St. Clair also included Washington in a group of eminent Virginians invited to dine with Braddock at the *Raleigh* and discuss the prospects of obtaining horses and supplies in Winchester for the army.[100] At this dinner Braddock saw Washington for the first

time, a tall, thin, flat-chested Virginian with a grace, a judicious
manner, and a humorless face.[101] He was the only man Braddock
had met who had a personal knowledge of the wilderness through
which the expedition would pass. He may have been the first to
correct Braddock's misconception of the country which lay before
him. From the maps he had seen, Braddock had been led to believe that he had only about 15 miles of rough country to cross. He
was dumfounded when told that more than fifty miles of mountain
lay between Wills Creek and Fort Duquesne.[102]

He offered Washington a captain's commission by brevet, the
highest he had authority to issue. Washington was not too clear in
his own mind as to what Braddock would expect of him or what
his relations might be with other members of the General's staff.
Furthermore, he had just taken over Mount Vernon, and as a cautious, thrifty, ambitious, young planter, he hesitated to become so
deeply involved in a military campaign that he would have no time
for personal business affairs. Braddock told him his time would
be his own, to think the offer over.[103]

Two transports, each carrying 100 British regulars, anchored in
the Chesapeake on Sunday, March 2, 1755. Braddock rode down
to Hampton to get a report from his troop commanders. Not above
two or three of those aboard ship were sick, he was told, and there
had been no deaths. Five more transports arrived within the next
five days with H.M.S. "Seahorse." Sailors as well as soldiers were
sick on these vessels, scarcely a man on the "Seahorse" being fit for
duty.[104] But that was not the sort of sickness that counted with
Braddock who had suffered a slight spell of illness himself. By
March 13, when the three ordinance ships and all but one of the
remaining transports had arrived in convoy with seven war vessels,[105] he returned to Williamsburg and dictated a long letter to
Robinson in which he said:

> All the transports are arrived except the *Severn,* which has one com-
> pany of Sir Peter Halkett's regiment aboard. There is not, as yet, one
> sick man amongst all the forces.[106]

The tantalizing sight of land was more than some of Keppel's
sailors could bear. They jumped ship. Governor Dinwiddie ran an
advertisement in the Virginia *Gazette,* warning people against entertaining or encouraging deserters, and offering 40 shillings reward
for their return.[107]

Three were caught, and Keppel's squadron, still anchored in Hampton roads, gave the waterfront an object lesson in British naval discipline. One deserter from the "Norwich," court-martialed and sentenced to 24 lashes on his bare back with a cat-of-nine-tails alongside five of His Majesty's war ships, was whipped from ship to ship. That is, he was placed in a small boat, rowed from alongside one vessel to another and lashed within full view of all hands who had been called on deck to see his punishment. Two deserters from the "Centurion" were given heavier penalties of 240 and 350 lashes. The sailor sentenced to 350 got 48 alongside each of the five ships on a Monday morning and was due the remainer on the following Friday "or when he shall be in condition to receive them." [108]

Braddock's original plan—at the suggestion of St. Clair and, probably, Governor Sharpe—had been to canton his troops for a short time in southern Maryland and Virginia towns to refresh them after a long, hard transatlantic voyage.[109] But the lack of wagons and the haphazard manner in which the transports had been loaded changed these plans. He ordered the whole convoy up the Potomac to Alexandria, as soon as the winds were favorable. The regulars would disembark there, unload the ordnance ships, and encamp.[110]

After January's snow the weather had turned remarkably warm, more like June.[111] Mr. Hunter, the expedition's agent at Hampton, had put fresh meat aboard the ships when they anchored in the Roads.[112] Eight hundred barrels of pork, some bacon and butter delivered on contracts made by Dinwiddie, were shipped to Alexandria.[113] Rare foresight on the part of the Admiralty had stowed another 1,000 barrels of beef and ten tons of butter on His Majesty's ships as emergency rations for the troops.[114] These with other supplies on which Dinwiddie expected future deliveries should sustain an army of four thousand for six months, according to the calculations of Braddock's staff. But the stubborn province of Pennsylvania, the key stone of Braddock's logistics, showed no inclination to supply anything.[115]

In a letter replying to Braddock's angry outburst of February 28, Governor Morris wrote:

> I am, sir, almost ashamed to tell you that we have in this province upwards of 300,000 inhabitants; that we are blessed with a rich soil and temperate climate, and besides our own consumption raise provisions enough to supply an army of 100,000 men, which is yearly ex-

ported from this city, and with other commodities employes upwards of 500 vessels, mostly owned by the merchants of our town. From a province so circumstanced what might not reasonably have been expected, especially as we are burthened with no taxes and are not only out of debt but have a revenue of £7000 a year and £15000 pounds in bank, all at the disposal of the House of Assembly. And yet when their *ALL* is invaded they refuse to contribute to the necessary defense of their country, either by establishing a militia or furnishing men, money or provisions.[116]

Braddock learned of the arrival of the last of the transports, the "Severn," on March 18.[117] That day he wrote a long report to Robinson. Knowing how tightly the King pinched pennies, the General was worried by the colonies' disregard for the Secretary of State's suggestion that they establish a common fund to meet military expenses.

"I am almost in despair of complying with it, from the jealousy of the people and the disunion of the several colonies, as well among themselves as one with another," he told Sir Thomas.[118] He wrote:

Governor Dinwiddie has obtained £20,000 currency and is in hopes of prevailing upon his assembly to raise a further supply which he has for that purpose summoned to meet on the first of May next. The province of North Carolina has granted £8000, and Maryland six in the currency of their respective governments. Pennsylvania, though by far the richest and most prosperous colony of any upon the continent, as well as most nearly interested in the event of the expedition, as yet, contributed nothing. . . .

As soon as I can assemble the troops, provide forage, provisions and other necessaries for their march, I shall proceed to attempt the reduction of the French forts on the Ohio; it is doubtful whether there will be grass on the other side of the Allegheny mountains before the latter part of April which is indeed as soon as it will probably be in my power to be there.

But he had no doubt as to the success of his expedition. He asked Sir Thomas to see that instructions were issued to Keppel for the disposal of French prisoners turned over to the Commodore by the army. To Newcastle and Halifax he dispatched shorter letters, making this request of Newcastle:

As small coined silver will be greatly wanted for the payment of troops, and as no considerable quantity of it can be got in this province, I must beg of Your Grace to direct the contractors, Mr. Hanbury and Mr. Tomlinson, to send over as soon as possible, if they have not already done it, four or five thousand piastrines and half piastrines which is the more necessary as all the money already brought over by the regimental paymasters is in Spanish gold and dollars.[119]

From Williamsburg, Braddock also disposed of a bombastic half-pay captain-lieutenant, William Dalrymple, who had turned up in Hampton to pester both him and Dinwiddie. The General sent him to command Fort Johnson in North Carolina.[120] In a letter to Governor Dobbs, Braddock said frankly that he would not trust Dalrymple with a hogsty and that the best thing Dobbs could do with him would be to hang him on the first convenient tree—that he was giving Dalrymple the command, an unimportant post, "as a feather to get rid of him." [121]

Dinwiddie explained, in an apologetic note to Dobbs, that Dalrymple would have been appointed to England "but a delicacy in regard to General Braddock prevailed. He is recommended by Lord Halifax, Anson and several others to me and the General." [122] Dinwiddie was not happy these days. The transports had brought news of the death of the Earl of Albemarle at Paris on December 21. Albermarle was still titular governor of Virginia. Lieutenant Governor Dinwiddie was anxious to keep his post.[123]

Even more provoking than Dalrymple, to Braddock, was the disappearance from the *Raleigh Tavern* stable of a bay horse the General had bought. Finnie, the embarrassed landlord, advertised in the *Gazette* of March 21:

> Strayed or stolen from my stable, a bay horse, belonging to his Excellency General Braddock. Was bought in Princess Anne county and is supposed to have gone toward Hampton. Whoever brings him to me shall have a pistole reward.[124]

Within the week Braddock, Keppel, and Dinwiddie set out for Alexandria, a new Potomac river port where the convoy was unloading.[125] The ocean-weary soldiers, who had seen Hampton only from a distance, must have gazed in dismay at the little settlement where their transports dropped anchor. There was not even a church steeple to indicate that the place was a town. Most of the houses were unpretentious wooden structures, strung along a lane leading back from the river bank where a flatboat served as a ferry to the opposite Maryland shore. Low tide exposed a belt of mud flats along the Virginia side of the river.[126]

The largest building in sight was a three-story brick house, the home of Col. William Fairfax, a cousin of Thomas, Sixth Lord

Fairfax and proprietor of the Northern Neck of Virginia, which was all the land lying between the Potomac and the Rappahannock rivers. For years the Colonel had been resident manager of his cousin's vast holdings, a royal grant of Charles II, originally comprising more than five million acres or nearly one quarter of the province east of the mountains.[127]

The next biggest building in town, a solidly constructed two-story stone house with protruding dormers in its high steep roof, was the home of Maj. John Carlyle, a Scotch merchant who did considerable business in connection with three tobacco warehouses at the lower end of the town.[128] The Major was married to a daughter of Col. Fairfax, a magic name in colonial gentry, and had enjoyed the profits of an army contractor while serving as commissary of supply for Washington's unfortunate expedition of a year ago. Both the Colonel's son, George, and his son-in-law, the Major, were active members of the Ohio Company. All three were incorporators of the new town of Alexandria, with building lots for sale on its grid-ironed plot.[129]

The troops, put ashore by the transport crews, marched up the lane from the river landing, drums thumping, fifes a-squeal. Frightened hogs and geese, which had the run of the place, scattered. Townsfolk, children, a few farmers, and Negro servants watched their first British regulars swing past. Never before had they beheld anything as gorgeous as those yellow-faced red uniforms with their big shining buckles and white lace—slightly soiled. Never before had they heard so many drums—twenty to each regiment. The regimental colors of fringed yellow silk, emblazoned with rose-and-thistle wreathed Roman numerals, were another curiosity.[130]

The soldiers, wrinkled by cramped quarters aboard ship, their pigtails smeared with a regulation mixture of flour and tallow, regarded the Alexandrians with much less satisfaction. The blacks were the first Negro slaves some of the soldiers had ever seen. But the long confinement of a transatlantic voyage had aroused more interest in the town. The redcoats marched past a court house, a jail, a whipping post, and a pillory—grouped around the market square. They looked for alehouses—and saw *one* small tavern! No cook shops. No pastry shops. No coffee houses. No signboards. Along the lane leading to the site of their encampment, the edge of a marsh to the northwest of the town, they passed not more than half a dozen coaches and those with unmatched horses and as plain and dusty as any country carriages they had ever seen in Ireland.[131]

Royal artillerymen and two infantry details were put to unloading the thirteen transports and the three ordinance ships of the convoy.[132] This was more of a task than they had expected. The weather had turned unusually warm. The ships, which also carried arms and clothing for the Shirley and Pepperell regiments, had been loaded in such haste that the baggage and equipment of Braddock's two regiments were hopelessly mixed with those of the other two. It would be necessary, Keppel said, to make a complete clearance of all the ships before any one regiment could be fully equipped.[133] The work began at 6 o'clock every morning and continued all day for a week.[134] The mate of one of the ordinance ships fell overboard and was badly hurt. He was bled, but he died.[135]

Major Carlyle put his own house, which stood beside the market square, at the General's disposal, and Braddock established his headquarters there, mounting a general's guard of one lieutenant and thirty privates at the gate.[136] The house stood on a stone platform with a terrace overlooking the river. It was a new house. Carved in the keystone of an arch above the fanlight of its river front entrance was the date, *1752*. The General was shown to a bedroom on the second floor, a corner room with a small fireplace, a built-in closet for his gear, and two deep windows overlooking the river.[137]

Here, on Thursday, March 27, Braddock issued his first orders to the troops in camp. Captain Roger Morris of Dunbar's regiment was named a second aid-de-camp to His Excellency. Sir Peter Halkett's eldest son, Francis, a captain of the Forty-Fourth, was appointed brigade major. As published to the troops the General's orders said he expected the regulars, well acquainted with military discipline after having served under the Duke of Cumberland, to set "the most soldier-like example" for American recruits. Any soldier who deserted, even though he returned, would be hanged without mercy. Any soldier found drunk, negligent, or disobedient would be put on short rations. "To promote diligence and activity," extra salt and bread or flour would be issued.[138]

The next day was Good Friday. The General named Lieut.-Col. Thomas Gage of Halkett's Forty-fourth, president of a court martial to try James Anderson, a private of Dunbar's regiment, probably on a charge of desertion. The court sentenced the soldier to a thousand lashes.[139] On Easter Sunday each regiment held divine services at the head of its colors.[140] On Monday the two regiments were mustered, the officers in boots and the men in brown gaiters, and inspected right down to the commissions of the newly com-missioned officers who had been forewarned to have their papers in their pockets.[141]

More than a thousand British soldiers meant trouble in any town the size of Alexandria. Aboard ship they had complained about their rations. Now they complained that Alexandria's water was unwholesome.[142] And the shopkeepers' stocks were neither large nor varied. Throughout Virginia it was difficult sometimes to buy such simple things as stockings and candles.[143] In Alexandria it was almost impossible for a thousand British soldiers to buy any-thing except cider and a peach brandy called whiskey.[144] "For their encouragement, so they may do their duty like good soldiers," Braddock posted an Easter Sunday order that every man enlisted or drafted into the two regiments from Ireland should be credited with 20 shillings pay. The response to this was a rip roaring drunk. In an effort to sober up the worst men of his regiment after nearly a week of carousal, Sir Peter Halkett ordered seven days' provisions withheld from any sergeant, drummer, or private appearing in camp under the influence.[145]

A few of the soldiers had brought along their wives.[146] Other female camp followers, a larger number than allowed by the gov-ernment, had been brought over as washerwomen and hospital at-tendants. In the absence of other women some of these became so popular and prosperous that they entered into an agreement among themselves not to serve as washerwomen or hospital attend-ants for the stipulated wage of sixpence a day and their keep. The General ordered that all who refused to work for the sixpence wage should be turned out of camp and others hired in their place.[147]

Other women arrived later from England, including a Mrs. Browne, a merry London widow travelling with her brother, a commissary attached to the hospital. Only after seeking lodgings at every house in town did Mrs. Browne find a tiny room, barely big enough for her bed and without so much other furniture as a chair. In the evening the downstairs parlor of the house was cleared for the soldiers who drank cider and danced jigs. There wasn't a spare room in the town.[148]

The General's headquarters was the central attraction. Its guard, usually provided by a different regiment on alternate days, was a model, with its booted lieutenant and its thirty redcoats in brown gaiters. Under the personal attention of Bishop, his body servant, Braddock himself cut a military figure in his ruffled cravat, a rosette fastening the upturned brim of his hat. The drummers turned out to salute him with the customary two ruffles, the guards resting on their arms. The drummers also were under orders to beat two ruffles for the Governor.[149]

Braddock discredited himself with the Lees of Stratford, one of the first families of Virginia, by rejecting the tendered services of twenty-three-year-old Richard Henry Lee, one of six sons of the late Thomas Lee, an acting governor of Virginia and a founder of the Ohio Company. Young Richard Henry had marched up to Alexandria with some of Westmoreland county's militia, a would-be volunteer under Braddock's command. Evidently Richard Henry was not too soldierly in appearance, because Braddock took one look at him and told him to go home. The name "Lee" conveyed nothing to Braddock. He had an insignificant lieutenant by that name—Charles Lee—in the Forty-Fourth.

But Mr. Richard Henry Lee was not accustomed to brusque dismissal. He hung around headquarters and walked down to the river with the General, Commodore Keppel, and a group of officers. A boat from a British man-of-war, which had sailed up the Potomac with the transports and anchored off shore, was waiting to take the party out to the vessel. Everybody except Mr. Lee stepped aboard the boat, and though he saw the young Virginian standing there, Braddock ordered the oarsmen to push off. Commodore Keppel sensed something was wrong, told the boatmen to wait, and invited Mr. Lee to accompany them. Mr. Lee accepted. Braddock gave him no second thought but the Lees of Virginia never forgave Braddock.[150]

Apocryphal stories relate how the General and officers of his staff went hunting with Washington, presumably at Mount Vernon, attended by slaves and a pack of hounds, the General floundering through the Virginia woods in his great boots, puffing and blowing and crying out:

"Great God, sir! What would Sir Robert have said in Norfolk, to see a man hunting with a fowling piece in his hand, and a pack of dogs actually laid on to a turkey!" [151]

Sir Robert Walpole, the rough, roystering old Squire, had kept a fine pack of hounds at Houghton, his palatial country home in Norfolk. Two brothers of Braddock had lived in Norfolk, and it is possible that the General had been entertained in the Hunting Hall at Houghton, where Sir Robert and his old friend, Col. Charles Churchill of the Coldstream, were central figures in a six-by-eight hunting piece painted by John Wooton, an artist devoted to dogs and horses.[152]

Legend grew, describing the General as having a jolly round face, scarlet as his coat, with eyes as innocent as a baby's. It was said that he swaggered, swearing at every word. Such conflicting reports have come down that he was ignorant of every point of parade, except the merits of a bottle and the looks of a woman, brave as bulldog, savage, lustful, prodigal, generous, gentle in soft moods, easy of love and laughter, dull of wit, utterly unread, believing his country the first in the world and he as good a gentleman as any in it, and why not? [153] These became legends, born of bitterness and rancor over defeat and of provincial disdain for the failure of a professional British soldier, often repeated by those whose criticism of the mother country centered in the ill-starred Braddock.

Stories have been told of Braddock, seated at the dinner table of a great plantation—not Stratford—being helped to most dishes more than once and forever holding out his glass for a drink.[154] He certainly enjoyed good food, and the Fairfaxes, like the Carlyles, did their best to feed him well. A Mrs. Wardrope won his favor with a gift of potted woodcocks and a cake.[155]

"I was invited to supper by a rich planter," [one officer wrote home to London] "and the heat of the climate, the dim light of the myrtle wax candles and the number of black half naked servants that attended us made me think of the infernal regions, and that I was at supper with Pluto only there was no beautiful Proserpine, for the lady of the house was more like one of the Furies; she had passed through the education of the college of Newgate, as great numbers from thence arrive here yearly; most being cunning jades, some pick up foolish planters; this lady's husband was far from a fool, but had married not only for the charms of her person but because her art and skill was quite useful to him in carrying on his business affairs.[156]

It is not unlikely that this letter-writer's estimate of his hostess had been influenced by reading Defoe's popular *Moll Flanders*. But he had another reason for his judgment. All the newly arrived British officers were buying their own horses. In this case the host "made me pay for my supper by selling me a horse upon honor which, soon as it was cool, showed itself dog lame and moon-blind." [157] Good horses were becoming scarce. There was a demand for bat horses as well as mounts. The General needed a team of six carriage horses for his coach. Virginians laughed at the General's coach. They thought it ridiculous that he should take one to war, but a coach was regulation for an officer of his rank in the British army.[158]

Washington came up from Mount Vernon to see a review at the camp and visit the General at his headquarters.[159] Braddock told him he might join the expedition at Wills Creek if he liked. Washington put himself on fairly intimate terms with the three younger members of the General's "family," Roger Morris, Shirley, and Orme.[160] Morris, twenty-seven years old, had been in the army ten years and was something of a ladies' man.[161] Shirley, the Massachusetts governor's son, was a kindly and worldly-wise but moody bachelor,[162] becoming disenchanted with his post as military secretary. Orme, pure Coldstream guardsman, moved in the same London social circles as Horace Walpole and was a man who would marry well.[163]

Orme had begun his military career as an ensign in the Thirty-Fourth Foot under Walpole's friend Conway, transferring to the Coldstream in 1745, and now was a Coldstream lieutenant of four years' standing. As a lieutenant of the footguards, Orme ranked as a captain among officers of the line regiments. This made him an object of constant jealousy among junior officers of the expedition. Braddock, himself a veteran guardsman, confided in Orme and often relied upon his judgment, a situation which gave currency to camp gossip about Orme being the General's favorite.[164] Naturally enough, Braddock also showed some partiality toward Lieut.-Col. Burton, recently promoted from major, who occasionally wrote to their mutual friend, George Anne Bellamy.[165]

Daniel Dulany, a young lawyer member of the Maryland General Assembly, who came to Alexandria from Annapolis with Governor Sharpe to see the troops, took an instant and intense dislike to Orme. Dulany had been educated at Eton and Cambridge and had studied law at the Middle Temple. He marked Orme down as an insolent, arrogant, worthless upstart, lording it over all the other officers.[166] But Washington and Orme got along very well.

Sharpe and Dulany had come to Alexandria after the Maryland assembly had been prorogued because it refused to vote any additional funds for the expedition against the French.[167] Sharpe was embarrassed. He had been instructed by Lord Baltimore, proprietor of the Maryland colony, to show Braddock all possible respect and obedience.[168] Not only as a provincial governor, but also as a former regional commander-in-chief he was anxious to please Braddock. One purpose of his journey to Alexandria was to escort Braddock and Dinwiddie back to Annapolis for the council Braddock had called there with the governors of Pennsylvania, New York, and Massachusetts.[169]

Sharpe was a tall man, a bachelor in his late thirties, with a nose as big as Keppel's and a firm, straight mouth—a cheerful fellow but not easily deceived. He had fairly good connections in England, one brother in Parliament and another a former chaplain to the Prince of Wales and master of the Temple, now a prebendary in Salisbury Cathedral. The new Duke of Albemarle, in a letter to Braddock, had mentioned Sharpe favorably and Sharpe hoped to merit the Duke's commendation.[170]

"The men are all well and hearty," Sharpe reported after seeing Braddock's troops, but he found the General "somewhat dissatisfied" with the action of the Maryland assembly, and anxiously concerned with the problem of land transport.[171] No horses had been brought from England for his army: it had been assumed they could be procured in America. With the troops had come sixteen artillery wagons, but many times that number would be needed to haul general supplies. The artillery wagons, fourteen pieces of artillery on travelling carriages, powder carts, tool tumbrils, and a rolling forge would require practically all the horses for which Dinwiddie had contracted. Where were the other horses and wagons coming from for the quartermaster? Dinwiddie had promised 200 wagons and 2,500 horses by May 10 but as of April 10 Braddock could find none for hire.[172]

There was also a recruit problem. Since the arrival of the two regiments of regulars, both under strength, Braddock had received orders from London to recruit each to a strength of 1,000 men. They were not up to 700 each now.[173] The "best" of the Virginians enlisted by Dinwiddie had been assigned to the two regiments, and even the "best" left much to be desired. To fill out the ranks of his regulars with more volunteers Braddock had had to send recruiting officers into Maryland, Virginia, and Pennsylvania.[174]

As a group the Virginia recruits were long, lank, yellow-faced and dirty, looking as if they were half-starved.[175] Many were culls from the thousands of "transports" shipped to the colonies from English jails during the past ten years.[176] In America, as in England, most men joined the army only when they could find nothing more profitable. Idle and ragged, some without shirts, some without shoes, they had been waiting for Braddock at Alexandria when he got there.[177] Until tents could be brought ashore and pitched for them they were quartered in the jail, where many, no doubt, felt at home. Those inducted in the Virginia companies were issued short uniform coats.

"Bobtails," the British called them.[178]

"Very indifferent men," said Braddock.[179]

And always there was the question of feeding them, of feeding the whole army on a march through the wilderness. It was a simple matter to subsist any army in Europe, even in enemy territory. The troops foraged and lived on the countryside. But the American countryside, from what Braddock had seen of it, was not nearly so thickly settled as that of Europe. What did Sharpe know of the supply situation at Wills Creek?

Well, the first time Sharpe had been there he had found the troops without salt, flour, or blankets. But he thought that had been corrected now. A trader named Cresap, who lived near the fort, had bought up some 29,000 pounds of pork, about 8,000 pounds of flour, and a herd of beeves. Sharpe understood Cresap had about 13,000 pounds of beef already cured in barrels at his house. But he warned the General against trader-contractors.[180]

"A parcel of dirty fellows," Sharpe said.[181]

As for transport, he suggested that some of Braddock's troops cross the Potomac and march westward on a road through Maryland. He was confident he could find at least a hundred farmers in Maryland who would provide horses and wagons for the army.[182]

A company of carpenters from the Virginia levies was ordered to march to Wills Creek where they would be put to work by St. Clair, who had gone ahead to repair the roads. At 7:30 o'clock Easter Monday morning, March 31, the Virginians were under arms. The other company of carpenters and two companies of Virginia rangers were attached to Dunbar's regiment, and the remaining three companies of rangers, to Halkett's. Six corporals of the two regiments were assigned, one to each company, to help a lieutenant of the regulars drill the provincials.[183]

This was to be the camp's first busy week. The artillery made up sample cartridges with ball and sent them around to make sure they fit the men's firelocks. All infantrymen were issued two good spare flints, twenty-four rounds of powder and ball. The new recruits were read the articles of war, instructed in the use of their arms, and warned that their firelocks must not be used as tent poles or otherwise encumbered while on the march. The regiments went through the exercise of wheeling up into line to fire by platoons.[184]

The word was passed, in order form, for officers to provide themselves with bat horses but, because forage was scarce, to carry no more baggage than necessary. It was recommended that inasmuch as their espantoons would be useless in the woods, the officers arm themselves with fusils. For the same reason the sergeants of the two regiments would leave their halberts behind and carry firelock and bayonet. To lighten their packs and enable each man to carry seven or eight days' rations the privates would shed shoulder belts, waist belts, and hangers and take with them into the field only one spare shirt, one pair of spare stockings, one spare pair of shoes, and one pair of brown gaiters.[185]

> Commanding officers of regiments are directed by His Excellency to inform their men not to suffer themselves to be alarmed upon a march by any straggling fires from the woods, they being of no consequence nor liable to any inconvenience but what arise from their misbehavior. Any soldier by leaving his company or by words or gestures expressing fear shall suffer death and the General will greatly approve and properly reward those men who by their coolness and good discipline treat the attempt of those fellows with the contempt they deserve.[186]

On Thursday, April 3, the General's guard at headquarters was reduced to one corporal and nine men.[187] The General had gone to Annapolis for his Governors council. With Keppel, Dinwiddie, and Sharpe he had crossed the Potomac on the ferry in Dinwiddie's coach and driven through upper Marlboro to Maryland's elegant little capital. Orme, Shirley, Keppel's secretary, Dinwiddie's clerk, and their servants rode horseback.[188] They expected to meet the

other governors in Annapolis over the weekend but a heavy snow
storm farther north blocked the roads between Boston and New
York, and Morris waited in Philadelphia for his colleagues, Shirley
and De Lancey.[189]

Sharpe entertained Braddock and his party as best he could. The
mansion he rented as a residence was equipped with a greenhouse
and surrounded by acres of gardens nearly ready to bloom. Gar-
dening was his hobby.[190] His two journeys to Wills Creek and his
visit to the camp at Alexandria had given him other things to talk
about with the General, and as a former captain of Powlett's
marines (he mentioned having served in the "twentieth regiment")
he could speak the language of military men.[191]

But Braddock was restless, impatient to put his army into motion. A long weekend at Annapolis, waiting for the three northern
governors, increased his agitation. Pacing the floor of Sharpe's
house, he asked again about those horses and wagons. Sharpe assured him they would be available whenever his troops crossed the
Potomac. The logical point to cross would be at the mouth of
Rock Creek, on the Maryland side, eight miles above Alexandria.[192]

Braddock waited through Sunday for the Northern governors,
still delayed by that snow storm. On Monday he returned to Alexandria. He left instructions with Sharpe to bring the three governors to his headquarters there when they arrived. He could wait
no longer. His army was moving.[193]

X

LOGISTICS

April, May 1755

A<small>ND NOW</small>, of a sudden, winter died. The salty tinge of the tide-water country faded in the breath of early spring. Where the tents of the regulars were pitched by the marsh, the ground was still soft and wet and darkness brought a penetrating chill. But the days were brighter. Early morning haze on the Potomac lost its sting. Sunset lingered. The willows by the river turned feathery green.

Here in Virginia the spring came later but swifter than on the Thames. And there was no mistaking it. Old soldiers felt April in their bones. This was the time of year, in the old days, when the barges loaded at the Tower, and the transports dropped down stream with troops for another campaign in Flanders.

For younger soldiers it was homesick season, breeding memories of golden gorse in Cornwall, budding pear trees in Kent, primroses and daffodils in the country lanes of Devon. The fresh scent of white hawthorne blossoms and of ploughed earth out of doors, the scrunch of sand in a patch of sunshine on an alehouse floor—that was spring in England.

"I reckon the day I bought my commission the most unhappy in my life excepting that in which I landed in this country," the offi-cer who had been sold the moonblind horse wrote home. "And there is no comfort in the spring; none of those months of gentle, genial warmth. . . . As soon as the severe frosts go off the heat of the neighboring sun brings on summer at once, one day shall be frost and the next more scorching or sultry than the hottest dog day in England." [1]

Virginia hospitality, the novelty of hominy, the absence of London smoke could not make up for the fact that "the worst English country town exceeds all they have in this whole province." There was no burgundy, or champagne. The claret was poor stuff, the madeira second-rate, and the rum punch monotonous. Flat tobacco fields, Negro slaves and their overbearing masters made sensitive, melancholy Englishmen yearn for meadows, blooming maid servants, and sedate livery men who shunned loud laughter and bad manners. They were tired of talk about tobacco. Could Virginians talk of nothing else? They worked too hard, aged too quickly.[2] "A Virginian is as old at thirty as an Englishman at sixty," a provincial coquette whispered behind her fan.[3]

The days of such whispers were numbered. On Friday, April 4, 1755, while Braddock was still in Annapolis, an advance detail of a corporal and six men from Dunbar's regiment had been ordered to Frederick with hospital stores and six days' provisions. On Monday an officer and twenty men of Halkett's were told to be ready to march to Winchester next morning. Thirty more men were detailed to load artillery wagons for Winchester and boats for Rock Creek. The army would move in two columns—one through Frederick and the other through Winchester—to ease congestion on the roads and utilize limited colonial transport as widely as possible.[4]

But the detail to load stores for shipment up the river to Rock Creek could find no boats. Impress boats, if necessary, Braddock ordered.[5] Keppel said the boats of the "Seahorse" and the "Nightingale," which had sailed up the Potomac with the transports, could be used.[6] Lieut. Spendlowe's detachment of seamen was sent to Rock Creek to help load wagons there with the stores ferried across the river. The sailors encamped under the trees on the wooded Maryland shore near a boatyard where a small sailing vessel was on the stocks.[7]

All that sunny, sultry April week,[8] unseasonably warm for the Potomac, boats plied between the Alexandria landing and the Rock Creek boat yard, carrying army baggage and provisions. Because of the intense heat the soldiers were issued light weight Osnabrig breeches and waistcoats, and officers were ordered to provide them with bladders or thin leather to put between the lining and crown of their hats as a protection against the sun.[9]

On Thursday morning, April 10, at 6 o'clock, Sir Peter Halkett marched for Winchester with six companies of his Forty-Fourth. He was cautioned to use no more wagons than absolutely necessary. Four of his companies, left in Alexandria with Lieut.-Col. Thomas Gage, would escort the train later. On Friday the General's guard was taken off and Dunbar's men began to strike their tents. They were under orders to begin crossing the Potomac for a march through Maryland at 5 o'clock Friday morning. A sergeant and twelve men of Dunbar's would move the General's baggage. All troops would be fully equipped for the field with blankets, knapsacks, and haversacks, each man carrying eight days' rations.[10]

Officers were still trying to provide themselves with bat horses.[11] There was a shortage of wagons, wagoners, carters, and batmen. Dunbar advertised in the Virginia *Gazette* for men willing to serve as drivers and batmen, offering them the same pay, provisions, and quarters as soldiers.[12] An order was issued:

> No person whatever to press or employ any wagons without an order from General Braddock, the Quartermaster General or his assistant.
> This order to be read not only to soldiers but to officers, servants and followers of the army as anyone who shall be found guilty of disobeying it shall be severely punished.[13]

Drunken redcoats continued to be a nuisance in Alexandria. Townsfolk complained that they abused people and hurt horses. The four companies of Halkett's regiment remaining in camp were warned that any soldier found selling liquor to the rest of the men would be "severely punished." Any soldier's wife caught in the act would be drummed out of camp.[14]

On Sunday, April 15, Sharpe arrived in Alexandria with the three northern governors who had not reached Annapolis until Friday. With them was Col. William Johnson, New York agent for Indian affairs.[15] Braddock and Keppel met with the governors for their long-awaited council of war in the "Blue Room" of Carlyle house, a crowded little parlor, high-ceilinged, with shallow windowseats and blue marble fireplace facings and pilasters that were the pride of Alexandria.[16]

The first proposition put forward by the General, after laying his letter of instructions before the group, was a proposal to establish a common fund to bear the expenses of the war. Unanimously the governors voted this down. Their own experiences with their assemblies during the past few months had convinced them that such a fund could never be set up in the colonies without the aid of Parliament. But they approved all three of Braddock's other proposals: (1) the appointment of Col. Johnson as an envoy to treat with the Indians and try to persuade the Six Nations to fight as English allies against the French, (2) simultaneous attacks upon the French forts in Nova Scotia, at Crown Point, Niagara ("the most important of all our actions," Braddock said), and the Forks of the Ohio, and (3) the construction of two 60-ton war vessels on Lake Ontario.

Some of the northern governors thought Braddock's projected march across the mountains an unnecessary hazard and expense, considering that the enemy was more accessible from New York. Privately they suspected some misrepresentation on the part of Virginia was responsible for this, but there was no argument, no protest on this point for the record. Braddock's orders from London were positive.[17]

Braddock was surprised at the importance which the governors attached to winning over the Six Nations. Of all the subjects brought up on the carpet this seemed to be regarded as the one of greatest consequence. So far he had had no direct dealings with Indians and had not troubled himself too much about them. None had volunteered to join his expedition, but Dinwiddie thought they would come in. The General asked Morris to do what he could to prevail upon friendly Indians of Pennsylvania to join the army at Wills Creek, but to leave their women and children behind.[18] "They will be very troublesome in camp," he said.[19]

At Braddock's dictation his secretary, young Shirley, drew up a formal commission appointing Col. Johnson to superintend and manage the affairs of the Six Nations and their allies. Two speeches to the Indians were prepared. The Colonel was to take presents to the Indians (for which the General would advance £2,000) and deliver the two speeches in the General's name.[20]

Their conference over, Sharpe and the three northern governors left Alexandria on Thursday morning for Annapolis.[21] Governor Shirley had an army of his own to get under way. If his reunion with his son had been brief, young Shirley had made a new and valued friend in his father's Pennsylvania colleague, Robert Hunter Morris, the son of a former governor of New Jersey. Morris was nearer the age of young Shirley's father. He and William probably had met in England where Morris had been working on New Jersey land claims when the Penns offered him the governorship of their colony in 1754.[22]

In a letter to Newcastle, enclosing the minutes of the council, Braddock wrote:

> As very little assistance has already been offered me by the provinces and still less is to be expected from them, it is necessary for me to apprise your grace that my contingent account will be much greater than I had persuaded myself, or than, I believe, Your Grace imagines; not only as several articles expected from the provinces must be comprehended in it, but from the excessive service of labor, the great number of stores, wagons, boats, etc., and innumerable other circumstances peculiar to the nature of the service in America. . . .
>
> Upon application from Gov. Shirley acquainting me that he had the greatest reason to fear a mutiny from the general discontent of the men in the two American regiments at paying for their provisions which are allowed to all H. M.'s other regiments upon this continent I have directed him to make no deductions from their pay on that account till H. M.'s pleasure shall be known: and with H. M.'s views on this head I must beg to know his pleasure whether I am to allow provisions to Sir. Peter Halkett's and Col. Dunbar's regiments when those furnished by the colonies are expended or to put them under stoppages upon which I must beg leave to observe to Your Grace that the duty of a soldier here is very great and that it is impossible for them to subsist upon their pay.[23]

Tuesday night the weather had changed. The warm south wind had shifted to the north. The temperature dropped. Thunder gusts swept the Potomac. Early Wednesday morning it began to snow and by 7 o'clock the Maryland countryside, between Rock Creek and Frederick, was covered to a depth of 18 inches. During the day the snow melted rapidly. But Dunbar's regiment, on the road to Frederick, remained in camp near Dowden's ordinary, a dormer-windowed country tavern, about 15 miles below the town. There were no villages in which the troops could be billeted along the way, only forest with occasional cabins in clearings where farmers lived.[24]

Next morning Spendlowe's sailors ferried the regiment across the muddy Monocacy river—high and swift as a result of Wednesday's snow—on a flatboat, and on Friday the troops encamped north of Frederick, a town of about two hundred houses, two churches (one English and one Dutch), a stone tavern, and a one and one-half-

story wooden courthouse, still under construction. Most of the townsfolk were "Dutch" as far as the British were concerned.

"Ich weiss nicht," was the reply to many English questions.

But the Dutch were good farmers. Food and forage were abund-
ant, at a price. Soldiers who could afford it ate well—eggs, chicken,
lamb, fresh pork, pie, and milk, a welcome variation from the
army's salt meat and biscuit.[25]

St. Clair had gone ahead to Wills Creek [26] to make sure that
boats and floats had been collected for river crossings, that supplies had been laid in along the way, and to look for wagons. He
reached the log fort at the foot of Wills Mountain—the fort re-
named Fort Cumberland in honor of the Captain General—about
3 o'clock Wednesday afternoon, April 16.[27] The Virginia road he
had traveled from Winchester was incredibly poor for an army's
main line of communication. A stock of flour for which Dinwiddie
had contracted in Pennsylvania, to be carted down from Lancaster
to an old Indian trader's stone storehouse at the junction of Conococheague creek and the Potomac, had not yet been delivered. And
there simply were no wagons.[28]

The deputy quartermaster general was tired, discouraged, and
disagreeable when he dismounted at the gate of the stockade and
was told that five men from Pennsylvania had been waiting for
him since Saturday.[29] From *Pennsylvania?* Bring them out!

Their spokesman, George Croghan, Pennsylvania's best known
Indian trader and interpreter, introduced himself and the other
four as commissioners appointed by Governor Morris to run a road
from Carlisle to the Youghiogheny.[30] That was all St. Clair needed.
He did the talking.

"He is extremely warm and angry at our province," Croghan
wrote to Morris later that day. "He would not look at our draughts
nor suffer any representation to be made to him in regard to the
province but stormed like a lion rampant." [31]

Croghan and his party had left Carlisle on March 29, following
a trail across the mountains of western Pennsylvania to within
eighteen miles of the Three Forks of the Youghiogheny. They
thought the trail could be widened into a road. Deserted by their
guides, who had become frightened by reports that war parties
from the French fort were aprowl, the road commissioners had
turned south to Fort Cumberland. They had been kindly received
by the commandant, by Col. James Innes, a veteran of Cartagena,

and Capt. John Rutherford of the independent New York company in garrison at the fort.[32] They were completely unprepared for the blast which St. Clair let fly. Croghan's letter summarized it:

He said our commission to lay out the road should have been issued in January last upon his first letter, that doing it now is doing of nothing, that the troops must march on the first of May, that the want of this road and the provisions promised by Pennsylvania has retarded the expedition, which may cost them their lives because of the fresh numbers of French that's suddenly like to be poured into the country; that instead of marching to the Ohio he would in nine days march his army into Cumberland county to cut the roads, press horses, wagons, &c; that he would not suffer a soldier to handle an axe, but by fire and sword oblige the inhabitants to do it, and take every man that refused to the Ohio as he had yesterday some of the Virginians; that he would kill all kind of cattle and carry away the horses, burn the houses &c and that if the French defeated them by the delays of this province that he would with his sword drawn pass through the province and treat the inhabitants as a parcel of traitors to his Master; that he would tomorrow write to England by a man-of-war, shake Mr. Penn's proprietaryship, and represent Pennsylvania as a disaffected province; that he would not stop to impress our assembly his hands were not tyed, and that we should find, ordering us to take these precautions and instantly publish them to our governor and assembly, telling us he did not value anything they did or resolved, seeing they were dilatory, retarded the march of troops and hang an arse (as he phrased it) on this occasion, and told us to go to the General if we pleased, who would give us ten bad words for one that he had given.

When St. Clair stopped, probably out of breath, Croghan tried to speak.

"But all in vain," he told Morris. "Our delays were unpardonable, he would do our duty himself and never trust us, but we should pay dearly for it; to every sentence he solemnly swore and desired that we might believe him to be in earnest." [33]

Braddock was still in Alexandria with Colonel Gage and four companies of Halkett's, waiting for teams for fourteen artillery pieces and horses and wagons for the fifteen cohorn mortars. There was also a shortage of wagons on the Maryland shore, in spite of Sharpe's promises. Heavy ordnance and hospital stores had not yet been moved from Rock Creek. Braddock sent an express to St. Clair, at Wills Creek, to meet him in Frederick [34] and wrote a letter to Napier in which he said:

I shall set out tomorrow for Frederick in my way to Fort Cumberland the new name for the fort at Wills's Creek, where I shall join the two columns which are now upon their march at about fifty miles distance: this disposition I was obliged to make for the conveniency of horses and wagons, by which means I employ those of Maryland which would not be prevailed upon to cross the Potomac. I have met with infinite difficulties in providing carriages etc., for the train nor am I as yet quite relieved from one, a great part still continuing here which has delayed me for some time; I shall get them dispatched tomorrow or the next day. I am impatient to begin my march over the mountains. . . . I am to expect numberless inconveniences and obstructions from the total want of dry forage, from the being obliged to carry all our provisions with us which will make a vast line of baggage and which though I reduce as much as possible will nevertheless occasion great trouble and retard me considerably. . . . I have been greatly disappointed by the neglect and supineness of those assemblies of those provinces with which I am concerned; they promised great matters and have done nothing whereby instead of forwarding they have obstructed the service. When I get to Wills's Creek I will send you . . . whatever other information or intelligence I shall get there, it being impractical to get any here, the people of this part of the country laying it down for a maxim never to speak the truth upon any account.[35]

Saying good-bye to those at the Carlyle house next morning, Braddock tried his soldier's best to be jovial. To a young Negro maid named Penny, he said:

"You are only a Penny now but I hope on my return you will be two pence." [36]

He rode into Frederick on Monday morning, April 21, with Orme, Morris, Shirley, and a bodyguard, a small mounted troop of Virginia horse.[37] Once again the weather was fine—warm days but cool nights with heavy dew.[38] Frederick's stone tavern, a two-story house at the top of a hill on the far side of town, had been reserved as a headquarters for the General. Four miles to the west lay the Kittochtinny hills, first range of mountains crossing the line of his march. From the tavern door they were mild mountains, almost English in appearance, a chain of wooded humps that turned blue in the April twilight.[39]

Contrary to his hopes after that long weekend at Annapolis with the obliging Governor Sharpe, who had promised to meet him in Frederick that evening, Braddock found no cattle corralled for the army, no park of wagons waiting to bring up the stores remaining at Rock Creek.[40] St. Clair, reporting to Braddock at his tavern headquarters, brought no better news from Wills Creek. George Ross, who said he had been appointed a commissary for the Army, was still waiting on his farm at the Conococheague for the flour supposed to be delivered there from Pennsylvania. The quarter-master had found no wagons. Some of the farmers near the Cono-cocheague were German Dunkers beset with conscientious objections to warfare. They wanted nothing to do with an army.[41]

"I have great promises," said the General, perhaps with a note of sarcasm.[42] "What the performances will be a little time will tell."

Sharpe drove in from Annapolis that evening in a six-horse chariot. Braddock laid the question of cattle, horses, and wagons before him. The Governor had no ready answer. So limited was his authority, to say nothing of his funds, he could only suggest that the General try to buy beeves from the farmers around Frederick and, if necessary, impress their wagons.[43]

The army had to have more wagons. Practically all those with Dunbar's column and now loaded with artillery stores had been sent ahead to the mouth of the Conococheague from where it might be possible to boat the stores up the Potomac to Wills Creek. The wagons would return to Rock Creek for another haul. At that rate it would be a month before all the stores at Rock Creek could be transported as far as Conococheague. Wheel and hand barrows at Rock Creek, intended for siege operations, were ordered to be left there.[44]

Mindful of his instructions to cultivate harmony and friendship, Braddock so far had taken pains to avoid any action which might be regarded as highhanded. But now he was beginning to grow desperate. Transports were vital to his expedition. He sent out staff officers to show the county justices of peace copies of his orders from the King, empowering him to impress transport for his army. But there were not many wagons in Frederick county to impress. Threats, entreaties, money at the rate of fifteen shillings per day for a four-horse team with a driver, produced only about twenty-five, and not all of those in serviceable condition.[45]

"This drear and desolate country," groaned Braddock.[46]

Buying cattle was not too difficult. The countryside through which the troops were marching was dotted with cowpens, patches of woods of eighty to a hundred acres enclosed with rail fences. Cows, calves, and steers seemed to run wild in the woods. Normally the herdsmen did not round up their cattle for market until fall. All the animals were lean, but the herdsmen were as eager to sell as the army was to buy.[47]

While Braddock waited for St. Clair and his assistants to round up transport and beef, Benjamin Franklin, deputy postmaster general of the North American colonies, and his son, William, arrived in Frederick from Philadelphia. The elder Franklin's immediate business with the General was a system of special posts which Braddock proposed to establish in order to speed the movement of dispatches between his headquarters and Annapolis, Philadelphia, and Williamsburg, as well as letters from the army to England. Braddock already had discussed this with the governors of the colonies involved.[48]

Franklin, now forty-nine years old, was of Braddock's physical build, with a big head, steady gray eyes, and a mouth lined for amusement.[49] His popularity as a provincial journalist and his ability at practical politics in the Pennsylvania assembly had made him the most influential man in that colony.[50] His son's only claim to fame was brief service as an ensign in an expedition against Canada during the last war. It is not likely that Braddock was aware either of the elder Franklin's growing eminence as a natural philosopher, or of his stature as a colonial politician. But Sharpe, no doubt, paid due deference to the Postmaster General, whose personal charm, quiet self confidence, and wide acquaintance with public affairs can have left little doubt in the General's mind as to his capabilities.[51]

Less than a year ago Franklin had been Pennsylvania's representative at an Albany meeting to draw up a treaty with the Six Nations. The principal Indian spokesman had been the Mohawk sachem Hendrick, one of the four Indian kings who had visited London when Braddock was a boy. But it was Franklin's natural gifts for diplomacy—a disarming simplicity and seeming humility—which had recommended him to the Pennsylvania Assembly as a special envoy to Braddock. The assembly had been stung by Braddock's harsh criticism and alarmed by a warning from Keppel that trading with the enemy must cease. It could not prudently risk the continued disfavor of a general commissioned by the King as commander-in-chief of all forces in America.[52]

The Franklins stayed in Frederick for several days. Benjamin dined with the General daily "and had full opportunity of removing all his prejudices, by the information of what the assembly had before his arrival actually done, and were still willing to do, to facilitate his operations." [53] The Franklins were on the point of returning to Philadelphia when the returns on the impressment of wagons reached Braddock's headquarters.

"The General and all the officers were surprised, declared the expedition was then at an end, being impossible, and exclaimed against the ministers for ignorantly landing them in a country destitute of the means of conveying their stores, baggage, etc., not less than one hundred and fifty wagons being necessary," Franklin remembered in later years.[54]

"I happened to say I thought it was a pity they had not landed rather in Pennsylvania, as in that country almost every farmer had his own wagon."

Braddock snapped at this ingenuous bait.

"Then you, sir," he said, "who are a man of interest there, can probably procure them for us, and I beg you will undertake it."

Franklin asked what terms he could offer the owners. Braddock told him to suit himself, whatever he thought necessary, and gave him £800 then and there to be disbursed in advance payments.[55]

"After taking Fort Duquesne," Braddock told Franklin, outlining his plan of campaign,[56] "I am to proceed to Niagara; and, having taken that, to Frontenac, if the season will allow time; and I suppose it will, for Duquesne can hardly detain me above three or four days; and then I can see nothing that will obstruct my march to Niagara."

Franklin thought about the woods and trails ahead of the General. In his mind he pictured Braddock's British regulars marching through those woods, over the mountains, a long red line weaving among the trees and brush of the solitude that lay beyond Frederick.

"To be sure, sir," he said "if you arrive well before Duquesne, with those fine troops, as well provided with artillery, that place not yet completely fortified, and as we hear with no very strong garrison, can probably make but a short resistance. The only danger I apprehend of obstruction to your march is from ambuscades of Indians, who by constant practice are dexterous in laying and executing them; and the slender line, near four miles long, which your army must make, may expose it to be attacked by surprise in its flanks, and to be cut like a thread into several pieces, which from their distance, cannot come up in time to support each other."

Braddock must have smiled.[57]

Evidently Franklin was not a student of Bland. Because it was all in old Humphrey's book, Chapter VII, "General Rules for the

marching of a regiment of foot." Any good officer should be able
to quote it from memory:

> When a regiment, or detachment, marches through an enclosed or
> wooded country, the danger which they are to apprehend must be
> from foot, and not horse; and lest a partisan party should escape the
> discovery of the van guard, it would be proper to have small parties,
> commanded by sergeants, marching on the flanks with orders to exam-
> ine all the hedges, ditches and copses which lie near the road, those
> being the places in which they generally conceal themselves."
> [And so on for three or four pages, into the subject of ambuscades.] [58]

"These savages may, indeed, be a formidable enemy to your raw
American militia," Braddock told Franklin, "but upon the King's
regulars and disciplined troops, sir, it is impossible they should
make any impression." [58]

Franklin subsided, conscious of the impropriety of a printer dis-
puting military tactics with a professional soldier, and said no
more.[59] He and his son supped with the officers of Dunbar's Forty-
Eighth. Dunbar told them he was concerned for his subalterns. The
Forty-Eighth was a regiment of the line. Few of its officers were
gentlemen of independent means. In a country where the simple
luxuries were as dear as in America, many of his younger officers
could not afford to supply themselves even with the sugar, tea, and
wine to which they were accustomed at home and which would
soften the rigor of a campaign in the wilderness.

Franklin knew how to handle that. His son, with a firsthand
knowledge of camp life and its wants in America, drew up a list of
suggested parcels:

6 lbs. loaf sugar	1 kegg containing 20 lbs.
6 lbs. good Muscovado do	good butter
1 lb. good green tea	2 doz. old Madeira wine
1 lb. good bohea do	2 gallons Jamaica spirits
6 lbs. ground coffee	1 bottle flour of mustard
6 lbs. chocolate	2 well-cured hams
1-2 Cwt. best white biscuit	1-2 dozen dried tongue
1-2 lb. pepper	6 lbs. rice
1 quart best white wine vinegar	6 lbs. raisins
1 Gloucester cheese	

Franklin enclosed the list in a letter written next morning to a
Pennsylvania assembly committee, which had the disposal of some
public funds, warmly recommending the case of Dunbar's subal-

terns to their consideration and proposing that the officers be made a present of these "necessaries and refreshments." [60]

The only person the amiable postmaster general had not appeased was St. Clair. The deputy quartermaster general was still bristling.

"Sir John St. Clair complains very loudly of your not having caused a road to be made as he desired through your province to Wills Creek," Braddock's secretary, Shirley, told Robert Morris in a short note which he gave Franklin to carry back to Pennsylvania's governor.[61]

After talking with Franklin the General also wrote Morris:

> It will be necessary to contract for horses and wagons in Pennsylvania, and the want of a road from Philadelphia to Wills Creek will prevent their joining me there as quickly and as in good condition. It is likewise of great importance to have a free communication with your province to facilitate the march of any assistance or convoys I may require from thence, but I don't see how I can with safety move from Fort Cumberland till that work is finished or in great forwardness. I must, therefore, desire you to give your orders to have it immediately made, and if you cannot prevail on your assembly to bear the expense of it, nevertheless have it done and I must be obliged to charge it to the public account.[62]

With something less than blind loyalty to the General's family, young Shirley sent Morris another note, along with this letter. He told Morris:

> I think it necessary to apprize you that Sir John St. Clair has conceived great resentment at your neglect (as he calls it) for his application to you for the road. If no delay has happened in this matter through your default, as I should not apprehend it had, I make no doubt you will answer any letter he may write you upon it in such a manner as a Governor of a province should do to a deputy quartermaster general, and I would advise you in your next dispatch to the Secretary of State to get this business in its fair and proper light. I mention this not to make any difference between Sir John and you, but that if he should be wrong-headed enough to take upon himself to make any representation of it at home, your character should not suffer for want of the truth being known.[63]

From Frederick the Franklins went to Lancaster, called on a printer to arrange for the printing of handbills directed at the farmers of Lancaster, York, and Cumberland counties:

Lancaster, April 26, 1755.
Whereas, one hundred and fifty waggons, with four horses to each waggon, and fifteen hundred saddle or pack horses, are wanted for the service of his majesty's forces now about to rendezvous at Wills Creek, and his excellency General Braddock having been pleased to empower me to contract for the hire of the same, I hereby give notice that I shall attend for that purpose at Lancaster from this day to next Wednesday evening, and at York from next Thursday morning till Friday evening where I shall be ready to agree for waggons and teams, or single horses. . . .

Under the signature, *B. Franklin,* the advertisement set forth the terms—fifteen shillings per diem for each wagon with four good horses and a driver, and two shilling per diem for each able horse with a pack--saddle, the pay to commence at the time of their joining Braddock's expedition at Will's Creek, which must be on or before May 20, with seven days' pay in advance to seal the bargain at the time of contracting, if required, and the remainder from the army paymaster when discharged.

Appended to the advertisement was a note that William Franklin was empowered to enter into like contracts with persons in Cumberland county, and a letter addressed by the elder Franklin to "Friends and Countrymen," describing Braddock's exasperation with the failure of the province of Pennsylvania and its inhabitants to supply him with horses and wagons. The letter implied that if transport were not provided voluntarily for the expedition, an armed force might be sent into the province to seize what was needed.

I apprehend that the progress of British soldiers through these counties on such an occasion, especially considering the temper they are in, would be attended with many and great inconveniences, but the king's business must be done; so many brave troops, come so far for your defense, must not stand idle through your backwardness to do what may be reasonably expected from you. . . .
. . . If this method of obtaining the waggons and horses is not likely to succeed, I am obliged to send word to the general in fourteen days; and I suppose Sir John St. Clair, *the hussar,* with a body of soldiers, will immediately enter the province for that purpose. . . .

No Dutchman who had immigrated to Pennsylvania within the last generation or two had to be enlightened on the subject of hussars, a type of light cavalry, originally Hungarian, that had pillaged western Europe during a century of recurrent war. Applying that title to Sir John St. Clair was a clever calculation by Franklin.

"I cannot but honor Franklin for the last clause of his advertisement," laughed Shirley when he saw it.[64]

Braddock had remained with Dunbar's regiment in Frederick, the soldiers sweating out an April heat wave that broke with hard showers and cold, high winds. Eighty recruits arrived from Rock Creek with a wagontrain load of ordnance stores. Officers who had not yet provided themselves with Negro or mulatto batmen were instructed to take their pick from among the recruits unfit for duty, as none suitable for soldiers could be spared. The seamen were told to look around for packhorses to carry their baggage, since wagons would no longer be available to them for that purpose. Transport was too scarce.[65]

Governor Sharpe had remained in Frederick with Braddock after the departure of the Franklins. After the wagon fiasco he was more zealous than ever to perform any other possible service. Col. Washington arrived to join the General's family. The tavern headquarters were overcrowded. Accommodations for the Colonel had to be found in a small house about half a mile away.[66]

At 6 o'clock Tuesday morning, April 29, the troops had resumed their march. Lt. Spendelowe's sailors were somewhat dejected by having to leave behind their hammocks with other gear for which they could find no pack animals. The army had impressed every horse St. Clair could find, including those used by contractors who were hauling materials for a new Frederick court house. Construction work on the building ceased as the army moved out of town. The column made eighteen miles that day over a fairly good but lonely road that crossed Kittochtinny and South Mountain by easy ascents. Both mountains were heavily wooded and infested with a species of chigre that set the soldiers to scratching. The sailors had never seen so much game—deer, birds, rabbits. But there were few cabins along the road and no ordinaries.[67]

At 3 o'clock in the afternoon the troops halted for the night at a cabin in a clearing in the wooded valley beyond South Mountain. At 6 next morning they marched again, crossed a succession of low ridges called "The Devil's Backbone," forded the shallow Antietam and, early in the afternoon, came out on the bank of the broad, placid Potomac near a stone warehouse at the mouth of the Conococheague. Here the seamen were faced with their biggest ferrying operation since Rock Creek. The river was nearly a quarter of a mile wide, but with little current. Two floats and five bateaux were moored at the river bank. Well before the following day Dunbar's regiment and wagons were on the Virginia shore.[68]

Braddock, his staff, and bodyguard of Virginia horse did not leave Frederick until May 1 when they set out for Winchester where the General expected to meet the Indian chiefs, who Dinwiddie had said would hold a council there. Still itching to square himself with Braddock, now damning the route through Frederick as a useless diversion, Sharpe pressed the General to share his chariot as a lighter and more comfortable conveyance for American roads than the General's own heavy coach.[69]

Sharpe left the General's party at Swerengen's ferry on the Potomac and returned horseback to Annapolis, insisting that the General keep his chariot, with spare pole and axle tree, as long as he pleased. Braddock allowed himself to be persuaded on condition that Sharpe sell him the whole turnout.[70]

Washington noted that once Dunbar's regiment was back across the Potomac, it proceeded to Wills Creek by the same road it would have followed had it marched directly from Alexandria through Winchester, as Halkett had done. Washington thought Braddock had been imposed upon either by Sharpe or St. Clair in being induced to use the Frederick road.[71]

Winchester, a Scotch-Irish frontier village of forty or fifty houses, mostly log, was another disappointment.[72] The road up the valley from the Potomac was no carriage road and there were no Indians at Winchester when Braddock got there.[73] Unknown to him, any plans which may have been laid for a meeting there with the Indians had been cancelled.[74] For four hot days Braddock waited, cursing Dinwiddie for having misinformed him, but reluctant to leave until convinced that a longer stay would be a waste of time.[75]

"I am very happy in the General's family, and I am treated with a complaisant freedom which is quite agreeable," Washington wrote to his mother.[76] He was not concerned with Indians.

In other letters from Winchester to his brother Jack and Col. Fairfax, Washington expressed doubt that Braddock's army would be able to proceed beyond Wills Creek before the end of May, for want of wagons.[77]

Braddock wrote to Dinwiddie, complaining that the Virginia commissary of stores had called on him for three or four thousand pounds to buy provisions which he had expected to find laid in along the road or at Wills Creek. There was also a matter of £100 which he had been obliged to advance to Capt. Steuart, of his mounted Virginia bodyguard, to buy horses.[78] In another letter, to Governor Morris, Braddock enclosed a complaint from an officer at Wills Creek who accused two Irish traders in western Pennsylvania of supplying the French with gunpowder and information.[79]

On May 7 Braddock was back on the road to Wills Creek with his aides, his light horse bodyguard, his coach, and Sharpe's chariot, two days' journey behind Dunbar. Every mile the dusty, crooked road grew worse, the mountains higher. Within one three-mile stretch the road crossed and recrossed a shallow stream twenty times. It crossed another, nineteen times in two miles. Sometimes the streams were bridged. Generally they had to be forded.[80]

"There is no describing the badness of the roads," said the Widow Browne, who followed the rough, twisting route behind Braddock, riding part of the way in a wagon.

"I am almost disjointed," she said. She got out and walked until her feet were blistered.[81]

Capt. Charles Lewis, a Virginia volunteer, admitted that the road was bad but admired the mountains and their winding runs.

"A beautiful prospect," he said, "and the best land I ever yet saw." [82]

"There is nothing round us but trees, swamps and thickets," a less cheerful British officer wrote home. "I cannot conceive how war can be made in such a country. There has not been ground to form a battalion since we left the settlements. I cannot conceive how we must do if attacked, nor how we can get up to attack; but the best is what the General said, to reassure the old soldiers who are all uneasy for fear of being attacked on the long march in defiles. His Excellency with great judiciousness says, that where the woods are too thick for as to hinder our coming at them, they will hinder their coming at us." [83]

Snake stories began to circulate. Several soldiers, reported sick, were said to have died from snake bites. Swampy areas along the road were full of snakes. A more general and less exaggerated complaint arose from a pest new to the Englishmen, a kind of tick, or forest flea, which got into their legs, causing inflammation and an unmerciful itching. The Americans knew about these tiny insects which flourished in the mountains. They called them "chigres." The next tall story to sweep the column was about a soldier bitten so badly by chigres that the flesh on his leg mortified, and he was obliged to have it amputated.[84]

Eighteen miles below Wills Creek a float ferried Braddock's party back across the Potomac from Virginia into Maryland territory, and along about 6 o'clock on the rainy day of May 8 they overtook Dunbar's column, encamped on the river bank around a stockade enclosing the log house of Col. Thomas Cresap, an Indian trader and army commissary of dubious reputation.[85] Cresap was a Yorkshireman by birth. He had emmigrated to Maryland as a youth, fighting a private war with the colony of Pennsylvania in an unsuccessful effort to keep title to a 500-acre grant from Lord Baltimore in disputed territory. Then he had gone west, up the Potomac, where he got along better with the Indians, who called him "Big Spoon" because the ladle of the kettle in his cabin fireplace was always at their service. Cresap was almost 60 now, a sort of lengendary knave, if a person believed all he heard.[86]

"A rattlesnake colonel," some said.[87]

One of the original partners of the Ohio Company, Cresap had been involved in various questionable deals to build storehouses, to open roads, and to persuade German settlers from Pennsylvania to take up Ohio Company land. He had provided emergency supplies for Washington's expedition of the previous summer, and now was in charge of the stone storehouse at the mouth of the Conococheague, where the Pennsylvania overdue flour for Braddock's army was to be delivered. As far as Braddock could see, Cresap was simply another army contractor, and the General remembered Sharpe's warning about all contractors being "a parcel of dirty fellows." [88]

Braddock spent the night in Cresap's house. As was customary in the British army, Dunbar halted every third day to rest his men, and May 9 was a rest day. To pass the time and amuse the General, officers of the Forty-Eighth staged a horse race, no horse over eleven hands and each to carry 14 stone. During the day Orme discovered that some of the Virginia troops were still using tents lent them by Sir Peter Halkett. The Virginians were supposed to provide their own tents. The Captain got off a letter to Dinwiddie, asking an explanation.[89]

Next morning, May 10, the column resumed its march, a last lap over low ridges, past the cabin of John Fraser, a Scot gunsmith, and down across the river flats toward the high, steep slopes of

Wills mountain, not far ahead. Braddock, making a later start, caught up with the troops and passed them when they halted at noon. The drums of the Forty-Eighth beat the *Grenadiers March* as the General's coach and its mounted escort trotted by and disappeared up the road.[90]

Dunbar formed his men in a circle. Within an hour or so, he told them, they would arrive at Wills Creek. They would see Indians there, friendly Indians. It was the General's orders that the Indians were not to be molested, that the troops were not to have anything to say to them, directly or indirectly, for fear of affronting them. That was all. The column reformed and marched on.[91]

Presently they heard the sound of cannon. The seventeen booms of a General's salute echoed back and forth among the hills. Braddock had reached Fort Cumberland.[92]

XI

FORT CUMBERLAND

May 10–29, 1755

EVEN AS strengthened and enlarged after Governor Sharpe's visit the previous November, Fort Cumberland was not an imposing work. A palisade of raw green logs, stripped of their bark and planted in the ground to stand twelve feet high, it crowned a hill on the far side of narrow, knee-deep Wills Creek at the confluence of the creek and the Potomac, now winding sharply through the wooded mountains. Embrasures for twelve cannon and loopholes for small arms had been cut in the stockade, an enclosure about two hundred yards long and fifty wide. The Union Jack hung from its flagpole.[1]

Six companies of Halkett's regiment and the Virginians who had marched with him had pitched camp on the stumpy river hillside behind the fort.[2] Directly beyond the white pattern of their tents rose a wooded wall of mountain, leafy green, sheer, and forbidding. Wills Creek flowed into the river from a gray rocky narrows in the mountain wall, 1500 to 1700 feet high. Scattered along the creek and the Maryland side of the river, at the foot of the fort-topped hill, were half a dozen cabins and shanties. In a lonely clearing across the Potomac, in Virginia territory, stood another large cabin, the storehouse of the Ohio Company.[3]

There was no bridge. The so-called "Virginia road," which the army had followed, crossed Wills Creek at a stoney ford and climbed the hill on the other side of the stream to the fort's gate.[4] Tumbling away in all directions, and broken only by the bending river, stretched a wilderness of heavily forested mountains.

"The most desolate place I ever saw," said the Widow Brown when she arrived.[5]

Harry Gordon, a Scottish engineer who had served under Cumberland in Flanders and had been recommended by the Duke to Braddock as a good man for laying out and supervising road construction, thought it useless to talk of putting such a place in a posture of defence.

"Three pieces of 6-pound cannon, with the advantage the ground would naturally give them, could knock the fort to pieces," he said.[6]

The last mile of road, cut through the trees from Cresap's place, had been level and shady but breathless for Dunbar's tired, sweaty Forty-Eighth in the burning brightness of that hot May afternoon. The soldiers splashed through the ford, glad to wet their feet with cold mountain water and pitched camp on the hill behind the fort, beside Halkett's regiment.[7] A detachment of Dunbar's relieved the fort guard, ordered to march back to Fraser's place as a grass guard with a squad of Virginia carpenters to build fences. The fort provided no pasture for the army's horses. Officers' mounts, pack animals, wagon teams were turned loose in the woods.[8] Braddock, who had noticed the lack of forage and grass along the road, dispatched Matthew Leslie, an assistant quartermaster, to Pennsylvania to buy oats.[9]

About a hundred Indians—men, women and children—had built huts and lean-tos of bark at the edge of the woods a quarter of a mile from the fort. The men were tall, greasy, and naked except for breach clouts and deerskin moccasins, their inflexible faces daubed with red, yellow, and black paint. The outer rims of their ears were slit and their tufts of hair stuck with feathers. The women, shawled in sleazy blankets, were well proportioned and seemed to have many children, the youngest bound to boards slung on their mothers' backs.[10]

The soldiers stared at the Indians. The Indians stared at the soldiers—from a distance, at first, spellbound by the regular movements of so many men, all dressed exactly alike, in cocked hats, red coats, white breeches, and tan gaiters, and all manipulating their muskets in unison. After the soldiers had pitched their tents the boldest of the Indians peeked inside. And the soldiers, forgetting the orders they had received back along the road, traded pennies and buttons for bear claws. Hardened old redcoats leered at the squaws and tried to talk to them.[11]

To the men of the Forty-Eighth who relieved the fort guard, the inside of the stockade was as disappointing as the outside. During their fourweek march from Alexandria they had subsisted almost entirely on salt provisions. Now they looked around hopefully for a sutler or a cookshop that might be selling cheap ale and mutton chops. There was not even a well in the fort. The garrison lugged its water up the hill in buckets from Wills Creek.[12]

The General's tent was pitched outside the gate, but he was lodged in a room in the fort.[13] Mrs. Browne applied to Col. Innes, the fort's provincial commander, for quarters inside the fort. The Colonel was glad to oblige the lady but as she later wrote in her diary:

"I was put into a hole that I could see daylight through every log, and a port hole for a window; which was as good a room as any in the fort." [14]

The tired, chigger-bitten malcontents of the English army she had followed across the ocean complained that no sane British ministry would send British troops to campaign in such a god-forsaken wilderness. They grumbled that they were freeborn Englishmen, not obliged to obey orders if not properly fed. Inexperienced younger officers, who thought such mutterings mutinous, retorted that the men had been in Ireland too long, that they had been tainted by factious popish pamphlets and Jacobite agents.[15]

"We will get the better of that," said one bumptious subaltern. "We will see which will be tired first, they of deserving punishments or we of inflicting them. . . . In Europe they were better fed than taught; now they must be better taught than fed." [16]

Braddock himself was greatly concerned about the want of fresh meat. There were no cattle at the fort. Dinwiddie had assured him that 500 head of beeves would be waiting, that 1,100 would be delivered to the army in June and August.[17] Maj. Charles Dick, a Dinwiddie-appointed colonial commissary who was supposed to have bought beef and flour and arranged for delivery to the army, could not be found. He had gone to Williamsburg to settle his accounts.[18] Braddock ordered a public market established at the fort under the supervision of the captain of the picket, and prices fixed at a penny in the pound above prevailing rates to encourage "the peasants," as Captain Orme described the backwoodsmen who came to the fort.[19] But "the peasants" had little fresh food for sale. They dealt almost exclusively in fiery, colorless homemade whiskey, as popular with the Indians as it soon became with the troops.[20]

Most of the Indians at the fort had been brought down from Pennsylvania by George Croghan,[21] the same George Croghan to whom St. Clair had denounced the Quaker colony and its governor a month ago. Braddock had expected more Indians to be waiting for him.

"Where are the rest?" he asked Croghan.

"I don't know," said the trader.

"Governor Dinwiddie told me at Alexandria that he had sent for four hundred which would be here before me."

"I know nothing of that," said Croghan.[22]

Those he had brought down from Pennsylvania were all he could gather at his home near Carlisle when he had received orders from Governor Morris to take them to Braddock's camp, Croghan said.[23] He added that Captain Montour, a Virginia interpreter, was at the fort. Maybe Montour could answer His Excellency's question. Braddock sent for Montour.[24]

Andrew Montour, an Indian whose maternal grandfather had been a Frenchman, wore brass pendants in his ears and dressed in grotesque colonial fashion, shirt tail out and hanging over his trousers under a bright red satin waistcoat. His half-breed mother, a native of Canada, had been taught that Christ was a Frenchman crucified by the English, but Montour preferred the English to the French. He spoke the language of both, as well as several Indian dialects, and the Indians held him in high esteem.[25]

Brought to Braddock's tent, Montour told the General that another trader-interpreter, Nathaniel Gist, had set out some time ago to bring in the Cherokees. Whether they would come, Montour could not say.

"What about the Delawares and the Shawnees?" Braddock asked.

Croghan had already sent a messenger, telling them to meet him at Wills Creek.[26] Braddock told him to send another message.[27] Washington cautioned Braddock privately not to trust Croghan too far. Washington had had dealings with him the previous summer. "Not to be depended upon," Washington told the General.[28]

But the Indians seemed to like Croghan. They called him "our brother, the Buck." For years they had traded with him, often for rum. And one of them, a chief variously known as Monacatootha and Scarouady, liked his liquor well enough to stay drunk for two days at a time. He was a tough old warrior, a veteran of thirty fights in which he boasted of having killed seven men and taken eleven prisoners. Into the skin of each of his cheeks was cut a crude bow and arrow, and on his breast, a tomahawk.[29]

At dark all the Indians returned to their camp. Later that night they danced around a fire, yelling to the beat of an Indian drum and the rattle of gourds. Lieut. Spendlowe's sailors, watching the dancers and listening to their hideous noise, were interested mostly in the women. Once or twice a year, the seamen were told, the women danced with men of their own choosing, lay with them for a week, then returned to their own husbands.[30]

This information, like a current report that English traders rarely lacked an Indian female bedfellow, passed rapidly through the camp. Most of the soldiers had never thought of female Indians, only of heathen warriors, paid £3 Sterling by the French for every English scalp they took. The stern, implacable faces of the men, apparently insensible to pleasure or pain, made it easy to believe some of the stories told about them.[31]

Perhaps because Washington knew more about Indians, Indian traders, and interpreters than any officer on his staff—Nathaniel Gist's father, Christopher Gist, had been one of Washington's guides over the mountain to the forks of the Ohio in 1753—Braddock formally appointed the tall Virginian an aide-de-camp the day they reached Fort Cumberland.[32] A sort of gentleman adventurer with no military responsibility except keeping an orderly book, Washington was without rank and subject only to the General's orders, but eager to learn anything professional soldiers could teach him. One of the first things he learned about was boots. "As wearing boots is quite the mode and mine in a declining state," he wrote his brother John, back in the tidewater country, "I must beg you to procure me a pair that is good and neat." [33]

On Sunday, the day after his arrival at the fort, the General's guard was remounted. Braddock announced that he would hold a levee at his tent every morning from 10 to 11 o'clock, that the troops would immediately begin field days, and that each man would be issued twelve rounds of powder for practice firing.[34] The

uproar in the Indians' camp the previous night led to the publication of a special order inscribed in Washington's orderly book:

"It is His Excellency General Braddock's orders that no officer,
soldier or others give the Indian men, women or children any rum
or other liquor or money upon any account whatever." [35]

Braddock now had had his first good look at the illimitable woods
and 2,500-foot mountains beyond Wills Creek. The narrow, unim-
proved "Virginia road" which wound away behind the stockade,
through the trees and up the side of Wills Mountain to a gap 600
feet above the river, was not a road. It was a mountain trail, an
Indian trail, widened a little the year before by Washington as far
as he got on his way to Fort Duquesne.[36] Unless it improved vastly
after its steep drop down the other side of the mountain, the trail
would be impassable for Braddock's coach, much less a train of
artillery. A return was ordered sent in to the Major of Brigade on
the number of men among the troops who understood the spring-
ing of rocks. Three hundred were put to work on the road.[37]

On Monday, May 12, the General held a council of war and congress for the Indians at his tent. Officers waited on him in full regimentals. The General's guard, drawn that day from Dunbar's
Forty-Eighth, received the Indians with rested arms. Croghan cere-
moniously presented the Indians first with a string, then with a
belt of wampum, while interpreting a speech by the General. In
his speech Braddock extolled the redcoats as friends and brothers of
the Indians. He said he and his army had come from England to
settle the Indians happily in their own country and to make the
French ashamed and hungry. All misunderstandings of former times
had been buried under the great mountain behind the fort, Braddock said, but any Indians who did not come into camp would be
treated as an enemy. Braddock also told the Indians, through his
interpreter, that he would have presents soon for them.[38] Gage was
bringing a wagon load—red and black stockings, gold and silver
tassels, looking glasses, beads, buttons, small brass kettles, brass
wire, ribbons and men's cheap ruffled shirts. At the end of the council Bishop and the General's batmen served drams around.[39]

Over the week-end the food situation had not improved. Braddock, who understood good eating as well as any man, had two
cooks—Bishop and Delboux—reputedly competent to produce an
excellent ragout from a pair of old army boots.[40] But neither fresh
meat nor flour was available. The troops complained of mouldy

biscuit. Twenty casks of salt beef opened that day for distribution to the Forty-Eighth regiment were found to be dry and without pickle.[41] The soldiers refused to eat the musty, stinking meat.[42] Braddock ordered the beef surveyed. Lieut. Spendlowe and Gordon, the engineer, condemned all twenty casks.[43]

The beef, drawn from supplies at the fort, had been packed by Col. Cresap on instructions from Maryland's Governor Sharpe.[44] Spendlowe and Gordon remembered . . . the log house with the stockade on the river bank, the last halt before Wills Creek—the Big Spoon, the Rattlesnake Colonel.

"A damned rascal," said Spendlowe.[45]

The market which Braddock had ordered established in the camp failed to materialize. There was no question of money. The army was willing to buy. But any backwoodsman with as much as a little Indian corn for sale found ready purchasers as soon as he reached the outer picket lines of the fort. This resulted in the issuance of another order: no soldier, under pain of death, should stop anybody bringing either food or forage into camp. But none came to market.[46] No farmers, no millers, no drovers looked for markets in the woods that far beyond the larger settlements.

That Monday ended with a gust. To many British soldiers, unaccustomed to western Maryland weather, the thunder and lightning of the summer storm and the wind sweeping down the mountains seemed unusually violent. Insecure tents were blown down and their occupants drenched.[47] Early next morning the sun was out again, bright, and the day grew so excessively warm that no effort was made to exercise the regulars until evening. Ensign Allen of the Forty-Fourth tried to drill the American recruits in platoon firing. British officers, watching the languid, unsoldierly performance of his bob-tailed squads, said it was hopeless. Most of the American officers seemed to be as ignorant as their men of military fundamentals.

"Make them as useful as possible," said Braddock in despair.[48]

The Americans were brigaded with the regulars. Two companies of Virginia rangers, one of Maryland rangers, and one of Virginia carpenters were placed under Halkett's command, along with two independent New York companies and a South Carolina detachment which had garrisoned the fort before the other troops arrived. The other Virginians and a North Carolina contingent, not yet accounted for but on its way to the fort, according to Dinwiddie, were assigned to Dunbar.[49]

Neither regiment of regulars had been recruited yet to the recommended strength of 1,000.[50] There had been no rush of Americans to join the army. And when rattlesnake Colonel Cresap arrived in camp from Annapolis with letters from Governor Sharpe asking that eight Maryland recruits be sent back to where they came from, he was almost as welcome as if he had delivered another barrel of bad beef. In his letters, one addressed to Braddock and another to Orme, Sharpe said four of the eight were convicts and the others indentured servants, all runaways enlisted by Lieut. Brereton of the 48th while loading stores at Rock Creek.[51]

Capt. William Poulson, a Scotsman commanding the company of Virginia carpenters attached to Halkett's brigade, waited on Braddock to complain that he had been slandered. Reports had been circulated that Poulson had served with the Jacobites in 1745.[52] The Captain previously had asked Governor Sharpe that a court-martial inquire into his character.[53] Now he made a similar request of Braddock. A general court-martial was sitting at the moment with Major William Sparke of Dunbar's as its president. But Braddock turned down Poulson's request. No inquiry into the Captain's past was necessary, he said. He did not question it. Let Poulson's traducers come forward or keep their mouths shut.[54] Sparke's court-martial had other things to do.

Private Luke Woodward of Dunbar's had been arrested for desertion. Three other soldiers of the same regiment were charged with the theft of a keg of beer valued at thirty-three shillings in colonial currency, but a priceless treasure in a wilderness without a tavern. The court found Woodward guilty and sentenced him to death. Braddock approved the sentence but pardoned the deserter. The other three soldiers, found guilty of stealing the keg of beer, were sentenced to be lashed by the drummers of the Forty-Eighth at the head of the line.[55]

Discipline was becoming difficult. Indian women and raw frontier whiskey demoralized the discontented redcoats. Some of the soldiers had picked up women on their march from Alexandria. Others had taken Indian squaws into their tents and were drawing extra rations for them.[56] Even officers grew scandalously fond of Indian women, buying their favor with money that led to quarrels with husbands and fathers.[57] One Indian girl, Bright Lightning,

the daughter of a chief, White Thunder, was in a fair way to become the mistress of a regiment when Braddock issued orders forbidding Indian women to enter the army camp.[58]

As a practical soldier Braddock had no intention of continuing
his march over the mountains until assured his column could be
supplied. Obviously the troops could not live upon the country,
as armies did in Europe. Before them lay nearly a hundred miles of
wooded mountains with neither towns nor cultivated countryside
to pillage. Until provided with beef, flour, forage, and with transport to carry stores and supplies, the army would either remain
where it was or return to the settlements.[59]

For a short time this delay was not serious. The complete column had not yet closed. In addition to the troops reported on
their way from Carolina and others expected from New York,
Lieut.-Col. Gage was still toiling up around the dreadful bends of
that dusty mountain road from Winchester with the artillery and
forty-two wagons of powder, wheel barrows, sand bags, and other
ordnance stores Braddock thought he needed for a successful attack on the French fort.[60]

Once Gage pulled into camp at Wills Creek, the situation of
Braddock's army would become acute. There would be more troops,
more horses to be fed. Assuming that adequate supplies reached
Braddock by the time Gage arrived, permitting the army to resume its march, the column still would be dependent upon horse
and wagon for the transport of those supplies to the troops on their
march from Fort Cumberland to Fort Duquesne. When the road
climbed the mountain behind Fort Cumberland, it swung away
from the Potomac river. Water transport was out of the question.
More teams were needed. The forty-two coming with Gage and
those already in camp were not enough to carry half the supplies
Braddock had hoped to take on the next leg of his march.[61]

Some of the provincial teamsters who reluctantly had hauled
stores and supplies from Alexandria to Fort Cumberland already
had gone home with their wagons. Others disappeared every night.
So did the army's horses, presumably in charge of a grass guard
but actually—because the army had no forage—running loose in the
woods to live on leaves and underbrush or starve. The carpenters
had found fences impractical. The horse and wagon masters tried
hobbles. But horses continued to vanish after dark. And the camp

was still far short of the 200 wagons and 2,500 horses Dinwiddie had promised to have there by May 10.[62]

"I see no prospect of moving from this place soon, as we have neither horses nor wagons enough and no forage except what is expected from Philadelphia," Washington wrote to his brother. "Therefore, I am convinced, that the troubles and difficulties we must encounter in passing the mountains, for the want of proper conveniences, will equal all the difficulties of the campaign; for I conceive the march of such a train of artillery in these roads to be a tremendous undertaking. As to any danger from the enemy, I look upon it as trifling, for I believe the French will be obliged to exert their utmost force to repel the attacks to the northward where Gov. Shirley and others, with a force of 8,000 men, will annoy their settlements and attempt their forts." [63]

On May 13 a short string of belled packhorses came jingling up the trail from Philadelphia, loaded with sugar, tea and some of the other delicacies which the Franklins had purchased for Dunbar's officers, ostensibly the gift of a "committee." Dunbar immediately got off a note of acknowledgment to the elder Franklin: "I am desired by all the gentlemen who the committee have been so good as to think of in so genteel a manner, to return them their hearty thanks." [64]

Next day another string of horses arrived with more gift-packs for the gentlemen of the officers corps, but the ordinary soldiers were no better off than before.

Twenty-two more casks of Cresap's barrelled beef had been condemned when Major Dick, the Virginia commissary, rode in from Williamsburg, his accounts there still unsettled.[65]

And where were the five hundred beeves promised by the Governor of Virginia? General Braddock wanted to know.

Dick blamed a Virginia contractor named Hite. He told the General that Hite had failed to make deliveries because a Virginia Assembly committee would not confirm his contract. Dick said the trouble lay in the manner in which the cattle were to be weighed up and paid for after slaughter. The contract had specified that the so-called fifth quarter of heads, hides, and hoofs should be paid for at the same rate as the other four. Dick spoke his mind freely about the assembly committee refusing to approve the contract, one point at least upon which he and Braddock were in agreement.[66]

Where was this fellow Hite? As Orme understood it, he had been paid part of his money for the beeves.[67] Was that true? Bring in Hite. This was not difficult. Hite was in camp. Called to Braddock's headquarters he told the General that because of the assembly's refusal to approve his contract the agreement was void. Braddock told him to forget contracts and drive in the cattle. The army would pay for them. Hite said he was sorry, but he had recalled his factors, as far away as Carolina. He could promise no deliveries earlier than September and then only at a higher price, one third down now.

Braddock lost his temper.[68]

A letter which Dick had brought him from Williamsburg did not restore it. Dinwiddie had written: "I hope the deputy paymaster brought along a good supply of money." [69]

The Governor's letter was a reply to the one Braddock had written from Winchester. It expressed regret that Captain Steuart should have dunned him £100 for horses. Dinwiddie had given Steuart £325 for horses—but the £100 would be repaid at Braddock's pleasure. As for the commissary calling upon the General for three or four thousand pounds, it should be understood that the colony of Virginia would pay for the subsistence of no troops but its own.[70]

Shirley took down a sharp reply from Braddock's dictation:

What was all this nonsense about fifth quarters—hides, heads and horns—in a contract to provide army beef? What did the Governor of Virginia expect the army to eat? How was it to move without wagons to carry its stores? Regardless of who was to pay for it, Dinwiddie had permitted himself to be deceived by his own people. There was no integrity in any of them and, apparently, their magistrates lacked authority. A Governor should force a people to obey his edicts.[71]

Garbled accounts of the General's angry letter became the talk of the camp.

> Just as I wrote this [said one homesick British officer in the midst of a letter home] we hear the best news I ever heard in my life. The General hath declared to the Virginians that if they do not furnish us with wagons and provisions in two days he will march back; he has just upbraided them for exposing the King's troops, by their bragging and false promises. They undertook to furnish us with horses, bread and beef, and really have given nothing but carrion for meat, Indian corn for bread, jades for horses which cannot carry themselves. These assurances of furnishing everything has deceived the General hitherto,

and he, out of zeal for the service, hath undergone the utmost difficulties; but now it is impossible to go farther without they comply with the promises, they are weak or wicked enough to make, for certainly they were never able to perform them; it is surprising how much they bragged before we left the settlements of what plenty they would furnish us with at the cowpens and in the woods; these circumstances has brought the General into the present difficulties, and he has very justly told them, that if he marched any farther without a supply, he should be justly charged with destroying His Majesty's troops in the deserts, and thereby occasion the destruction of Virginia by encouraging the French; that if he was not supplied in two days he would march back and lay their breach of faith before His Majesty.

I now begin to hope that I shall once more have the pleasure of seeing you and the rest of my friends. Pray acquaint my dear Mr. M——
that I desire him not to sell my farm since I hope soon to be over.⁷²

Satisfied that he could depend no longer upon Dinwiddie or the Virginia commissaries for supplies but must provide them himself, Braddock packed Washington off that night to Col. Hunter, the agent at Hampton, with an order for £4,000 sterling. Riding down the way toward Winchester next day, Washington met Lieut.-Col. Gage, still on the march with two companies of Halkett's and the last division of the train, field pieces, howitzers, cohorns, and wagons. Gage reported that he had gotten away from Alexandria only by impressing horses, and that he found neither forage nor pasture on the way. Drought was ruining pastures everywhere.⁷³

Gage's column reached the fort that afternoon. He and the officers of Halkett's two companies with him found brother officers of their regiment dejected. Captain Bromley of the Forty-Fourth, had just died. The camp was hot and dusty. The troops were dispirited over the lack of fresh food. Salt rations were short. The commissaries had orders to issue provisions only in strict accord with strength returns sent the brigade major by commanders of each unit.⁷⁴

Another public congress of Indians, announced for Saturday, had been postponed until Sunday.⁷⁵ The Indians were still a problem, drunk, sulky, and so unnaturally noisy after nightfall that another order published that day said:

> Any Indian, trader, soldier, or follower of the army who shall dare to give liquor to any of the Indians or shall receive or purchase from them any of their presents made to them by His Majesty through General Braddock, shall suffer the severest punishment a court-martial can inflict.⁷⁶

Sunday, May 18, was unusually warm.[77] Except for occasional gusts, no rain had fallen for weeks.[78] Both Wills Creek and the Potomac lay low on their mud-cracked banks. At 10 o'clock that morning the drums of the Forty-Fourth beat the *Dead March* in the lifeless air along the river flats at the head of Captain Bromley's funeral procession. A captain's guard marched before the corpse, firelocks reversed. All the officers in camp followed, two and two. At the grave, outside the palisaded fort on the hill, the guard formed two lines, facing each other, rested on their arms, muzzles downward. The coffin was carried between the lines, Bromley's sword and crimson sash on top. Chaplain Philip Hughes of the Forty-Fourth read the service. The guard fired three volleys over the grave.[79]

At noon the Indians gathered again at the General's tent.[80] Braddock made a speech, urging all of them to take up the hatchet against the French by serving his army as scouts, and asking those with families in camp to send their wives and children home. Rings, knives, paint, pieces of cloth, some of the presents brought to the Fort by Gage, were handed out, along with strings and belts of wampum. The Indians promised an answer next day. That night they danced in their own camp and kept the sailors awake with another "terrible noise." [81]

Walpole's godson, Captain Horatio Gates, the young officer who had served with Cornwallis in Nova Scotia and whose advice on North American affairs had been sought by Newcastle the previous summer, arrived at the fort next day with another independent company from New York. They were just in time for the final pow-wow.[82] As soon as retreat had beat, the drum majors of the two regiments marched their drummers and fifers to the artillery park.[83] The Indians congregated around the General's marquee, banked with red coated officers waiting to hear what they had to say.

It took them a long time to say it, in their ceremonial fashion, but they finally reached the point: they would take the war path against the French. When Braddock replied, through Croghan, that he was their friend, he would never deceive them, the Indians seemed to go wild, bellowing war whoops, arching their bodies into intense, grotesque postures and screaming. Croghan explained that the French were their perpetual enemies. Braddock led the way to the artillery park where three howitzers, three 12-pounders, three cohorns were fired for the Indians' benefit while the fifes and drums of the two regiments thumped and shrilled a spirited strain called a *point of war*.[84]

The sun went down red behind the mountains. The first stars glittered in the east. The Indians went back to their camp where they ate a bullock.[85] Later that night they danced a war dance, treading a large ring around two fires while the squaws and old men not dancing beat time to a savage chant on drums of deerskin over small brass kettles. The redcoats stood around and watched silently, as they had watched a cricket match by daylight back home.[86]

Into the firelit ring leaped war-painted braves, their oily, naked bodies gleaming, some wearing the heads and skins of forest beasts. They divided into two war-whooping groups, charged each other in mock battle with wild, unearthly cries, and ran off to leave a single warrior flay the ground with his tomahawk. In a mimic life-and-death struggle with an imaginary enemy, this lone warrior finally triumphed and went through the motions of scalping his victim. He held up a real scalp, a dry one, chanting the achievements of his tribe, the names of its warriors, the number of scalps each had taken in feats of war against the French.[87]

To British soldiers watching him, this was a new and terrifying revelation of Indian character. They knew now what Americans ment by the "scalp halloo," what an Indian looked like when painted and stripped for battle. Now they could believe all the frontier atrocity stories they had heard. How Indians tore off women's breasts, shook bloody scalps of murdered husbands in their faces, took children by the heels and beat out their brains against a tree. How they cut off the heads of their victims, ripped open their bellies and tore out their bowels. How they buried mutilated captives up to their necks and built scorching fires near their faces until their brains boiled and their eyeballs burst and gushed from their sockets. This was the cruel, inhuman savage, merciless and stealthy, the ferocious enemy who lay in the woods on the other side of the mountain, waiting.[88]

Earlier that day an express from Winchester had delivered a packet from Philadelphia at the General's headquarters.[89] In the packet were a draft of Evans's new map of Pennsylvania and two letters, one from Morris to Braddock and the other from Richard Peters, the Pennsylvania provincial secretary, to young Shirley.[90]

Braddock was glad to see the map, although it convinced him that a route through Shippensburg would have been shorter than the road through Wills Creek. But the letter from Morris was disturbing. After informing him what progress had been made on the new road toward the Youghiogheny, the Pennsylvania Governor went into the history of the project at some length, making it plain that he did not care for the attitude of the General's quartermaster general. He wrote:

> I should not have been so particular as to this matter had not Sir John St. Clair taken the liberty to speak of my conduct in it in a very improper way to the persons I am employed upon this service, which may lessen me in the eyes of those I am appointed to command but cannot in the least contribute to His Majesty's service. Had he wrote me on this head, I should have been obliged to him, but as he took another method I think it unbecoming me to take any other notice of it than what I have done in answer to your letter being satisfied that you want no proofs of my attachment to the crown or zeal for His Majesty's service.[91]

Shirley's letter from Peters in the Philadelphia packet was in reply to a note which the General's moody military secretary had written while in low spirits. In an effort to cheer him up Peters said:

> Mr. Franklin has had excellent success and I suppose you may have not only wagons enough but single horses, and then your march over the hills will be pleasant—don't take your notions of the country from that dismal inhospitable place, Will's Creek—the farther you advance the more grass you will find, and a finer country.[92]

The two-day ultimatum reportedly served on the Virginians was still uppermost in the minds of some of Braddock's British subalterns on Tuesday, May 20, when five sober "Quakers" rode into camp, plump men on fat horses. They went directly to the General's tent and curiosity drew a group of young officers after them.[93]

Braddock recognized one of the five as Benjamin Franklin's son, William. William had ridden ahead of the promised wagons, now coming up the road from Conochocheague. Within two weeks after the appearance of their advertisement, the Franklins had disbursed Braddock's £800 and another two hundred of their own in advance horse-and-wagon hire. They would have done even better had not half the wagons in York county failed to pass inspection. The wagons arrived in camp that night—ninety-one sturdy Pennsylvania farm wagons. Eleven from Philadelphia were loaded with the parcels of butter, cheese, wine and spirits suggested by young Franklin. These and twenty more pack horses were the gift of a Pennsylvania assembly committee to Braddock's subaltern officers who, for the first time in weeks, sat down to a decent mess.[94]

"A duty so long disused that it was a tour of fatigue to the teeth," said one after supper.[95]

Dunbar wrote the elder Franklin another letter of thanks:

> Your kind present is now all arrived, and shall be equally divided tomorrow between Sir Peter Halkett's subalterns and mine, which I apprehend will be agreeable to the committee's intent. This I have made known to the officers of both regiments who unanimously desire me to return the generous benefactors their most hearty thanks to which be pleased to add mine.[96]

Halkett wrote Franklin:

> The officers of my regiment are most sensible to the favors conferred on the subalterns by your assembly, who have made so well-timed and so handsome a present. At their request and desire I return their thanks, and to the acknowledgement of the officers I beg lef to add mine, which you, I hope, will do me the favor for the whole to offer to the assembly and assure them that we shall on every occasion do them the justice due for so seasonable and well-judged an act of generosity.[97]

"Though this was good news, I did not like it," one pessimistic subaltern wrote home, after describing the arrival of the gift.[98] "I feared it would occasion our stay and prevent our marching back. Besides, it was ominous, your cheese and your bacon being the bait that draw rats to destruction."

The same night the Pennsylvania wagons rolled into camp, a lone Delaware Indian appeared with a story of having left the French fort only six days past. He said the post had a garrison of only fifty men but that a reinforcement of nine hundred was expected. When Braddock's army had advanced across the mountains, he said, the French planned to fall on the back settlements of the English and massacre their inhabitants, blowing up their own fort when the British troops appeared before it.[99]

"I believe this fellow is a villain," said Gordon, the engineer.[100]

In view of the failure of the Delawares to answer Groghan's message there was no reason to trust this man. But Braddock dutifully passed the warning on to the governors of Maryland, Pennsylvania, and Virginia, at the same time informing them that if his operation against the French was successful, he would expect them

to be prepared to arm, man, and provision the captured work.[101]
In his letter to Sharpe he added:

> As I find it impractical to take my chariot with me, if you will send
> for it and the harness for the six horses I shall be much obliged to you
> and you will make use of it till I want it. I shall be still more so as I
> am sure it will be less damaged by good usage than by lying still and
> will also save you the trouble of sending for another to England as it
> shall be at your service at your own price when I leave this part of the
> world. Let your servants take care of harness and have it oiled if you
> don't use it. I shall leave directions with Col. Innes to deliver chariot,
> harness, spare axel and pole to your order.[102]

The General's secretary was disturbed by the whole Indian situation[103] With the exception of that lone Delaware, no other member
of his tribe, no Shawnees, no Cherokees had come into camp in
response to Croghan's messages.[104] Replying to the personal letter
he had received from Peters, Shirley remarked that only about fifty
Indians were expected to go with the army. He added with his
usual frankness:

> Upon our arrival at this fort we found Indian affairs so ignorantly
> conducted by Col. Innes, to whom they were committed, that novices
> as we were, we have taken 'em into our management. It is not for me
> to remark what might have been done or what ought to have been
> done for the security of the General's service or for his ease in con-
> ducting the present expedition (as it is called) in the most effectual
> manner for the purposes intended by it. Here we are and I imagine
> we will move from here in about a fortnight. The difficulties which
> have unavoidably attended our motions, and such as have been occa-
> sioned through ignorance in some and insolence in others are in-
> numerable; with the assistance we have had from Mr. Franklin, who
> is almost the only person to whom the General is indebted for either
> horses or wagons, we hope to get over the mountains. Governor Mor-
> ris has taken a very sensible and proper notice of Sir John St. Clair's
> behavior in his letter to the General. Sir John begins to find that he
> has mistaken himself and to draw in his horns.[105]

To his friend Morris, Shirley wrote:

> You have wrote very properly to the General with regard to the
> road to the Youghiogheny, and set your conduct in a very fair light,
> and such a one, as at least, cannot deserve censure. I am persuaded Sir
> John will not be in a hurry in making representations to England. He
> has received what is called in the language of the camp, a *set down.* . . .
> It is not easy to give you a picture of the business we do, or the
> manner in which it is done. I do not look upon it to be always trans-

acted in the most masterly way, but considering all circumstances, believe it may have its merits.[106]

That rattlesnake Colonel Cresap's son, Michael, had been told to load the Pennsylvania wagons with the army's flour when they passed the stone storehouse at Conococheague. But only a few were loaded and some of the flour was in green timber casks that would soon turn it sour.[107]

"Had he been a French commissary he could not have acted more to their interest," stormed Braddock when told of young Cresap's failure to obey his instructions.[108]

He ordered thirty wagons back to Winchester for forage and three hundred packhorses to Conococheague for the rest of the flour. A detachment of light horse from the general's bodyguard, to escort the pack animals, was ordered to arrest Cresap and bring him in.[109] But they never found him. Someone told him they were after him and he made off.[110]

The people of Pennsylvania appreciated the protection of the army against the French and Indians, the Quakers with young Franklin told Braddock, but they themselves were opposed to warfare and thought he should try to make a treaty with the French, as Oglethorpe had done with the Spaniards in the south. Young Franklin shared his father's apprehensions of a surprise attack on Braddock's marching column by the French and Indians. He reminded Braddock that the deeper his army advanced into the wilderness, the more difficult it would become to supply him, even after the proposed new Pennsylvania road had been cut.

Impressed by the wagon train and the gifts brought from Philadelphia, and noting that even the shabbier Pennsylvania teamsters had a well-fed look in contrast to the army's lean, lank Virginians, Braddock's officers closed in on the Quakers with questions about their colony and their sect.[111]

"They are a very frugal people," one officer concluded after talking to them,[112] "and if not so would be as beggarly as their neighbors, the Virginians."

Next day the visitors left, young Franklin carrying a note of thanks from Braddock to his father, and a letter from Braddock to Governor Morris complimenting him on the zeal he was showing for the success of the expedition. Shirley's notes to Morris and Peters also were in the packet.[113]

Peters, having set out from Philadelphia to see for himself what progress had been made on the new road beyond Shippensburg, was coming down over Sidling Hill, on the Maryland-Pennsylvania, border, on his way to Wills Creek.[114] The day after Franklin's party had gone Peters rode into camp, a pious, polished English gentleman of fifty who had been ordained a priest in the Church of England and whose amiability and good sense quickly endeared him to both Orme and Shirley.[115]

With Peters was Sheriff John Potter of Cumberland County, Pennsylvania, and two prisoners. On the strength of Braddock's complaint in his letter from Winchester to Governor Morris about those two Irishmen trading with the French in western Pennsylvania, warrants had been issued for their arrest. Potter had brought in both men and was ready to turn them over to the army provost. Braddock suggested that the Sheriff take them back to the Pennsylvania county jail. Should a court martial find them guilty as charged, Braddock said, he might feel obliged to punish them too severely.[116]

The sheriff's prompt action, coming so soon after the delivery of the Pennsylvania wagons, put Braddock on the defensive. As for the Pennsylvania road, Peters had actually seen it under construction, 12 feet wide, now extending 20 miles west of Shippensburg and advancing toward the Youghiogheny at the rate of almost a mile a day. A hundred men were at work on it, and the number would be doubled. Original plans called for a fork in the road, one branch to Wills Creek and the other to the Turkey's Foot on the Youghiogheny, intersecting Braddock's route to Fort Duquesne. The proposed fork to Wills Creek would be useless after the army had left Fort Cumberland, Peters said. Why not abandon the fork and press forward with one main road? [117]

Braddock was agreeable, but repeated firmly that he would not budge from Fort Cumberland until assured by the Governor of Pennsylvania that the road to the Turkey's Foot would be completed in time for a summer campaign. Peters said the only way to be sure of that would be to provide an armed escort to protect the workmen. He doubted that they could be kept together a single day in case of an alarm from the Indians, and Indians might be expected to appear any time after the road crossed the mountains. Braddock said that was no business of his. It was up to the province of Pennsylvania to protect its own road workers.

Peters was not sure the General realized how annoying the Indians could be. He ventured to say that even the army would have its difficulties on the march, that it would need the practiced protection of both rangers and friendly Indians to get safely through the mountains to the French fort. The General was contemptuous of such danger, scorning the capabilities of an Indian attack. His primary concern was logistics. He complained at length of the failure of everybody with whom Dinwiddie had contracted for army provisions, forage, wagons, and horses.[118]

In his last letter from Williamsburg, Dinwiddie had said that he thought St. Clair was to take care of the wagons. As for beeves, Major Dick talked too much. Governor Dobbs of North Carolina was sending along five or six hundred cattle next month and Hite's contract, of course, amounted to jobbery.

"I should be sorry the expedition should suffer from trifles," wrote Dinwiddie. "At the same time I hate jobs. As there are large quantities of salt provisions provided, I cannot see the march of your forces will be delayed for want of provisions, and I doubt not of your having a sufficient supply of beeves in a proper time." [119]

Another note from Dinwiddie to Orme, regarding the shortage of tents for Virginia troops, suggested that the General's aide take up that matter with the Virginia quartermaster. The note concluded:

> I hear that provisions at Fort Cumberland begin to be scarce. Surely if Pennsylvania has performed their promise, flour cannot be wanting and if salt provisions are wanting you know there is a good quantity at Alexandria which can be sent if wagons can be had. My little family join me in kind regards to you and Mr. Shirley, sincerely wishing you health and all other felicity.[120]

In spite of the arrival of Franklin's wagons, his supply situation was still unsatisfactory, Braddock told Peters. Peters understood that only too well after a meal in the General's tent. The beef was not sweet. Only the highest ranking officers in camp had butter on their tables. Fresh meat was scanty and Peters heard a general complaint among officers of the want of "necessaries." [121]

Peters was fairly certain that all the flour ordered from Pennsylvania had been delivered by this time at Conococheague. There might have been a delay about milling it. And if necessary that already sent up by young Cresap in green barrels could be repacked in dry casks and sacks. Furthermore, Governor Morris had advanced £500 to St. Clair's assistant, Leslie, to buy army oats in the back counties.[122] But more than this was needed. Braddock proposed that Morris and Peters undertake contracts to lay in additional supplies of flour, wheat, beeves, salt beef, pork, or fish at Shippensburg by July 1 for three thousand men, promising to be accountable for all charges and expense.[123] Peters was reluctant to commit himself. It had been hard enough to provide flour and bacon for the road workers at Shippensburg, to say nothing of cooks, overseers, wagons, tools—and whiskey to keep them happy.[124]

From the General's tent Peters went over to the Indian camp to talk to Croghan, Montour, and Scarouady. The Indians were unhappy. They said Braddock never consulted them. Their wives dallied with his officers, plentifully supplied with rum and money. Even Braddock's protege Burton was wooing a squaw with promise of a repeater watch and other presents. Disturbed by what he heard and saw, Peters urged Braddock to put an end to the "licentiousness" which prevailed in camp, insisting that the Indian women be sent home to Pennsylvania. The General expected a certain amount of looseness among so many soldiers but he said he would forbid Indian women to enter the army camp.[125]

After Franklin's visit the troops had been told:

It is His Excellency's order that no sutler give any liquor to the Indians on any account; if anyone does, he will be severely punished.

The Provost is to go his round every day through all the roads leading to the camp. Every soldier or woman that he shall meet on the other side of the river, or beyond the advanced piquets without a pass from the regiment or the officer commanding the company to which they belong, he is to order his executioner to tie them up and give them fifty lashes and march the prisoners through the camp to expose them.

One gill of spirits mixed with three gills of water may be allowed every man per day, which the officers of the piquet are to see delivered out every day at 11 o'clock. Any sutler who shall sell any spirits to the soldiers without an officer being present shall be sent to the Provosts.[126]

Now, as a result of Peters' complaint, a further order was posted:

If any officer, soldier or follower of the army shall dare to give any strong liquor or money to the Indian men or women, if an officer he shall be brought to a general court martial for disobedience to orders, if a non-commissioned officer, soldier or follower of the army he shall receive 250 lashes without a court martial.[127]

Shirley was occupied as the judge advocate of the court-martial trying Lieut. McLeod of the Royal Regiment of Artillery, con-

fined to quarters by order of General Braddock, when Peters left
the Fort after a two-day visit.[128]

"Make my excuse for not taking leave of Mr. Shirley," Peters
told Orme.[129]

A congenial trio, the three of them looked forward to reunion
in Philadelphia when the army went into winter quarters at the
end of the campaign.[130] Braddock was thinking of Philadelphia,
too. In a packet of letters Peters carried away from the fort was
this one from Braddock to Morris:

> Dear Morris:
> You will, by the bearer, Mr. Peters, be informed of the situation I
> am in by the folly of Mr. Dinwiddie and the roguery of the assembly,
> and unless the road of communication from your province is opened
> and some contracts made in consequence of the power I have given, I
> must inevitably be starved. Sir John St. Clair (who by the way is
> ashamed of having talked of you in the manner he did) has employed,
> by the advise of Governor Sharpe, a fellow at Conochocheague, one
> Cresap, who behaved in such a manner in relation to the Pennsylvania
> flower that had he been a French commissary he could not have acted
> more to their interest. In short, in every instance but my contract for
> the Pennsylvania wagons, I have been deceived and met with nothing
> but lies and villany. I hope, however, in spite of this that we shall pass
> a merry Christmas together.
>
> E. Braddock.[131]

In another note to Morris, separately sealed, young Shirley
wrote:

> . . . I don't know what description Mr. Peters will give you of our
> camp and the principal persons in it, but as this goes in his packet I
> will give you mine, grounded upon the observation of several months.
> We have a G—— most judiciously chosen for being disqualified for the
> service he is employed in, in almost every respect. He may be brave
> for ought I know and he is honest in pecuniary matters. But as the
> King said of a neighboring governor of yours when proposed for the
> command of the American forces about a twelfth month ago, and rec-
> ommended as a very honest man though not remarkably able, "a little
> more ability and a little less honesty upon the present occasion might
> serve our turn better."
> It is a joke to suppose that secondary officers can make amends for
> the defects of the first. The main spring must be the mover. The
> others in many cases can do no more than follow and correct a little its
> motions. As to them, I don't think we have much to boast. Some are
> insolent and ignorant; others capable but rather aiming at showing
> their own abilities than making a proper use of them. I have a very
> great love for my friend Orme, and I think it uncommonly fortunate

for our leader that he is under the influence of so honest and capable a man, but I wish, for the sake of the public, he had some more experience of business, particularly in America.

As to myself, I came out of England expecting that I might be taught the business of a military secretary, but I am already convinced of my mistake. I would willingly hope my time may not be quite lost to me. You will think me out of humour. I own I am so. I am greatly disgusted at seeing an expedition (as it is called) so ill-concerted originally in England and so ill-appointed, so improperly conducted since in America; and so much fatigue and expense incurred for a purpose which, if attended by success, might better have been left alone. I speak with regard to our particular share.

However, so much experience I have had with the injudiciousness of public opinion that I have no little expectation, when we return to England, of being received with great applause. I am likewise further chagrined at seeing the prospect of affairs in America which, when we were at Alexandria I looked upon to be very great and promising, through delays and disappointments which might have been prevented, grown cloudy and in danger of ending in little or nothing. I have hopes that the attempt against Niagara will succeed.

I don't know whether there is any man but yourself to whom I would have wrote some parts of this letter or could at present have justified myself in doing it, but there is a pleasure in unburdening oneself to a friend. I should be glad you would burn it as soon as you have read it. I shall be very happy to have reason to retract hereafter what I have said here, and submit to be censured as moody and apprehensive.

I hope, my dear Morris, to spend a tolerable winter with you. Pray take no notice of any part of this letter in your answer, for fear of accident.[132]

Braddock could delay his advance no longer if the plan of campaign agreed upon at Alexandria was to be carried out in accord with his instructions. Two thousand New England troops had sailed for Nova Scotia under convoy of three men-of-war. Governor Shirley's regiment was under orders to move from Boston to Providence, whence transports would carry it to Albany, the rendezvous for the projected attack on Crown Point. There had been a delay in recruiting Pepperill's regiment, but another corps, raised in New Jersey by Col. Philip Schuyler, was on its way to Albany.[133]

The last of Braddock's own troops had closed up—two companies of Halkett's which had been left at Winchester and a company of North Carolina volunteers commanded by Capt. Edward Brice Dobbs, son of the Governor of North Carolina.[134] With Dobbs's company was a twenty-one-year-old wagoner, Daniel Boone. Quiet, serious, mild-mannered Boone was intensely curious about the country beyond the mountains. Any provincial soldier or frontiersman who had seen it found Boone an eager listener.[135]

Counting those sent back to Winchester and Conococheague, nearly 200 wagons with 300 teams or pack horses, 50 provided by Croghan, had been collected in the woods and on the flats along the river where Boone unhitched the teams. The horses were not the best looking beasts. All the weak, spavined, wind-broken cripples of the western settlements had been rounded up by army contractors. But provincial teamsters said work horses were not to be judged by looks alone, that many poor in flesh were as good as any draft animal that ever stretched a chain. A call went out for smiths and soon their hammers rang an anvil chorus around the forge cart of the artillery detachment.[136]

Carpenters, superintended by the ship's carpenter of the "Seahorse"—one of Spendlowe's sailors—built a float and squared timbers for a wagon bridge across Wills Creek. About a hundred wagons were loaded with provisions. Extra pay, ranging from sixpence per day for privates to three shillings for subalterns, was promised volunteers to help dig, cut, and blast away the worst spots marked by the engineers on the road up the mountain behind the fort. Bakers, relieved of all other duties, sweated over oven-pits, baking army bread of Pennsylvania flour.[137]

"Half sand, half dirt," they said.[138]

The regiments exercised daily. The mountains echoed platoon practice firings, sometimes at the rate of three a minute.[139]

At a council of war held in his tent, Braddock outlined his general plan of march to Halkett, Dunbar, St. Clair, Burton, Gage, Sparks, and Maj. Russell Chapman of Dunbar's regiment, asking them to be frank in comment and criticism. He said a party of 300 men, commanded by St. Clair, would move ahead to cut and clear the mountain road to a width of 12 feet. The companies would march two men deep, either side of the road, baggage in the middle, with advance and rear guards and flank parties to prevent surprise. Sir Peter Halkett would lead the main column and Dunbar would bring up the rear. At night the wagons would be drawn up in close order, the roadsides cleared of saplings and underbrush, and tents pitched in a single row along the line of baggage, facing outward.

Control of the column, extended along a narrow road through the woods and encumbered by horses and baggage, was an important part of Braddock's plan. Troops were to turn out in the morning when the drums beat the *General*. Tents would be struck on order and horses and wagons loaded when the drummers beat *Assembly*. Upon the beating of the *March* the column would move forward. While on the march, he said, command would be decentralized to some extent, each capain being responsible for the security of his own flank.[140]

Copies of this overall plan, approved by the council of war unanimously, were distributed to all field officers with instructions to discuss it with their captains.

Three more Delawares who had come into camp and waited over night to see him were received by Braddock in his tent on Wednesday, May 28. They asked him when he expected to move against the French fort. Within a few days, he said. They told him they would go home, gather more warriors, and meet him on the way— but no one believed them.[141] Nothing had been heard yet from the Shawnees. Gist's son, sent south to bring in the Cherokees, returned alone. He said he had fallen in with another trader, well supplied with liquor, who persuaded the Cherokees that Gist was an imposter because he had no written document, no seal from the Governor of Virginia.[142]

Arms and clothing had been given to the fifty warriors still in camp, but Col. Innes advised Braddock to take no more than ten with him on his march. They would be troublesome and of no service, Innes said. Croghan admitted that an Indian would eat twice as much as a white man, but thought Braddock should take all who were willing to go as scouts to prevent surprise. Innes' counsel prevailed. Braddock ordered all the Indians home except ten picked as scouts. Included in the ten were Scarouady's son, and Montour.[143]

Braddock had intended to set out on the next lap of his march with 70 days' supply of flour and 50 days' supply of meat, his own calculated minimum safety of provision. Informed by the wagon masters that there were not enough horses and wagons in camp to carry that big a load, he called another council of war. At this meeting, also attended by Orme, Braddock proposed that a party of 600 men go forward carrying eight days' provisions for 3,200 troops, that it march five days toward the first crossing of the Youghiogheny —about 30 miles beyond the fort—establish a magazine there, unload its wagons and send them back for more supplies.[144]

Again the council gave Braddock its approval, but Sir Peter Halkett, irritated by the presence of Orme, who seems to have done most of the talking, suggested that "everybody might afterwards sign their opinion." Braddock was offended by this remark, but Halkett, who probably had a line officer's prejudice against all guardsmen, made no secret of his dislike of the General's Coldstream aide. He privately hinted that Orme's advice might be the ruin of both Braddock and the expedition, and declared that if he ever succeeded to the command he would sack the handsome captain of the Coldstream as an aide.[145]

The delay caused by this change of plans did not improve troop discipline, which remained a problem even after the Indians left. Gaming had got so far out of hand that it was forbidden among enlisted men under a penalty of three hundred lashes without a court-martial. Young Shirley, as a judge advocate, was kept busy. Four of seventeen soldiers listed as deserters were arrested, found guilty by the court, and sentenced to the lash. Another was tried and found guilty of theft. He, too, got the lash, then was drummed out of camp with a halter around his neck.[146]

At daybreak Thursday, May 29, an usually cool morning, St. Clair started up the Wills Mountain road with the advance party of 600 men under Major Chapman's command, two field pieces, 50 wagons, a party of Indian guides, Engineer Gordon, Lieut. Spendlowe, and half a dozen seamen. The steepest ascent was almost a perpendicular rock, and a drop on the other side of the mountain was equally sharp. Three of the 50 wagons slithered off the rocky road and were smashed.

Braddock was not at all sure, after taking another look at the road, that it would be possible to get his heavy artillery up and down its steep grades safely. He called Gordon back, told him to go to work on the road again and see what he could do. Three hundred men were detailed for pick and shovel work.[147]

But all troops in camp remained under orders to hold themselves in readiness to march within twenty-four hours.[148]

Back at Hampton Roads, where Keppel's squadron still lay at anchor, Captain Samuel Hood, of the sloop Jamaica, wrote to a friend and patron, Admiral Thomas Smith, in England:

> . . . We are all in high spirits, as everything seems to go as can be wished. . . . I could wish the French stronger than they are, as I am afraid they will quit all the forts as fast as our troops can get to them. . . .[149]

XII

THE LONG MARCH

May 30–July 8, 1755

THE WARM SUNSHINE of western Maryland's early summer withered Gordon's working party on the mountain road. Even those who had volunteered became unhappy. The sixpence per day extra pay promised privates—drummers were to get ninepence, and sergeants a shilling—would be withheld, they were told, "as at present there is no public market and of course the men will have no opportunity of making use of the ready money." Forbidden whiskey was almost the only thing for sale in the camp around the fort at the foot of the mountain.[1]

It would be impossible to pass the entire army and all its baggage over that one narrow road in a single day. Troops and train would march in three divisions. Halkett would command the first, taking about a hundred wagons of stores, provisions, and powder. Burton would follow with the independent companies, artillery, and ammunition. Dunbar, last to leave, would take all remaining wagons and carrying horses. Innes had been appointed governor of the fort and would resume its command on Braddock's departure.[2] Some of the wagons were loaded, ready to go.[3]

Back from Williamsburg with the £4,000 for which he had been sent, Washington was elated at the prospect of getting on with the march, but young Shirley had no heart in it.[4]

"I shall be very glad when the campaign is over," said the General's moody military secretary.[5]

Washington had had some difficulty getting the £4,000 he

brought back to the General. A Mr. Johnson, paymaster of the forces, had arrived in Virginia from London at the end of March with £16,000 sterling. But Mr. Hunter, to whom Washington had been sent, had gone to Philadelphia before Washington reached Hampton. Dinwiddie had come to the rescue by providing the necessary cash.[6]

And when would the men in Gordon's working party receive their promised extra pay?

"His Excellency is so kind as to promise that he will see that they are punctually paid whatever is due them when they arrive in winter quarters," said an order read to the troops.[7]

In other words, when they arrived in Philadelphia, at the end of the summer's campaign.[8]

"I am hurried to death," Orme wrote hastily to Morris in the midst of last minute preparations to march, "and want the refreshments of Philadelphia." [9]

With a population of 30,000, Philadelphia was the largest town in the colonies and, from what Braddock's officers and men had been told, the most desirable. Captain Thomas Ord of the Royal Regiment of Artillery, finding the weather warm in Philadelphia when he arrived there from Newfoundland, on his way to join Braddock and take command of the train, had not hesitated to ask for a carriage for himself and wagons for thirteen non-commissioned officers and their baggage. (The Captain was fatigued and not used to horseback.) Leslie, St. Clair's assistant, sent to Philadelphia to buy forage, had enjoyed the luxury of a quarrel at a *billiard table!* Braddock's cook, Delboux, looked forward to opening a tavern in Philadelphia when his soldiering days were done.[10]

"As there will be an express going in a few days," said a notice from headquarters, "any officers that have *any* letters to send to Great Britain are desired to give them to either the General's aide-de-camp or to Mr. Shirley."[11]

Letters to Great Britain . . . where the English spring, almost as dry as Maryland's in 1755, had sapped lawns and leaves to a faded green. Rose bushes had put out fewer blossoms than usual.[12] The words of a song sung to a favorite tune at Vauxhall related how

> *The fatal shafts unerring move,*
> *I bow before thy altars, Love!*
> *I feel that soft resistless flame*
> *Glide swift through all my vital frame. . . .*[13]

Parliament had been prorogued. The King had gone back to Hanover.[14] The night before he went there had been a ball and supper at Bedford House. The Duchess of Bedford probably repeated a phrase she had heard Lord Herford use:

"I don't think a little war would do us any harm." [15]

Captain Gates' godfather, Horace Walpole, entertained the Bedfords at breakfast at Strawberry Hill. His goldfish were greatly admired.

"The war is quite gone out of fashion and seems adjourned to America," [16] Walpole wrote to his friend, Richard Bentley.

To America . . . where Spendlowe and his seamen, who had gone ahead with St. Clair, returned to Braddock's camp by the fort on Wills Creek. The road beyond the mountain was even worse than that over its crest. St. Clair had advanced only about fifteen miles when they left him.

Gordon, Spendlowe, and Burton went out next morning to look for a better route. By 2 o'clock Spendlowe was back saying he had found one. He had simply followed Wills Creek, up around the foot of the mountain, through the beetling narrows of cleft gray rock. Gordon rode out to look it over. When he came back he said he thought it would do. It would be only a mile or two longer than the old route over the top.[17]

So another working party of a hundred grumbling soldiers, with an armed guard of thirty against possible Indian attack, marched up the creek to open a 12-foot lane which Gordon had marked by blazing trees along the stream. It was a fairly level route but rough, steep, and swampy in spots. Gordon said it would be impassable in wet weather, but it was all right now.[18]

Braddock was beginning to believe that he had been on the wrong road from the start, that he should have landed his troops at Philadelphia, and marched across Pennsylvania.[19] His eagerness and anxiety for the success of his expedition, his impatience with provincial apathy and politics, often led him into sweeping denunciation of provincial honesty which provoked both Washington and Shirley. The General had not yet recovered from what he sarcastically termed "the fine promises" of Sharpe and Dinwiddie.[20] Together, he said, the two governors had produced only about 200 horses and twenty wagons. Excepting Franklin, "almost the only instance of ability and honesty I have known in these provinces," the General declared that until he left Frederick "the falsehood of every person with whom I was concerned" had been his daily experience.

Challenged by Washington or Shirley to sustain his wholesale indictment, Braddock had this answer: "It would be endless, sir, to particularize the number of instances of the want of public and private faith, and the most absolute disregard of all truth which I have met with." [21]

He had not changed his opinion of provincial recruits, now constituting about 1,100 of his 2,000 effective troops. They had so little courage and disposition for army life "that scarce any military service can be expected of them," he said. "It has cost indefinite pains and labor to bring them to any sort of regularity and discipline." [22]

Mindful that provincial officers drew on their provincial government for the expense of their recruiting, he added: "I am told they have made a very good hand of this year's recruiting affair, although I can get no proof of it." [23]

As for the fifty or so Indian warriors around the camp:

> When I arrived in America [Braddock recalled], I was assured that I might depend upon a great number of Indians from the southward, but the bad conduct of the Governor of Virginia has turned them entirely against us; in effect they [evidently he included all the colonial governors] behaved to the Indians with so little discretion that we must at present be at great expense to regain their confidence, and there is no trusting even those who have embraced our cause.[24]

With a Virginian's pride in all things Virginian, Washington was annoyed when Braddock made exceptions of Franklin, Morris, and other Pennsylvanians in his criticism of American lassitude.

"The chosen people," Washington scoffed. "They have furnished what their absolute interest alone induced them to do." [25]

Shirley found it easy to disagree with all professional soldiers. His position as Braddock's secretary burdened him with no official responsibility. No ghosts of Johnny Cope, Hawley "the Hangman," or the unlucky Ingoldsby haunted his camp bed. And his friendship for the governor of Pennsylvania kept him in almost constant hot water with Braddock's quartermaster general.[26]

In any argument at headquarters Sir John found it expedient to side with Braddock, but he was reluctant to make an exception of Morris among the Americans for whom he felt contempt. Sir John never forgot that he had urged the immediate construction of a new road across Pennsylvania as soon as he reached Virginia. And what happened?

"That road has not been set about until very lately," he said, and he held Morris responsible for the delay.

No magistrate in Virginia or, to the best of Sir John's recollection, in Maryland, had given himself the least trouble to collect country people to work on the roads or provide wagons for the army.

"On the contrary," he said, "everybody laid themselves out to put what money they could in their pockets." [27]

Braddock's normal anxiety as a commanding officer, his petulance under repeated delays and disappointments, were aggravated by the strain of a personal crisis. Approaching the end of an undistinguished but unblemished career, he was making his first and last cast for fortune. A wound at Blenheim had won Lieut.-Col. Alexander Spotswood, of the Earl of Bath's Tenth Foot, the governorship of Virginia.[28] Albemarle, the last governor of Virginia, and a former colonel of the Coldstream, was dead. Was it too much to hope that another Coldstreamer, defeating the French in North America, might reap a reward similar to Spotswood's? Morris had heard Braddock mentioned for the government of New York. . . .[29]

With other members of his staff Braddock's relations were those of any commanding general. Lower ranking officers, who may have resented his superiority as the veteran of an elite corp, thought him peevish, inclined to indolence, and glad to have subordinates take detail off his hands. With no social pretentions and his bad habit of spilling snuff on his waistcoat, he was regarded by some uncouth, but the fair-minded agreed he was sensible and good-natured.[30]

It was easy to understand why Orme was his favorite. Only Orme of the Coldstream measured up completely to Braddock's own rigorous standards for an officer. At the same time Braddock respected rank. Burton was his choice for the colonelcy of a regiment he planned to form later of the provincial companies. Orme was to succeed Burton as lieutenant-colonel of the Forty-Eighth. Morris, Braddock's aide from the Forty-Eighth, was to be Burton's lieutenant-colonel, and Capt. Robert Dobson of the Forty-Eighth, another Braddock favorite, was to be Burton's major.[31] Washington was still "Mr. Washington" but on the best of terms with Braddock, who already had granted two requests for special favors—the ap-

pointment of Townsend Washington, a cousin, as an assistant commissary and the bestowal of an ensign's commission in the Forty-
Eighth to young Anthony Strother, the son of one of Washington's
friends.[32]

Braddock seemed to sense that he had a weak regimental commander in Dunbar, who complained of ill health and wanted to
go home.[33] But the old Coldstreamer knew he could depend on Sir
Peter Halkett, the long-beaked colonel of the Forty-Fourth. Halkett
had the stern, disdainful face of a pompous fellow, and he might
despise Orme, but he had held a company together against the
Scots at Preston Pans.[34]

Gordon's working party, relieved from day to day by fresh details, was a week building the new road around the foot of the
mountain.[35] This gave everybody ample time to get letters in that
outgoing express. Braddock wrote to Sir Thomas Robinson on
June 5, explaining the delay and warning the Secretary of State
that expenses of the expedition would exceed original estimates.[36]
The failure of the provincial governments to provide horses and
wagons would halve the planned capacity of his train and increase
the charges of transporting army supplies over the mountains
"many times more than double the original cost of them," Braddock wrote. St. Clair put the total figure at near £40,000. The
teamsters were getting fifteen shillings a day.

"The behavior of the governments appears to me to be without
excuse," Braddock wrote, "but it may be some extenuation of the
guilt of the lower class of people, that upon former occasions their
assistance in public has been ill rewarded, and their payments
neglected; the bad effects of which proceeding we daily experience."

He cited Hite's beef contract and Dinwiddie's bungled management of Indian affairs as examples of his vexations. He deplored
the slothful, languid disposition of his provincial recruits, in whom
he expressed little confidence.[37]

To the Duke of Newcastle he sent a similar letter:

> I know not, my Lord, whether to express a greater surprise at the
> supineness and . . . unreasonable economy of the governments and
> people of the southern colonies, or at the general falsehood and dis-
> honesty that prevails amongst them; I have already acquainted your
> grace that the expense attending His Majesty's service under my direc-
> tion would be greater than I had apprehended, and I must here in-
> form you that this inexcusable behavior of the provincial governments
> will greatly increase it: the consequences of it are that I have been

obliged to send to a great distance for forage, and to contract for and lay in stores of every kind in order to prevent future disappointments, and upon every occasion to comply with higher terms than I might otherwise obtain.[38]

Shirley evidently showed this letter to Washington, or told him about it, because Washington came close to repeating some of Braddock's phrases two days later in a letter of his own to Col. Fairfax:

The General, by frequent breeches of contracts has lost all degree of patience; and for want of that consideration and moderation which should be used by a man of sense upon these occasions, will, I fear, represent us in a light we little deserve; for instead of blaming the individuals as he ought, he charges all his disappointments to public supineness; and looks upon the country, I believe, as void of both honor and honesty; we have frequent disputes on this head, which are maintained by warmth on both sides, especially on his who is incapable of arguing him out; or of giving up any point he asserts, let it be ever so incompatible with reason.[39]

And Shirley unburdened himself in a letter to Morris:

I wrote you some time ago a letter full of complaints, and forget at present who it went by; the truth is I have many things that give me much uneasiness, which I had rather tell than write to you, and which put me almost beyond my stock of patience; I never expected the most perfect conduct with regard to some friends of yours and mine, but I could not have imagined it would have been so intolerable. On Monday we move from this place with 200 wagons: how we shall get that number over such roads and through such weather as we have had for some time past I know not, however I doubt not we shall get through it; we compute that we shall be before Fort Duquesne in a little more than three weeks.[40]

Another violent thunderstorm broke over the hot, dry mountains. The fury of the gust split army tents,[41] and other letters in the outgoing express probably carried to Great Britain more than one account of "the heat of the country, which occasions such faintness that the men can hardly carry their arms; and sometimes when these heats are a little relaxed there come such storms of rain, thunder and lightning that all the elements seem on fire; numbers of pine trees are struck to shivers, and such effects of lightning that if not seen one could scarcely believe." [42]

At 2 o'clock Friday afternoon, June 6, Gordon pronounced the new road around the mountain ready. Next morning Halkett marched with his brigade, Spendlowe's sailors, two field pieces, and some of the loaded supply wagons. They got caught in another thunderstorm.[43] To put some heart in his drenched men when they reached their next camp site, a glade behind Wills Mountain, Sir Peter told his officers to see that the sutler delivered one pint of spirits to every three soldiers.[44]

The number of women marching with the troops was restricted to six per company for each regiment, four or five for each of the smaller units. No soldier's wife following the army was to be permitted the luxury of a horse of her own.[45] Although this order was not enforced as rigidly as it might have been, many husbands and wives had been separated by the time Burton marched on Sunday with his division. At Braddock's direction, Shirley made out a pass for twenty-eight wives left behind, and Braddock wrote Morris a note asking him to subsist them and promising to make the necessary stoppages in their husband's pay to defray the cost of their keep.[46] One of Dunbar's friends, Captain Rutherford, the English officer commanding the independent New York company, remarked that Braddock might have gotten away sooner from Fort Cumberland had he himself been less interested in women, but no one else seems to have taken notice of this.[47]

On Sunday, June 8, Braddock wrote out a long report for Napier, enclosing a return of all troops encamped at Wills Creek and on the march, a total of about 2,300, or, as the General put it, "about two thousand effectives, the greatest part Virginians very indifferent men, this country affording no better."

"With these I flatter myself to be able to drive the French from the Ohio," he told the Duke's adjutant. He wrote:

> It would take up too much of your time were I to tell you particularly the difficulties and disappointments I have met with from the want of honesty and inclination to forward the service in all orders of people in these colonies, which have occasioned great delays in getting hither, as well as my being detained here a month longer than I intended. . . . Nothing can be worse than the road I have already passed and I have an hundred and ten miles to march through an uninhabited wilderness over steep rocky mountains and almost impassible morasses. From this description which is not exaggerated you conceive the difficulty of getting good intelligence, all I have is from the Indians whose veracity is no more to be depended upon than that of the borderers here; their accounts are that the number of French at the fort at present is but small, but pretend to expect a great reinforcement; this I do not entirely credit, as I am very well persuaded they will want their forces to be northward.[48]

Braddock was not wholly dependent upon the Indians for information on enemy movements. Robert Morris had relayed a message from Oswego that 34 large French batteaus carrying 300 men had passed up Lake Ontario on May 13, and that more were expected to follow. Provincial newspapers put the number at 900.[49]

"We shall have more to do than go up the hills to come down again," said Washington.[50]

Monday's weekly express from Winchester brought Braddock a letter from Governor James Glen of South Carolina containing a bill of exchange payable to Braddock for £4,000. This was the only money raised so far by an American province to pass through Braddock's hands. He sent it on to Morris to reimburse him for the forage Leslie had bought, and to be applied to future contracts. In a postscript to the letter of transmittal Braddock wrote:

> If you should have it in your power to employ some of the money in raising recruits for me I should be obliged to you, and desire you to send 'em after me as soon as the road from your province is opened. I want 'em to complete the English regiments. You may allow £3 sterling per man; arms and clothing will be ready for 'em, and if you have anybody you can confide in to bring 'em up he shall be rewarded for his service.[51]

That night an express from Philadelphia brought Braddock two letters from Morris. One assured him that the supplies he had requested would be gathered on the new road at Shippensburg. The other reported 20 loads of forage purchased by Leslie, 50 fat oxen and "a parcel of fat sheep" on their way to the army, but informed Braddock that the 200 workmen on the new road, now at Sidling Hill, had refused to proceed farther than Rays Town unless provided with a guard to protect them from Indians. Morris reminded Braddock that the province of Pennsylvania maintained no militia. It was difficult to buy a musket in Quaker Philadelphia. If the workmen were to be given armed protection it must be provided by the army. Braddock grumbled, having refused such a guard to Peters, but ordered Captain Hogg's company of Virginia rangers to Ray's Town.[52]

Braddock had hoped to get away from Fort Cumberland on Monday, June 9, with Dunbar's regiment and the rest of the train. The General's guard, drawn from Dunbar's Forty-Eighth and reduced to twelve men, one sergeant, and a corporal, was under orders to remain with Braddock's baggage. Other guards had been recalled from up the river, from the flats east of Wills Creek. Those on duty at the fort had been told to rejoin their regiment as soon as Col. Innes took up his duties as governor with a garrison of the most infirm officers and men in camp. About sixty soldiers, suffering from fever and a sort of bloody flux, would remain in a hospital at the fort.[53]

At the last moment on Monday, marching orders were withheld. Burton had had trouble getting the artillery over the new road after Saturday's rain. Dunbar's men did not strike their tents until Tuesday morning. The last of the officers' field beds and portmanteaus then were loaded into baggage wagons or roped to batsaddles, and the twenty drums of the Forty-Eighth beat the *March*. This, at last, was good-bye. Up the road went Dunbar's Forty-Eighth. Behind it crawled a long procession of heavily loaded wagons and carrying horses.[54]

The raw road through the narrows, crossing and recrossing the stony bed of Wills Creek, had not been cut for rapid marching.[55] The tan-gaithered redcoats took it as they found it, wading the shallows by the sheer rock walls of the deep defile. The wagons behind them could move no faster than the men in front. By the old road, over the mountain, it was four miles from the fort to the glade where the two first divisions were encamped. Around the foot of the mountain was a good five miles.[56]

Later that afternoon, when the dust had settled behind the last of the wagons and carrying horses, Braddock got into the saddle of his bay and rode after them. With him went his staff, his mounted bodyguard of Virginia troopers, and his body servant, Bishop.[57]

It had been June—June of 1704—when Marlborough began his famous march to the Danube. Maj. Gen. Edward Braddock was just about old enough to remember it. In the tradition of the great Duke, Braddock was reputed to wear a coat of mail at times.[58] Breastplates were still issued in the British army. Three sets of armour—backs, breasts and head pieces—for the service of the engineers had been listed in the stores inventoried at the Tower for his expedition.[59] With or without a breastplate the General who rode up the road toward Fort Duquesne was a short, thickset British officer, booted and sashed, in a brown tie-wig, who kept reaching for loose snuff in his waistcoat pocket.[60]

Burton was waiting for him when the General's party rode into

the glade behind the mountain. Halkett's regiment, the independent and provincial companies, were still there. Dunbar's men were
shaking out their tents. The woods were fairly open, more like a
grove than a forest. There was even grass for the horses.[61]

But it was plain to Burton, looking up the valley toward a green
tumble of mountains ahead, that the narrow track cut through the
forest would grow harder and harder. Burton could see tree-covered
crests at least 2,400 feet high.[62] Guns and wagons would never make
those grades behind their present teams of small, lean, worn-out
nags.[63] Five English cart horses to an eight-inch howitzer on the
hard, flat roads of Flanders was one thing. Five jades with the same
gun on a mountain Indian trail was another.[64]

The wagons, particularly the King's army wagons, were almost
as much of a problem as the artillery. Washington suggested fewer
wagons, more packhorses.[65] Packhorses with pack saddles and sur-
cingle were the most practical means of carrying freight over these
mountains. The fur traders had learned that.[66] But the packhorses with Braddock's army were no better than the draft horses
of the wagon teams. Each packhorse was supposed to carry two
hundredweight, a light load for a good English horse, but many
of Braddock's were cast-off's, sold to army contractors by Indian
traders, Orme observed.[67]

"A parcel of banditti who call themselves Indian traders,"
snorted Braddock.[68]

"There has been vile management in regard to the horses," Washington admitted.[69]

At a meeting of all line officers, held in his tent at 11 o'clock
next morning, Braddock explained the horse and wagon problem.
He recommended that all baggage except absolute necessities be
sent back to Fort Cumberland and that each officer limit himself
to one riding horse. The generosity of any officer who spared a
horse of his own for army use would not be forgotten. Such horses
should be paraded in the rear of Col. Dunbar's regiment where
Major Sparkes would look them over. Any spare batsaddles should
be sent along with the pack horses.[70]

"This is a good scheme and the way to do our business," said
Shirley after the meeting.[71]

"Which is what I recommended at first," said Washington.[72]

British officers were not accustomed to campaigning without
baggage wagons and bat horses, but many agreed to forego private

tents and other comforts.[73] That released about 80 horses. Wash. ington cheerfully discarded half his kit to provide another. All told, the General and his headquarters contributed 20 more, but the combined total of 100 was far below the required number. Seven of the heaviest and strongest horses in the train were needed for each howitzer, 5 for each two-pounder and 4 for each wagon, although wagonloads were ordered reduced to 14 hundredweight each.[74]

At a council of war held in the General's tent next day it was de-cided to send two of the six-pounders, four cohorns, and some of the ordnance stores back to the fort. They would clear about twenty wagons. In the train were sixteen of the King's wagons, heavy, Eng-lish-built wagons with a lot of ironwork, brought over from Lon-don to carry bread or ammunition. They were just too big for the light work horses that struggled to pull them. Between the shafts of a King's wagon, shafts as massive as those of an artillery timber, a light American horse looked like a runt.[75] So all sixteen of the King's wagons were unloaded into ordinary farm wagons and pulled aside to be taken back to the fort by fifty of the less desirable men from the independent and ranger companies.[76]

And there were still too many women around camp to suit the General. No more than two per company would be permitted to continue the march from here on, he decided. The brigade major would list their names. Any woman who persisted in remaining without authorization would be shot, said an order which nobody believed.[77]

Since early morning a 30-man detail had been weighing out back-loads of flour and bacon for the carrying horses. All was to have been in readiness by 2 o'clock that afternoon, but the task of fitting oilcloth covers to the farm wagons that were to be used to carry powder, and of shifting and redistributing other wagon loads, took more time than expected. The army did not march that day. Some of the advance pickets, not knowing how long they might remain in the woods where they had been posted when the column halted, built themselves shelters of boughs and bark. These the General ordered destroyed and he forbade the erection of any more. Nothing should interfere with the vigilance of his pickets.[78]

The drums beat *reveille* at 4 A.M., next morning, Friday, June 13. The troops, each man with four days provisions in his haversack, moved up the narrow forest trail two by two on either side of the long procession of limbers, gun carriages, powder carts, wagons, and pack horses.[79] The first mile of the trail was swampy but level, the next two and a half, rough and steep. Frequent halts were called behind the hatchetmen and carpenters who had gone ahead with a trumbril of tools to cut and dig and bridge. The path they cleared through the woods, breathlessly hot, damp, and gloomy, could not properly be called a road. It went weaving among the trees, around stumps of fallen timber, over rotting logs, rocks, and roots of a virgin woodland whose matted boughs shut out the summer sunlight.[80]

Halkett's brigade, leading the column, encamped for the night at Martin's plantation, a log cabin in a clearing by George's Creek at the foot of Big Savage mountain.[81] Officers, men, and horses were exhausted. They rested next day, the men getting orders to help the wagons in any pinch over a hill.[82] Sourly the soldiers surveyed Big Savage, whose 2,900-foot humps extended the length of a thickly timbered horizon. It was 11 o'clock that morning before Dunbar's straggling regiment closed in from behind. They, too, were tuckered out.[83]

Braddock was far from satisfied with march discipline. Orders were issued that hereafter the troops would turn out, accoutre, and form two deep at the head of their respective encampments along the road in the morning when the drums rolled the *General*. No tents would be struck until specific orders had been given. As soon as tents had been struck and loaded in the wagons with the officers' baggage, the troops would lay on their arms until ordered to march. They would march on the beating of the *March*—a beat to be taken up by other drummers from those of Halkett's regiment at the head of the column. They were to face outward, two deep, at every halt.[84]

The carrying horses now became a matter of concern. They had suffered on the march to Martin's, standing loaded in the previous camp for an hour after the main body moved out, and bearing their loads continuously all day. It was not practical to unload them at every halt, and they strung the column out to a dangerous, unwieldy length.[85]

Next morning, an hour before the main column resumed its march, the carrying horses were sent off with a guard of two companies. There was no obstruction on the trail to impede pack horses and they were ordered to continue to Little Meadows, where St.

Clair's advance guard was encamped, ten miles beyond Martin's plantation.[86] Batmen were warned to take care to prevent their horses eating laurel when they reached the Savage river on the other side of Big Savage Mountain. "It is certain death to them," they were told.[87]

The first four miles of that day's march were up and down a succession of rocky ridges. Half the main column, falling far behind the pack train, grounded arms to help the trembling, winded teams of hot, boney little horses drag their 12-pounders and heavy howitzers over the mountain crest. The last of the wagons did not pull away from Martin's until almost noon and three of them, going down the western slope of the mountain toward the Savage river, slipped off the precipitous road and smashed to pieces against the rocks and trees.[88]

The Savage river, winding through the laurel and rhododendron of its wooded upland valley, was an insignificant stream that summer because of the drought. In the winter time, the Indians said, it was broad and deep. The tired column that forded it that warm June afternoon was strung out for a distance of three or four miles. Halkett's regiment, still leading the way, advanced only about three miles beyond the river, camping for the night at the top of another steep ascent that delayed the wagons for three hours. Next day the regiment marched on, through three miles of dense white pine—a gloomy track known to frontiersman as "the shades of death"—across another boggy stream, up through the laurel thickets of another mountain side and down into the lap of a prairie grass plateau called Little Meadows.[89]

St. Clair's vanguard was encamped here, behind an abbatis they had built. The Quartermaster and his fifty wagons had been eight days getting that far.[90] He had stopped to blast boulders out of the road, rarely more than 10-feet wide now, to ditch swamps, and lay corduroy bridges. Little Meadows was a natural pasture, normally springy, lush and green, where the fur traders stopped their pack trains to rest. But in June 1755 the high treeless valley was dry, almost parched. A stream running through it had fallen to a trickle.[91]

Waiting for the main column to catch up with him, St. Clair had written a letter to Col. Napier:

> I am not at all surpised that we are ignorant of the situation of this country in England, when no one except a few hunters knows it on the spot; and their knowledge extends no farther than in following

their game. It is certain that the ground is not easy to be reconnoitered for one may go twenty miles without seeing before him ten yards. . . .

What was looked on at home as easy is our most difficult point to surmount, I mean the passage of this vast tract of mountains; had we a country we could subsist in after we got over them, the thing would be easy. . . .

One of our Indians who left the French fort the 8th instant tells me that there are only 100 French and 70 Indians at that place; that they were preparing to set out the day after to dispute the passage of the mountains. I have seen nothing of them as yet, nor do I expect they will come so far from home. . . .[92]

Miles behind Halkett's regiment and its convoy came Dunbar with the rest of the train. The thin, haggered, underfed little horses, cursed and lashed by their weary drivers, were beginning to wear out. The weakest had broken down along the way and been shot.[93] The men of Dunbar's regiment, too, were close to collapse. In nine days they had advanced only 20 miles but they had been under arms almost continuously, protecting the long line of wagons strung out over three or four miles of mountain trail.[94]

"The soldiers guarding them were so dispersed that if we had been attacked either in front, center or rear, the part so attacked must have been cut off and totally dispersed before they could be properly sustained by any other corps," Washington wrote to his brother Jack.[95]

And they were moving too slowly. Braddock knew that. He called Washington aside. The Virginian had been over the route before. He knew what to expect. Privately, Braddock asked him, what did he think should be done?

"Push on," said Washington.[96] But push on with a lighter column, unencumbered, taking only what was absolutely essential. Leave the baggage and the train with the rest of the army, to follow by slow marches as best they could.

"Marching to the French fort is certainly practicable with this present convoy," said St. Clair.[97]

Practicable maybe, but too slow, said Washington. Cut down the number of wagons. Increase the carrying horses.

Everything they had heard, including the story told St. Clair by the Indian who claimed to have left the French fort less than two weeks ago, indicated that the enemy force on the Ohio was weak but expecting reinforcements. These, to the best of Washington's knowledge, could not arrive as long as the prevailing drought continued. The headwaters of the streams between Lake Erie and the fort, Duquesne's only means of communication with Canada, would be too low for big canoe or batteau navigation.[98] Now was the time to attack, before the weather changed.

"Push on!"

Braddock, mindful of St. Clair's professional opinion that siege operations would be necessary to reduce the fort, was not going to do anything rash.

"Your greatest difficulty will be the subsisting of your troops," the Duke had said in his instructions. "Give your chief attention to this." [99]

Dunbar, asked his opinion, began by saying it had been the practice of other commanders under whom he had served—

"Stuff!" interrupted Orme, who had little respect for any of Dunbar's former commanders and less for Dunbar. "You might as well talk of your grandmother." .

"If she were alive," retorted Dunbar, resenting Orme's interruption, "she would have more sense, more good manners, and know as much of military matters as you do."

"Gentlemen," interrupted Braddock, "you are both warm."

"General, you see the provocation I got," said Dunbar.[100]

Next day, while the army rested, Braddock told Dunbar, Halkett, and St. Clair that he had made up his mind to push ahead with a light, picked detachment of his best troops.[101] To clear and cut the road, St. Clair would march the following morning with 400 men, two companies of Virginia rangers, and the Indian scouts. Braddock himself would march the morning after with 550 rank and file from the two British regiments, Spendlowe's sailors, and Captain Stewart's Virginia light horse troop. The men from the British regiments would be picked from among those brought over from Ireland.[102]

"The commanding officer of each regiment to be answerable to His Excellency that this is complied with," Washington wrote in his orderly book. "No women to be victualled upon the detachments that march tomorrow and Thursday." [103]

A cryptic order was posted in the camp area of Halkett's Forty-Fourth:

"At half an hour after 12 o'clock the Twenty to be at Dr. McKenley's tent, and any woman who shall be absent will be sent back." [104]

This time most of the women positively would be left behind.[105]

Sir Peter Halkett, Lieutenant Colonels Gage and Burton, Major Sparke, 8 captains, 20 lieutenants, and 9 ensigns were listed by name as the officers to go with the special detachment. St. Clair was to take two 6-pounders and three wagons of tools. Braddock would take the howitzers, the 12-pounders, and thirteen wagons, one loaded with Indian presents, the others with ammunition. Each column would carry thirty-five days' provisions on pack horses. Dunbar would remain behind in command of the rest of the army, the poorest troops and most of the wagons, to follow as fast as he could.[106]

St. Clair marched at 4 A.M., Wednesday morning, June 18, with Gage as his second in command, and Braddock on Thursday with the rest of the special detachment. Braddock's column carried the King's colors, Forty-Fourth Regiment, and the second color, Forty-Eighth. Each of the wagons had a six-horse team, each howitzer a team of nine, and each 12-pounder a team of seven sound horses. Four hundred of the ablest carrying horses had been picked for the detachment and about a hundred extras were taken along in case of accident. Light horsemen of the Virginia troop led the line of march, protected by the usual flanking parties.[107]

At least one sick man rode with Braddock's column. Ever since the halt at Martin's plantation Washington had been suffering with headaches and fever. Once he had quit his saddle for a jolting army wagon of the train. His symptoms were those of the bloody flux, which had hospitalized most of the sick left at Fort Cumberland, but he was determined to go on.[108]

When the last of the special detachment had moved out of the Little Meadows camp, Dunbar called his wagon masters to discuss a plan of march for the rest of the force. To his dismay they told him he had been left with only about a hundred four-horse teams for a hundred and fifty wagons, and about a hundred and fifty carrying horses for double that number of backloads of bacon and flour. The only way he could follow Braddock would be to shuttle forward as many wagons and backloads as his horses could move at one time, then unhitch teams, unload pack horses and return for another haul. Allowing no rest for the extra efforts of man or beast, three days would be needed to advance his complete command the distance of a one-day march.[109]

The vexed and worried colonel thought he remembered Braddock having said something about never being more than one day's march ahead of him. Was the General aware of the transport problem he had created by going off with so many of the horses? Never very adept at letter writing, Dunbar scratched off a note to Braddock, explaining his situation and requesting further instructions. The courier returned with a curt reply. Dunbar was to do his best, be on his guard, expect to be answerable for his conduct, and not tease the General with complaints.[110]

Braddock's main column then was crossing the Casselman river, a knee-deep stream of mountain water snaking down a wooded valley west of Little Meadows. Indians and backwoodsmen called the ford the soldiers used "the little crossing" to distinguish it from "the great crossing" of the broader Youghiogheny river, farther west.[111]

Two miles the other side of "the little crossing" the guides at the head of the column ran back in alarm. They said a large body of enemy was advancing to attack. Croghan's Indians had seen their tracks. Actually, the guides had overtaken St. Clair's advance party, at work cutting a traverse road over the next ridge. To be safe, Gage's battalion was posted along the top of the ridge and remained their under arms for two hours. No enemy appeared.[112]

From St. Clair's men Orme heard that on the previous day Scarouady had been surrounded and captured by a party of French and Indians. The chief's son, who was with his father, had escaped and made his way back to the English. A rescue force led by the son had found the chief tied to a tree. The chief said he had been left there by the French who had been inclined to kill him but had spared him when the Indians with the French threatened to desert and join Braddock.[113]

Both columns encamped that night at the foot of the ridge where St. Clair's men had been working. When all the guns and wagons had been drawn up closely along the trail, the line of tents pitched on either side did not extend over three hundred yards. Underbrush was cleared and pickets posted. The light horse pitched their tents in a protective semi-circle behind the General's, and the grenadiers put theirs across the trail, horizontally, at either end of the encampment.[114]

The pace was still too slow to suit Washington. Too much time was being taken to repair the road. "Halting to level every mold hill and to erect bridges over every brook," he complained.[115]

But Braddock thought he knew what he was doing. He believed communication essential to the conquest of an inaccessible country. The military roads which old General Wade had built in Scotland, after the Jacobite rebellion of 1715, had done as much to win Wade a marshal's baton as any battle he had fought.[116] A couplet about it was familiar to Braddock's generation:

> *Had you seen these roads before they were made*
> *You would lift up your hands and bless General Wade* [117]

Braddock also knew that his Virginia aide was too ill to travel farther. He told Captain Morris to take care of this. That evening Morris sent a note:

Dear Washington:
    I am desired by the General to let you know that he marches tomorrow and the next day but that he shall halt at the Great Meadows two or three days. It is the desire of every particular in this family and the General's positive command to you not to stir but by the advice of the person under whose care you are till you are better which we all hope will be very soon. . . .[118]

The sick man was promised, on Braddock's word of honor, that he would be brought up to the front before the army reached the French fort. Until then he was to put himself in the care of Dunbar's surgeon, Dr. Murdock, and try a dose of Dr. James's Powder, a popular British cure-all.[119]

Next morning Washington was left at the overnight camp site with a sergeant and a wagon, to wait for Dunbar.[120] At daybreak a force of a hundred redcoats had occupied the ridge to the west, and they stayed there until all the artillery and baggage had passed. No enemy was seen. The column, now half a mile long, marched through a chain of rocky passes and stoney ravines whose steep turnings and thicket undergrowth forced halt after halt while St. Clair's men chopped and dug.[121]

It was 7 P.M., three hours past their usual marching time, before they reached a hollow in the mountains with either enough water for the horses or enough open ground to erect their tents. Here, in the heart of the Alleghenies, 2,300 feet above sea level, hemmed in by an overtowering forest of oak and hemlock, Braddock's task force rested for two days while St. Clair's men opened a zig-zag trail over the next hump.[122]

Another packet of letters overtook them. One, from Robert Morris, told Braddock that fifty-two wagons of oats and Indian corn were on their way to the army, and that the new Pennsylvania road had reached Rays Town. Morris enclosed a letter from Oswego with a detailed account of French troop movements up the lake from Montreal, one force with several small cannon. Braddock wrote Morris a note, thanking him for his trouble.[123] According to Christopher Gist and St. Clair's maps, the expedition was approaching the Turkey Foot, the confluence of the Casselman river and Youghiogheny.[124] The new Pennsylvania road was supposed to link up with the old Virginia trail someplace near here. In a postscript to his note of thanks, Braddock reminded Morris:

> As it is not perfectly understood here in what part the road making in your province is to communicate with that through which I am now proceeding to Fort Duquesne, I must beg that you and Mr. Peters will immediately settle it and send an express on purpose after me with the most exact description of it, that there may be no mistake in a matter of so much importance.[125]

A wagon from Philadelphia also caught up with Braddock near this mountain camp, arousing more enthusiasm on the part of the General's cook, Delboux, than he had shown since arriving in America. The wagon was loaded with good things for the General's table.[126] A note from Morris to Orme contained a complete inventory "which you will order received" from the driver:

12 hams	2 chests of lemmons
8 cheeses	2 kegs of spirits
2 dozen flasks of oil	1 cask of vinegar
10 loaves of sugar	1 barrell of potatoes
1 cask of raisins	8 kegs of biscuit
1 box of spice and currents	1 box of pickles and mustard
4 kegs of sturgeon	3 tubs of butter (to be taken
1 keg of herring	up at Shippensburg)

Regimental officers and soldiers subsisted largely on salt rations, occasionally varied by wild turkey or lean deer shot along the road. Somewhere Halkett's mess had bought a calf for £3, and a talebearer's story that Halkett was living better than some of his officers, who had exhausted their Pennsylvania parcels, led to unpleasant words at headquarters.[127] The ordinary soldiers' fare was salt beef, salt pork, salt fish, Fort Cumberland bread and beans. The sutler had rum, but it was 20 shillings a gallon.[128]

The monotony of the forest, its leafy silence, and its woodsy smells, were beginning to tell on the heavily uniformed British regulars. They were weary of cramped little tents. They yearned for taverns and straw-stuffed paillasses. They were tired of hauling on drag ropes, helping tired horses pull a train of artillery over a crooked mountain trail. They were tired of scratching "jiggers," of crawling through bushes in three-cornered hats and wide-skirted coats. They were tired of bark dust on the back of their necks. They were tired of the sound of hatchets, pickaxes, spades ringing out in that godforsaken wilderness. They were tired of the dry daylight heat, and of mountain nights so fresh that a man sometimes wished for an extra blanket. They were tired of the whole bloody business.[129]

"A desolate country uninhabited by anything but wild Indians, bear and rattlesnakes," William Johnson, a commissariat officer wrote home to England.[130]

Orme noticed that the troops had lost a cheerfulness they had shown earlier in their march. This was to be expected. So was a certain coolness, indifference, and jealousy among the officers, denied regulation comfort and restricted to the limited association of their corps. Any discontent among the officers was bound to reach the ranks, but there was no acute disciplinary problem.[131]

Once again Braddock cautioned his officers on vigilance, the control and disposition of flanking parties which, he said, must remain at least a hundred yards from the line while on the march. At every halt, however brief, the men were to form two deep, face outward and stand shouldered.

"The officers and sergeants are to be very attentive to the beat of the drum, taking care always to halt when they hear the *long roll* at that part of the line from which they are detached, and to march upon the beating of the *long march*," said an order to correct some of the slackness the General kept noticing.[132]

There was no excuse for lack of vigilance in Braddock's book, which was Bland's, Chapter VII, page 132—general rules for the marching of a regiment of foot, or a detachment of men, where there is a possibility of being attacked by an enemy:

> There is not anything in which an officer shows his want of conduct so much as in suffering himself to be surprised, either upon his post or in marching with a body of men under his command, without being prepared to make a proper defense, and by not having taken the necessary precautions to prevent it.[133]

When the road had been cleared for another six rough miles, they broke camp and marched through a long defile toward what the guides called "the great" or "the middle crossing" of the Youghiogheny. Three Mohawks came into the camp they made that night. The Indians said they had left the French fort only a few days ago. Taken to the General's tent and questioned, they said reinforcements had reached the fort from Montreal and more were expected, but provisions were scarce because low water had stopped river navigation between the Ohio and Lake Erie. During the night the Mohawks sneaked off, taking with them one of Croghan's ten Indians, a fellow who had been seen lagging on the flanks, looking as if he wanted to desert.[134]

"We could not punish him," said Orme, to explain what appeared to be another bit of carelessness.[135] "The Indians are so extremely jealous that we feared it would produce a general dissatisfaction."

At 5 next morning, June 24, they marched again and forded the Youghiogheny, a swift-flowing mountain river of blue-green water. The stream was a hundred yards wide but only three feet deep at the riffle where they crossed. Along the trail, later that day, they came upon the deserted huts of an Indian encampment which looked as if it had just been abandoned. Croghan's scouts estimated that there had been about 170 French and Indians in the party. Some of the trees around the huts had been stripped of their bark. Scrawled in French on the bare white wood were scurrilous threats and taunts which few of the redcoats could read.[136]

That afternoon Braddock's column again overtook St. Clair's, and again the two detachments encamped together for the night. The General was still dissatisfied with the operation of his outlying flanking parties, commanded by subalterns and sergeants. They were not keeping within sight of the line, he said.[137] "The General is determined to put the first officer under arrest whom he shall find negligent in these duties," said an order written up that night.[138]

Any doubt that the column now was under enemy observation was removed next morning when three batmen, wandering beyond the sentinels, were shot and scalped. A horse and a wagoner also were killed. Immediately parties were sent out to scour the woods and drive in any stray horses. But the scalping party had vanished. Morbid soldiers looked on the butchery, three gory heads, and shuddered. Obediently, at beat of drum they fell into line again and toiled across another rolling upland valley called the Great Meadows.[139]

They passed the ruined palisades and feeble breastworks of Washington's Fort Necessity, captured and destroyed by the French and Indians the previous summer. The fort was a little thing, already grass-grown and forlorn, at the bottom of the valley. Its location did not recommend it to Braddock's officers as a piece of military engineering. The place could be swept by musket fire from almost any of the hills around it.[140]

Some of the Virginians with St. Clair had been in the fight at Fort Necessity. Presuming to speak on the subject of Indian warfare with more authority than British regulars, they predicted trouble for anybody who depended entirely on the platoon firing drilled into them at Alexandria and Fort Cumberland. Capt. Thomas Waggener, a veteran of the past summer's campaign, now commanding a company of rangers, was one of those who knew how the French and their Indian allies fought. He had seen them, right here. They had scattered, used cover, fired at will at anything that moved.[141]

Two miles west of the Great Meadows the trail descended so abruptly that the sailors were obliged to get out their block and tackle to ease guns and wagons safely down an incline. Here the column stopped for the night, in a small stream valley overgrown with crabapple trees. The memory of that morning's three scalpings was still uppermost in soldiers' minds. They cleared all brush from the camp site with alacrity. The light horse and a small body of volunteers searched the woods around the camp for any lurking Indians. Nervous sentinels fired at every rustling. As a sporting proposition, to ease their tension, Braddock promised five pounds to any man who took an enemy scalp.[142]

On the next day's march a British soldier picked up a written commission which mentioned a party under the command of *Sieur Normanville,* and that night they halted among the chestnut trees near the foot of a high, rocky cliff where the fires of another Indian camp were still burning. On barked trees they read more French names and taunts scrawled in charcoal.[143] Waggener and Scarouady knew the rocks of this cliff well. Just about a year ago, with Washington and the Half King, a sachem friendly to the English, they had surprised a small party of French and Indians here. The Half King had revenged himself with scalping knife and tomahawk on the French who, he said, had boiled and eaten his father.[144]

The trail divided at the rocks, one track running off through the hills in a northwesterly direction, along a stream called Redstone Creek, toward the Monongahela, and the other turning northeast, along the crest of another high and mighty mountain range—the last, according to the guides. The tracks of the Indians who had abandoned the camp at the rocks also seemed to divide, some going one way, some the other. That night ninety volunteers set out along the creek trail, hoping to overtake the Indians who had gone in that direction. In the morning the rest of the troops swung north-easterly, following a route taken earlier by St. Clair's men.[145]

That night, Friday, June 27, the entire force reassembled at Christopher Gist's deserted plantation, a stumpy clearing on the other side of the mountain. Heaps of ashes and charred logs were all that remained of plantation cabins burned a year ago by the Indians. The volunteers returning from Redstone Creek had found a quantity of provisions and a batteau, which they had destroyed, but no enemy.[146] Bacon was issued that night, and some of the more energetic soldiers baked what they called bread before they left Gist's next morning. The last of the army rum, which His Excellency was "pleased to give to the men in consideration of their good behavior," was doled by Leslie, the assistant commissary. The sutler's price was up to four shillings a pint now, almost beyond an officer's reach.[147]

On Friday, June 27, they were back on the west bank of the looping Youghiogheny. For the first time in a week they rested. The French fort was only fifty miles away. An engagement with the enemy could be expected at any time. Some of the soldiers were growing nervous, firing at imaginary Indians. The General said there was entirely too much shooting in an irregular and unmilitary fashion. Even if it were necessary to fire the men's pieces when old charges could not be withdrawn, officers should apply to the General, through one of his aides, for permission to shoot. He wanted no unnecessary alarms.[148]

Sunday, June 29, 1755, was the day Lieut.-Col. James Wolfe, whose Twentieth Foot had been shifted from Exeter to Winchester, in England, wrote his father:

> I have some letters from Braddock's army, giving a very favorable account of the General's proceedings, and of his good behavior to the people under his command; this gives me high hopes of his success if

Baron Dieskau does not arrive in time, with his succours, to stop the progress of our arms.[149]

Lieut.-Gen. Baron Ludwig August von Dieskau, a German-born cavalry officer who had served under Marshal Saxe, commanded three thousand French regulars on their way to Canada. The troops were aboard a fleet of eighteen vessels that had sailed from Brest on the third of May.[150] Braddock knew something of this. The weekly Maryland *Gazette* had been printing items about the preparation of a French fleet to put to sea, 30 ships with 10 battalions, perhaps 6,000 men. The paper said Governor Dinwiddie had told the Virginia Burgesses that six French men-of-war with transports had arrived at Louisburg. The *Gazette* also reported parts of the Maryland colony burned up with drought. Oats and flax were hard hit. But the weather was still against any French reinforcement of Dusquesne by canoe.[151]

On the last day of June, Braddock's advanced force re-crossed the Youghiogheny. This was "the main crossing," twice as broad as "the great crossing," but a placid ford not more than three feet deep. The river crossing was executed in precise military fashion. An advance guard waded through the stream and posted itself on the far bank until all baggage and artillery had cleared the ford safely. A rear guard of four hundred redcoats was the last unit over. The column moved only about half a mile beyond the ford, pitching camp until St. Clair's men could widen the trail up a high bluff.[152]

Four days' supply of bacon and flour was issued here so that the troops might cook and bake the victuals they would carry on the next leg of their march. The men also drew and cleaned their arms that day, sending damaged cartridges back to the ammunition wagons. Fires were forbidden in front of the pickets, a precaution against enemy Indians stealing up on them unobserved, guided by flame or smoke.[153] After dark sentries were doubled. The last courier to come up the trail from Fort Cumberland had brought news of an outbreak of Indian attacks in the back settlements. About twenty people had been killed, scalped, or carried off.[154]

Still awaiting word as to where the new Pennsylvania road would connect with the old road and, perhaps, with some apprehension as to the possibility that his line of communication with Wills Creek might be cut, Braddock wrote another letter to Morris at Philadelphia:

As I shall soon be in want of supplies from your province, I must beg you would order all possible dispatch to be made use of in finishing the new road as far as the Crow Foot of the Youghiogheny and afterwards send forward to me such articles or provision as shall be in your power.

Some of the inhabitants near Fort Cumberland having been killed and taken prisoner by straggling parties of Indians, the people in these parts have been deterred from coming to the camp. My chief dependence must therefore be upon your province, where the road will be secure from insults and attacks of that kind. . . . I hope soon to have an express from you with an exact account of the place fixed upon for the communication between the two roads.[155]

The five miles Braddock's troops marched the next day were the muddiest they had travelled. Long overdue rain had softened the trail and they halted on the edge of a wide swamp extending up and down a wooded valley. They were two days getting through this muck. A lot of old timber had to be cut away before St. Clair's carpenters could build a bridge and lay a corduroy road.[156]

The rain also damaged some of the backloads of flour on the carrying horses. Braddock sent Dunbar orders for a hundred horses with more flour, and for some of the Pennsylvania beeves promised by Morris, if the drovers had delivered them. St. Clair proposed that when the advance force went into camp on July 3, they stay there until Dunbar could bring up the train.[157] Dunbar was coming slowly, advancing only 6 or 7 miles every three days.[158] Braddock, habitually open to suggestions, called a council of war to hear the opinion of his other field officers on St. Clair's suggestion. Halkett, Gage, Burton, Sparkes, St. Clair, and Orme attended. Orme set down the circumstances for consideration:

Dunbar's most advanced units probably were no nearer than the Great Crossing of the Youghiogheny, eleven days' march by the light detachment. The road had been improved as they went along but it was unlikely that Dunbar, short on horses, could cover the distance within less than eleven days.

Any horses sent back to help Dunbar would be at least two days on the way and too tired and weak to be of much assistance when they reached him. Even if reunited the two commands would be unable to proceed together because of the shortage of good horses.

It would be impractical to detach any more troops from Dunbar to increase the strength of the advance column.

Dunbar was in much less danger of attack where he was than he would be in a more advanced position.

Time lost waiting for Dunbar would further deplete existing stocks of supplies and, perhaps, force another halt for re-supply farther on.

Any delay now would be to the advantage of the French who would use the time to strengthen their defences and, in the meanwhile, might receive reinforcements and supplies from Canada.

The conjecture was that the enemy must be weak at this time. Otherwise he would have made some effort to defend defiles and stream crossings which the British had passed without opposition.[159]

The council agreed to proceed without waiting for Dunbar. Braddock sent for Croghan and asked him to try to persuade some of his Indian scouts, who had stuck close to the marching troops ever since the Great Meadows' scalping, to range ahead and take a look at the French fort. Croghan talked to the Indians. Neither promises nor presents would overcome their reluctance to go that far ahead.[160]

But additional precautions were taken against surprise. The men were told that the bell tents, ordinarily put up at every encampment to protect their arms against the weather, would no longer be erected. From now on the soldiers would sleep with their arms in their own tents, pitched in a single row along the trail, facing outward. Company officers were instructed to inspect arms every evening before the beating of retreat, to be sure they were in good working order. Half of the advanced pickets would remain constantly under arms with fixed bayonets, and during their two-hour relief they should stay at their posts, lying down on their muskets.[161]

All troops loaded with fresh cartridges when the drums beat *assembly* next morning. That day they marched six miles through a fairly open forest of white oak. All the way from Little Meadows the carrying horses and their batmen, each armed with a firelock, had been a drag, falling in behind the main body. But now that the woods had thinned, batmen with horses were ordered to march on the flanks, between the pickets and the line, falling in at the rear only when the undergrowth became too thick or the trail too narrow.[162]

Next day, Saturday, July 5, the troops rested again. A train of flour-laden packhorses and a herd of beeves came up, sent forward by Dunbar in obedience to Braddock's order. Some of the officers' women left behind with Dunbar came up, too.[163] Croghan talked again to his Indians and this time prevailed upon two of them to go up the trail and look for the enemy. Christopher Gist set off quietly on a scouting expedition of his own.[164] They were now within twenty miles of the forks of the Ohio.

In the pallid dawn of the Sabbath the drums again beat *reveille* in the forest. Down came the tents. Teams were hitched up. The Redcoats fell in. A company of grenadiers tramped off with the advance guard, and the batmen led their carrying horses to either side. At proper interval behind the grenadiers the drummers thumped the march,—when gunfire echoed sharply through the woods. Somebody screamed—three men were screaming.

Enemy Indians had waylaid three stragglers behind the advance guard. The grenadiers turned back. They were too late. Three bodies, scalps torn and ripped from the crowns of their heads, lay bleeding in the tangled honeysuckle and black leaf mold beside the trail.

Firing broke out at the head of the column. Some of Croghan's Indians had caught sight of the scalping party and had scattered among the trees, shooting at them. In the excitement the Virginia rangers mistook Croghan's men for the enemy and began shooting at their own Indians. They shot and killed Scarouady's son.[165]

They came into camp shaken that evening. The body of the chief's son lay in an ammunition wagon. Braddock sent for Scarouady and the other Indians and expressed his condolence. Officers were asked to attend the funeral of the chief's son, held that evening. A firing squad discharged a volley over his grave. This appeared to please the Indians, but they probably obtained more genuine satisfaction from the scalp of a French officer brought back by Croghan's two Indian scouts, who claimed Braddock's bounty, the £5 he had promised for an enemy scalp. They said they had killed the Frenchman while he was shooting game within half a mile of Fort Duquesne.[166]

The two scouts told Braddock they had seen few tracks, few men, and only a few boats on the river near the fort, and that no new defenses had been built. The enemy held none of the passes along the trail between the British camp and the fort. Gist, who also returned to camp that evening, told the same story. He said he had tried to get close to the fort the night before but had been discovered and nearly captured by two Indians. The only other sign of a human being he had seen between the camp and the fort had been a single wisp of smoke. But Braddock relaxed none of his vigilance.

He put out an order that during any halt, while on the march, half
of each of the advance parties should remain under arms with fixed
bayonets, the other half sitting down by their weapons.[167]

Next day the column advanced cautiously. Small parties occasionally quit the trail to look for a crossing over Turtle Creek, a
Monongahela tributary that cut across their line of march. The
creek turned and twisted between precipitous hills which rose a
sheer three hundred feet on either side. Descent was impossible
for wagons and artillery. At Braddock's suggestion Sir John St.
Clair rode off with a hundred men, the Indian guides and light
horse to search for a route across the gulch.[168] Two hours later the
Quartermaster returned. He said he had found a ridge which apparently led all the way to the fort, avoiding dangerous defiles.
Some work would be necessary to make it passable for wagons and
artillery. It was too late to begin work that day. The army encamped
for the night where it was.[169]

Braddock talked with Gist and the other guides, who knew the
ground between them and the French fort. They told him the
Monongahela flowed through a narrows just ahead of them, a hazardous pass for a marching column. If the troops followed a trail
on this side of the river, they would have the river close to their
left and a sharp bluff on their right. At the end of the narrows
they would again face the Turtle Creek ravine. But the river was
shallow, its banks low, and it had two good fords, the guides said.
A safer and easier way for wagons and artillery, and the only route
by which they could avoid the Turtle Creek ravine, would be to
ford the Monongahela above the narrows, follow the river's com-
paratively broad and flat left bank to a second ford, below the
mouth of Turtle Creek, and recross the river there. A bend in the
river would make this route fairly direct.[170]

Braddock thought the double river crossing a logical plan, but
Scarouady advised him not to enter the narrows until both sides
of the river had been thoroughly reconnoitered. The chief warned
the General that a better spot for an ambuscade could not be
found.[171] Braddock thought he could take care of that. In the
morning he moved his force nearer the river bank, pitching an
overnight camp on some rising ground near a big spring, within
less than a mile of the upper ford.[172]

Here Washington rejoined the General's staff. His fever was
down, but he was still so weak that he had made the trip from

Dunbar's camp in a covered wagon. At the rate Dunbar was moving, it would be another three weeks before the train caught up with the advance. That is, if his horses held out. They were so weak that Washington had come away doubting they would last.[173] "I believe shortly he will not be able to stir at all," he said.[174]

Officers and men at Dunbar's camp had been stricken with the flux. Their communication with Fort Cumberland had ceased since the Indian raids on the settlements. In one of the most savage of these, said to have occurred near Wills Creek, a boy had been knocked down and scalped for dead, then regained consciousness to see an Indian scalping his mother. Dunbar's only brush with the enemy had been harassing night alarms.[175]

Washington tried, without much success, to impress upon Braddock and his staff the pecularities of Indian warfare. The Virginian doubted that platoon firing, even by regulars, was an adequate defense against Indian attack. But the British officers were confident that their men could meet any battle situation. Braddock himself had a guardsman's contempt for the French as an enemy. Regularity and discipline were what counted. Some of Braddock's soldiers had been shocked by the scalpings they had seen, but there was no indication they had lost their nerve.[176]

Even Shirley was optimistic of the outcome. So far the enemy had shown no strength, no inclination to give battle. Awed by the approach of an overwhelming force, it was always possible they might not stand and fight at all. Maybe the British would reach the forks of the Ohio to find the French fort dismantled and abandoned. There had been reports of a French withdrawal to Canada. Orme suspected, from what scouts and observers had told him, that the French were alarmed by Braddock's approach.[177]

St. Clair suggested the feasibility of sending a detachment on a night march to invest the fort that night, before its garrison had time to blow it up. He begged Braddock to give him command of a force of 400 men "to go ahead and hinder any sortie to be made on the convoy." But after some discussion of the distance—the fort was still ten miles away—he agreed it might be prudent to wait until the next camp.[178]

Halkett wanted Braddock to order a reconnaissance by his Indian scouts that night. But the camp gossip was that Halkett and the General were not on speaking terms. Sir Peter disapproved of the line of march, thought more men should be trained as cannoneers, and had suggested that blockhouses and stockades be built along the road they had made. According to one story Braddock had told Halkett publicly that "he was a fool and wanted leading strings." Another story was that Braddock had threatened to take away his regiment, that Halkett had retorted he was not dependent upon it for a livelihood, and that if his honor had not been concerned he would never have come on the expedition. Orme told Washington he had had a time trying to keep peace at headquarters.[179]

The troops received two days' meat and two days' flour that day. Each soldier was to have twenty-four rounds of powder and ball. Officers inspected their ammunition. Tomorrow, the men were told, they would wear knapsacks and haversacks, and leave tents behind for the quartermaster.[180] Other orders issued before the drums beat *retreat* that night were:

> Lieut. Co. Gage would parade at 2 A.M. with two companies of grenadiers, 160 rank and file from the 44th and 48th, Gates' independent company, two 6-pounders and proper guides. They would pass both fords of the river and take post, after the second crossing, to secure the passage for the rest of the troops.
>
> St. Clare would march at 4 A.M., with 200 men to clear the way for the baggage and artillery.
>
> All troops except those on the night's picket duty would draw & clean their pieces and all would load with fresh cartridges at the beating of *The General* in the morning.[181]

Bishop would look to the General's pistols, a beautiful pair of brass-fitted flintlocks—officers' light weight holster pistols made by Gabbitas, a Bristol gunsmith. Their shining eight-inch brass barrels, belled toward the muzzle, were set in polished walnut stocks. Engraved on the monoplate of each were the General's initials, "E. B." Must have cost at least £8 or £12 the pair.[182]

XIII

INTO BATTLE

July 8–12, 1755

THE MOUNTAINS crossed by the forest trail from Wills Creek to the Ohio made observation easy for the French and their Indian allies. They could not mistake the smoke of Braddock's campfires in the solitude of an uninhabited wilderness. In its silence they could not lose the beat of his drums, or the peal of axes in St. Clair's working party, much less the blasts set off by Gordon and his men to blow boulders from the bed of the road they were building.

From the time the Redcoats waded across the Casselman river their movements had been watched by the enemy.[1] As the column neared the Monongahela, runners were dispatched to the French fort to keep its commandent advised of the progress of Braddock's troops and the formations in which they marched.[2] French scouts estimated the British to number about 3,000 men, a force "si bien sur leur gardes, marchant toujours en bataille," that efforts to harass them with small detachments had been futile.[3]

Pierre Claude Pecaudy, Sieur de Contrecoeur, who had occupied the forks of the Ohio in the spring of 1754 and built the fort named for his governor, the Marquise of Duquesne, was still on the post,[4] but during the winter he had asked to be relieved. Duquesne had sent Captain Daniel Hyacinth Mary Lienard de Beaujeu from Quebec to replace him but asked Contrecouer to stay on at the fort until after the expected British operations.[5]

Captain Beaujeu, forty-four years old, was the Canadian-born son of a former mayor of Quebec, Louis Leinard de Beaujeu. The father had been born at Versailles, son of an officer of the royal guards, and had come to Canada before the end of the past century. He had prospered, rising from an ensign to a captain of the French marines in Canada. He had received grants of land on the Chambly river and had been decorated with the cross of St. Louis. The elder Beaujeu was not one of those rough, roving bushrangers content with an Indian squaw for a wife. He had married the widow of Charles Juchereau, sieur de St. Denis.[6]

Beaujeu's second son, Daniel, born August 9, 1711, was one of five children. He had followed his father into the service and married a French Canadian wife. By 1748 young Beaujeu also was a captain of marines, sufficiently experienced in Indian affairs to attend a Quebec conference which the French governor held with the sachems of the Six Nations. In time young Captain Beaujeu became the French commandant at Detroit and, later, at Niagara. He was awarded the Cross of St. Louis.[7]

The French fort which he now commanded at the forks of the Ohio was garrisoned by an inadequate force of probably less than 300 regulars and militia. Only a few small cannon, brought down from Canada by canoe, were mounted on its ramparts. The design of the fort, with four bastions, was more impressive than its construction. Its ramparts were cribs of squared logs filled with earth. Outside the fort, where the forest had been cleared away for the distance of a musket shot, about 800 Indians had built wigwams and bark sheds.[8] Some were "French praying" Indians [9] from Canada and the lakes where they had been baptised by French missionaries. Others were from western Pennsylvania, Virginia, and the Ohio valley. None were reliable in time of battle.[10]

With or without the Indians the fort was in no condition to withstand the sort of siege Braddock was prepared to lay. Under these circumstances a cautious commander had a choice of two well-established alternatives: he could wait for Braddock's attack, make a token resistance, and surrender with honors of war, or he could destroy the fort and withdraw before the attack was delivered. But at least one of his subordinate officers, Captain Jean Dumas, was not a cautious man. He urged Beaujeu and Contrecoeur to attack the British before they reached the fort.[11]

To arms, to arms! my jolly grenadiers!
Hark, how the drums do roll it along! . . .

were the opening verses of a ballad popular in southeastern Pennsylvania's Chester county,[12] a safe three hundred miles from the French.

March on, march on, brave Braddock leads the foremost;
The battle is begun, as you can see. . . .

But out in the border country, where the battle had begun at the end of June, with a series of Indian raids, no songs were being sung about it. Brave Braddock was beyond the frontier, too far west to provide any protection for settlers in the mountain valleys behind him.

Within a fortnight, nine Virginia families had been murdered by bands of Indians near Fort Cumberland. Twenty-six back country Maryland settlers had been killed or carried off. The road beyond Fort Cumberland, traveled almost daily during the past month by teamsters, drovers and messengers, was deserted. On the trail between Dunbar and Braddock a soldier had been found scalped and with his throat cut. The last letter received at the fort from Braddock's camp was dated July 1.[13]

On the third of July three Indians waylaid Arnold Virgoras, a hired man and 18-year-old James Smith on the new Pennsylvania road between Rays Town and the Turkey Foot. Young Smith, the brother-in-law of a road superintendent, had been sent out to hurry along provision wagons for the road workers. Virgoras was shot and scalped before his eyes, and the youth was carried off a prisoner. About 9 o'clock that night Indians attacked a fortified storehouse used by the workmen beyond Rays Town. Next night there was another alarm. Fourteen men already had deserted Captain Peter Hogg's understrength company of forty Virginia rangers, detached by Braddock to guard the road cutters and their provision wagons. Thirty frightened laborers, who had no arms, quit their job the following morning and started home.[14]

On July 7, the day Braddock reached Turtle Creek, the three Indians who had captured young Smith arrived at Fort Duquesne with their prisoner. The boy was ready to drop after a four-day journey over the mountains at Indian pace. Blinded with sand and clubbed into unconsciousness when forced to run the gauntlet through the Indian village outside the fort, he was bled and re-

vived in the fort hospital by a French doctor, then questioned
about the number of men at work on the new Pennsylvania road.[15]

Threatened with death if he lied, young Smith told the truth.
He said there were about 300. Asked if they were well armed, he
lied. He said they were, although he knew they had no more than
thirty-five guns among them, not counting those of Hogg's rangers.
He was not asked about Braddock, but the boy wondered where
the British were. Not far away, he hoped. They were his only hope
of rescue.[16]

One of the Indians who had captured Smith was a Delaware who
spoke imperfect English. The youth asked him what the news was
from Braddock's army. The Delaware replied that the Indians
spied on the British every day and showed him, by making marks
on the ground with a stick, how the soldiers were advancing in
close order, how the Indians would surround them, taking cover
behind trees.

"Shoot um down all one pigeon," said the Delaware.[17]

An ensign with a detachment of French and Indians, sent out
by Beaujeu to pinpoint Braddock's position, had returned with
word that the British were within eight leagues of Duquesne. A
second scouting party had come back to report them within six
leagues and approaching in three columns.[18] By that time Beaujeu
had made a decision: he would ambush Braddock.

But he was having trouble persuading the Indians at the fort to
help.

"What, my father, do you wish to die and sacrifice us?" one
warrior asked the French captain. "The English are more than
4,000 and we are but 800 and you wish us to attack them. You
know very well you have no hopes."

Beaujeu argued otherwise. He was not afraid. He had a French
Canadian wife and a son to consider, too.[19]

"Give us until tomorrow to make up our minds," a chief told
him.

That night, while Braddock's troops encamped near the Monongahela, the Indians at the fort held a council.[20]

Early next morning Smith was awakened by a great stir in the
fort. Barrels of gunpowder, bullets, and flints were rolled out of
the magazine and upended at the gate of the fort where the barrel
heads were knocked in. In the fort's log chapel of the Assumption
of the Blessed Virgin at the Beautiful River, Beaujeu knelt in con-

fession before the gray-robed chaplain, the Reollect Father Denys Baron. With other French officers and soldiers the Captain received the holy communion. Stripped to the waist, Indian fashion, with his silver gorget around his neck, Beaujeu then led his men from the fort, a force of about 200 French and Canadians. Contrecoeur was left in command of the post with what remained of its garrison.[21]

"I am determined to meet the English," Beaujeu told the Indians. They said they had not changed their mind in council. They would not go with him.

"What! Will you let your father go alone?" he cried. "I am certain of defeating them." [22]

Some of the more reckless braves, naked except for breech clouts, already had daubed themselves with red, blue, black, and brown war paint. Smith watched them, huddled at the gate of the fort. A Huron chief, Anthanases, and another named Pontiac wavered.

As they hesitated, a party of Indian scouts who had been up the river watching the British came into the fort. They told Beaujeu they had left the troops near the upper ford of the Monongahela. Apparently the British were going to follow the trail along the river.

"You see, my friends," said Beaujeu, turning back to the hesitant chiefs, "the English are going to throw themselves into the lion's mouth. They are weak sheep who pretend to be ravenous wolves. Those who love their father, follow me! You need only hide yourselves in the ravines which line the road, and when you hear us strike, strike yourselves. The victory is ours!" A flutter of excitement burst into a frenzy. Suddenly braves crowded around the bullet and powder kegs at the gate, scooping in with their powder horns, filling their bullet pouches. The Indians had changed their minds.[23]

Beaujeu led the way up the forest track toward the lower ford. Smith, watching them go, fixed the number of Indians at around 400. He wondered how they dared set out against Braddock with so small a party, and hoped the British would send them back aflying.[24]

Braddock also was on his way toward the ford. Gage had marched with the advance guard, but not until well after daybreak. Fiddling with tents and baggage, his men had been delayed. The light horsemen rode ahead, over a hill and down the trail toward the Monon-

gahela. The grenadiers followed, four abreast, with the usual flanking parties. About 7 o'clock a band of maybe thirty Indians burst
out of the bushes beside the road but scattered among the trees
before the troops could fire.[25]

Where Gage and his men came out on its bank, the Monongahela
was about three hundred yards wide, a shallow stream of glittering,
gurgling riffles in the hazy morning sunshine.[26] This was the upper
ford. The river came around a bend, a mile above the soldiers, and
turned the other way half a mile below. Cliffs and wooded hills
hemmed it in except for a stretch of bottom land where the soldiers were, and another flat farther down on the other side in the
wide sweep of another bend.[27]

If French or Indians intended to dispute the crossing, this was
the place to be ready for an attack. The light horsemen rode out
into the stream, cautiously. The water was unusually low because
of the drought, not more than a foot or two at its deepest.[28] The
grenadiers waded in. The pebbly river bottom was firm. The tired,
famished little horses hitched to two brass 6-pounders splashed in.
If chains slackened and heads went down to drink the teamsters
shouted and laid on their whips. This was no time, no place to
dally.

Safely across, the foot soldiers wet to their knees, Gage's column
marched down the river bank and around its broad bend to the
second ford, generally opposite but slightly downstream from the
mouth of Turtle Creek. Here the sandy banks on either side of
the river were about twelve feet high and almost perpendicular.
Gage left his two 6-pounders on the left bank and recrossed the
river with his infantry. St. Clair, following closely with tool wagons,
carpenters, and pioneers, put his men to work sloping both banks
down to the ford so wagons and artillery could cross more easily.[29]

It was about 11 o'clock. Except for some footprints on the bank
at the lower ford, no sign of an enemy had been seen since Gage
flushed the Indians above the upper ford. Braddock had crossed
the upper ford about 8 o'clock with the main body, wagons, artillery, packhorses and a drove of cattle.[30] He and his staff had ridden
a mile or so down the west bank when they met a horseman with
a note from Gage informing Braddock that he had recrossed the
river without interference and taken a position on the right bank
commanding the lower ford.[31]

By the time Braddock reached the lower ford St. Clair's working party had finished on that side and crossed to complete the job of grading an incline up the opposite bank. Braddock ordered guns and wagons drawn up along the river and pickets posted on the steep hillside behind.[32]

As far as Braddock and his aides could see, the other side of the river was a deserted mass of wooded hills.[33] Almost directly opposite, just below the incline where St. Clair's picks and shovels clinked and grated, lay the charred logs of a cabin which both Gist and Washington recognized as that of John Fraser, the Scot trader and gunsmith.[34] They had stopped there in December, 1754, on their way back to Virginia after delivering Dinwiddie's ultimatum to the French commander at Fort Le Boeuf. The river had been high then, its banks icy and deserted. The trees on the surrounding hills had been brown and bare.[35]

Now the river valley was warm and green—too warm to suit the heavily uniformed Redcoats of the two regiments, momentarily grateful for any shade.[36] The hills ahead looked no cooler than those they had been climbing for the last month. Avidly they surveyed the river bank for some signs of habitation, something more than Fraser's cabin. After all, the French were a civilized people. Maybe, when they reached the French fort, the British would find at least one tavern, a decent place for a good thick slice of meat and a stiff tot of cheap rum.[37]

Shortly after noon St. Clair's workmen on the other side of the river tossed their tools into a tumbril. The slope up the bank from the edge of the river had been finished. Braddock sent Morris over to Gage and St. Clair with orders to march on until 3 o'clock when, it was presumed, the entire column would bivouac for the night. They would invest the fort in the morning. The artillerymen of the two 6-pounders, which had been guarding the ford, limbered up their pieces and forded the river with their ammunition wagon.[38]

Then the main body began to cross, drums beating, and fifes playing the *Grenadiers March*. First went the Redcoats of Halkett's Forty-Fourth, bayonets a-gleam, and the great union of the King's colors whipping in the sunshine. Next, the sailors, barefoot, with their pants rolled up to their knees. Then the tired artillery teams with the 12-pounders and the heavy brass howitzers, the little horses plunging ahead and straining at their chains to get a footing and a start up the bank on the other side. Then the wagons, the carrying horses, the cattle, and finally the detachment of the Forty-Eighth with its buff regimental flag—boots, bare feet, hoofs, wheels splashing through the riffles, churning up the pebbles in a spectacle calculated to dishearten any French or Indian scout looking down from the wooded hills on either side.[39]

When the recrossing had been completed without the firing of a single musket, officers and men began to think their campaign must be almost over. If the enemy lacked courage or strength to attack them here, where the British were at a disadvantage, would he be so foolhardy as to risk battle on less favorable ground?[40] They were within six or seven miles of the French fort now. Some of the British officers crowed that they would not be surprised to hear an explosion, the sound of the fort being blown up by its own garrison, at any moment now. The only other choice of its defenders was to wait for Braddock's cannon to knock it to pieces.[41]

Gage and his advance party had gone ahead, the grenadiers still four abreast. Guides and horsemen from Stewart's Virginia troop were about two hundred yards in front. The flank pickets of Grenadiers, upon which Braddock insisted, had been put out on either side of the trail.[42] The trail curved around Fraser's house and slanted up the hillside at an easy grade, away from the river and through a tangle of walnut trees and bushes.[43] Two companies of carpenters in St. Clair's working party, close behind Gage, cut away underbrush and chopped down trees marked by Gordon, the engineer, to widen the way. A covering company of rangers marched with the carpenters, their tool cart, the two 6-pounders, and the ammunition wagon.[44]

The main body, halting on the river bank near Fraser's house at the foot of the trail, formed up in its usual marching order. Light horse led the column. Sailors and pioneers followed the troopers with a tumbril of tools. Then came three of the 12-pounders, the General's guard, and the convoy of howitzers and wagons with the main body of troops marching two by two on either side. Twenty-man flanking parties moved off through the woods to the right and left. Batmen led the baggage and provision horses among the trees between the flanking parties and the convoy, and herdsmen drove the cattle with the carrying horses. The fourth 12-pounder tailed the convoy, its downcast muzzle a guide for the column's rear guard of a hundred men commanded by Sir Peter Halkett.[45]

A quarter of a mile from the river the forest undergrowth

thinned away and the woods became so open that guns and wagons could have driven almost anywhere under the trees. Gordon was riding ahead of Gage's grenadiers, looking for the guides, when he saw them running back toward him, shouting.

French and Indians were coming down the trail ahead.[46]

Looking through the trees Gordon saw maybe three hundred coming on the run, led by an officer dressed like an Indian except for his hat and a silver gorget at his throat. Catching sight of the grenadier's red coats through the forest green, the officer snatched off his hat and waved it at the men behind him, motioning right and left. They scattered, the Indians war-whooping an unearthly screech that sent a chill through Gordon.[47]

The vanguard of Gage's advance party did a right-about. They would have run back with the guides, but an officer's command to fix bayonets steadied them. They faced about, hurriedly formed in line of battle across the trail.[48] Front rank kneeling, they sent an ear-splitting blast of musketry into the bushes where the enemy had opened irregular fire.[49]

"God save the King!" cried a British subaltern.

Some of the older soldiers shouted a half-hearted "Huzza!"

They fired a second and a third volley into the bushes without having seen more than one or two of the enemy. The crashing roar of these volleys through the woods was as terrifying to French and Indians as were the enemy's war-whoops to the British. At the third volley Beaujeu went down, shot through the head. Most of the Canadians began to run. *"Sauve qui peut!"* [50]

Some of Gage's men also retreated. They fell back on St. Clair's carpenters and rangers, fifty or sixty paces behind them.[51] Sir John ran forward to see what was happening. He saw ten or twelve British soldiers in grenadier caps lying in the road. He felt the hard hot stab of a bullet in his own body. His shoulder blade was broken, but he stayed on his feet.[52]

Gage, with bullet holes in his hat and a musket ball's streak across his waistcoat,[53] was trying to form a platoon to advance up a hill on the right, a double breasted slope already partly occupied by the grenadier flanking party which had been scouring the woods on that side of the trail. He bellowed his commands, but the soldiers standing in the road refused to budge. Baffled by the popping gunfire—it was not a roar—of an enemy hidden in the woods around them, the Redcoats kept loading and firing at trees and bushes.

They shot at men of their own flanking parties, at grenadiers cut off in the first attack and now trying to rejoin the main detachment.[54]

The wounded St. Clair managed to walk back to his Virginia carpenters and rangers. He posted them to protect the two 6-pounders, now unlimbered, loaded with case shot, and primed. Gage's men also fell back.[55] The 6-pounders were touched off, blasting the bushes. French and Indians scrambled out of their range, shifting farther to right and left, firing into the flanks of the now muddled St. Clair-Gage detachments. Bullets sang and sliced through the foliage. Black powder smoke billowed under the trees where the Indians shrieked their raw, shrill scalp-halloo.[56]

The last of the grenadiers on the flank had retreated from the hill on the right. The enemy took over that high ground undisputed. Other French and Indians crept back through the woods on the left, between the trail and the river, keeping out of sight in the undergrowth. Skulking in gullies, stretched out on their bellies behind trees and stumps, in the bushes, anywhere they could find concealment, they poured a demoralizing cross fire into the bunched Redcoats behind the 6-pounders. Within a few minutes most of Gage's officers were killed or wounded. Polson's company of Virginia carpenters was almost shot to pieces.[57]

Indian war whoops from the rear spread fresh alarm. Somebody, maybe the teamsters with the 6-pounder limbers back under the trees, said the baggage had been attacked. Gage's disorganized grenadiers gave way. If the French and Indians were behind them, they feared they were surrounded; they would be massacred, scalped alive. They fell back along the trail, the carpenters and rangers with them. The gunners manning the two 6-pounders quit their cannon and ran.[58]

A quarter of a mile down the trail Braddock had halted at the sound of the grenadiers' first volley. He sent an aide forward. When the firing continued, growing heavier, he knew they had met an enemy force, that Gage's advance party was under attack. He ordered Burton ahead with 800 men and the three 12-pounders in line behind the sailors. Other teams of the convoy closed up. The 300 men remaining with them obeyed standing orders, facing outward with bayonets fixed, a double file on either side of the road. Halkett's rear guard of a hundred was extended across the trail behind the convoy in small detachments to protect the carrying horses and the cattle.[59]

Burton's battalion moved forward, but in some disorder when the files came together after clearing the convoy which had separated them. Most of the men were four abreast, but one officer had understood an aide-de-camp to say he should double his front to eight. The mix-up increased under enemy rifle and musket fire from the hill to the right. Burton halted to form a line. He ordered his three 12-pounders posted on the lower side of the trail to protect his rear.[60]

Before Burton's battalion could wheel and shuffle into position, Gage's retreating grenadiers and St. Clair's Virginia irregulars backed into them. The narrow road through the forest became a tangle of rangers, carpenters, grenadiers, wounded men on improvised litters, mounted officers, Virginia troopers, and artillery teams. Those behind pushed forward. Those in front pushed back. And the fire of the unseen enemy increased on a target mass growing bigger every moment. Fortunately many of the French and Indians fired high.[61]

Braddock and his aides rode up, Bishop behind them. St. Clair staggered toward the General.

"For God's sake," cried the baronet in his bloody hussar jacket, "the rising ground on our right!"

That was the last Sir John remembered for the next hour or two. He fainted.[62]

The road was jammed, the soldiers packed twelve, fourteen, twenty deep, some facing right, some facing left.[63]

"Tell off a hundred and fifty men and advance up the hill," Braddock told Burton.[64]

Another party was needed on the left to support artillerymen trying to get two of the 12-pounders into firing position.[65]

"March on my lads, and keep up your fire," said an officer.[66]

March where? Fire at what? The road was blocked with frightened, bewildered redcoats, out of order, out of control. Bewildered veterans of the Forty-Fourth, in yellow-faced red uniforms, were jumbled with stupefied American recruits in blue, with surly Irishmen who wore the white facings of the Forty-Eighth, all looking for file leaders or sergeants or company officers. Braddock had been afraid of that, but it was too late now.[67] To sort out the mixture, the King's colors of the Forty-Fourth and the Forty-Eighth's regimental flag of yellow silk were advanced in opposite directions, waved under the trees, and Burton finally got a hundred men of the Forty-Eighth together.[68]

He started up the hill with them, a perfect target—a red-coated officer on horseback—and was promptly shot out of his saddle. The hundred men of the Forty-Eighth draggled back to the trail, loading and firing at the enemy they could not see. Another officer went down under his horse. His men pulled him out.[69]

Braddock, his hat tied on with a big white handkerchief knotted under his chin,[70] roared orders at other officers to form their men into small divisions and advance.[71] The power of the British army was its platoon fire power, its heavy rolling musketry, invincible at Minden and Fontenoy. If the French and Indians had no line of battle, no exposed front to attack, they must be blown out of the bushes.[72]

Captain Waggener, remembering the French at Fort Necessity, tried to lead his Virginia rangers up the hill, using the trunk of a great fallen tree as a parapet. He got that far with the loss of only three men; but the British, mistaking the fire of Waggener's concealed riflemen for that of the enemy, began shooting at the rangers. Some of the regular officers, who distrusted the provincials, thought the rangers were trying to get away.[73]

Washington, like Waggener, wanted to fight the French and Indians on their own terms. He asked Braddock's permission to scatter three hundred men among the trees. Bill Brown, Burton's Negro servant, thought he heard Braddock curse and reply: "I've a mind to run you through the body. We'll sup today in Fort Duquesne or else in hell!" [74]

Then Braddock noticed that the tall Virginian had a cushion on his saddle, and remembered that he was sick.

"Bishop," called Braddock to the old Coldstream guardsman behind him, "this young man is determined to go into action today, although he is really too weakened by illness for such purpose. Have an eye to him and render him any assistance that may be necessary."

"Your honor's orders shall be obeyed," said Bishop.[75]

Scarouady, who had an Indian's respect for ambuscades and was one of the few British scouts who had not disappeared, thought they should retreat. Otherwise the army would be destroyed, he said. He tried to catch Braddock's attention. He looked around for someone to intercede with the General. St Clair had come to. Scarouady asked him to talk to Braddock.[76]

"I would be of little use, being never listened to," said St. Clair.[77]

A few of the regulars took to the trees without being told. But Braddock, riding back and forth, hat tied under his resolute chin, beat them over the shoulder with the flat of his sword, ordering them back into line.

"Cowards!" he cried.[78]

He was determined that his orders should be obeyed, that the men should form under their officers, that they should advance in strength, shoulder to shoulder.[79]

Officers pleaded with men to obey. They threatened them. The French and Indians kept shooting.[80]

"One bold attack" was all Gage wanted.[81]

But his grenadiers had had enough of boldness. Less than a dozen of the Forty-Fourth's grenadier company seemed to have escaped gunshot wound. On the troop-crowded trail men still toppled over, falling hard with a jingle of belt buckles and bullet pouches and canteens, some of them gory, groaning or crying, some silent in sudden death. And not all the grenadier caps, with their little red flaps and white horse, had "GR" embroidered on yellow facings of the Forty-Fourth. Some of those lying around in the dirt had "GR" on the Forty-Eighth's white.[82]

"We would fight if we could see anybody to fight with," muttered one soldier.[83]

Gage could not say that he himself had seen more than one or two of the enemy. A few officers and men had seen as many as half a dozen.[84] Gordon and the guides, who had had a better view than anyone else, estimated that they did not exceed a total of 300.[85] But the French kept out of sight. Occasionally an Indian slithered out of the bushes to scalp some Redcoat shot down at a safe distance, but he did his cutting quickly and vanished again in the black gunpowder-smoked forest.[86]

Most of the British shooting was aimless. The Redcoats kept firing at smoke puffs and muzzle flashes. But they had gone into battle carrying only twenty-five [87] rounds and at times their gunfire grew thin and unsteady. Only when enough soldiers could be lined up to fire by platoon did the battle roar. But platoons, improvised and then disintegrating before they advanced twenty yards, never could be persuaded to charge the hill on the right or try to recapture the two lost 6-pounders.[88] Officers and groups of officers jumped out in front. Their example was unconvincing. Too many were shot. An ensign carrying the Great Union of the Forty-Eighth tried to lead. He was shot down. John Hamilton, the regimental chaplain, rescued the colors. A captain of the Forty-Fourth went down with two wounds, retrieving the King's colors dropped by too bold an ensign of his regiment.[89]

Lying dead under the walnut trees were the Forty-Fourth's colonel, Sir Peter Halkett, and his younger son, James, the major of brigade. Braddock had left the elder Halkett back on the road in command of the convoy, but Sir Peter had ridden up to see if he could do anything with the men of his own regiment. He knew panic. He had met it at Preston Pans where the Scot broadsword and lochaber ax had been as dreadful as the scalping knife and the tomahawk. He did not agree with Braddock's tactics. He thought the troops should take cover, in extended order, like the enemy.[90] But he tried to obey orders, to form his men into small parties, to make them fire by platoons. He was shot through the body. His son received a death wound going to his father's aid, and Sir Peter's servant was killed while looking to see if his master's wound was mortal.[91]

Captain Tatton of the Forty-Eighth was dead, shot by the grenadiers of his own regiment. So was Captain Chomondeley of the Forty-Eighth.[92] Lieutenant Spendlowe was dead. Braddock's secretary, young Shirley, was dead, shot through the head.[93] Both Orme and Morris had been wounded, Orme, with a bullet in his thigh. A ball had shattered Gordon's forearm, halfway between wrist and elbow, but the engineer was too anxious over the outcome to quit the field.[94]

Braddock pressed Captain Thomas Ord, commanding the Royal Regiment of Artillery detachment with the three 12-pounders, to clear the thickets within point blank range. Washington, dismounted, his thumbs hooked in the armholes of his waistcoat, while the General told Ord what to do, circled around, and said:

"General, be assured, even if you cut away the bushes, your enemy can make enough of them artificially to answer the purpose of shelter and concealment."

"What do you think of this from a young hand, from a beardless boy?" Braddock asked Ord.[95]

The beardless boy, now in the midst of his second battle with

French and Indians, had bullet slits in his hat and coat. He was still so weak from his illness that Bishop had lifted him out of the saddle of the second horse shot from under him, and he was Braddock's only remaining aide until joined by Captain Dobson of the Forty-Eighth, hastily assigned to replace the wounded Orme.[96]

Braddock's sabre swipes at skulkers, to drive them back into line and get them moving, had angered Americans unfamiliar with the code of the British officer corps. Some of the officers threatened men at sword point.[97] Private Tom Fausett, a big, rough Pennsylvania backwoodsman enlisted at Shippensburg by a recruiting party for Captain Chomondeley's company, gripped his King's musket with murderous intent when he saw a British officer's sword thrust through his brother, Joseph, when Joseph refused to face about.[98]

Until almost 4 o'clock, when half of his officers and men had been killed or wounded and the persistent fire from the French and Indians indicated that they had suffered no serious losses, there was always a possibility that Braddock might be able to get enough of his troops in hand to organize a counter attack and sweep the woods.[99] But as the forest battlefield became thick with dead and disabled redcoats, Braddock reconciled himself to retreat. An order was given to withdraw to the wagons. They would fall back with as much of the convoy as they could save. The drums began to beat *Retreat.*[100]

Four horses had been shot under Braddock during the hour and a half he had been riding up and down the woods, trying to whip fear-frozen foot soldiers into fighting fettle. He was about to mount his fifth horse when a bullet struck his right arm and penetrated his side. The pain was agonizing. He could not even sit erect.[101]

Bishop, ever close at hand, unwrapped the scarlet sash of silken net from around the General's waist. Almost as long as a hammock when stretched to its full length, the sash now served its ultimate purpose. In it the wounded Braddock was carried from the field by Bishop, Capt. Robert Stewart of the Virginia horse, and Col. Gage.[102] They carried him down the trail toward the baggage convoy where they lifted him into a wagon.[103]

Some of the horses and drivers had been shot. The column's rear guard, the South Carolina detachment, had beaten off an attack, but teamsters and batmen, standing around the horses and wagons and howitzers, were frightened.[104] They listened to the shooting farther up the trail. Wounded soldiers came walking back to the wagons. Half a dozen women, who had persisted in following the troops, helped dress injuries unseen or disregarded by an over-worked surgeon and his mates. Six of the surgeon's own party had been killed and five wounded.[105]

Most of the shooting up front now was that of about two hundred men commanded by a few officers who had either escaped injury or returned to duty after having their wounds tied up.[106] They kept loading and firing until they had exhausted all their ammunition and all they could find in the cartouche boxes of the dead and wounded strewn around them.[107] For a while Ord's cannoneers, ramming their 12-pounders with round shot after they had used all case shot in the ammunition wagon, kept firing, too. But the foot soldiers gave the gunners no protection and so many were picked off that one by one the 12-pounders were silenced.[108]

Stragglers sneaked away, down the trail through the woods to the baggage convoy. They hung around the wagons, talking about what they had seen—men killed and scalped! Fresh outbursts of musketry up the trail and a rising chorus of war whoops along the high ground on the right sent shivers through the wagon drivers.[109] Most of them were farmers. They had not been hired to fight, or to get scalped. They began unhitching the best of their horses, mounting and riding down the trail toward the river. One who rode away was Daniel Boone.[110]

Some of the soldiers standing around the wagons started down the trail on foot after the wagoners. Others had a better idea. They unhitched the remaining wagon horses. They unhooked the horses of the four howitzer teams. Then off came the surcingles and batsaddles of the carrying horses. Up went the batmen and anyone else who could lay hands on a packhorse. Soldiers still on foot began to run after those on horseback. Down the trail through the trees toward the river they ran, throwing away muskets, bayonets, belts.[111]

Washington watched some of them go.

"Sheep pursued by dogs," he said, knowing it would be useless to try to stop them.[112]

Left along the trail with more than a hundred other helpless wounded, unable to run, was the homesick young British officer whose disenchantment with America had begun with the Virginia planter who sold him a moonblind horse. Shot in one leg and in the heel of his other foot so he could not even hobble, he sat at the foot of a tree, imploring everyone who passed to help him.

The whole army seemed to be on the run, but an American who heard him paused a moment.

"Yes, countryman," he said, "I will put you out of your misery. These dogs shall not burn you."

He leveled his musket at the officer's head. The terrified Englishman yelled and ducked—heard the gun roar and felt its blast but no other pain; and knew the bullet had missed him.

Moments later a Lieut. Gray came along with men of the South Carolina detachment. They, too, were on their way to the river but they picked up the wounded officer and carried him with them.[113]

Capt. John Treby of the Forty-Fourth, lay writhing on the ground, wounded so desperately he could not crawl. Another volunteer, Thomas Farrell, took Treby up on his back and carried him toward the river.[114]

Near the wagon in which Braddock lay stood a small two-wheel covered cart, which had been used on the march to carry some of the General's equipage. It had shafts for one horse. Washington thought the cart a better conveyance than the wagon for the wounded Braddock. It would be lighter, faster. He and Stewart lifted the General into the cart.[115] Croghan came up to see if he could be of any help. Braddock looked longingly at the Irishman's pistols. Bishop or Washington carried the General's pistols. Braddock said he had no wish to live. Give him a pistol, look to their own safety, and leave him on the field.[116] They started for the river with Braddock in the cart.[117]

One of the last to leave the battleground up in the woods was Gordon, the engineer. Remembering the toil that had gone into building more than a hundred miles of road, all the way over those mountains from Wills Creek, he hated to run away now and abandon a whole train of artillery, a string of wagons and all those tools to a band of wild Indians. Nobody else seemed to have thought of saving anything but his scalp. Three bullets had crippled Gordon's horse. He shifted his saddle to a stray without a bridle.[118]

When he reached the ford at the river, at the foot of the trail near Fraser's house, he found the slope which the working party had cut in the bank that morning choked with soldiers, some on horseback, some on foot helping or carrying wounded. He put his own bridleless horse over the 12-foot sandy bluff. Sand caved in and tumbled with him as he hit the water. His horse nearly lost his footing and Gordon nearly lost his seat, but he managed to stick on and the horse stumbled through the shallow water toward the opposite shore.

Forty yards out in the stream he heard Indians yell behind him. He looked back and saw them tomahawking wounded soldiers and struggling with some women near the wagons. Other Indians fired at the troops crossing the river. Gordon got another bullet through his right shoulder before he reached the other side of the stream.

A short distance up the river bank he caught up with Burton,[119] Orme, Washington, and the two-wheel cart in which the General lay. About a quarter of a mile back from the river, perhaps 200 yards off the road, was a hill where Orme thought the wounded might be collected and protected until help came up. Burton talked to some of the soldiers who seemed less demoralized than others. He persuaded them to post pickets and organize a guard.[120]

Braddock was in great pain but fully aware of all that was happening. He asked Washington to ride ahead to the upper ford and try to rally more of the retreating troops. Washington rode as far as the hill on the other side of the upper ford, where he found Gage, who appeared to have reestablished discipline over 80 or 100 soldiers. Gage seemed to be doing everything that could be done to halt the fleeing men, so Washington left the General's order with him and turned about. At sunset he recrossed the river and unexpectedly met Burton, Orme, and the others coming up the road with Braddock in a hand litter.[121]

The soldiers of Burton's provisional guard for the General had run away soon after Washington had left them.[122] They had changed their mind about remaining so near the lower ford, with Indians whooping just across the river. Braddock had been placed in a litter, because he could no longer stand the pain of being moved in a springless cart. The bullet through his arm and side had penetrated his lungs. But he was conscious. He could think and talk. He asked Washington to set out immediately for Dunbar's camp, to send back food, rum, and hospital supplies for the wounded. The stuff should be sent back under an escort of grenadiers. Braddock would meet them at Gist's plantation, or nearer if possible.[123]

Still weak from his own illness, Washington had been in the sad-

dle since early morning. At the end of the battle he had been doing
the work of three aides. Dunbar's camp was forty miles away. But
Washington knew the road. With two mounted guides for company
he turned his horse about, crossed the upper ford for the fourth
time that day, and started back along the forest trail. Even that
far from the battlefield the road was dotted with dead and dying.
He would never forget the groans, the lamentations, the cries of
wounded for help as he rode past in the gathering darkness. Night
fell. There was no moon. The thick shade of the trees shut out the
starlight. Once, when they lost the trail in the dark, the guides dismounted and groped around on the ground with their hands until
they left the wagon wheel ruts that marked the way.[124]

But Washington was not the only man living a nightmare. Late
that afternoon an Indian runner had carried tidings of the battle
back to Fort Duquesne. Young Smith was as eager as anyone to
know the outcome. Some of the older French soldiers at the fort
spoke Dutch. Smith knew enough Pennsylvania Dutch to ask them
what news the runner brought. They told him the French and
Indians had surrounded Braddock, that unless the British took to
the river not one would be alive by sundown.[125]

Later that evening Smith heard the scalp-halloos of a returning
war party. He looked out and saw them coming down the trail toward the fort, Indians in grenadier caps, harnessed with British
bayonets and canteens, waving fresh scalps in their bloody hands,
firing muskets in the air. They were answered by yells and gun
blasts from the French and Indians at the fort, who went out to
greet the returning warriors.

Behind the first war party came a second of about a hundred
Indians with more scalps. Then a third, some riding captured
wagon horses, whooping, shooting, and waving scalps. About sundown another small party brought in a dozen naked prisoners,
hands tied behind their backs, faces and parts of their bodies black-
ened. Finally came the last of the pillagers, Indians ludicrously
dressed in ill-fitting red uniform coats, disarrayed scarlet sashes, the
laced hats and burnished gorgets of British officers.

One of the prisoners was tied to a stake on the river bank opposite the fort. A fire was kindled at his feet. Indian tormenters kept
poking him with blazing sticks and red hot irons. The tortured
man's cries of agony were too much for Smith. Horrified, he
climbed down from the wall of the fort and went back to his prison

lodgings. The whooping Indians must have burned all their prisoners at the stake that night. Smith never again saw one of them
alive.[126]

Braddock must have gone through the night in spirit with Hawley, whose heart was broken at Falkirk—and with Johnny Cope, at
Preston Pans, where you feinted here and parried there against
wild Scotsmen. And with old Humphrey who had written in his
book, Chapter VIII, page 132:

> When an officer has had the misfortune of being beat, his honor will
> not suffer by it, providing he has done his duty, and acted like a sol-
> dier. But if he is surprised by neglecting the common methods used to
> prevent it, his character is hardly retrievable, unless it proceeds from
> his want of experience; and even in that case he will find it very
> difficult.[127]

Had Braddock been surprised? Had he done his duty? For a hundred miles he had marched by old Humphrey's book.

Gage had been talking to some of his soldiers. "The only excuse
I can get from them," he said, "is that they were greatly dispirited
from fatigue they had undergone and from not receiving a sufficient quantity of food, and further that they did not expect the
enemy would come down so suddenly." [128]

All night they retreated along the same dark lane of wretched
wounded that Washington had traveled ahead of them. They tried
to pick up the helpless who seemed to have a chance of surviving.
Those able to walk struggled on. Better order was established
among the soldiers after daylight, but hunger and fatigue were beginning to tell. By noon, only fear of the French and Indians kept
most of them going. Orme had difficulty persuading enough men
to carry the General's litter, at first offering thirty, then sixty, then
eighty guineas and rum punch. Braddock's officers carried him for
twenty miles. About 3 o'clock in the afternoon the old Guardsman
gritted his teeth and was lifted back into a saddle.[129]

Gordon, whose wounds had not yet been dressed, suggested they
halt at one of the more defensible of their old camp sites and wait
there for Dunbar.[130] But they kept on, hoping the relief convoy
might meet them at the main crossing of the Youghiogheny. It was
sunset of the following day, July 10, when they reached the river.
They had come more than forty miles. And no sign yet of a convoy. They crossed the river and went on until dark, another seven
miles, to the burned cabins of Gist's plantation, where they

dropped on the ground and slept in the open. There was not even a tent for the General.[131]

Braddock was dazed with pain and weariness. "Who would have thought it?" he murmured.[132]

Dunbar's column was encamped only six miles away, in a stoney hollow at Rock Fort, the British name for the cliff where Jumonville had been killed. Early that morning a drover's boy had started out from there for Braddock's advance party with a herd of cattle, but about 9 o'clock he reappeared in Dunbar's camp with vague rumors of "bad news." Apparently he had met some of the wagoners and packhorse drivers who had run away at the end of the battle. One had reached Dunbar's camp at 5 A.M. The boy may have seen Washington, who arrived too sick and exhausted to do more than deliver Braddock's orders that wagons and supplies meet him at Gist's.[133]

Three Pennsylvania wagoners saw a wounded officer—one saw two—carried through the camp on a sheet. At noon the drummers beat *To Arms.* By that time rumors had bred rumors that two officers on their way to join Braddock had found the trail blocked by the enemy, that Braddock's force had been wiped out by French and Indians who had dug a trench across the road and attacked the marching column with swivel guns; that Braddock was dead, fallen upon by Indians and murdered after he had been placed in a wagon wounded . . . and now the drums were beating *To Arms!* The alarm spread a fringe of panic that sent a few frightened teamsters and soldiers headlong down the trail toward Fort Cumberland before Dunbar's sentries could stop them.[134]

About 1 o'clock Sir John St. Clair was brought into the Rock Fort camp. He gave Dunbar his first full account of the battle.[135] St. Clair was bitter. He said Braddock had fallen into a trap after ignoring his advice to halt until Dunbar's division came up.

"I urged strongly that no General had hitherto marched up midday to the gates of the town he was besieging leading his convoy," said St. Clair.

"All I could say to General Braddock could not make him stop . . . his advisers were so much prepossessed that nothing was wanting at Fort Duquesne for the reduction of it but his presence. . . ." [136]

Dunbar said Braddock had told him that he would never be more than a day's march ahead.

"His orders to me was to fire a gun (a six-pounder) if I wanted his assistance, and if he wanted mine he was to do the same." [137]

The wagons and supplies Braddock had asked of Dunbar did not reach Gist's until 11 o'clock next morning. Gordon and others who had not yet seen a surgeon had their wounds dressed.[138] When everyone at Gist's had been cared for, Braddock ordered that a sergeant's party should go back along the trail as far as the other side of the Youghiogheny's main crossing and leave food along the road where it could be found by any soldiers who might have become lost in the woods during their flight.[139] Gordon again suggested that an end be made of the column's withdrawal, that Gist's place could be fortified with two or three redoubts to withstand any attack the enemy was likely to make upon them. But again this suggestion was ignored.[140]

That evening Braddock and the main body of his retreating force, both wounded and unhurt, dribbled into Dunbar's camp. Braddock was in no condition to talk. "We shall know better how to deal with them another time," was all he had to say of what had happened.[141]

But he showed no signs of relinquishing command.[142] Orders came from his tent to make preparations to begin a general withdrawal to Fort Cumberland next day. No one questioned the wisdom or authority of the order. His army had lost its will to fight.

Casualties were still being counted. Of sixty-nine grenadiers in the company from Halkett's regiment, all but eight were reported killed or wounded. Of seventy-nine in the grenadier company from Dunbar's regiment, less than a dozen seemed to have escaped injury. Every officer of the two companies had been killed or wounded. Only fifteen of the sailors had come through the battle unhurt.[143] As far as Washington could make out not more than thirty men were left of the three Virginia companies in the battle.[144] Of the 1,500 officers and men who had gone into action, it was estimated that a total of about 1,000 had been killed and wounded. Three or four of eight women with the advance party were missing.[145]

All artillery and wagons with the advance force, a hundred head of cattle, and between four and five hundred horses had been left on the battlefield. In one of the wagons were all the General's papers, including his secret instructions outlining the proposed plan of campaign against the French, and, some said, a military chest variously reported to have contained £1,000, £2,500, and £12,000. Later, Johnston, the commissary officer, said the military chest and vouchers were safe at Dunbar's camp, where they had been left with the train.[146]

The lost horses were an item of first importance to Dunbar. He complained that Braddock had taken all the best horses when the force was divided, and, in response to repeated requests to send some back, had returned only those that were worn out and could not go on. "I told him it was impossible I could get up with him unless his Goodness would halt and send me his horses to help me," said Dunbar.[147]

But Braddock's orders to continue the retreat left it up to Dunbar to find enough horses and wagons to haul the least ambulatory of about 400 sick and wounded to Fort Cumberland. There was only one solution: dump food, ammunition, and ordnance supplies with which the remaining wagons of his train were loaded. It was not necessary to consult the General, Dunbar was told. Provide transportation for the wounded and teams for the army's only remaining artillery, the two brass six-pounders left with Dunbar when the force separated at Little Meadows. If possible these guns must be saved. Destroy everything else he could not carry.[148]

Older officers, among the few still on their feet who had not lost their heads, looked at each other. Captain Ord, the artillery officer, did not question the wisdom of destroying what they could not carry rather than let it fall into enemy hands. But neither he nor James Furnis, the commissary of stores for the Ordnance Board with Braddock's expedition, were going to destroy anything without written orders. They were looking ahead to the day when they might be asked for explanations, when an official return would have to be submitted to the Ordnance Board of London. So an order was produced—or at least the copy of an order—signed by Captain Dobson, still serving as the General's aide.[149]

No one—not even Gordon—suggested that a stand be made at Dunbar's camp. Surrounded by hills, which commanded it from all sides, it was about the worst chosen piece of ground for a defensible camp site that could have been found in wild, mountainous country.[150]

Most of the next day was spent unloading wagons and disposing of stores and provisions freighted so laboriously up from the sea and over the mountains. The stout heads of 162 copper-hooped barrels of gunpowder were stove in and the powder dumped in a little stream below the camp. Fifteen hundred artillery shells were broken open. Cannon balls, musket bullets, barrels of flour, casks of salted meat were scattered over the ground. Pick-axes, spades, hatchets, even the blacksmith's tools and his horseshoe nails were flung into the bushes. One zealot threw away the engineer's instruments and stationery. When they were through, Dunbar still had 150 wagons for which he had no horses. These wagons were ordered burned.[151] By then it was too late to break camp that day. The retreat was delayed until the morrow. It was just as well. A great number of missing officers and soldiers, some of them wounded, came straggling in that afternoon.

One straggler, Private Duncan Cameron, an old soldier of Halkett's regiment who had been with Gage's advance guard, told of having hidden in a hollow tree after being left on the battlefield for dead and finding himself overrun by the enemy. He said the French had put a stop to the scalping of dead and wounded British soldiers, that the Indians then fell to plundering army baggage, found a small amount of rum, and got themselves drunk. There were still other wounded stragglers back along the trail, Cameron said, who had begged him for God's sake to be helped along.[152]

All evening the battle was refought, some officers blaming the cowardice of their men for their defeat.

"I hope never to live to see that argument hold good against our men unless some previous steps were taken to make them dilatory in doing their duty," was St. Clair's pontifical opinion.[153]

"I can't help thinking their misbehavior is exaggerated, in order to palliate the blunders made by those in the direction, as they make no allowance for regular troops being surprised," argued one of Dunbar's officers.[154]

"It was the pride and ignorance of that General that came from England," said Scarouady. "He looked upon us as dogs, and would never hear anything what was said to him. We often tried to tell him of the danger he was in with his soldiers, but he never appeared pleased with us, and that was the reason that a great many of our warriors left him and would not be under his command."

British soldiers, said the Indian chief, "were unfit to fight in the woods." [155]

If Braddock made any excuses they were in confidence. But Bishop said that while holding the General in his arms on the battlefield, he had heard him say to Washington:

"Oh, my dear, had I been governed by your advice we never should have come to this." [156]

The column had not moved far from Rock Fort next morning when some footsore invalid discovered that one wagon of the shortened train was loaded with powder and seven cohorns. Captain Dobson ordered a squad of pioneers to dig a pit beside the road and bury the cohorns.[157]

Braddock was still giving orders. His mind was clear, but he was in no condition to command. He was a dying man, weak from loss of blood and the fatigue of travel in pain.[158] He seems to have suggested that 200 Foot and what remained of Stewart's light horse troop push ahead with the wounded.[159] And then, about a mile beyond the Rock Fort, he called Dunbar and told him to take command.[160]

They did not march far that day. Intending to make use of their old camp sites they had a choice of one, three-and-half miles from the Rock Fort, or another, seven miles farther on. They chose the nearer, halting for the night by a brook in a glade to the west of Fort Necessity, where Braddock had encamped his advance detachment three weeks before.[161] Many bivouacked in the open that night, giving their tents to the wounded.[162]

Dr. James Craik, a friend of Washington and the surgeon of the Virginia troops, looked in on Braddock.[163] Braddock knew he had not long to live. And now that he had seen them fight, he thought better of all Virginians. He asked that Captain Stewart of the light horse be commended to Dinwiddie.[164]

To Bishop, his body servant, the General said:

"Bishop, you are getting too old for war. I advise you to remain in America and go into the service of Mr. Washington. Be as faithful to him as you have been to me." [165]

Braddock also talked to the wounded Orme. As soon as Orme was able to write, Braddock told him, he must send an account of the action to Henry Fox. Fox would tell George Anne. Tell Fox, said Braddock: "The behaviour of the officers deserved the very highest commendations." [166]

Orme must, of course, also inform Keppel. Orme was already framing the letter in his mind. . . . "A few hours before his death . . . the General directed me, sir, to tell you from him that. . . ."

"Nothing could equal the gallantry and conduct of the officers nor the bad behavior of the men," said Braddock.[167]

It was all according to the book, in which Old Humphrey had written that when private soldiers go into battle they look for their notions of danger to the conduct of their officers, and that "fortune may fail us if we trust too much to her, but a prudent conduct never will. It is true we may be overpowered and conquered, notwithstanding all our care; but never shamefully beat if we act as we ought; and a man may gain reputation, though he is overcome." [168]

It was sunset. The drummers beat *Retreat*.

"Is it possible?" murmured Braddock.[169]

He had only until about 9 o'clock that night to wonder. He was dying.[170]

"All is over," he said.[171]

In the morning the drums beat the *General*. Up the road, beyond the head of the column, in the middle of the trail where the troops would march, a squad of pioneers had dug the General's grave. He had been buried there at midnight, decently though privately, with honors of war. And now the drums beat the *March*. Off moved the column on the next stretch of its retreat, the soldiers' boots, the horses' hoofs, the broad rims of the wagon wheels obliterating all signs of the grave.

Washington had advised it to be done that way. He was fearful that French and Indians, hearing of Braddock's death, would try to find his body and desecrate it.

They did hear, and they did try to find his grave. But the marching column had stamped it out.[172]

XIV

REQUIEM

NINETEEN FRIGHTENED SETTLERS, seeking refuge from Indian war parties after the border outrages of June, moved into Fort Cumberland. Some of the wives left behind by Braddock's soldiers were still there. They blanched at the ghastly stories the settlers told. One man had been killed within three miles of the fort. A boy who had been scalped alive was brought to the fort hospital. He died four days later. The soldiers' wives were terrified.[1]

The widow Brown's brother was sick with fever, flux, and fits, and her maid was ill with fever on July 7—the day Braddock reached Turtle Creek—when a party of Indians professing to be friendly appeared before the fort. Col. Innes ordered the gates shut. The Indians stood outside for four hours. It was a hot Monday. There was no water in the fort, and still no well. Mrs. Brown was thankful when the Indians left. Ill herself before her brother and her maid had been taken sick, she had worn herself out nursing them.[2]

Four days later, about noon, a boy rode into the fort. He had come from Dunbar's camp. He said Braddock had been killed and nearly all of Sir Peter Halkett's regiment cut off and massacred by French and Indians hiding in the woods four miles from the French fort. Later in the afternoon wagoners and camp followers arrived at Wills Creek from Dunbar's camp with much the same tale. But they could give Innes few details. What they told him was what they had heard early that morning.[3]

Soldiers' wives at the fort went into hysterics. Mrs. Brown packed her things, expecting the Indians every hour. Her brother tried to persuade her to leave the fort immediately and start back toward Frederick and Winchester, but she refused to go. She would not leave her brother.[4]

Col. Innes wrote a note:

> Sir: I have this minute received the melancholy account of the defeat of our troops, the General killed and numbers of our officers, our whole artillery taken in short the account I have received is so very bad, that, as please God I intend to make a stand here, it's highly necessary to raise the militia everywhere to defend the frontiers.
>
> Your humble servant
James Innes
>
> To all to whom this may concern
> Fort Cumberland, July 11th, 1755 [5]

The distracted Colonel handed this note to a mounted messenger and told him to ride east and spread the alarm. Next day a horseman delivered the note to Col. William Fairfax at Belvoir, the Fairfax estate just below Mount Vernon. Fairfax made a certified copy which he sent by express, across the Potomac and through Marlboro, to Gov. Sharpe.[6] He sent the original on to Williamsburg; it reached Dinwiddie the night of July 14.[7] The Virginia governor could not believe what the note said. He had predicted the French would surrender without a fight.[8]

A fortnight passed before another messenger from Fort Cumberland arrived in Williamsburg with letters for the Governor from Washington and Orme.[9] With these came a letter from Orme addressed to Napier, and as complete a casualty list as the General's wounded aide could compile.[10] Dinwiddie wrote out reports of his own to Sir Thomas Robinson and Lord Halifax, delivering the entire packet to Commodore Keppel at Hampton Roads.[11]

Keppel had transferred his flag to the "Seahorse." On July 26 the "Seahorse" sailed for England, in company with the "Norwich" and the "Centurion." She put in at Portsmouth one month later.[12]

From his Gothic rococo villa at Strawberry Hill, Horace Walpole already was circulating malicious gossip about the unlucky Braddock.

"He has not yet sent over to claim the surname of Americus," Walpole had written to Bentley on August 15.[13]

And a few days later, in a letter to Mann:

The Duke, who is now the soul of the Regency, and who on all hands is allowed to make a great figure there, is much dissatisfied at the slowness of General Braddock, who does not march as if he were at all impatient to be scalped. It is said of him, that he has had bad guides, that the roads are exceedingly difficult, and that it was necessary to drag as much artillery as he does. This is not the first time, as witness in Hawley, that the Duke has found that brutality did not necessarily consummate a General. I love to give you an idea of our characters as they rise upon the stage of history. Braddock is very iroquois in disposition. . . .

Walpole then proceeded to rehash the tragedy of Braddock's sister, Fanny. He related the story of the General's affair with Mrs. Upton.

"Now you are acquainted with General Braddock," he told Mann.[14]

The news of Braddock's disaster reached Whitehall on Tuesday, August 26. It was published next day in *The Public Advertiser*. The newspaper account stated that Braddock had been defeated by an entrenched force of 2,100 French regulars and irregulars, and that according to rumour most of the British officers lost in the action had been fired upon and killed by "European troops" while attempting to rally their men.[15]

At a summer house she and Calcraft now maintained at Holwood, about ten miles southeast of London, George Anne Bellamy was recovering from a broken shoulder, a compound fracture of her left arm and a broken hand—injuries received in a riding accident—when Calcraft walked into her room with a long face.

"Bad news from America!" exclaimed George Anne, prompted by what she called her second sight.

Calcraft nodded.

"My fears are too prophetic," she said, "and I have lost a second father." [16]

Walpole summarized the newspaper reports in a letter to Mann.

"I have already given you some account of Braddock," Walpole wrote. "I may complete the poor man's history with a few words."

He devoted those words to the Braddock-Gumley duel.[17]

Fed by private letters from America, the London newspapers chewed on Braddock's defeat for the next two months. Especially critical was *The Public Advertiser* which said Braddock was universally disliked by reason of his overbearing, rough, haughty disposition, and that the failure of his expedition, badly conducted from the start, attested to his own obstinacy in insisting that his soldiers fight in formation.[18] *The Gentleman's Magazine* said Braddock was by natural disposition the most unfit person in the world to command in a situation where cool circumspection and affable behavior were necessary to success. But the magazine also printed some verses on his death:

> *Beneath some Indian shrub, if chance you spy*
> *The brave remains of murdered* Braddock *lie,*
> *Soldier, with shame the guilty place survey,*
> *And weep, that here your comrades fled away.*
> *Then, with his brother-chiefs* * *encircled round*
> *Possess the hero's bones of hostile ground*
> *And plant the English* ** *oak that gave his name,*
> *Fit emblem to his* valour *and his* fame!
> *Broad o'er this stream* *** *shall this his honors grow,*
> *And last as long as e'er the waters flow.*

———

* His officers.

** *Brad* in old Saxon English is the same as *broad* and *Brad-oke* is the same as *Broad-oak.*

*** The Ohio.[19]

And this "apology for the Men who deserted General Braddock when surprised by the ambuscade":

> *Ah!* Braddock *why did you persuade*
> *To stand and fight each recreant blade,*
>   *That left thee in the wood?*
> *They knew that those who run away,*
> *Might live to fight another day,*
>   *But all must die who stood.*[20]

"Braddock's defeat still remains in the situation of the longest battle that ever was fought with nobody," Walpole wrote Bentley at the end of August.[21]

On the third day of September, John Calcraft appeared before Andrew Colbee Ducarel, a London surrogate, to prove the General's will and be sworn as an administrator of Braddock's estate, like powers being reserved to Mary Yorke, the other executor, "when she shall apply for the same."[22] Sometime later the Treasury made a demand for the return of government plate left by the General. The demand was rejected and a suit was instituted but failed. The plate remained on George Anne's table.[23]

Until they became fully aware of the extent of Braddock's defeat, Morris and Dinwiddie both assumed that Dunbar would reorganize the force under his command and make another attempt to capture the French fort that summer.[24] Sharpe was less optimistic.[25] But the least any of them expected of Dunbar was that he would protect the frontier.[26] Dunbar had no such intentions. He was going into winter quarters. He reached Fort Cumberland on the afternoon of July 22 with three hundred wounded officers and men. Court Martials convened. Soldiers accused of mutiny and desertion in the battle were lashed. On August 2 Dunbar marched on to Philadelphia, leaving the wounded in the fort hospital.[27]

"I must confess the whole conduct of Col. Dunbar appears monstrous to me," Dinwiddie told Sharpe.[28]

To the inhabitants of western Maryland, Pennsylvania, and Virginia, left to the mercy of the French and Indians, Dunbar's withdrawal was both cowardly and heartless.[29] Hot heads like Daniel Dulaney, to whom all British officers were obnoxious, took out their resentment on Braddock.[30] Private Tom Fausset, a deserter from the Forty-Eighth Foot after the battle, boasted that he had killed Braddock to avenge the death of his brother.[31]

But even in towns as far west as Frederick, people were not reduced to utter panic. The Widow Brown, following Dunbar's column through Frederick, attended a ball there where the ladies danced without hoops or stays, a ball which ended with a jig from each lady.[32]

As soon as he had recovered enough from his wound to travel in the General's coach, still at Fort Cumberland with Sharpe's chariot, Orme started home. From Fort Cumberland he drove to Philadelphia.[33] Backbiting had become an occupational disease of his fellow officers there with Dunbar.[34] Somebody—possibly Gage or one of his friends—published an advertisement in the *Pennsylvania Gazette* stating that the main body of Braddock's troops had been in confusion before going into action the day of the battle.[35] Gage had applied for the colonelcy of the Forty-Fourth, vacated by the death of Sir Peter Halkett.[36] Other officers were still writing letters home about the battle. Anxious to uphold their own reputations in the shame of defeat, they used Braddock and his favorites as scapegoats on whom to lay the blame for every error of the campaign.[37]

It was the same with Virginians, fiercely proud of their rangers who had suffered such heavy losses in the battle. Washington, home again at Mount Vernon, wrote to Orme in Philadelphia:

> It is impossible to relate the different accounts that was given of our late unhappy engagement but all tended to the disadvantage of the poor deceased General, who is censored on all hands.[38]

In a long and rather melancholy reply to Washington, Orme wrote:

> That part of your letter mentioning the reflections upon the General gives me much uneasiness though I feel a contempt for the detractors which alleviates in some degree my concern. I know the ignorant and rascally C—— D—— is one promoter through resentment and malevolence and the thick headed baronet another, intending to build his character upon the ruins of one much more amiable than his can be. For my part I judge it a duty to vindicate the memory of a man whom I greatly and deservedly esteemed and I think every man whom he regarded should be his advocate, keeping literally to the facts which must always improve the goodness of his disposition. I am convinced the affection he bore you as well as your integrity and good nature will make you assiduous in removing these abominable prejudices the generality of people have imbibed and publish. It is very hard the bluntness and openness of a man's temper should be called brutality and that he who would hear opinions more freely than any man should be accused of obstinacy and peremtoriness. In short in a thousand particulars I find such lies and opposites that I will say no more.[39]

"This general was, I think, a brave man, and might probably have made a figure as a good officer in some European war," Franklin wrote in his *Autobiography*. "But he had too much self-confidence, too high an opinion of the validity of regular troops, and too mean a one of both Americans and Indians." [40]

Recalling the circumstances of Braddock's death in a biographical memoranda which he made twenty-eight years later, Washington wrote:

> Thus died a man whose good and bad qualities were intimately blended. He was brave even to a fault and in the regular service would have done honor to his profession. His attachments were warm. His enmities strong, and having no disguise, both appeared in full force. He was generous and disinterested, but plain and blunt in manner, even to rudeness.[41]

Later, when he had become the first President of the United States, Washington one day got to talking about Braddock's expedition with William Findley, a Pennsylvania congressman. Findley, who was 14 years old at the time of Braddock's defeat, remarked that from the time of his Pennsylvania boyhood he had had a bad impression of Braddock.

"True, true," said Washington, "he was unfortunate, but his character was much too severely treated."

Washington said he himself had gone back along the trail and looked for Braddock's grave, intending to erect a monument. But the route of the road had been changed. He could not tell where Braddock was buried.[42]

Sometime around 1820, workmen repairing the road dug a skeleton from the bank of the little stream near the site of the camp where the General died. From metal buttons and other insignia said to have been found in the grave, it was assumed that the bones were Braddock's. Those of one hand were sent to the Peale Museum, in Philadelphia.[43] The others were buried again at the foot of an oak tree beside the road. In time the oak died. The site was enclosed with a board fence painted white. Pine trees were planted inside the fence. The fence rotted and disappeared. Not until 1913 was a granite monument erected to mark the supposed burial place.

"Here lieth the remains of Major General Edward Braddock . . ." says a bronze plaque on the granite, which bears the crest of the Coldstream Guards.

NOTES

II. ANCESTRY AND EDUCATION OF A GUARDSMAN

1. *Memoirs of John Evelyn,* ii 148
2. *Bishop Burnet's History of His Own Times,* 31, 125; *The Stuarts,* Sir Charles Petrie, 78ff; *The Royal House of Stuart,* Samuel Cowan, ii 148
3. The London *Times,* January 29, 1949, 5 ("January 30, 1649," G. Kitson Clark); *Evelyn,* ii B2, 4
4. *The Works of King Charles the Martyr,* Eikon Bsailike, 208ff
5. *Evelyn,* ii 148-9; *Diary of Samuel Pepys,* i 150ff; *London in the Time of the Stuarts,* Sir Walter Besant, 74ff; Cowan, ii 199; *Continuation of the Memoirs of the Court of England,* John Heneage Jesse, 1 207; *The Life of General Monk,* Thomas Gumble, 252, 388ff; *Royalty Restored,* J. Fitzgerald Molloy, i 24ff; *Origin and Services of the Coldstream Guards,* Daniel MacKinnon, i 95
6. *Evelyn,* ii 148-9; Gumble, 252; *England Under the Stuarts,* John Heneage Jesse, iii 41ff; MacKinnon, i 12ff; Gumble, 1ff; *Angliae Notitia,* Edward Chamberlayne, Part II, 195
7. MacKinnon, 1 96; JHC viii 171-2, 318, 321
8. Burnett, 54ff; Petrie, 215ff; *Social England,* ed. H. D. Traill, iv, 338; *A Short History of the English People,* by John Richard Green, ii 165; *The History of England from the Accession of James II,* Thomas Babington Macaulay (Everyman's Edition), i 123ff; *A Detection of the Court and State of England,* Roger Coke, ii 60; *The Last Years of the Protectorate,* Charles Harding Firth, i 7ff, 122ff, 134ff; *Oliver Cromwell and His Times,* Thomas Cromwell, 425ff; *Oliver Cromwell,* John Banks, 174
9. MacKinnon, 1 98ff; *A History of the British Army,* J. W. Fortescue, i 289ff; Burnet, 78-9
10. MacKinnon, i 85ff; Gumble, 172ff
11. Fortescue, i 291; Gumble, 402
12. MacKinnon, i 95; *Angliae Notitia,* 250, 251; Burnett, 66; *England Under the Stuarts,* John Heneage Hesse, iii 41ff
13. MacKinnon, i 129ff, 201
14. *Ibid.,* 105, 114ff; *Angliae Notitia, 1684,* 135; *The Origin and History of the First or Grenadier Guards,* F. W. Hamilton, i 4ff, 143; *The Military Forces of the Crown,* Charles M. Clode, i 364

15. *English Army Lists and Commission Registers*, Charles Dalton, i 296; *Calendar of State Papers*, (Domestic Series), 1682, F. H. Blackbourne Daniell, ed. 251

16. *Staffordshire Pedigrees* (Harleian Society Publications, Vol. 63), 31; seal on the will of Edward Braddock, Esq., late Major General of His Majesty's Forces, Principal Probate Registry, London.

17. *The Visitation of Norfolk* (Harleian Society Publications, Vol. 32), 46

18. *A Register of the Parish of St. Peter's Upon Cornhill* (HSP, Register Section, Vol. 1), 184; *The Parish Registers of St. Michael*, Cornhill (HSP, RS, Vol. 7), 212; *The Registers of Christ Church*, New gate (HSP, RS, Vol. 21), 284; *The Registers of St. Mary the Virgin*, Aldermanbury (HSP, RS, Vol. 61), 44-5-6-7; *The Register of St. Martin-in-the-Fields* (HSP, RS, Vol. 66), 287, 289; *The Register of St. Lawrence Jewry* (HSP, RS, Vol. 70), 113, 135; *The Registers of St. Michael Bassishaw* (HSP, RS, Vol. 73), 101; *Allegations for Marriage Licenses Issued by Dean and Chapter at Westminster* (HSP, Vol. 23), 232; *Allegations for Marriage Licenses, Etc.* (HSP, Vol. 25), 109, 193, 209; *Allegations for Marriage Licenses, Etc.* (HSP, Vol. 26), 318; *Calendar of Marriage Licenses Issued by the Faculty Office* (Index Library, British Record Society, Vol. 33), 19, 96, 161; *Calendar of Marriage License Allegations in the Registry of the Bishop of London* (I L, BRS, Vol. 62), 78, 162; *Calendar of Marriage License Allegations, Etc.* (IL, BRS, Vol. 66), 18, 24; *Administrations in the Archdeaconry of Northampton* (IL, BRS, Vol. 70), 124; *Calendar of State Papers* (Domestic Series), Charles II: Addenda, 1660–1685, F. H. Blackburne Daniell ed., 419; *Calendar of State Papers* (Domestic Series), May 1690–October 1691, John Hardy ed., 445-6; *Calendar of Treasury Books*, prepared by William Shaw, ix Part 5 1910, Part 4 1831, 1935; x (1935) Part 2 691; xxi (1952) Part 2 422

19. *Staffordshire Pedigrees*, 31

20. *A List of Scholars of St. Peter's College*, Westminster, Joseph Welch, 18

21. *Staffordshire Pedigrees*, 72, 116, 260

22. *Ibid.*, 31

23. *Allegations for Marriage Licenses Issued by the Vicar General of the Archbishop of Canterbury* (HSP, Vol. 33), 105-6

24. "The Will of Edward Braddock of the Parish of St. Margaret's, 1708," Principal Probate Registry, London; *The Marriage, Baptismal and Burial Registers of the Collegiate Church or Abbey of St. Peter*, Westminster (HSP, Vol. 10), 263n; Angliae Notitia, 1682, 234, 288; *The Old Cheque Book of the Chappel Royal from 1561 to 1744*, edited from original manuscript etc., Edward F. Rimbault, printed by the Camden Society, 12

25. *Angliae Notitia 1682*, 229; Whitehall, W. J. Loftie, 68; Letter from the Lord Chamberlain's office, St. James's Palace, July 27, 1956

26. *Allegations for Marriage Licenses Etc.* (HSP, Vol. 33), 106

27. *Westminster Registers* (HSP, Vol. 10), 263n

28. *Ibid.* (The Will of the elder Edward Braddock of St. Margaret's [*Op. Cit.* 24] mentions a granddaughter, Arabella Braddock. There is no record of his son, Edward, having had a daughter by that name, hence the uncertainty about the number of the elder Braddock's children.)

29. *Allegations for Marriage Licenses Etc.* (HSP 23), 232; *Cheque-Book*, 15

30. DNB, ii 723ff; *Westminster Registers*, 266n; *Cheque Book*, 16, 23

31. Clode, ii, 75ff

32. MacKinnon, ii, 464ff

33. *Ibid.*, ii 385, 405ff; Fortescue, i 310ff

34. Clode, i 106; ii 115-6; Fortescue, i 315; *English Social History*, G. M. Trevelyan, 309

35. Clode, i 36-7, 67-8
36. Traill, 512ff; Fortescue, i 316ff
37. MacKinnon, ii 384-5; Fortescue, i 318; *Social England*, H. D. Traill, iv 512ff; *Historical Memoirs of His Late Royal Highness William Augustus Duke of Cumberland*, 467; Macaulay, 1 713
38. MacKinnon, 1 161ff; *The Microcosm of London*, ii 162; Clode, i 57ff, 221ff
39. Loftie, 15ff; *Memoirs of Count Grammont*, Anthony Hamilton, i 142
40. Jesse (*England Under the Stuarts*), ii 493; Molloy, i 203; MacKinnon, i 167
41. *Theatre Royal Drury Lane*, W. J. Macqueen Pope, 44ff; *The Story of Nell Gwynn*, Cecil Chesterton, 61ff; *Nell Gwynn*, Lewis Melville, 194ff; *The Story of Nell Gwynn*, Peter Cunningham, xxxv, 55ff; *Evelyn*, ii 339; *Some Account of the English Stage*, the Rev. John Genest, i 380ff
42. Macaulay, i 353ff; *Memoirs of the Duke of Marlborough*, William Coxe, i 1ff; Grammont, ii 151ff; Burnet, 486; *A Brief Relation of State Affairs from September 1678 to April 1714*, Narcissus Luttrell, i 242
43. Macaulay, i 195ff; Burnet, 116-7; Luttrell, i 215, 222
44. Petrie, 306; Burnet, 114-5, 244-5, 401
45. *Evelyn*, ii 436, iii 92, 195; Luttrell, i 346ff; Burnet, 272-3, 366
46. Burnet, 114ff; Petrie, 302, *James the Second*, Hillaire Belloc, 157ff; Macaulay, i 162; *British Plays From the Restoration to 1820*, Montrose J. Moses ed., 334; *Works of Thomas Otway*, Thomas Thornton ed., iii 7; DNB, xiv 1243, 1681-2; Genest, 352; Luttrell, i 227
47. Macaulay, i 207ff; Burnet, 346ff; Luttrell, i 228, 263ff
48. *Evelyn*, iii 85ff; *Cobbett's Complete Collection of State Trials*, ix 353ff, 1010; Burnet, 358ff; Luttrell, i 271
49. *Evelyn*, iii 128ff; Macaulay, i 332; Burnet, 391ff
50. *The Last Days of Charles II*, Raymond Crawford, 48; *Evelyn*, iii 136; Mac-Kinnon, i 190, ii 452; Luttrell, i 327
51. MacKinnon, i 176, 178; Luttrell, i 339
52. MacKinnon, i 178; *Queen Mary of Modena*, Martin Haile, 128-9; Burnet, 403; Luttrell, i 371, 375ff
53. *Evelyn* iii 162; Macaulay, i 401ff; *King Monmouth*, Allen Fea, 219, 223; Burnet 401, 404-5, 410ff
54. MacKinnon, i 179, 180n.; Luttrell, i 346ff; Fea, 276ff
55. Luttrell, i 355-6, 459ff; Burnet, 435, 447, 487; Clode, i 80; Green, ii 264; Macaulay, i 512, 585
56. Luttrell, i 399; Belloc, 209; Clode, i 80
57. Luttrell, 402ff; Burnet, 448, 452ff; *Evelyn*, iii 220ff
58. *Evelyn*, iii 220-1; DNB, ii 724
59. Burnet, 476ff; Belloc, 207; Macaulay, ii 9; Luttrell, i 377, 422, 426, 429
60. Macaulay, ii 78ff; Fea (Mary of Modena), 186ff; *James the Second and His Wives*, Allen Fea, 156ff; Burnet, 469, 475ff, 491; Luttrell, i 442, 449, 469
61. Green, ii 281; *Evelyn*, iii 251, 253, 255; Burnet, 484ff, 942ff; Luttrell, i 433, 441, 445, 455ff
62. *Evelyn*, iii 258; Burnet, 499; Luttrell, i 473
63. *Evelyn*, iii 259; Burnet, 500; Luttrell, i 474ff; Macaulay, ii 75ff; Green, ii 284ff
64. Macaulay, ii 91
65. *Evelyn*, iii 259; Sheppard, 69; Burnet, 501; Luttrell, i 476ff; *An Apology for His Life*, Colley Cibber (Everyman's Library) n. d., 40
66. Burnet, 502n
67. *Evelyn*, 260, 261; Belloc, 217ff
68. Macaulay, ii 90, 104ff; Luttrell, i 474ff

69. Macaulay, ii 111ff, 131ff; *Evelyn*, iii 259, 261; Luttrell, i 486
70. Macaulay, ii 125; Fea (Mary of Modena), 218-9; Burnet, 504; Luttrell, i 485
71. Macaulay, ii 127ff; Burnet, 504; Luttrell, i 485; MacKinnon, i 192ff
72. Macaulay, ii 128
73. *Ibid.*, 139ff; Burnet, 505
74. Macaulay, ii 146; Clode, i 485; MacKinnon, i 193-4; Burnet, 506ff
75. Macaulay, ii 149-50; MacKinnon, i 196; Luttrell, i 488
76. MacKinnon, i 197
77. *Evelyn*, iii 262
78. MacKinnon, i 197; Burnet, 509; Luttrell, i 489
79. MacKinnon, i 194n
80. *Evelyn*, iii 262
81. Burnet, 508ff; *Evelyn*, iii 262
82. Burnet, 512ff; Macaulay, ii 164ff, 192ff, 218; *Evelyn*, iii 264ff; MacKinnon, i 197; Hamilton, i 337ff
83. Clode, i 195-6; Burnet, 511
84. MacKinnon, i 191, 199; ii 387, 465
85. *Ibid.*, i 201; DNB, xix 924ff; Luttrell, i 434, 509
86. Clode, i 142, 497; MacKinnon, i 199; Luttrell, i 494, 507ff; Coxe, i 24
87. Fortescue, i 338; Macaulay, ii 260-261; *Encyclopedia Britannica*, Ninth edition, xi 643; Clode, 486, 487; Luttrell, i 494ff; MacKinnon, i 199; i 389; Dalton, iii 43
88. *The Registers of Marriage of St. Mary le Bone*, Middlesex (HSP Registers of Section, Vol. 47), 132; MacKinnon, i 202ff; ii 416-7; Hamilton, i 344; Luttrell, i 582; ii 36, 37, 41, 73, 130, 165, 282
89. MacKinnon, ii 416-7
90. *Westminster Registers*, 208, 227
91. *Angliae Notitia 1692*, 172; *Westminster Registers*, 263; *Cheque Book*, 18, 115ff, 210; *Memorials of St. James Palace*, Edgar Sheppard, London 1894, ii 287, 325
92. MacKinnon, i 202ff; Fortescue, i 351ff; Luttrell, i 572
93. Macaulay, ii 768; Fortescue, i 351ff; MacKinnon, i 207
94. Hamilton, i 352-3; MacKinnon, i 211ff
95. Macaulay, iii 44; *Evelyn*, iii 313
96. Macaulay, iii 42; Burnet, 574-5; Coxe, i 34ff
97. Macaulay, iii 43ff, 110, 344-5; Luttrell, ii 443, 445, iii 455, 457; Fortescue, i 359; Burnet, 577-8, 584
98. Macaulay, iii 129ff; Fortescue, i 360ff; Hamilton, i 361ff; MacKinnon, i 218ff
99. Macaulay, iii 146ff; Fortescue, i 366, 368; JHC, x 775
100. Fortescue, i 369ff; MacKinnon, i 230ff; Hamilton, i 372ff; Macaulay, iii 224ff, 303ff
101. MacKinnon, i 241
102. *Evelyn*, iii 338; Burnet, 606-7
103. *Evelyn*, iii 338; Luttrell, iii 420
104. Macaulay, iii 327
105. *Baptismal Register, St. Margaret's Church*, Westminster (All previously published biographical sketches of Edward Braddock [1694–1755] which have ventured to give the place of his birth have suggested that he was born in Perthshire, Scotland. This error appears to have been based upon information contained in a New Orleans newspaper clipping which was reprinted in *Notes and Queries*, Third Series, XII 5. In 1946 the author visited Perthshire in search of some verification of this claim but could

find none. A subsequent search of Scottish marriage and baptismal records in the Register House, at Edinburgh, failed to produce any information indicating that any Braddocks were living in Scotland circa 1695. Later the London baptismal record was found at St. Margaret's.)

106. Sheppard (The Old Royal Palace at Whitehall), 304; Luttrell, iii 446, 447; *Evelyn*, iii 339; Macaulay, iii 323

107. DNB, v 376ff, xviii 1017ff; Dalton, iv 173; *Poetical Miscellanies*, Sir Richard Steele, 247; *The Life of Sir Richard Steele*, George A. Aiken, 49ff; *Richard Steele*, Austin Dobson, 14ff

108. Luttrell, iv 15

109. *Calendar of State Papers (Domestic Series) 1694–1695*, 63

110. Luttrell, iii 462

111. MacKinnon, i 247-8n., 254ff; Hamilton, i 393ff; Fortescue, i 378-9; Luttrell, iii 498; DNB, 376ff; Macaulay, iii 309, 359

112. Macaulay, iii 377f; Luttrell, iii 536-7; *A Catalogue of the Royal and Noble Authors of England, Scotland and Ireland*, Horatio Walpole, v 219

113. MacKinnon, ii 417; Macaulay, iii 378; Luttrell, iii 537

114. Luttrell, iii 537; Add Mss., 38, 700f, 229

115. Macaulay, iii 519, 524; Greene, ii 308; Burnet, 641ff; Luttrell, iv 277, 285ff, *Evelyn*, iii 362; HCJ, xiii 1

116. DNB, ii 724; *Evelyn*, iii 362

117. Luttrell, iv 304; MacKinnon, i 272-3, ii 307

118. *The Will of Dr. John Blow*, Principal Probate Registry, London; *Calendar of Treasury Books*, xvii II 1006

119. *Notes and Queries*, First Series xii 72

120. Letter from the Headmaster, Westminster School, May 3, 1950

121. *The Works of Jonathan Swift*, ix 369, 370

122. *The Life and Opinions of Tristram Shandy, Gentleman*, Lawrence Sterne (Modern Library Edition), 68ff, 105, 114, 395, 462ff

123. *The Life of Lawrence Sterne*, Percy Fitzgerald, i, 7, 9

124. DNB, xiii 607

125. DNB, v 368-9

126. Macaulay, iii 529ff, 545; Fortescue, i 384ff; Hamilton, i 414ff; *Robert Harley, Earl of Oxford*, E. S. Roscoe, 21; i 390

127. *Evelyn*, iii 367; Burnet, 645-6, 653; Luttrell, iv 280, 311, 313, 317ff, 330, 333, 472, 473, 478, 486, 487; *Evelyn*, iii 367; *Journals of the House of Commons*, xii 5, 7, 18, 30ff, 37, 44, 51, 52, 55, 75ff, 86; DPHC London, 1742, iii 77-8

128. Luttrell, iv 293

129. Macaulay, iii 635-6; *Evelyn*, iii 367; Burnet, 653; Luttrell, iv 282, 481; HEJ, xii 603, 614

130. Macaulay, 576-7; Luttrell, iv 327-8; *Evelyn*, iii 363

131. MacKinnon, i 275; Luttrell, iv 495, 498

132. Corner, 128; Burnet, 525; Luttrell, iv 326, 353ff, 361, 377, 401, 458, 529, 553, 562, 565, 575, 577; *Evelyn*, iii 284, 290

133. *Evelyn*, iii 338; Luttrell, iv 525, 574, 711

134. MacKinnon, ii 308-9, 417; Luttrell, iv 347, 348, 375, 486, 712; *The Microcosm of London 1808–11*, iii 110; *Blenheim*, G. M. Trevelyan, 82

135. Sheppard, ii 203-4, 209-11

136. Trevelyan (Blenheim), 175

137. *Evelyn*, iii 343

138. Trevelyan (Blenheim), 62-3, 118ff; Jesse, i 250; Luttrell, iv 671, 672; Burnet, 668-9, 683-4

139. Fortescue, i 389; Luttrell, iv 455, 499, 510, 605, 610, 623, 644, 679 etc; HCJ, xii 18, 48, 53, 54, 59, 60, 69 etc

140. Fortescue, i 389; Traill, iv 742; Macaulay, iii 608; Luttrell, iv 382, 392, 395, 402-3, 419, 420, 424, 437, 455, 490, 499, 510, 518, 540, 541, 577, 587, 601, 610, 618, 679

141. *Mr. Steele's Apology for Himself and His Writings*, 80

142. DNB, xviii 1018; *The Funeral, of Grief a La Mode*, Richard Steele, 72, 73; Luttrell, iv 657

143. Macaulay, iii 731ff; *Evelyn*, iii 392; Luttrell, v 87; MacKinnon, i 277; Burnet, 695ff

144. Trevelyan (Blenheim), 143ff; Coxe, i 73ff

145. Dalton, v 100-1

146. Trevelyan (Blenheim), 160-1; Macaulay, iii 744ff; *Evelyn*, iii 393; Burnet, 700ff

147. Luttrell, v 166

148. MacKennon, ii 309-10; Trevelyan (Blenheim), 164; Burnet, 704ff; Coxe, i 1-77; Hamilton, i, 428; Luttrell, v 172

149. Trevelyan (Blenheim), 204; HEJ, xii 905-7

150. Luttrell, v 118

151. MacKinnon, i 279ff, ii 311-12; Hamilton, i 434ff; Fortescue, i 407; Trevelyan (Blenheim), 262ff; Ashton, 158; Dalton, v XV, Burnet, 717-8

152. Fortescue, i 401ff; Trevelyan (Blenheim), 241ff; Luttrell, vi 152; Burnet, 713-4

153. MacKinnon, ii 465; Dalton, v 46

154. *Calendar of Treasury Papers*, xix 170, 209, 217

155. Marlborough Dispatches, i 212

156. Trevelyan (Blenheim), 218ff; Fortescue, i 399, 411ff

157. *The Commedies of George Farquhar*, ii; *The Recruiting Officer*, 22

158. Trevelyan (Blenheim), 407ff; MacKinnon, i 286, ii 314ff

159. MacKinnon, ii 465; Luttrell, v 420; Fortescue, i 434

160. MacKinnon, ii 465

161. Fortescue, i 341ff; Hamilton, i 443ff; Coxe, i 156ff; Burnet, 751ff; Trevelyan (Blenheim), 421; Luttrell, v 462-3

162. Luttrell, v 497-8

163. Hamilton, i 457; Coxe, i 250ff

164. Trevelyan (Blenheim), 422; *English Poets of the Eighteenth Century*, Ernest Bernbaum ed., 9

165. Trevelyan (Blenheim), 421; Luttrell, v 509, 515-6, vi 125; Dalton, v Part II 1-73; Coxe, i 251-2

166. Trevelyan (Blenheim), 422-23

167. MacKinnon, i 296ff, ii 317; Fortescue, i 450ff; Hamilton, ii 7ff; Luttrell, v 555, vi 37, 61; Trevelyan (Ramillies), 63ff, 295ff; Green, ii 323ff; DNB xiii 840ff

168. Luttrell, vi 31, 42, 50, 52, 136, 172, 176, 690-1; MacKinnon, i 296ff; Fortescue, i 480ff

169. Dalton, v II, i 159; Luttrell, 535, 560

170. Luttrell, vi 134

171. DNB, iv 308

172. MacKinnon, i 315-6; *Calendar of Treasury Books*, XXIII ii 178

173. *Ibid.*, 315ff; Hamilton, ii 28, 33; Dalton, i 329

174. Hamilton ii

175. *Westminster Abbey Registers*, 263, 265; *Cheque Book*, 25; Luttrell, vi 366

176. Will of Edward Braddock, of the Parish of St. Margaret's, Principal Probate Registry, London
177. MacKinnon, ii 469; Dalton, vi 321; *Sir Richard Steele*, Willard Connely, 34, 45
178. Dalton, vi 18
179. Luttrell, vi 542ff, 547, 551, 554, 559ff; Green, ii 330; Burnet, 846ff; Coxe, iii 4ff, 21ff
180. *Queen Anne's American Kings*, Richmond P. Bond, Oxford 1953, III, 1, 2; Tatler No. 171; Luttrell, vi 571; *American History and Government*, Willis Mason West, 146; *A Basic History of the United States*, Charles A. and Mary R. Beard, 84; Luttrell, vi 572, 576
181. Bond, 2ff
182. Bond, 94-5
183. *Ibid.*, 12ff; Luttrell, vi 574; *History of the Dress of the British Soldier*, John Luard, 94; *British Military Uniforms*, James Laver, 27, Plate I
184. MacKinnon, i 347
185. Clode, ii 77, 608
186. Dalton, vi 56

III. MORE EDUCATION ETC.

1. Dalton (George), ii XV; Fortescue, i 577-8
2. Clode, ii 609-10
3. *Annals of Philadelphia and Pennsylvania*, John F. Watson, ii 140
4. *Swift's Works*, ix 371-2
5. *Memoirs of Jonathan Swift, D. D.* (Swift's Works), Walter Scott, 463; *Journal to Stella*, Jonathan Swift, Harold Williams ed., i XXff, 3, 24
6. *Journal to Stella*, 13
7. Coxe, iii 77ff; Burnet, 856; Trevelyan (*The Peace*), 65ff; Jesse (Memoirs), ii 39ff; *Journal to Stella*, i XVIIIff, 25; *Marlborough: His Life and Times*, Winston S. Churchill, iv 257ff
8. DNB, xii 1295; Trevelyan (Blenheim), 83; (Ramillies), 326; Jesse (Memoirs), ii 36ff; *A History of the Reign of Queen Anne*, John Hill Burton, London, 1880, iii 70ff; *Marlborough*, v 32ff, 311ff, 348ff; Coxe, i 59, ii 97, 490ff; *The History of Great Britain During the Reign of Queen Anne*, Frederick William Wyon, i 137, 238ff; JHC, xvi 398; *Debates and Proceedings*, iv 168
9. *Op. Cit.*, 6
10. *Journal to Stella*, i 7
11. *Ibid.*, i 40; Trevelyan (Blenheim), 78; Burnet, 857; Churchill, vi 327; *The Review of the State of the British Nation*, vii Nos. 84, 85, 86, 87, 90, 91; Tatler No. 232
12. Luttrell, vi 639ff; *Journal to Stella*, i 42, 52; Burnet, 857-8; Marlborough, vi 348; Trevelyan (Blenheim), 52, 79; *Walpole*, John Morley, 19; Wyon, ii 251; Burton, iii 79; *Memoirs of Lord Bolingbroke*, George Wingrove Cooke, i 76
13. *Journal to Stella*, i 67; Luttrell, vi 643
14. *Journal of Stella*, i 120; Luttrell, vi 664; Marlborough, vi 339ff; Trevelyan (*The Peace*), 114-5
15. *Bolingbroke and His Times*, Walter Sichel, 15-6; *The Life of Henry St. John Viscount Bolingbroke*, Thomas Macknight, 104-5; Coxe, ii 94ff; Green, ii 328
16. DNB, lx 847-8, xii 1296-7; Burton, iii 52ff

17. DNB, xii 1295; Jesse (Memoirs), i 286-7, ii 242ff; Coxe, 94ff; Churchill, v 316ff; *Robert Harley, Earl of Oxford*, E. S. Roscoe, 94ff

18. Coxe, ii 487; Macaulay, ii 639ff; Jesse, i 320; *Sarah Churchill*, Frank Chancellor, i 142ff; Marlborough, vi 228, 265, 414, 650; Corner, 159; DNB, iv 334; Trevelyan (*The Peace*), 63, 115; Jesse, iii 450-1; *An Account of the Conduct of the Dowager Duchess of Marlborough*

19. DNB, xii 1296; Luttrell, vi 75; Dalton, iv 173, vi 18, 224; MacKinnon, ii 470-1; Sichel, 76

20. DNB, xii 1295, ix 847-8; Coxe, ii 348; iii 6ff; Churchill, vi 212-3, v 316; Dalton, v 46, 66, 157, vi 18, 365; MacKinnon, ii 468-9; Burton, iii 62-3

21. Marlborough, vi 212ff; Dalton, ii 299n., vi XXV, v 38; *Swift's Works*, iii 229

22. Churchill, vi 212; Coxe, iii 7

23. Churchill, vi 268ff; Fortescue, i 538; Dalton, v 18

24. Coxe, iii 6ff; Green, ii 328

25. *Journal to Stella*, ii 401

26. Macknight, 149, 214; Sichel, 212

27. Luttrell, vi 655; *Journal to Stella*, i 104, 113, 116ff; Churchill, vi 650; Campbell, 233

28. Churchill, vi 272

29. *Swift's Works*, iii 317ff; Wyon, ii 259

30. *Five Queer Women*, Walter and Clare Jerrold, London 1929, 83ff; Marlborough, v 386, 442, vi 48, 72, 482, 534

31. Luttrell, vi 671, 672; Coxe, iii 172ff; *Journal to Stella*, i 145; Marlborough, v 225, vi 352

32. Luttrell, vi 680, 682; Burnet, 862

33. Luttrell, vi 682

34. Luttrell, vi 687, 689-90, 693-4; *Journal to Stella*, i 183, 192, 195-6

35. Bond, 49ff; Dalton, vi 20, v 157; Coxe, iii 203n.; Luttrell, vi 707; Fortescue, i 541

36. Spectator No. 2

37. Luttrell, vi 709; Swift's Works, v 30; Bond 50; Fortescue, i 540; Burnet, 871; Dalton, vi XXV; *Journal to Stella*, ii 380

38. Luttrell, iii 429; Fortescue, i 559, 580

39. *Journal to Stella*, i 276, 288

40. *Ibid.*, i 304

41. MacKinnon, ii 420

42. Wood, 448

43. GM, January 1731, 25

44. *Ibid.*, 263

45. Portrait by Bartholomew Dandridge, National Portrait Gallery.

46. Wood, 447

47. *Ibid.*

48. LHW, Mrs. Paget Toynbee ed., iii 334

49. *Political State of Great Britain*, xiii 350-1

50. Melville (Bath), 200

51. *Lord Hervey and His Friends*, Earl of Ilchester, 9

52. *Ibid.*, 94-5

53. Wood, 446

54. *Ibid.*, 449

55. *Journal to Stella*, i 255, 328, 335, 350, ii 557, 567, 561, 615, 623, 629, 639

56. *A History of the Four Georges*, Justin McCarthy, i 14ff; *A History of*

England in the Eighteenth Century, W. E. H. Lecky, i 136ff; *England Under George I*, Wolfgang Michael, 29; Luttrell, vi 716, 724

57. Hamilton, ii 59, 60; Dalton, iii 189n; iv 191-2, 268n; v. 42; vi 51, 53n,, 197, 318-9

58. Hamilton, ii 60; *Hannibal Not at Our Gates*, 28; Trevelyan (*The Peace*), 297

59. *London in the Eighteenth Century*, Sir Walter Besant, 121, 435

60. *Hannibal at the Gates*, Daniel Defoe; *The Art of Restoring*, John Toland; *Neck or Nothing*, John Dunton; *Plain English*, Daniel Defoe; *Ancient Precedents for Modern Facts; A View of the Real Danger of the Protestant Succession*, Daniel Defoe; *Britain's Alarm; The Public Spirit of the Whigs*, Jonathan Swift; *The Succession of the House of Hanover Vindicated*, Mr. Asgill; *The Revolution and Anti-Revolution Principles Stated and Compared*, John Shute Barrington

61. MacKinnon, ii 421

62. Sichel, 485ff, 492ff; Macknight, 414ff; Trevelyan (*The Peace*), 293ff; Coxe, iii 362ff; Lecky, i 163ff; McCarthy, i 53ff

63. Michael, 19, 20, 37ff; Ashton, 403; Marlborough, vi 604ff

64. Hamilton, ii 60

65. Macknight, 418; Lecky, i 165; Trevelyan (*The Peace*), 305; Sichel, 494, 497; Michael, 53

66. Trevelyan (*The Peace*), 310ff

67. MacKinnon, i 341, ii 328; *The First George in Hanover and England*, Lewis Melville, i 232

68. *Caroline the Illustrious*, W. H. Wilkins, 115; *England Under George I*, Wolfgang Michael, 76; MacKinnon, i 342 and n.; Hamilton, ii 62

69. Wilkins, 19, 54, 131; Melville, i 216, ii 1ff; Michael, 80ff

70. Michael, 107

71. Wilkins 54; Melville, 47ff, 74; Michael, 78-9

72. Coxe, iii 378; *George the First's Army*, Charles Dalton, i XXI; Hamilton, ii 62; Michael, 95

73. Dalton (*George the First*), i XXIV

74. *Ibid.*, ii 159; Dalton (Army Lists), vi 55, 57, 318, 320; Hamilton, ii 64; MacKinnon, i 343-4

75. Dalton (*George*), XXIV; MacKinnon, i 454

76. Macknight, 222-3; Sichel, 482; Michael, 122ff; Wyon, ii 530

77. *England Under the House of Hanover*, Thomas Wright, i 23; Morley, 42ff, Michael, 115-6, 123

78. Michael, 126; Wilkins, 160

79. Hamilton, ii 64; Coxe, iii 382-3

80. Michael, 126; Luard, 96

81. Michael, 130; Coxe, iii 382

82. Michael, 88, 132; MacKinnon, ii 330

83. Michael, 130, 132; Dalton (George), i 19, XXII, XXIII; MacKinnon, i 344-5; Hamilton, i 65-6; Melville, ii 68ff

84. Michael, 163; Hamilton, ii 66; Churchill, vi 636

85. Dalton (George), i 191; MacKinnon, 134ff, ii 421

86. MacKinnon, i 347, ii 466-7

87. Fortescue, ii 29

88. *Notes and Queries*, First Series XII 517

89. MacKinnon, ii 421; Hamilton, ii 65-6

90. Dalton (George), i XXVI, XXVII, XXXIII; Hamilton, ii 67; Michael, 178ff; Wilkins, 186, 189; *Prince Charles Edward*, J. Cuthbert Hadden, 22ff

91. Michael, 220ff; *Frederick Louis Prince of Wales*, Averyl Edwards, 12; *History of Frederick II of Prussia, Called Frederick the Great*, Thomas Carlyle, i 431
92. Michael, 223
93. MacKinnon, ii 455; Dalton (George), i 29n
94. Skrine, 58; *Evelyn*, ii 440
95. Fortescue, ii 32ff
96. MacKinnon, ii 330ff, 421
97. Wilkins, 226
98. *Ibid.*, 227; Melville, ii 58-9
99. *Ibid.*
100. Edwards, 11ff
101. Wilkins, 226ff; *Leicester Square*, Tom Taylor, 225ff; *The Life of Lord Chesterfield*, W. H. Craig, 61ff; *Court Life Below Stairs*, J.　Fitzgerald Malloy, 114ff, 183
102. *Complete Works of Alexander Pope*, W. C. Armstrong ed., 66-7; *Representative English Dramas from Dryden to Sheridan*, Frederick Tupper and James W. Tupper ed., 262; Craig, 63ff; Taylor, 237; Wilkins, 240; Dalton (George), i XXIII; *Theatre Royal Drury Lane*, W. Macqueen Pope, 133
103. *Journals of the House of Commons*, xviii 627, 653; DNB, xviii 217; Dalton (George), i XXXVIII, XXXIX, Fortescue, ii 15
104. MacKinnon, ii 473; Dalton (George), i 159n; DNB, xx 584ff
105. DNB, xi 44-5; MacKinnon, ii 476-7
106. MacKinnon, i 345; *Political State of Great Britain*, xvii 404
107. *Ibid.*, 409-10, 623ff
108. *Ibid.*, xviii 317, 395ff; MacKinnon, i 346, ii 334-5; Hamilton, ii 71
109. MacKinnon, ii 242, 335-6, 339, 423ff; *Political State of Great Britain*, xvii 511, 627ff; Hamilton, ii 75
110. *Political State of Great Britain*, xxi 433
111. Fortescue, ii 52; I Charters, 12
112. *The Life and Letters of Lady Mary Wortley Montague*, her grandson Lord Wharncliffe ed., i 126, 469; DNB, xiii 707; DNB, ix 739
113. Wharncliffe, i 469; *Letters to and From Henrietta, Countess of Suffolk, and Her Second Husband*, i 50
114. Melville, 144ff; Wilkins, 315ff; Carlyle, ii 58ff; MacKinnon, ii 349-50
115. Marlborough, vi 649; Coxe, iii 398ff; MacKinnon, ii 348; Fortescue, ii 11ff; Hamilton, ii 78
116. Campbell, 251
117. Edwards, 15ff
118. *Ibid.*, 16, 115; *Portrait of Frederick Louis, Prince of Wales*, Philip Mercier, National Gallery, London; *Poor Fred: The People's Prince*, Sir George Young, 30-31; *The Forgotten Prince of Wales*, Captain Henry Curties, 50; Egmont, i 290, 412

IV. SCANDAL AT BATH

1. *And So to Bath*, Cecil Roberts, 53ff, 215; *A Picturesque Guide to Bath, Bristol, Hot Wells*, Messrs. Ibbetson, Laporte and J. Hassell, 7
2. Roberts, 56
3. Jesse, i 141, 185

4. Roberts, 55ff; *Walks through Bath*, P. Egan, 4ff; *The Bath Road*, Charles G. Harper, 56ff; Ibbetson, Laporte, Hassell, 33

5. Trevelyan (*English Social History*), 302

6. *The New Bath Guide, 1778*, 63; Ashton, 373-4; Ibbetson, Laporte, Hassell, 27

7. Jesse, i 340; Marlborough, vi 651; Coxe, iii 429ff

8. Traill, iv 512; Fortescue, 584-5

9. *Life and Letters in Bath*, A. Barbeau, 79ff, 168; *A Guide to the Knowledge of Bath*, John Earle, 161ff

10. *The Life of Beau Nash, Esq.*, Oliver Goldsmith, 41ff

11. Melville (Bath), 103ff

12. *Round the Shires*, Martin S. Briggs, 278

13. Barbeau, 63; Melville (Bath), 112ff

14. Barbeau, 26ff; Melville (Bath), 42ff

15. Barbeau, 154

16. *Bath Under Beau Nash*, Lewis Melville (L. S. Benjamin) London 1907, 155

17. Edwards, 29; Melville (Bath), 153ff; Barbeau, 90n

18. Barbeau, 169, 32n

19. *The Life and Letters of James Wolfe*, Beckles Willson, 238

20. DNB, ix 740; *Lord Hervey and His Friends*, the Earl of Ilchester ed., 94; Jesse, i 365ff, 383ff

21. *Lord Hervey's Memoirs*, XVIIIff, 986-7; DNB, iv 217-8; *The Eighteenth Century Architecture of Bath*, Mowbray A. Green, 102

22. Melville (Bath), 153-4

23. DNB, x 22-3

24. *Letters to and From the Countess of Suffolk*, i 182-3

25. Jesse, ii 188ff

26. Melville (Bath), 163

27. The Will of Edward Braddock (1725); *An Essay Towards a Description of Bath*, John Wood, 334

28. Green 17, Plate IV

29. *Bath Abbey Registers*

30. Will of Edward Braddock (d. 1725); *Gentleman's Magazine*, September 1731, 397; *The History of Gambling in England*, John Ashton, 66

31. Will of Edward Braddock (d. 1725)

32. *Bath Abbey Registers*

33. Will of Edward Braddock (d. 1725). Letter to author from G. M. Kirkwood, Principal Probate Registry, London, August 26, 1955

34. Letter to author from Beverly A. Hackett, Curatorial Assistant, Mount Vernon Museum, August 29, 1955

35. Goldsmith, 83ff. A footnote on page 199 of Melville's *Bath Under Beau Nash*, states that there is an account of Fanny Braddock's death in *Modern Amours* with a key prefixed, but an examination of a copy of this book (London 1733) in the British Museum revealed no identification of the "celebrated S----." A semi-fictional article entitled "Frances Braddock's Only Love," by Eugene F. Coughlin in *The American Weekly* for September 19, 1948, identified her lover as Hugh Boadley, "commonly regarded as one of the most eligible bachelors in England," but Coughlin can recall no basis of fact for the identification, and source materials he used in the Library of *The American Weekly* provide no information on the subject.

36. The Works of Oliver Goldsmith, ii 5, 16

37. Wood, 447

38. Goldsmith, 86

39. *Bath Abbey Registers*
40. GM, September 1731, 397
41. Goldsmith, 89; Wood, 448
42. Wood, 448
43. Wood, 447
44. *Ibid.*
45. LHW, Mrs. Paget Toynbee ed., iii 334
46. *Political State of Great Britain*, xiii 350-1
47. Wood, 446
48. *Ibid.*, 449
49. *Ibid.*
50. *Lord Hervey's Memoirs*

V. COVENT GARDEN

1. Ashton, 150ff
2. Besant (*London in the 18th Century*), 236ff; *Mr. Gay*, Oscar Sherwin, 161; Luttrell, iv 687
3. Besant, 276; *Poems on Several Occasions*, John Gay, 163, 188, 191
4. Summerson, 13ff, 248ff
5. *The Life of Henry Fielding*, Frederick Lawrence, 45n
6. *Clubs of the Georgian Rakes*, Louis C. Jones, 4ff, 11ff
7. DNB, xxi 1312ff
8. Lang, 106
9. DNB, xii 438; *Works of Jonathan Swift* (Scott Edition), xiii 412; *The Complete Peerage of England, Scotland, Ireland, Great Britain and United Kingdom*, Vicary Gibbs, iii 217
10. *Hogarth's London*, H. B. Wheatley, 38
11. *Hogarth*, Austin Dobson, 49
12. Wheatley, 285-6
13. Sherwin, 113ff; *John Gay*, William Henry Irving, 241ff
14. Lawrence, 44; *Some Account of the English Stage*, the Rev. John Genest, ii 656
    Daily Post, June 1, 1732
15. *The Covent Garden Tragedy, As It is Acted at the Theatre Royal in Drury Lane by His Majesty's Servants*, 13, 14; *The Georgian Theatre*, W. S. Scott, 25ff; Genest, ii 334-5; Mezzotint frontispiece, *The Complete Works of Henry Fielding*, iii
16. Wheatley, 286; *The History of Henry Fielding*, Wilbur L. Cross, 128
17. *Ibid.*, 133
18. GM, June 1732, *A Register of Books*, 13; *Covent Garden Tragedy* etc.
19. Cross, 129
20. *Letters of Horace Walpole*, Mrs. Paget Toynbee, ed., Oxford 1903 (Hereafter referred to as *LHW*), iii 334-5
21. LHW, iii 337
22. *Ibid.*
23. *An Apology for the Life of George Anne Bellamy, written by Herself*, i 36-7, 188 (Hereafter indicated as GAB.)
24. DNB, xvi 337; Dalton (George), i 253, 309; ii 205-6, 269; MacKinnon, ii 476; GAB,
25. GAB, i 3ff
26. Dalton (George), XLVI; Fortescue, ii 8

27. Hervey, XI, 156, 278, 340ff, 508, 650, 922, 987; *Memories of the Court and Times of George II*, Mrs. K. B. Thomson, 231; Wilkins, 241
28. Edwards, 16; Wilkins, 364
29. Hervey, 205ff, 628ff; Edwards, 70
30. Jesse, 209; Hervey, 98, 919
31. Hervey, 340-1, 445; Kelly, 15
32. *Political State of Great Britain*, xlii 9ff
33. Green, ii 349
34. Edwards, 25ff, 41ff 61, 81ff; Wilkins, 489ff; Egmont, ii 267, 308, 325, 352, 462, 415, 421; Hervey, 553, 613, 95-6, 205, 207, 255-6, 553, 613
35. Edwards, 116; Young, 71, 177, 190; GM, xii 217
36. Edwards, 19, 23ff; Wilkins, 494ff; Egmont, 192, 93, 208, 218, 225, 235, 236, 265; *The Forgotten Prince*, Captain Henry Curties, 71-2
37. Fortescue, ii 53; Skrine, 68; Portrait by Charles Jervas, facing p. 22 II Charteris; Kelly, 10
38. Jesse, iii 172; *Caroline of England*, Peter Quennell, 79; Edwards, 18-19; GM, xii 538; Kelly, 8; I Charteris, 22
39. Thomson, ii 264ff
40. MacKinnon, ii 471-2; Fortescue, ii 14ff
41. Hamilton, ii 98
42. *Common Sense*, July 2, 1737, *The Gazetteer* quoted in GM 1737, 427ff
43. *GM 1737*, 427ff, 437; 1738, 202
44. MacKinnon, ii 339
45. Egemont, ii 424-5
46. Hervey, 614ff; Edwards, 91ff; Young, 115ff
47. Edwards, 111ff; Young, 122ff
48. Edwards, 120; MacKinnon, ii 339
49. Edwards, 114ff, 119
50. Hervey, 816; Edwards, 112
51. *Memoirs of St. James*, 89
52. Edwards, 125; Young, 136-7; *GM*, 1737 699-700; *LM*, 1737 644-703
53. MacKinnon, ii 339-40
54. Genest, iii 523, 547
55. Genest, iii 547
56. *GAB*, i 26
57. Dalton, (George), ii 27
58. *GAB*, i 29
59. *Ibid.*, ii 194
60. *Ibid.*, ii 55, 56
61. *Loc. cit.*

VI. JENKINS'S EAR

1. GM 1737, 635, 699; 1738, 217, 273, 303ff, 423, 424; 1739, 68ff, 104-5, 118ff, 159, 472ff; 1740, 146; *Craftsman*, March 4, 1738, March 10, April 28, 1739; *Common Sense*, February 24, March 10, 17, April 14, 28, 1739; Green, ii 345ff; McCarthy, ii 198ff; Hayes, i 308-9; *Debates and Proceedings of the British House of Commons*, x 96ff, 102-3, 174-5, 176-7, 182ff
2. GM 1738, 162
3. Fortescue, ii 55; *Gazetteer*, August 25, 1739; *Craftsman*, September 9, 1738; *The Negotiators; The Convention, London 1739; Sir . . . Speech upon the Peace; Hirco and Dunno*
4. *Life of Samuel Johnson*, James Boswell, i 79; *London: A Poem*

5. GM 1739, 382, 383; DNB, xx 267ff
6. GM 1739, 551-2; *LM* 1739, 517-8; HCJ, xxiii 382
7. LM 1739, 518; McCarthy, ii 236; Edwards, 130
8. McCarthy, ii 236; Fortescue, ii 57
9. Watson ii 140
10. Unsigned Portrait, Fort Necessity Museum, Farmington, Pa.; Fortescue, ii, 57
11. GM 1739, 606; HCJ, xxiii 389
12. Dalton, ii 271; *GM* 1739 309, 659; MacKinnon, ii 476, 471
13. GM 1739, 664
14. GM 1740, 37; Hervey, 750; Egmont, iii 105, 107
15. MacKinnon, ii 470, 471; Hamilton, ii 95; *LM* 1740, 147
16. GM 1740, 91; *LM* 1740, 101; Hamilton, ii 101
17. GM 1740, 142, 143; DNB, xx 269
18. GM 1742 368, 379; *History of British Journalism*, Alexander Andrews, i 138; *English Newspapers*, R. H. Fox Bourne, i 116ff
19. MacKinnon, ii 482, 483
20. Charteris, I 77; Egmont, iii 163; *GM* 1740, 356
21. Hamilton ii 95; MacKinnon ii 430
22. GM 1740, 569
23. *Maria Theresa*, Constance Lily Morris, 17, 44ff; *GM*, 1740 127; Green, ii 345; Hayes, i 346
24. GM 1741, 53; Morris, 46ff
25. GM 1740, 570, 623; HCJ, xxiii 547ff, 705, xxiv, 40, 41, 407, 723
26. GM 1740, 623; *The Succession of Parliaments, Being Exact Lists of the Members etc.*, Charles Whitworth; Dalton, i 292; *GM* 1741, 235, 616ff; Clode, ii 93; *History and Proceedings of the House of Lords*, vii 60ff
27. Egmont, iii 219, 220; *The Craftsman*, May 23, 1741; *GM* 1741, 275, 304; Hamilton, ii 103
28. GM 1741, 304; DPHE, xiii 14, 49, 53
29. GM 1741, 275; *LM* 1741, 252
30. Carlyle, iv 3ff; Morris, 77ff; Hayes, i 354ff
31. GM 1741, 667; Carlyle, iv 71
32. GM 1741, 445, 501
33. *Ibid.*, 542
34. Ketton-Cremer, 79-80
35. GM 1741 277, 446, 502, 552-3, 557, 607, 610-11, 667; *LM* 1741, 100, 415, 467; *The Craftsman*, August 1, 1741; *Old English Journal*, April 16, 1743; *London Gazette* April 20, 1741; Carlyle, iv 36, 55-6, 98-9; LHW, i 112, 113
36. LHW, i 127
37. Ketton-Cremer, 56ff
38. DNB, xvii 49ff
39. LHW, i 114ff
40. *Ibid.*, 109, 170ff; *GM* 1742 103, 105, 107; Egmont, iii 248; Edwards, 135, 136; Ketton-Cremer 82
41. *Historical Memoirs of His Late Royal Highness William Augustus, Duke of Cumberland*, Anonymous, 14; *GM* 1742, 163, 217; Hamilton, ii 104-5; Carlyle, iv 187ff; *William Augustus Duke of Cumberland; His Early Life and Times*, Evan Charteris, 115ff
42. LHW, i 216
43. GM 1742, 108; Dalton (George), i 59ff; MacKinnon, ii 482, 483
44. GM 1742, 108; DNB, xviii 757ff
45. GM 1742, 273, 498; MacKinnon, i 353, ii 430; LHW, i 278, 285, 288-9

46. Fortescue, ii 84; GM 1742 390
47. LHW, i 308, 322; Dalton (George), ii 27
48. GAB, i 31ff; Dalton (George), ii 27
49. GAB, i 18, 38ff
50. Wyndham, 1 81; Genest, iv 9
51. GAB, 21ff
52. *Ibid.* i 34, 37, 38
53. *Ibid.* 38
54. *Ibid.* ii 60; Molloy, 1 87ff; Genest, iii 631
55. Scott, 49-50
56. Pope, 103
57. Scott, 55
58. GM 1743, 218, 219; Hamilton, ii 107; Kelly, 20
59. MacKinnon, ii 473
60. LHW, i 352, 360; Charteris, I 125ff; MWDC, 58ff; GM 1743, 534; Carlyle, iv 255ff; Hamilton, ii 109ff; Skrine, 75ff; MacKinnon, i 356ff; Kelly, 22ff
61. LHW, i 365
62. Egmont, iii 274
63. *Ibid.*, 275; MWDC, 117; GM 1743, 552; MacKinnon, ii 483
64. *Fontenoy*, Francis Henry Skrine, 70; MWDC, 131; GM 1743, 668
65. GAB, i 38, 39
66. *Ibid.*, i 42ff
67. *Ibid.*, 48ff, 55ff
68. Genest, iv 155ff; Gab i 67-8
69. GAB, i 69
70. *Ibid.*
71. GM 1744, 78; LHW, ii 2, 6; Egmont, iii 284ff
72. GM 1744, 79, 104
73. *Ibid.*, 103, 106, 107, 109, 212, 556; Dalton (George) ii 35ff; MWDC, 142
74. GM 1744, 102, 103, 104, 106, 165, 168, 221ff, 281; LM 1744, 257
75. MacKinnon, ii 431
76. LHW, ii 10
77. LHW, ii 11; MWDC, 144; GM 1744, 154
78. LHW, ii 9
79. GM 1744, 165
80. MacKinnon, ii 431; GM 1744, 221
81. Carlyle, iv 316, 333, 363-4; MacKinnon, i 426; Skrine, 119
82. GM 1744, 565; DNB, xi 37ff; MacKinnon, ii 476-7
83. Skrine, 116; MWDC, 169; GM 1744, 567
84. GM 1745, 109, 165; MWDC, 179; Skrine, 126; Carlyle, iv 414; WADC, 167; I Charteris, 163; Kelly, 28
85. WADC, 104ff, 116ff; DNB, xi 42-3; MacKinnon, ii 480-481
86. WADC, 116ff; LHW, ii 80; Dalton (George), i 355-56
87. WADC, 103
88. GM 1745, 162
89. *Ibid.*, 223; MWDC, 189
90. GM 1745, 223; MWDC, 156, 194; Fortescue, ii 116, 117; LHW, ii 87; Skrine, 137; Carlyle, iv 432ff; I Charteris, 177
91. GM 1745, 246ff; MWDC, 236
92. GM 1745, 247ff; MWDC, 236; WADC, 219; MacKinnon, ii 476-7, 482-3
93. GM 1745, 315
94. *Ibid.*, 315
95. *Ibid.*, 275; WADC, 208

96. WADC, 190; MacKinnon, i 368; Hamilton, ii 126
97. LHW, ii 88; WADC, 36-7
98. GM 1745, 277; WADC, 216; GM 1745, 332-333
99. LHW, ii 111ff
100. Hamilton, ii 127
101. GM 1745, 447; Skrine, 226ff; MWDC, 257ff
102. Skrine, 230; GM 1745, 433; MWDC, 260; Fortescue, ii 104
103. Skrine, 230
104. Hamilton, ii 127
105. LHW, ii 124; Skrine, 245, 270; Hamilton, ii 127; Fortescue, ii 108
106. MacKinnon, i 373n; Skrine 237; Hamilton, ii 128
107. *Journal of a Tour in the Netherlands in the year 1815*, Robert Southey, 5
108. Skrine, 143; LHW, ii 117
109. *A Year's Tour Through the Pais Bas*, Philip Thickness, 13; *An Hasty Sketch of a Tour Through Part of the Austrian Netherlands, by an English Gentleman*, 4ff; *The Papers of Thomas Bowrey*, 24; *The English Atlas*, 252; Southey, 6ff
110. Luard, 97; Hamilton, ii 115; MacKinnon, ii 340
111. LM 1745, 394-5; *An Hasty Sketch*, 4
112. Hamilton, ii 127, 128
113. *Ibid.*; Skrine 230
114. Skrine, 251
115. GM 1745, 385; Hamilton, ii 128
116. GM 1745, 391; Skrine, 252
117. GM 1745, 416; Skrine, 255-6
118. GM 1745, 386, 416; LM 1745, 398-9, 414
119. *Critical, Historical and Misc. Essays*, Thomas B. Macaulay, iii 192
120. GM 1745, 442
121. *Life and Times of Prince Charles Stuart*, Alexander Charles Ewald i 101; WADC, 45-6; *Memoirs of the Pretenders and their Adherents*, John Heneage Jesse, i 164; *Itinerary of Prince Charles Edward Stuart*, Walter Beggar Blaikie, 1, 2; Lockhart Papers, ii 439
122. GM 1745, 442
123. *Ibid.*, 419, 441
124. *Ibid.*, 385; Hamilton, ii 128
125. GM 1745, 497
126. *Ibid.*, 496
127. LHW, ii 128, 129; Skrine, 271; *Sir John Cope and the Rebellion of 1745*, Sir Edward Cadell, 27ff; GM 1745, 496, 500
128. Fortescue, ii 132; MacKinnon, ii 341
129. GM 1745, 499; MacKinnon, i 375-6
130. GM 1745, 600, 609; Skrine, 143-4
131. GM 1745, 497ff
132. Cadell, 200ff
133. *Ibid.*; GM 1745 499; LHW, ii 129, 136; Fortescue, ii 130
134. GM 1745, 597
135. *Ibid.*, 637
136. Cadell, 250
137. GM 1745, 500, 502; Dalton (George), i 28; Ewald, 279
138. *The Journal of the Rev. John Wesley* (Everyman's Edition), i 527
139. LHW, ii 144, 156, 199; GM 1745, 554ff, 606, 607, 609, 630, 633; Ewald, i 290
140. GM 1745, 557; MacKinnon, ii 341, 431
141. GM 1745, 604ff; Blaikie, 23

142. GM 1745, 605ff, 610ff, 620; Hamilton, ii 133; *Bonnie Prince Charlie,* Clennell Wilkinson, 119
143. GM 1745, 555ff; WADC, 244
144. GM 1745, 615; LM 1745, 564, 619; LHW, ii 152; Hamilton, ii 132
145. MacKinnon, ii 472-473
146. *Ibid.,* i 347, ii 474-5, 484-5; Hamilton, ii 121; Dalton (George), ii 263, 266
147. Hamilton, ii 132n
148. MacKinnon, i 341; Hamilton, ii 132; GM 1745, 614, 617; LHW, ii 151
149. LHW, ii 156
150. MacKinnon, i 381, ii 341-2-3
151. *Ibid.,* i 378; GM 1745, 620
152. WADC, 245
153. *Dr. Johnson's Lichfield,* Mary Alden Hopkins, 8ff
154. GM 1745, 665-6, 668
155. *Ibid.,* 613, 620ff; Hamilton, ii 133
156. GM 1745, 621
157. *Ibid.,* 1745 621; Wilkinson, 126
158. Blaikie, 30
159. Jesse, 321; *William Augustus, Duke of Cumberland, and the Seven Years War,* Evan Charteris, 47; Hervey, 539; Ewald, 292; Lang, 224
160. *Memoirs of the Pretenders and their Adherents,* John Heneage Jesse, i 153
161. GM 1745, 665-6; LM 1745 620; Wheatley, 405; Dobson, 129
162. WADC, 250; Greene, ii 363-4
163. Lang, 218; Blaikie, 30
164. GM 1745, 623; Hamilton, ii 135; *The Conqueror of Culloden,* Bernard W. Kelly, 45
165. Kelly, 47; GM 1745, 623
166. GM 1745, 666; LM 1745, 621
167. MacKinnon, i 380, ii 432; LM 1745, 623
168. Wheatley, 408; *Hogarth's Works,* John Ireland and John Nichols, ii 122

VII. FLANDERS

1. *Memoirs of Prince Charles Stuart,* Charles Louis Klose, i 354; *Life and Times of Prince Charles Stuart,* A. C. Ewald, i 311ff; LM, xiv 614ff, 625-6; GM, xv 667-8; MWDC, 316ff
2. LM, xv 36; GM, xvi 20
3. GM, xvi 41; LM, xv 48; Engraving, Royal Library at Windsor, reproduced in II Charteris facing 258
4. Charteris I, 241, 254; Kelly, 55; engraving Charteris II, 22
5. Edwards, 146; *Poor Fred: the People's Prince,* Sir George Young, 190
6. GM, xv 668; LM, xiv 630; Dalton (George), ii 41ff; Fortescue, ii 137; DNB, ix 243; LHW, ii 167-8
7. LHW, ii 170; GM, xvi 27-8, 41; LM, xv 42-3; Fortescue, ii 137ff
8. Ewald, i 336; Fortescue, ii 140
9. Dalton (George), ii 46; Fortescue, ii 141
10. Dalton (George), ii 47; MWDC, 325-6; GM, xvi 43, 81, 111; LM, xv 49; LHW, ii 170-1-2
11. LM, xv 210; GM, xvi 222; LHW, ii 185
12. GM, xvi 92ff; MWDC, 332, 342-3; LHW, ii 181
13. GM, xvi 105; LM, xv 97
14. GM, xvi 64, 145; MWDC, 352

15. GM, xvi 218; LM, xv 313
16. GM, xvi 209ff; LM, xv 199ff; MWDC, 346ff; Charteris I, 266ff; Kelly, 72ff
17. LHW, ii 189, 190, 215; GM, xvi 209; LM, xv 199; MWDC, 361
18. GM, xvi 211-2; Willson, 57-8
19. GM, xvi 210, 219-20, 263, 271; *The Lyon in Mourning*, ii 298ff; Ewald, ii 42ff; MWDC, 350; Fortescue, ii 144ff; McCarthy, ii 301
20. Ewald, ii 42ff; *The Lyon in Mourning*, 298ff; GM, xvi 383, 440, 531, 554; LM, xv 423-4
21. GM, xvi 326-7, 381, 438; LM, xv 15, 301; LHW, ii 222; MacKinnon, ii 343
22. Kelly, 88
23. *The Lyon in Mourning*, ii 301ff; MWDC, 360; GM, xvi 324, 374-5; LHW, ii 222, iii43; Kelly, 104; Charteris I, 289
24. GM, xvi 335ff, 382-8, 437; LM, xv 370, 393; Hamilton, ii 138; MWDC, 398-9; LHW, ii 233
25. LHW, ii 229, 238; Ewald, ii 62; GM, xvi 338, 358ff; 382-3, 439; LM, xv 374, 393, 395, 408ff, 431ff, 466, 645; MacKinnon, ii 343; Hamilton, ii 138; LHW, ii 235ff; GM, xvi 391ff; LM, xv 408ff
26. LM, xv 262, 477, 537; MacKinnon, i 387-388; GM, xvi 439, 491, 493; Hamilton, ii 138-9; Kelly, 274
27. MacKinnon, i 388; GM, xvi 493; Hamilton, ii 139
28. LM, xv 477; GM, xvi 493; MacKinnon, i 388
29. Charteris I, 295
30. GM, xvi 493
31. GM, xvi 600; MWDC, 429; Hamilton, ii 139-140
32. Hamilton, ii 139-140; MacKinnon, i 388-389
33. LM, xv 509, 580; GM, xvi 537, 542, 555, 595, 599ff; MacKinnon, i 388-389; Hamilton, ii 140; Fortescue, ii 156; LHW, ii 250-251; MWDC, 430-431; Kelly, 295; *Naval and Military Memoirs of Great Britain*, Robert Beatson, i 329ff
34. MacKinnon, ii 344
35. *Ibid.*, i 388
36. *Ibid.*, ii 344, 433
37. LHW, ii 251
38. MacKinnon, ii 344
39. Fortescue, ii 149ff; Hamilton, ii 142
40. *Historical Record of the First or Royal Regiment of Foot*, Richard Cannon, 130; LM, xvi 178, 200; GM, xvii 202
41. MacKinnon, i 389; *Britannica*, Ninth Edition, ix 350, xxiv 771-2
42. MacKinnon, i 389
43. *Ibid.*
44. *The English Atlas*, iv 38
45. LM, xvi 216, 220, 246; GM, xvii 250; Cannon, 130, 131
46. LM, xvi 244; DNB, x 322; GM, xvi 26-7, 241; MacKinnon, ii 474
47. GM, xvii 250; MWDC, 440
48. LM, xvi 246
49. MWDC, 347, 439, 443ff; WADC, 437; LM, xvi 229, 252ff, 323ff; GM, xvii 258ff, 308, 315ff, 345; Hamilton, ii 143ff; Fortescue, ii 159ff; LHW, ii 285ff
50. GM, xvii 328-9, 344, 401ff; LM, xvi 299-300, 342, 396; *An Authentic Journal of the Remarkable and Bloody Seige of Bergen-op-Zoom, by an English Volunteer* 9ff; *Historie Abregeé de la Ville de Bergen-op-Zoom*, M. Jean Favre, 235ff; Charteris I, 332ff; Kelly, 98-9.
51. *The English Atlas* iv 11ff, 191ff; *The Heart of Holland*, Havard, 305ff
52. WADC, 360

53. State Papers, Public Records Office, Military Expeditions 87/23; *The English Atlas* 191; WADC, 359
54. State Papers, 87/23
55. MacKinnon, i 389; Hamilton, ii 145; State Papers 87/23; GM, xvii 399; Dalton II, ii 269, 270 n5
56. State Papers 87/23; MacKinnon, i 390n
57. GM, xvii 410ff; LM, xvi 422; Hamilton, ii 145
58. LM, xvi 425; GM, xvii 410ff; Charteris I, 332ff; Kelly, 98
59. State Papers 87/23
60. *Ibid.*
61. MacKinnon, i 390, ii 433; Hamilton, ii 146
62. GM, xvii 541; LM, xvi 530; LHW, ii 336; Charteris II, 21
63. LHW, ii 303
64. GM, xviii 189-190; LM, xvi 192; Hamilton, ii 146; Fortescue, ii 163; Carlyle, v 66-7
65. MWDC, 455; Fortescue, ii 164; LHW, ii 307; LM, xvi 143, xvii 233; GM, xvii 286, xviii 238; Hamilton, ii 146
66. MWDC, 457; LM, xvii 503; GM, xviii 473; LHW, 347; HCJ, xxv 662
67. MacKinnon, i 391; Hamilton, ii 147
68. LM, xvii 571; GM, xviii 570-571
69. MacKinnon, i 391; Hamilton, ii 147
70. MacKinnon, ii 434
71. *Ibid.*, ii 401; Hamilton, ii 147; GM, xix 89
72. Hamilton, ii 147; GM, xviii 229, 312, 378; xix 522, 569; xx 41, 42, 378; LM, xviii 526; Charteris II, 30
73. LHW, ii 423; GM, xix 329, 522; LM, xviii 141, 334, 529; Ketton-Cremer, 130-131; Hamilton, ii 148, 149
74. Charteris II, 29; GM, xix 112, 138, 185, 235, 330, 378, 408, 426; LM, xviii 119ff, 181, 191, 238, 384; LHW, ii 367
75. GM, xix 378; LM, xviii 383-4
76. LHW, ii 398
77. *Ibid.*
78. GM, xix 42; LM, xviii 35, 142-3; Hamilton, ii 148-9
79. MGaz, February 20, 1755; PGaz, January 28, 1755; *Whitehall Evening Post*, Nov. 7-12, 1754
80. *Georgian London,* John Summerson, 49ff; *London,* G. H. Cunningham, 16, 17
81. Summerson, 49ff
82. *Recollections and Private Memoirs of Washington, by his adopted son,* G. W. Parke, 374
83. Sheppard (*Memoirs of St. James*), i 390; *The Connoisseur,* June 6, 1754; Luttrell, iii 513; Ashton, 142
84. GAB, ii 12; Genest, iv 215, 273, 275
85. Genest, vi 342ff; Bartolozzi engraving after Coates portrait in GAB, 1786 edition; *Their Majesties' Servants,* Dr. John Doran, ii 278; *A General View of the English Stage,* Thomas Wilkes, 303; *Romance of the Irish Stage,* J. Fitzgerald Malloy, i 179ff
86. Genest, iv 275
87. GAB, ii 19
88. *Ibid.*, i 66, 120, 136; ii 19, 22, 30; Malloy, i 189ff
89. GAB, ii 61
90. *Ibid.*, i 104, 107, 108, 115, 116; ii 3
91. *Ibid.*, ii 113

92. GM, xix 88, 185ff, 205; LM, xviii 94, 191ff; LHW, ii 368ff, 375ff, 382; Genest, iv 282ff; GAB, ii 18, 19, 43; HCJ, xxv 662; Charteris ii 354
93. GAB, ii 55ff
94. *Ibid.*, 93ff, 101ff
95. *Ibid.*, ii 33, iiiff, ii 14, 87, 106
96. McCarthy ii, 380; GAB, ii 112
97. Genest, iv 273ff, 309ff, 343
98. LHW, iii 18; GAB, ii 114; GM, xx 327, 422, 437ff; Pope, 171-2
99. GAB, ii 79, 80; Young, 215ff
100. *Ibid.*, 78, 79; GM, xxi 140; LM, xx 139; Dodington, 96; Edwards, 183, 186; Charteris II, 75, 76; LHW, iii 43; *Memoirs of George II*, i 78
101. GM, xxi 137; LM, 140; Genest, ix 326, 336
102. LHW, iii 43; Charteris II, 76; Edwards, 186; *Memoirs of George II*, i 78
103. LM, xx 183, 184, 190; GM, xxi 184, 185; Dodington, 110-111; Edwards, 187; LHW, iii 43; Charteris II, 77
104. Charteris II, 21ff; LHW, ii 367
105. *Memoirs of George II*, i 212; Fortescue i 566
106. GAB, iii 56
107. *Ibid.*, ii 62, 86, 92, 129, 139ff, iii 150
108. *Ibid.*, iii 176ff
109. Clode, i 74; Fortescue, i 316ff; MacKinnon, ii 406; LM, xv 331; DNB, iii 688
110. GAB, ii 186, 192, 193, 222, v 192
111. LHW, iii 142
112. GM, xx 43, xxii 40, 276ff; Green, ii 365; McCarthy, ii 373; Carlyle, v 251, 256; *Montcalm and Wolfe*, Francis Parkman (Everyman's Edition), i 25ff, 81-2; Charteris II, 86ff, 115ff, 121; *Memoirs of the Administration of the Right Honorable Henry Pelham*, William Coxe, 281-2; *Memoirs of George II*, 1 48-9, 394
113. LM, xxii 41; Parkman, 55-6; LHW, ii 365
114. LHW, ii 448; DNB, xi 44-5
115. McKinnon, i 393; *Army List (1770)*, 213ff
116. *The Letters of Philip Dormer Stanhope, Earl of Chesterfield*, ii 253
117. MacKinnon, i 347
118. LHW, ii 12; GM, xx 380; LM, xix 380
119. GM, xxiii 53; LM, xxii 45; Dalton (George), ii 363; *Army List (1770)*, 214
120. GAB, ii 193, v 192

VIII. GIBRALTAR

1. *The Historical Record of the Fourteenth Foot*, 9ff
2. *Ibid.*
3. Fortescue, i 560; ii 43ff; Ashton, 401; Trevelyan (Blenheim), 228; *The History of Gibraltar*, Captain Frederick Sayer, 481
4. LM, xvii 15, 54, 128-129; Sayer, 257; Egmont, iii 298
5. Sayer, 258-259
6. DNB, ii 658, 659; II Dalton i 115 n3; *A Treatise of Military Discipline by Humphrey Bland* (9th Edition); *The Life and Letters of James Wolfe*, Beckles Willson, 113
7. *A History of the Seige of Gibraltar*, John Drinkwater Bethune, 11; Dalton (George) ii 265-6; *Historical Record of the Nineteenth or the First Yorkshire Riding Regiment of Foot*, Richard Cannon, 12, 13; *History of the Herculean Straits*, Thomas James, ii 316
8. MacKinnon, ii 473; *Army List (1770)*, 219

9. Bland, 229
10. GAB, 130ff; Genest, iv 360; DNB, xxi 1286
11. GM, xxii 333
12. Fortescue, i 562
13. Bland, 237
14. Sayer, 458ff
15. *Ibid.*, 238, 433, 474, 483; *The History of Gibraltar, translated from the Spanish of Don Ignacio Lopez DeAyala with a Continuation to Modern Times by James Bell*, 172, 176-7; *A Voyage to Cadiz and Gibraltar*, Lieut. Gen. G. Cockburn, 16
16. Bethune, 23
17. *Historical Record of the Sixth or Royal First Warwickshire Regiment of Foot*, 68
18. *Ibid.*, 58, 109; LHW, i 250-1; DNB, viii 775; Hamilton, ii 28; Dalton (George), i 125, 127n; *Army List (1770)*, 217; Dalton (George), ii 265
19. GM, xxiii 249; LM, xxii 244; Dalton (George), ii 216-7n
20. Sayer, 238, 253ff, 267; Bethune, 34, 39; Dalton (George), ii 29; Bell, 172-3; Cockburn, 17
21. GM, xxiv 45, 98
22. Will of the Honorable Edward Braddock Esq., late Major General of His Majesty's Forces, Principal Probate Registry, London; *List of Officers of the First Royal Regiment of Artillery from the year 1716 to the Present* (Revised edition of J. Kane's List of Officers etc., published in 1815), 5
23. *List of Officers of the Royal Regiment of Artillery*
24. Braddock's Will (Op. Cit. 22); GAB, iii 192
25. Parkman, i 85; Freeman, i 274ff; Dinwiddie I, 210, 253, 326, 340, 382; GM 1754 321-2
26. *George Mercer Papers Relating to the Ohio Company of Virginia*, compiled and edited by Lois Mulkearn, 1ff, 167ff; *The Ohio Company of Virginia*, Kenneth Bailey, 17ff
27. Mulkearn, 52ff; Bailey, 73, 103ff
28. Mulkearn, 2ff, 168ff; Bailey, 64ff; Parkman, i 35
29. Mulkearn, 2ff, 168ff; Bailey, 25, 41, 35, 51, 58, 147, 148
30. Mulkearn, 52, 67, 68; Bailey, 74ff, 86ff; Parkman, i 29, 36ff
31. Mulkearn, 66, 70, 73; Bailey, 171-2
32. Mulkearn, 67, 72, 101, 253, 583; Bailey, 205ff
33. Parkman, i 86ff; Freeman, i 274ff
34. GM, xx 142; LM, xxiii 141; LHW, iii 212ff; *Memoirs of George II*, 378ff; Charteris II, 97ff; *Macaulay's Essays*, ii 388
35. GM, xxiv 191; LM, xxiii 188
36. GM, xxiv 190
37. GM, 1754 252ff
38. Parkman, i 92; Freeman, i 344; *History of an Expedition*, Winthrop Sargent, 40ff
39. *Walpole Memoirs*, i 399; GM 1754 399-400
40. *Walpole Memoirs*, i 400
41. LHW, iii 254
42. *Walpole Memoirs*, i 400
43. Freeman, i 422; Fortescue, ii 268; Dinwiddie I, 248; Parkman, i 107
44. British Museum Additional Manuscript 32850, f 289
45. *Memoirs of George II*, i 400-1; LHW, v 192-3
46. Freeman, i 436; v 337
47. Dinwiddie I, 353ff, 371; *Whitehall Evening Post* Dec. 21-24, 1755

48. *Memoirs of George II,* 401; *The French and Indian War in Maryland,* Paul H. Giddens, *Maryland Historical Magazine,* xxx No. 4 291-2; *Archives of Maryland* (II Sharpe), xxxi 52; GM 1754, 578

49. GM, xxiv 289, 386; LM, xxiii 190; Charteris II, ii 121; *Maryland Gazette,* Jan. 2, 1755

50. GM, xxiv 290, 386

51. GM, xxiv 386; *William Shirley, Governor of Massachusetts,* George Arthur Wood, 220ff; DAB, xvii 121; *The Conduct of Major General Shirley, Late General and Commander in Chief of His Majesty's Forces in North America,* William Alexander, 1ff

52. *Walpole Memoirs,* i 400; Charteris II, 106, 121ff

53. Add Mss., 35, 376 f 127; DNB, i 506

54. Newcastle to Murray, September 28, 1754, Br Mu Add Mss., 32, 736 f 591

55. Robinson to Newcastle, September 22, 1754, *Newcastle Papers,* British Museum, Vol. LI 32, 736 f 563

56. Clode ii 65; ColRec, vi 286

57. GM, xxii 144, 193, 290; DNB, vi 375; *The Naval Chronicle for 1809* xxii (engraving facing) 177; Publications of the Navy Record Society Vol. xlii, *The Loss of Minorca,* H. W. Richmond, 24, 46, 122, 135, 138, 146

58. Dalton (George), ii 28

59. Albemarle to Robinson, October 23, 1754, *Shelburne Papers,* 36:68, William L. Clements Library, University of Michigan

60. LM, xxiii

61. *Op. Cit.* 55

62. *Historical Record of the Forty-Fourth or East Essex Regiment of Foot,* Thomas Carter; Dalton II, 316; *Army List (1775)* 223; MWDC, 465; MGaz, January 2, 1755

63. Clode, i 128-129

64. HCJ, xxvii 86; Sargent, 162

65. Braddock to Newcastle, March 20, 1755, *Newcastle Papers,* clxviii 388ff

66. *Op. Cit.* 50

67. Robinson to Newcastle, September 23, 1754, *Newcastle Papers,* British Museum Vol. LI 32, 736 f 569

68. Charteris II, 128

69. *The British Empire Before the American Revolution VI: The Great War for Empire,* Lawrence Henry Gipson, vi 44ff

70. *Maryland Gazette,* January 2, 1755; GM, xxvi 484; LM, xxiii 484; Fortescue, ii 268

71. Albemarle to Robinson, October 9, 1754, *Shelburne Papers,* Clements Library, 36:64

72. LM, xxiii 481, 484, 522, 525; GM, xxiv 481, 484; DNB, xi 37-8; MGaz, January 2, 9, 1755, February 6, 20, 27, 1755; *London Public Advertiser, Evening Post, Whitehall Evening Post,* Oct.-Nov.-Dec. 1754; PGaz, April 3, 1755

73. *Ibid.*

74. LM, xxiii 477-8

75. *The Connoisseur* No. XXX; II Dalton ii 19n

76. LHW, iii 260; GM, xxiv 530

77. LHW, iii 334, 337

78. MGaz January 2, 9, 16, February 6, March 6, 1755

79. *Op. Cit.* 56

80. MGaz February 20, 1755; PGaz January 28, 1755; *Whitehall Post,* Nov. 9-12; *Advertiser,* Nov. 11, 1754

81. *Ibid.*

82. Instructions for General Braddock, Amherst Papers, 1 xxi P. R. O., W/O 34/71
83. Charteris II
84. *Military Affairs in North America, 1748–1765,* Stanley Pargellis ed., 12ff; Newcastle to Albemarle, September 27, 1754, *Newcastle Papers,* British Museum Vol. LI 32, 736 f 592
85. *Op. Cit.* 82; PaArch 203ff
86. PaArch 203ff; *Memoire Contenant Le Precis de Faits avec Leurs Pieces Justifcatives,* Jacob Nicolas Moreau, 16off; *MGaz,* January 30, 1755; *PaArch,* ii 249; ColRec, vi 177, 200ff; Sharpe II, 93; I Sharpe 160; *Op. Cit.* 82
87. *PGaz,* September 12, 1754; *The History of England,* Tobias Smollett, iii 446; *MGaz,* January 9, 1755
88. GM, xxiv 529; HCJ, xxvii 13ff, 27, 28, 34, 36, 86; *A Letter of the People of England,* by John Shebbeare, 33
89. GM, xxiv 485, 578; Genest, iv 419; GAB ii 192, 193, 211, 212
90. GAB, ii 193, 211; iii 2, 22, 114, 129
91. *Ibid.,* ii 193
92. Pope, 182
93. GAB, ii 136
94. Braddock's Will (*Op. Cit.* 22)
95. GAB, ii 92, 194, 212ff, iii 31, 32
96. Braddock's Will (*Op. Cit.* 22); GAB iii 95, 146
97. *Op. Cit.* 82
98. Pargellis, 53
99. GM, xxvi 269, 270
100. *Historic Highways of America,* IV; *Braddock's Road,* Archer Butler Hulbert, 57
101. GAB, 82
102. GAB, ii 62, 194; ii 29, 62, 194; *London Advertiser,* Nov. 11, 13, 1754
103. GAB, ii 194; *London Post,* Nov. 7-9, 1754; *Advertiser; Whitehall Post*

IX. COLONIAL PROBLEMS

1. GM xxvi 23
2. *The Barrington Papers,* D. Bonner-Smith ed. (Publications of the Naval Record Society, Vol. lxxvii), i 113, 116
3. *Ibid.,* 116
4. *Ibid.,* 117
5. *History of An Expedition to Fort Duquesne,* Winthrop Sargent, Philadelphia 1856, 137; *PGaz* March 11, 1755
6. Fortescue, ii 268; Sargent, 134-5; *Forty-Fourth Regiment Orderly Book,* Library of Congress, also known as *Halkett Orderly Book* and referred to hereafter as HOB; *PGaz* January 14, 28, March 4, 1755
7. *Walpole Memoirs,* iii 155; Fortescue, ii 32; Willson, 212, 223, 357
8. Willson, 239; *MGaz,* January 9, 1755
9. Willson, 274
10. Sargent, 138; I Sharpe, 155; *MGaz,* January 2, 9, February 6, 27, 1755
11. *Barrington Papers,* i 113; Dinwiddie, I 467
12. *Barrington Papers, op. cit.*
13. Sargent, 139; *Pa Mag.,* xxii 499; *PaGaz,* March 11, 1755
14. GM, xvii 468; *Moll Flanders,* Daniel Defoe (Modern Library), 302, 304; *Journal of a Voyage to Lisbon,* by Henry Fielding (Fielding's Works, xvi), 218ff
15. *Barrington Papers, op. cit.*

16. MGaz, March 13, 1755; Macaulay (*History of England*), ii 344, 345; *Britannica* (Ninth Edition), vi 405

17. *Robert Orme's Journal* (Reprinted in Sargent), 295; *Braddock's Orderly Books* (Reprinted in Lowdermilk). The original orderly books are in the Library of Congress. Hereafter in these references *Orme's Journal* is referred to as *Orme*, and the paging follows that in Sargent's reprint. Braddock's orderly books will be referred to as *BOB*, using the Lowdermilk paging.

18. GM, xviii 345

19. MG, March 13, 1755; *Johnson's England*, 46

20. *Roderick Random*, Tobias Smollett, 146ff; *The Sailor's Workbook*, Smith 478

21. *Barrington Papers*, i 113; Dinwiddie, I 511; *The Life of Augustus Viscount Kepple*, the Hon. and Rev. Thomas Keppel, i 203

22. LM, xv 572, 622; *Barrington Papers*, i 113

23. *Barrington Papers*, i 113; *VaMag*, xxxii 306

24. Pargellis, 58ff; Dinwiddie, I 466, 453; MG, February 6, 1755; St. Clair to Robinson, February 12, 1755, PRO c/o 5/46

25. Pargellis, 59

26. Keppel, i 203; Barrington, i 113

27. *Orme*, 283; *VaGaz*, February 28, 1755; MG, March 20, 1755

28. LM, xv 622; PaMag, xvi 278; *Travels in the American Colonies*, Newton D. Mereness ed., 403-4

29. Braddock to Fox, February 24, 1755, GM, xxvii 195; Braddock to Newcastle, March 20, 1755, Pargellis 80; *Newcastle Papers*, clviii 388ff; Moreau, 192ff

The conversation reproduced here and elsewhere in this narrative is based entirely upon letters and written records. Rather than introduce all this material, the author has taken the liberty to quote excerpts in dialogue form. None of the quotations has been knowingly or intentionally taken out of context. Sources are noted for each quotation.

30. Dinwiddie portrait, National Gallery, London; Watson, ii 140; Braddock portrait by unknown artist, Fort Neccessity Museum; Portrait of General Braddock (etching) by H. B. Hall, 1871, New York Public Library; History of the Early Settlement and Indian Wars of West Virginia, Wills de Hass, 114 (woodcut)

31. DAB, v 316-317

32. Portrait by Sir Joshua Reynolds, National Gallery, London; DNB, xi 39ff; Keppel i frontispiece (engraving)

33. Dinwiddie, II 4, 65

34. Dinwiddie, I 504; Sharpe, I 169; *Minutes of the Provincial Council of Pennsylvania* (hereafter designated as *ColRec*), vi 304

35. Dinwiddie, I 485, 461, 468, 501

36. St. Clair to Robinson, February 12, 1755, Public Records Office, London, C. O. 5/46

37. Dinwiddie, I 465

38. *Ibid.*, 474; MG, January 23, 1755

39. Dinwiddie, I 513

40. *Ibid.*, 480, 496, 513

41. Sharpe, I 167ff; DAB, vii 323-4; *An Englishman in the French Army in America*, James High ed., *Maryland Historical Magazine*, xlvii 103ff Ms. letter in Darlington Library, Pittsburgh

42. Orme, 287; *Friendship Valley Farm*, Ruth Gist Pickens, M.Hist.Mag., xlvii 122; Moreau, 180-181; Bailey, 86;

43. Dinwiddie, I 475, 496

44. *Ibid.*, 452, 469, 509; Orme, 287
45. Orme, 284
46. Dinwiddie, I 454, 455, 458, 460, 463, 465, 468, 484, 521, 522; Orme, 285, 287; VaG February 28, 1755; Md.Hist.Mag., vii 137ff
47. Dinwiddie, I 513, 523
48. *Ibid.*, 525
49. Parkman, i 93ff; Mercer, 4, 85
50. Sharpe, I 140; Parkman, i 126
51. Sharpe, I 140; Mercer, 4
52. Dinwiddie, I 473, 476; VAG, March 7, 1755; ColRec, vi 323
53. Gipson, 66; ColRec, VI 323
54. Dinwiddie, I 512, 513
55. This is an assumption, based upon the customs of the time, the limited accommodations of the Governor's Palace, the necessity of Braddock having a centrally located headquarters, and the notice published in the *Va.Gaz.* on March 21, 1755 (See Note 124)
56. *William and Mary College Quarterly* (1st Series), xiv 213, xvii. 170
57. VaG., April 25, 1755
58. Dinwiddie, I 515
59. Portrait, facing title page, PaMag, ix 1ff; GM, xxv 378
60. GM, xxvii 195; Moreau, 174ff
61. GM, xxvii 195; Moreau, 168ff
62. PaMag, ix 8
63. A Map of Pennsylvania, New Jersey, New York and Three Delaware Counties, by Lewis Evans, 1749. Reproduced in *Lewis Evans*, Henry N. Stevenson; Mercer, 226, 411; Pargellis, 66
64. St. Clair to Morris, Williamsburg, February 10, 14, 1755; ColRec, vi. 298ff
65. Pargellis, 62; Dinwiddie, I 461, 472, 493; Sharpe, I 136ff, 167, 168; MG, January 16, 1755
66. Pargellis, 63
67. *Ibid.*, 61
68. *Ibid.*, 63; Sharpe, I 168, 186
69. Dinwiddie, I 475
70. Pargellis, 60
71. Sharpe, I 168, 186
72. Orme, 288; Md.Hist.Mag., xxx 295
73. St. Clair to Robinson, February 12, 1755, P. R. O., C. O. 5/46
74. Pargellis, 62
75. *Op. Cit.*
76. *Ibid.*, 79
77. *Ibid.*, 61ff; Dinwiddie, I 464, 504; Orme, 285-6; Sharpe, I 172, 174, 202, 229
78. Pargellis, 62
79. Orme, 285; Braddock to Robinson, March 18, 1755, Newcastle Papers, British Museum, clxviii 346; Dinwiddie, I 515
80. BOB, II I
81. *Archives of Pennsylvania* (hereafter designated as *PaArch*), ii 203; Dinwiddie, I 518; Braddock to Robinson, March 18, 1755, British Museum, Newcastle Papers, cxlviii 346ff
82. ColRec, vi 299, 300
83. Dinwiddie, I 523
84. *Ibid.*, 406
85. ColRec, vi 307

86. PaArch, ii 258; Frank B. Need Documents, 447, Pennsylvania Historical Society
87. *Op. Cit.*, 63
88. *Ibid.*
89. ColRec, vi 300, 301
90. Pargellis, 79; Barrington Papers, 118, 119n; Braddock to Robinson *Op. Cit.*, 79
91. Barrington, 118ff
92. Orme, 289; Barrington, 113; Braddock to Robinson *Op. Cit.*, 79
93. Barrington, 118
94. *The Writings of George Washington*, John C. Fitzpatrick ed., Washington, 1931 (hereafter designated as Fitzpatrick), i 108
95. *Ibid.*, i 104ff; Freeman, i 440ff, xxix 41
96. Dinwiddie, I 355, 408ff
97. *MdG*, September 26, October 24, 1754; Fitzpatrick, xxix 41
98. Md.Hist.Mag., vii 140; Freeman, i 441ff; Hughes, i 174
99. *Letters to Washington*, Stanislaus M. Hamilton, ed., New York 1898 (Hereafter designated Hamilton), i 57, 58
100. PaMag, xvi 278, 279
101. Freeman, ii 383ff; Hughes, 31ff
102. Pargellis, 82
103. Fitzgerald, i 109ff
104. Barrington, i 113; VaG, March 7, 1755
105. Braddock to Robinson, *Op. Cit.*, 79; Fitzgerald, i 109-110
106. Braddock to Robinson, *Op. Cit.*, 79
107. VaG, March 21, 1755
108. Barrington, i 120, 121
109. Sharpe, I 186; Braddock to Robinson, *Op. Cit.*, 79; BOB, IV
110. Orme, 289; Braddock to Robinson, *Op. Cit.*, 79
111. MdG, January 30, 1775
112. Orme, 289; Pargellis, 59
113. Dinwiddie, I 523
114. Instructions to General Braddock, *Amherst Papers* lxxi PRO W/O 34/71
115. Orme, 288; Dinwiddie, II 12
116. ColRec, vi 336
117. Braddock to Robinson *Op. Cit.*, 79; VaG, March 21, 1755; MdG, March 20, 1755
118. Braddock to Robinson, *Op. Cit.*, 79
119. Braddock to Newcastle, March 20, 1755, Newcastle Papers, British Museum, clviii 388; GM, xxvii 197
120. Dinwiddie, II 2, 4, 18, 19
121. *North Carolina Colonial Records*, Raleigh 1887, v 571
122. Dinwiddie, II 4
123. MdG, March 20, 1755; Keppel, 201ff
124. VaG, March 21, 1755
125. Orme, 290, 291; Dinwiddie, II 4, 5; VaGaz. March 14, 1755
126. *Seaport in Virginia: George Washington's Alexandria*, Gay Montague Moore, 9ff; *Virginia: A Guide to the Old Dominion*, American Guide Series, 193ff; *History of Old Alexandria, Virginia*, Mary G. Powell, 33ff; *Plan of the Town of Alexandria, in the District of Columbia*, in 1798, published by I. V. Thomas, engraved by T. Clarke
127. *Appletons' Cyclopaedia of American Biography*, James Grant Wilson and John Fiske, ed., ii 401, 402; DAB, vi 255-56

128. Freeman, i 236n
129. Dinwiddie, I 53, 54, 150, 231, 264, 424, 431; Freeman, i 232
130. Army List (1770), 222; *Historical Record of the Forty-Fourth Regiment;* Skrine, 64
131. *Op. Cit.,* 126
132. BOB, XIII
133. Keppel, Braddock to Napier, March 17, 1755, Pargellis, 77; VaMag, xxxii 306
134. BOB, XIII
135. MdG, April 10, 1755
136. BOB, X, VIII
137. Local tradition. The house still stands.
138. BOB, VIIIff
139. *Ibid.,* Rider's British Merlin for the Year of Our Lord God 1755, London 1755; BOB, XII
140. BOB, XI
141. Dinwiddie II 5; BOB, IX
142. Orme, 297
143. Sharpe, I 188; Dinwiddie, I 462
144. VaMag, xxxii 306, 307
145. BOB, XIIff
146. *Ibid.,* VII, XVII
147. *Ibid.,* XVIII
148. VaMag, xxxii 307
149. BOB, VII; Dinwiddie, II 5
150. *The Lees of Virginia,* Burton S. Hendrick, 85, 93; DAB, vi 98ff; WPaMag, xv 210
151. *The Virginians,* William Makepeace Thackeray, 81ff. It should be noted that Thackeray wrote *The Virginians* after two visits to the United States. John Pendleton Kennedy saw much of the novelist (see Kennedy's manuscript Journal, February 27, 1853; January 8, 9, 15, 1856, Peabody Institute Library, Baltimore) and is credited with having later provided material for the fourth chapter of the second volume of *The Virginians.* (Kennedy Journal, September 26, 1858; John Pendleton Kennedy, by Edward M. Gwathmey, New York, 1931, 127ff.) Thackeray visited the neighborhood of Alexandria and talked with many Virginians. It seems not improbable that his description of Braddock in *The Virginians* was based partly upon legendary tales which he may have heard during his visits here.) He also talked with Parkman.
152. *Sir Robert Walpole,* Alexander Charles Ewald, London 1878, 5; *The Plans, Elevations and Sections, Etc., of Houghton,* Thomas Ripley, 2; *Anecdotes of Painting in England,* Horace Walpole, ii 706
153. *Op cit.*
154. *Op cit.*
155. Fitzpatrick, i 122-123
156. *The Expedition of Major General Braddock to Virginia with the Two Regiments of Halkett and Dunbar,* London 1755 (Hereafter designated as *Expedition*), 6, 7
157. *Ibid.*
158. Sharpe, I 210; WADC, 341
159. Fitzpatrick, i 112ff, 116, 122
160. *Ibid.,* BOB, IV, V
161. DAB, xiii 226

162. ColRec, vi 496; VaMag, xii 302
163. MacKinnon, 484-5 ii; LHW, iii 336-7, 421n
164. PaMag, (Military and Political Affairs in the Middle Colonies in 1755, by Daniel Dulaney), iii 20
165. GAB, iii 112-113
166. PaMag, iii 13ff; DAB, v 499; MdG, March 5, April 3, 1755
167. Sharpe, I 186, 189
168. *Ibid.*
169. Sharpe, I 186, 195ff
170. GM, xi 109; *Governor Horatio Sharpe Retires,* Paul H. Giddens, MdHist Mag, xxxi 218; *Governor Horatio Sharpe and His Maryland Government,* Paul H. Giddens, MdHistMag, xxxii 157; Sharpe, I 187, 207, 220, 228, 443
171. Sharpe, I 195
172. ColRec, vi 376; MdG, March 13, 1775; VAG, April 11, 1755
173. Sharpe, I 194; Dinwiddie, II 14; Pargellis, 83
174. Sharpe, I 194
175. Expedition, 22, 23
176. Sargent, 75
177. Sharpe, I 201; Parkman, i 92; Dinwiddie, I 450
178. Powell, 45
179. Pargellis, 84
180. Sharpe, I 144, 149, 138, 139, 201, 228
181. Sharpe, I 201
182. *Ibid.*, 205, 207; Orme, 297; Braddock to Napier, April 19, 1755; Pargellis, 82
183. BOB, XIIIff
184. *Ibid.*, XIff
185. *Ibid.*, Vff, XIX; Braddock to Napier, April 19, 1755; Pargellis, 83; Orme 298
186. BOB, V
187. *Ibid.*, VIIIff
188. Dinwiddie, II 5; MdG, April 3, 1755; PaG, April 17, 1755
189. *The Conduct of Major General Shirley,* MdG *op. cit.*
190. *Governor Horatio Sharpe's Whitehall,* Charles Scarlett, Jr., MdHistMag, xlvi 11
191. GM, xi 109
192. *Op. Cit.,* 182; Sharpe, I 77, 97
193. Sharpe, I 230; MdG, April 10, 1755

X. LOGISTICS

1. Expedition, 5, 6
2. *Ibid.*, 6ff; LM, xv 323
3. Expedition, 9
4. Orme, 296; Sharpe, I 77, 97; BOB, XVIIff
5. Orme, 299; BOB, XVIII
6. Orme, 299; Seamen's Journal (hereafter Seamen), 366 [84]; BOB, XXII
7. Seamen, 367; Sharpe, I 204
8. Seamen, 367; Orme, 298
9. Orme, 298; BOB, XXI
10. Orme, 298; BOB, XVff; MdG, April 3, 1755
11. BOB, XIII; Dinwiddie, II 12
12. VaG, April 11, 1755
13. BOB, XXII
14. *Ibid.*, XVI, XVII HOB

15. Sharpe, I 194; MdG, April 3, 1755; Orme, 300ff; DAB, x 124, 125
16. *Op. Cit.*, Chapter VIII, 126
17. Braddock to Robinson, April 19, 1755, Public Records Office c/o 5/46; *A Review of the Military Operations in North America*, William Livingston, 34-5
18. Pa Arch, ii 290
19. *Ibid.*
20. The Papers of Sir William Johnson, ed. James Sullivan, i 456-6, 468; ColRec, vi 365ff; Orme, 303
21. Sharpe, I 194; MdG, April 24, 1755
22. DNB, xiii 225
23. Braddock to Newcastle, April 19, 1755, Newcastle Papers, British Museum, clxix 188ff
24. Seamen, 367-8 [85]; PaMag, xxiii 324; Andrews, 55
25. Seamen, 367-8; VaMag, xxxii 319
26. Orme, 297
27. ColRec, vi 368
28. *Springfield Farm on Conococheague*, Mary Vernon Mish, MdHistMag, xlii 315, 318; Dinwiddie, I 454-5, 521-2; ColRec, vi 369, 373-4; 379; Sharpe, I 205, 207, 230
29. ColRec, vi 368
30. *Ibid.*, 323-4; DAB, iv 556
31. ColRec, vi 368
32. Pargellis, 86; Dinwiddle, I 125
33. ColRec, vi 368
34. Orme, 307
35. Braddock to Napier, April 19, 1755; Pargellis, 81ff
36. PaMag, iii 13
37. Seamen, 369
38. *Ibid.*, 368
39. *History of Western Maryland*, T. J. C. Williams, Baltimore i 25; Local Tradition; Pa Arch, ii 690
40. Orme, 307
41. *A Light in the Wilderness,* by Freeman Ankrun, The Brethren Evangelist, March 17, 1951
42. Pargellis, 83
43. Sharpe, I 194, 196, 203, 207; MdG, April 24, 1755; Orme, 307
44. Orme, 307-8; BOB, X; Pargellis, 482
45. *The Autobiography of Benjamin Franklin,* ed. Frank Woodworth Pine, 254; Orme, 308
46. Pargellis, 82
47. Orme, 307; *Expedition* 10
48. Franklin, 253; Braddock to Robinson, March 18, 1755; PaMag, xxxvi 125
49. Portraits of Franklin by Robert Feke or John Greenwood, Harvard University, Fogg Art Museum, and David Martin, Pennsylvania Academy of Fine Arts; *Benjamin Franklin,* Carl Van Doren, 90, 91
50. Van Doren, 205
51. *Ibid.*, 201
52. *Ibid.*, 205ff, 220ff, 227ff; Franklin, 253; ColRec, vi 323; Bond, 39
53. Franklin, 254
54. *Ibid.*
55. *Ibid.*, 254-5
56. Franklin, 263-264

57. Bland, 143
58. Franklin, 264
59. *Ibid.*
60. *Ibid.,* 260-61
61. Shirley to Morris, April 23, 1755, PaArch, ii 292
62. Braddock to Morris, April 23, 1755, ColRec, vi 377-8
63. Shirley to Morris, PaArch, ii 293-4
64. PaArch, ii 294-6
65. Seamen, 370
66. Fitzgerald, i 118; Sharpe, I 205; local tradition
67. Seamen, 368, 370; *History of Maryland,* James McSherry, 132; *Court Square,* Charles McC Mathias, Jr., MdHistMag, xlvii 110-111
68. Seamen, 370 [87]. Bracketed figures indicate paging of that version of the Seamen's Journal reproduced in Braddock's Road, by Archer Butler Hulbert, Cleveland 1903, as taken from an original manuscript in the Royal Artillery Library, Woolwich; *A Light in the Wilderness,* by Freeman Ankrum, The Brethren Evangelist, March 17, 1951
69. Orme, 309; Fitzpatrick, i 122; Sharpe, I 205, 208, 210, 254
70. Sharpe, I 205, 208
71. Fitzpatrick, i 118, 121, 122
72. MdG, March 17, 1755; *The Story of Winchester in Virginia,* Frederic Morton, 49, 52, 84; Winchester, *Virginia, Its Beginnings,* Katherine Glass Greene, 6, 43; Mereness, 334
73. Seamen, 371
74. PaArch, ii 308; ColRec, vi 372
75. Orme, 309; Seamen, 371
76. Fitzpatrick, i 120
77. *Ibid.,* 118, 119
78. Dinwiddie, II 34
79. PaArch, ii 299, 300; ColRec, vi 380
80. Seamen, 373 [89]; VaMag, xxxii 312
81. "Journal of a Journey from London to Virginia, 1754," VaMag, xxxii 311, 316
82. *Journal of Captain Charles Lewis, 1755,* 4, Draper Manuscript, 18 V 21 State Historical Society of Winsconsin
83. Expedition, 16
84. *Ibid.*
85. Seamen, 373 [89]
86. *Thomas Cresap, Maryland Frontiersman,* Kenneth P. Bailey, 96ff; ColRec, vi 379
87. VaMag, xxxii 316; Seamen, [89]
88. Bailey, 97ff; Orme, 312-313; Mulkearn, 141-2, 413, 421, 529-30, 653
89. Seamen, 373 [89]; Dinwiddie, II 37
90. Seamen, 373 [89]; *History of Allegany county, Maryland,* James W. Thomas and J. T. C. Williams
91. *Ibid.*
92. *Ibid.* [90]; Braddock to Robinson, June 5, 1755, PRO c/o 5/46

XI. FORT CUMBERLAND

1. *History of Cumberland,* Will A. Lowdermilk, 89ff; Sharpe, II (Archives of Maryland VI), 136ff; Seamen, 373 [90]
2. Seamen, 393 [90]

3. Hulbert, 47; Map in British Museum, reproduced in Hulbert
4. Seamen, 379; Lowdermilk, 130
5. VaMag, xxxii 316
6. Pargellis, 108
7. Seamen, 373 [90]
8. BOB, XXX
9. Orme, 313, 314; Fitzpatrick, i 127; ColRec, vi 379, 383
10. Seamen, 374 [90]
11. *Ibid.*
12. Orme, 311, 315; Lowdermilk, 90; Braddock to Robinson, June 5, 1755
13. Fitzpatrick, i 148
14. VaMag, xxxii 316
15. Expedition, 15
16. *Ibid.*, 14, 15
17. Orme, 311; Braddock to Robinson, June 5, 1755, PRO; Moreau, 199
18. Dinwiddie, I 418, 431, 432, 436, 514, 519, 521; II 34
19. Orme, 311; BOB, XXXI
20. *Whiskey Rebellion*, Leland D. Baldwin, 25; *History of the Western Insurrection in Western Pennsylvania*, H. M. Brackenridge, 17; PaArch, II 277; *Chronicles of Border Warfare*, Alexander Scott Withers, 30-1; VaMag, XXXII 313, 314; PaMag, XLVI 283; WPaMag, xvii 242
21. ColRec, vi 374-5; PaMag, XLVI 278ff
22. Sargent, 407
23. ColRec, vi 372, 374-5
24. Sargent, 407
25. Parkman, i 35, 37
26. ColRec, vi 375
27. Sargent, 407
28. Fitzpatrick, i 95
29. ColRec, vii 87; GM, xxvi 414-415; PaMag, xlvi 295
30. Seamen, 393
31. Bond, 55, 56, 77; LM, xv 207; Withers, 25ff
32. BOB, XXX
33. Fitzpatrick, i 123
34. BOB, XXXI
35. *Ibid.*, XX, XXXII
36. Hulbert, 20, 23; ColRec, vi; U. S. Geological Survey, Cumberland Quadrangle
37. BOB, XXXI; Orme, 323
38. Seamen, 375 [92]; HOB (unpaged)
39. Hamilton, i 89
40. Expedition, 15, 16
41. Orme, 313
42. GM, xxv 378
43. Seamen, 375; Porter, i 163, 171
44. Sharpe, I 149, 191-2
45. Seamen, 372 [89]
46. Orme, 311; BOB
47. Seamen, 375
48. Seamen, 376 [93]; Orme, 298, 312; Pargellis, 84; Add Mss 35593; BOB, VI; Braddock to Robinson, June 5, 1755, PRO c/o 5/46
49. Sharpe, I 168; BOB, XXXII, XXXIII
50. Dinwiddie, I 114-115n; Pargellis, 86-7; Braddock to Robinson, June 5, 1755

51. Sharpe, I 204
52. BOB, XXXII
53. Sharpe, I 142; Dinwiddie, I 428
54. BOB, XXXII
55. BOB, XXXIV; Ritenour, 132; ADB, xiii 166
56. BOB, XXXII; ColRec, vi 397
57. ColRec, vi 397
58. Seamen, 378 [95]; Lowdermilk, 123-4
59. ColRec, vi 400; Braddock to Robinson, June 5, 1755
60. Seamen, 377 [94]
61. Fitzgerald, I 123; Orme, 321; Braddock to Robinson, June 5, 1755
62. Orme, 313-4; Braddock to Robinson, June 5, 1755
63. Fitzgerald, I 123-4
64. ColRec, vi 635-636
65. Seamen, 377 [93]; Dinwiddie, II 34; Orme, 315
66. Dinwiddie, II 40
67. Orme, 315
68. *Ibid.*, 315; Braddock to Robinson, June 5, 1755
69. Dinwiddie, II 34
70. *Ibid.*
71. *Ibid.*, 40-41
72. Expedition, 16ff
73. Fitzpatrick, I 125; Seamen, 377 [94]
74. Seamen, 377 [94]
75. *Ibid.*
76. BOB, XXXV
77. Seamen, 377
78. Fitzpatrick, I 127
79. Seamen, 377 [94]
80. *Ibid.*, 377-8; Sargent, 407
81. Seamen, 378 [95]
82. *Ibid.*; DAB, vii 184
83. BOB, XXXVII
84. Seamen, 378 [95]
85. Seamen, 379; Expedition, 18ff
86. Expedition, 18
87. *Ibid.*, 18ff
88. Withers, 29ff, 76ff; Drake, 9ff
89. ColRec, vi 398; PaArch, II 317
90. ColRec, vi 380ff; PaArch, II 307ff
91. ColRec, vi 381
92. PaArch, II 309
93. Expedition, 22
94. Seamen, 379 [96]; Orme, 312-313; ColRec, VI 398; Franklin, 260
95. Expedition, 23
96. ColRec, vi 635-6
97. *Ibid.*, 636
98. Expedition, 22
99. Seamen, 379 [96-7]
100. *Ibid.*
101. Dinwiddie, II 41, 44; ColRec, vi 399-400; Sharpe, I 210
102. Sharpe, I 210
103. PaArch, ii 321-2

104. Sargent, 407; Orme, 314; Fitz., i 92
105. PaArch, II 321-2
106. *Ibid.*, 317
107. Orme, 312-313; ColRec, vi 408
108. ColRec, vi 400
109. Orme, 313
110. PaArch, II 330, 379
111. Expedition, 23ff
112. *Ibid.*
113. ColRec, vi 398; PaArch, II 317, 321
114. ColRec, vi 402-403
115. DAB xiv 508; PaArch, II 325
116. ColRec, vi 397ff; PaMag, xlvii 133; PaArch, II 299
117. ColRec, vi 396
118. *Ibid.*
119. Dinwiddie, II 40
120. *Ibid.*, 37-38
121. ColRec, vi 397
122. *Ibid.*, 374, 375, 379, 383, 394
123. *Ibid.*, 400
124. *Ibid.*, 379, 396, 402; PaArch, II 321
125. ColRec, vi 397; Van Doren, 206-7; Pargellis, 120; GAB, iii 112-113
126. BOB, XXXVIII; HOB
127. BOB, XXXIX; HOB
128. BOB, XXXIX
129. PaArch, II 330
130. PaArch, II 325; ColRec, vi 400, 403
131. ColRec, vi 400
132. *Ibid.*, 405-6
133. *Ibid.*, 410-411; Shirley, ii 199-200; DAB, xvi 377
134. Seamen, 381 [98]
135. DAB, ii 442, xiii 166; *Old Tom Fossit*, John Ritenour, 132
136. PaArch, II 311, 315, 347; Orme, 321; VaMag, xxx 310, 315; BOB, XXXVIIIff
137. Seamen, 379ff [97]; Orme, 321; BOB, XXXVIII; *James Wolfe*, W. T. Waugh, 37
138. Expedition, 15
139. BOB, XXXI, XXXVII
140. Orme, 317ff
141. Orme, 314; Seamen, 380 [98]; Sargent, 407
142. Sargent, 407; Orme, 314; Seamen, 380 [98]
143. Seamen, 379; Sargent, 408; ColRec, vi 398-399
144. Orme, 321; Seamen, 380 [98]
145. Orme, 322; Pargellis, 122
146. BOB, XXXIXff
147. BOB, XLII; ColRec, vi 443
148. BOB, XLIV
149. *Ibid.*

XII. THE LONG MARCH

1. BOB, XLI, XLII; Orme, 324, 330
2. *Ibid.*, XLVI, Orme, 322
3. BOB, XLIV

4. Fitzpatrick, i 131-2, 133; PaArch, ii 346-7
5. PaArch, ii 347
6. Fitzpatrick, i 125ff; Dinwiddie, II 41; ColRec vi 394, 408; VaGaz, March 28, 1755
7. BOB, XLII
8. ColRec, vi 499
9. PaArch, ii 325
10. *Ibid.*, 335; *The Dutch and Quaker Colonies in America*, John Fiske, ii 379; Franklin, 48; PaArch, ii 346, 356, 358; ColRec, vi 417; List of Officers of the Royal Regiment of Artillery, London 1890, 2; PaMag, xxii 499
11. BOB, XLIII
12. LHW, iii 309
13. GM, xxv 322-23
14. *Ibid.*, 185, 234; LM, xxiv 249, 250; HCJ, XXVII 296
15. Walpole, iii 299, 304-5
16. *Ibid.*, 302, 305
17. Seamen, 381 [98-99]; Orme, 324; Fitzpatrick, i 132
18. BOB, XLII; Seamen, 381
19. Pargellis, 92; Braddock to Robinson, June 5, 1755, c/o 5/46 PRO Moreau, 197ff; *A Letter to the People of England*, John Shelbeare, 35
20. Fitzpatrick, i 133-4; Braddock to Robinson, June 5, 1755
21. Braddock to Robinson, June 5, 1755, PRO, c/o 5/46
22. *Ibid.*
23. Braddock to Napier, June 8, 1755, Pargellis 84
24. *Op. Cit.,* 21
25. Fitzpatrick, i 134
26. DAB, xvii 120ff; DNB, xviii 142; PaArch, ii 330, 347; ColRec, vi 406; Correspondence of William Shirley, ed. Charles Henry Lincoln, i 397, 424n; ii 110, 146ff, 152ff, 232n
27. Pargellis, 94; St. Clair to Napier, June 13, 1755; WPaMag, xvii 240ff
28. *Old Virginia and Her Neighbors*, John Fiske, ii 432ff; II Dalton (George), ii 347, 348n; DAB xvii 467ff; DNB, xviii 177-8
29. ColRec, vi 286
30. Pargellis, 119
31. Sharpe, I 268
32. Hamilton, i 69; Fitzpatrick, i 140
33. Dunbar to Napier, July 24, 1755, Pargellis, 111
34. *Autobiography of the Rev. Dr. Alexander C. Carlyle, D. D.*, ed. J. H. Burton, 144
35. BOB, XLIVff (XLIV)
36. Shirley's correspondence, ii 202; Braddock to Robinson, June 5, 1755, PRO c/o 5/46
37. *Ibid.* ColRec, vi 437
38. Braddock to Newcastle, June 5, 1755, Newcastle Papers, CLXX 336
39. Fitzpatrick, i 133
40. PaArch, ii 346-7
41. Seamen, 381-2
42. Expedition, 15
43. Seamen, 381-2; BOB, XLVI
44. HOB
45. BOB, XLVII
46. *Ibid.;* Orme, 326; PaArch, ii 348; ColRec, vi 426

47. *Philadelphia Evening Bulletin,* September 19, 1849, *How The News of Braddock's Defeat Came to Town and What Followed.*
48. Braddock to Napier, June 8, 1755, Pargellis, 84ff
49. ColRec vi 411; Fitzpatrick, i 134, 137
50. Fitzpatrick, i 134
51. Orme, 325; Col.Rec, vi 426-7
52. ColRec, vi 406ff, 415; PaArch, ii 257
53. Fitzpatrick, i 136; Orme, 326; BOB, XLIV, XLVIIIff; Sharpe, I 245, HOB
54. Seamen, 382 [99-100]; Orme, 326; BOB, XLIX
55. A Sketch of General Braddock's March from Fort Cumberland Etc., Cumberland Maps, Royal Library, Windsor, reproduced in Pargellis. The Route of the Army Under the Command of General Braddock to the Place of Their Defeat, Laid Down by Christopher Gist, Henry Huntington Library, San Marino, Cal.; Pennsylvania State Survey Map, Fort Necessity Museum.
56. U. S. Geological Survey, Cumberland Quadrangle
57. Seamen, 382 [100]; Orme, 327
58. Watson, ii 142
59. Pargellis, 485
60. Watson, ii 140; primitive Braddock portrait, artist unknown, Ft. Necessity Museum
61. Orme, 331; Braddock Road Series, Photographic Post Cards, John Kennedy Lacock, Washington (Pa.) 1908, No. 7
62. *Op. Cit.,* 56
63. Orme, 331; VaMag, xxxii 310
64. Skrine 135; *A New and Enlarged Military Dictionary,* Charles James (unpaged), artillery; *A Treatise of Artillery,* by John Muller, 179-180
65. Fitzpatrick, i 140, 143
66. PaMag, xli 283
67. Orme, 331
68. *Op. Cit.,* 48
69. Fitzpatrick, i 144-45
70. Orme, 331; BOB, L
71. PaArch, 357
72. Fitzpatrick, i 140
73. Muller, 161
74. Orme, 332
75. Muller, Plate XX, 116ff; Orme, 332
76. Orme, 332
77. *Ibid.,* BOB, L
78. Orme, 332; BOB, LII
79. BOB, LIV
80. *Ibid.; Op. Cit.* 55
81. Orme, 333; U. S. Geological Survey, Frostburg Quadrangle
82. HOB
83. Orme, 333
84. BOB, LIV
85. Orme, 334, 350-351
86. Orme, 334; BOB, LIV
87. BOB, LX
88. Orme, 335; *Op. Cit.,* 55; Lacock Cards, Nos. 14, 15.
89. PaMag, xxxviii 16n, 17; *Op. Cit.* 55; Orme, 335
90. WestPaHistMag, xvii 117; Pargellis, 93ff

91. *Op. Cit.* 55; U. S. Geological Survey, Avilton Quadrangle; WPaMag xviii 117

92. Pargellis, 93ff

93. WestPaHistMag, xvii 261n

94. Fitzpatrick, i 142; Orme, 335

95. Fitzpatrick, i 129, 142-3; ColRec, vi 409, 422, 431; MGaz, June 5, 1755

96. *Ibid.,* 143

97. Pargellis, 95

98. Fitzpatrick, i 142-3

99. GM, xxvi 269-270; General Braddock's instructions, W/O 34/71, Amherst Papers lxxi PRO

100. Pargellis, 121-2

101. *Ibid.,* 102, 109

102. Orme, 336; BOB, LVI

103. BOB, LVI, LVIII

104. HOB

105. Fitzgerald, i 143

106. Pargellis, 113; Orme, 336; BOB, LVII; ColRec, vi 477; Sharpe, I 249

107. Orme, 336; BOB, LVI; Sargent, Plate III, facing 336

108. Fitzpatrick, i 141

109. Pargellis, 109ff, 113

110. *Ibid.*

111. Orme, 337

112. *Ibid.,* Lacock Card No. 18

113. Orme, 336-7; Sharpe, I 234

114. Orme, 337-8; Sargent, Plate iv

115. Fitzgerald, i 144

116. GM, xxiv 516ff; II Dalton (George), ii 13ff; DNB, xx 414-5; *James Wolfe, Man and Soldier,* W. T. Waugh, 64

117. Dalton, II 16

118. Hamilton, i 66

119. *Ibid.;* Fitzgerald, i 142

120. Fitzgerald, i 141-2; Niles Weekly Register, xiv (March 9, 1818) 180

121. Orme, 338; Lacock Cards Nos. 20, 21

122. Orme, 338; U. S. Geological Survey, Accident Quadrangle

123. ColRec, vi 414ff, 428ff, 445

124. *Ibid.,* 412; Evans' Map; Gist's Map, Henry E. Huntington Library and Art Gallery

125. ColRec, vi 445-6

126. *Ibid.,* 414-5

127. Pargellis, 121; PaMag, xxiii 324; Expedition, 27

128. HOB

129. *Ibid.;* Orme, 340, 342; The Correspondence of William Shirley, ed. Charles Henry Lincoln, ii 313ff; Inquiry into Behavior of Troops at the Monongahela c/o 5/46 PRO; GM 1755, 426

130. PaMag, xi 93

131. Pargellis, 123; Orme, 342; PaMag vii 431

132. Orme, 339

133. Bland, 114

134. Orme, 340

135. *Ibid.*

136. *Ibid.,* 340-1

137. *Ibid.,* 341; Lacock Cards, No. 30

138. Orme, 341
139. *Ibid.;* PaG, July 17, 1755
140. PaG, *Op Cit.;* Freeman i 400ff; Parkman 100ff
141. Parkman, i 101; Freeman, i 404; Fitzgerald, xxix 40
142. Orme, 342-3; PaMag, xxxviii 25n
143. Orme 343; PaMag, xxxviii 25, 26
144. Freeman, i 372-3; Fitzpatrick, i 73; Parkman, i 96
145. Orme, 343
146. Orme, 343-4; Moreau 153
147. HOB; PaMag, xxxiii 324
148. Orme, 344
149. Willson, 267
150. Shirley Correspondence ii 255ff; Nouveau Larouse Illustré, Directeur: Claude Augé, Paris 1898 iii 717; Parkman, i 117; MdGaz, April 16, June 5, 1755
151. MdGaz, May 1, 8, 15, 22, 1755; ColRec, vi 409
152. Orme, 345; Lacock Cards Nos. 46, 47
153. Orme, 345-6; HOB
154. ColRec, vi 454ff; Sharpe, I 237-8; Orme, 345-6; MdGaz, July 3, 1755
155. ColRec, vi 475-6
156. Orme, 346; Lacock Cards No. 48; PaMag, xxxviii 29n, 30
157. Orme, 346
158. Pargellis, 110, 111; PaMag, xi 93ff
159. Orme, 346, 347-8
160. *Ibid.,* 348
161. *Ibid.,* 345-6, 348
162. Orme, 348ff
163. HOB
164. Orme, 349, 350; Sharpe, I 246
165. Orme, 349, 350; Sharpe, I 250
166. Orme, 349, 350; HOB
167. Orme, 349, 351
168. *Ibid.,* 351; PaMag, xxxviii 34
169. Orme, 351-2
170. *Ibid.,* 352
171. PaMag, xxiii 325
172. Orme, 352; Lacock Card No. 58
173. Fitzpatrick, i 146-7; Pargellis, 110ff
174. Fitzpatrick, i 144, 146-7; Fitzpatrick, xxix 41; MdGaz, July 10, 1755
175. ColRec, vi 477; Sharpe, I 238, 239, 242, 243, 247; Shirley, ii 317
176. Watson, ii 141; Fitzpatrick, xxix 41-2; ColRec, vi 497
177. GM, xxv 235; Shirley, ii 181, 202-3; Fitzpatrick, i 146
178. Orme, 352; St. Clair to Robinson, Sept. 3, 1755 PRO c/o 5/46
179. Pargellis, 121; Hamilton, i 125; Entick, i 145
180. HOB
181. Orme, 353
182. The Braddock-Washington pistol in the collection of William G. Renwick, Weston, Mass.; Letter from F. B. Brandt, clerk to the Worshipful Company of Gunmakers, London, February 3, 1956.

XIII. INTO BATTLE

1. *Chronicles of Border Warfare,* Alexander Scott Withers, ed. Reuben Gold Thwaites, 66-67; *Tragedies in the Wilderness* (An Account of the Remark-

able Occurrences in the Life and Travels of Col. James Smith) Samuel G. Drake, 183; *Relations Diverses sur la Bataille du Malanguele,* Jean Marie Shea, 9ff

2. Parkman, i 134; PaMag, viii 121 (*Daniel Hyacinth May Leinard de Beaujeu,* John Gilmary Shea.)
3. Pargellis, 129
4. Sargent, 41ff; Freeman, i 374ff; Parkman, i 92ff, ii 271; Pargellis, 129ff
5. PaMag, viii 122
6. *Ibid.,* 122-3, 128
7. *Ibid.,* 123, 128; *Les Heroes de la Monongahela,* de Beaujeu, 4
8. *Ibid.,* 124; Parkman, i 133-4; ColRec, vi 160ff; I OT 39-40
9. ColRec, vi 445
10. PaMag, viii 124
11. *Ibid.,* 128; Sargent, 411; Shea, 10; Cudet, 24
12. Sargent, 414-5
13. Sharpe, II 234ff, 465ff; ColRec, vi 454ff; PaArch, ii 362-363; MdGaz, June 28, July 10, 1755
14. ColRec, vi 466-8; Pargellis, 88; Drake, 180-1
15. Drake, 182
16. *Ibid.,* 183
17. *Ibid.,* 183
18. Pargellis, 129-30; Parkman, i 135; Sargent, 409ff
19. PaMag, viii 128
20. *Ibid.,* 125; Sargent, 411; Parkman, i 136
21. Drake, 183; PaMag, viii 125; Shea, 11
22. PaMag, viii 128; Sargent, 411
23. PaMag, viii 125-6; Drake, 183; Parkman, i 136; Shea, 14
24. Drake, 183; Gage to Albemarle, July 24, 1755, Keppel, i 214
25. Pargellis, 120ff; Seamen, 384 [102]
26. Pargellis, 106; Sargent, 218
27. U. S. Geological Survey, Pittsburgh Quadrangle
28. Pargellis, 98
29. *Ibid.,* 106, 108
30. PaMag, iii 17-18
31. Orme, 353-4
32. *Ibid.,* 354
33. *Op. Cit.* 27; Sargent, 218-219; PaMag, xvii 212-213
34. Sketch of the Field of Battle of the 9th July upon the Monongahela, Etc., by Patrick MacKeller, No. 1, Cumberland Papers, Royal Library, Windsor Castle, reproduced in Pargellis, Parkman, etc. Duplicate set in New York Public Library.
35. Freeman, i 323; Parkman, i 88
36. *Serious Advice to the Inhabitants of the Northern Colonies,* New York, 1755.
37. Gage to Albemarle, July 24, 1755, Keppel, i 214
38. Pargellis, 106; Orme, 354
39. Pargellis, 98, 106; Orme, 354; Seamen, 385 [102]; Mackellar Map No. 1; PaMag, xlvi 212-213
40. Seamen, 385 [102]; Pargellis, 106
41. Freeman, ii 64
42. Pargellis, 106; Mackellar Map No. 1; Gage to Albemarle, *Op. Cit.* 37
43. Pargellis, 103; Mackellar Map No. 1; Sargent, 219
44. Seamen, 385 [102]

45. Orme, 355; Mackellar Map No. 1; Pargellis, 103, 117; de Beaujeu 16
46. Pargellis, 106; Seamen, 387
47. Pargellis, 106
48. Gage to Albemarle (*Op. Cit.*, 37)
49. Pargellis, 106
50. Audet, 24-25; Shea, 11; PaMag, viii 126
51. Pargellis, 106; Gage to Albemarle, *Op. Cit.* 37
52. St. Clair to Robinson, September 3, 1755, PRO c/o 5/46
53. *Op. Cit.*, 37; Pargellis, 117
54. *Op. Cit.*, 37; Pargellis, 99
55. Pargellis, 103, 106
56. *Op. Cit.*, 50
57. Seamen, 385; Pargellis, 106; Fitzpatrick, xxix 40; Add Ms 35593
58. Pargellis, 106, 115
59. *Ibid.*, 99, 115; Mackellar Map No. 2; Orme, 354
60. Orme, 355; Pargellis, 116; Mackellar Map No. 2.
61. Pargellis, 99, 106; *The Life, Adventures and Surprising Deliverances of Duncan Cameron*, 11
62. *Ibid.*, 103, 115
63. *Op. Cit.*, 37; Pargellis, 106
64. Pargellis, 107
65. *Ibid.*
66. *Ibid.*, 116
67. *Ibid.*, 83
68. *Op. Cit.*, 37; Orme, 355-356
69. Orme, 356
70. Sargent, 250
71. Orme, 355
72. Kelly, 8; WADC, 38; MdGaz, September 11, 1755; Add Ms 410f.
73. *Olden Times* ii 139; Whitehall Evening Post, October 9, 1755, quoted PaMag, xxiii 321; Fitzpatrick, xxix 43
74. Watson, ii 141; de Hass, 109; Public Advertiser, October 3, 1755, quoted PaMag, xxiii, 319
75. Custis, 374-5; Fitzpatrick, xxix 42
76. PaMag, xxiii 32
77. Pargellis, 103
78. ColRec, vi 501; PaMag, xxiii 325
79. PaMag, xxiii 325
80. Pargellis, 99, 107
81. *Op. Cit.*, 37
82. HOB; Fitzpatrick, xxix 42
83. GM, xxv 380; Parkman, i 140
84. *Op. Cit.*, 37; Pargellis, 117; Sharpe, I 253; Shea, 11; Fitzpatrick, i 150
85. Pargellis, 107; Sharpe, I 253
86. Watson, ii 138; Pargellis, 118
87. HOB
88. Pargellis, 107
89. *Public Advertiser,* October 31, 1755, quoted PaMag, xxiii 324
90. Pargellis, 121
91. Sharpe, I 253
92. Pargellis, 117
93. Sharpe, I 253
94. Pargellis, 100, 101, 107

95. Watson, ii 140
96. Pargellis, 119; Fitzpatrick, i 152, xxix 42-3; Custis, 375
97. GM, xxv 380
98. Sargent, 246-7; Ritenour, 113ff
99. Freeman, ii 74
100. Orme, 356; Shirley, ii 312-313; *Inquiry into Behavior of Troops at the Monongahela,* Albany, Nov. 21, 1755, PRO c/o 5/56
101. Pargellis, 99, 107; Seamen, 386 [104]
102. de Haas, 129-130n; Dinwiddie II 425
103. Pargellis, 107
104. *Ibid.,* 117; Orme, 355
105. Freeman, ii 76; PaMag, xxiii 311
106. Pargellis, 107
107. Orme, 356
108. Pargellis, 107
109. *Ibid.;* Shirley, ii 312-313
110. Franklin, 265-6; *Daniel Boone,* John Bakeless, 25; *Daniel Boone,* Reuben Gold Thwaites, 21
111. Pargellis, 107; Orme, 356; Shirley, ii
112. Fitzpatrick, i 149, 151
113. Expedition, 28ff
114. ColRec, vi 501
115. Fitzpatrick, i 43; *Niles Weekly Register,* May 9, 1818, 180
116. Sargent, 387n; Ritenour, 94
117. Fitzpatrick, xxix 43
118. Pargellis, 107-108
119. *Ibid.;* Shea, 15
120. Orme, 356; Fitzpatrick, xxix 43-44
121. Fitzpatrick, xxix 43-44; *Niles Weekly Register,* May 9, 1818, 179; Fitzpatrick xxix 44
122. Orme, 356
123. *Ibid.,* 356-7; Fitzpatrick, xxix 44
124. Fitzpatrick, xxix 44
125. Drake, 183ff
126. *Ibid.*
127. Bland, 114
128. *Op. Cit.,* 37
129. Dinwiddie, II 221ff; GM, xxv 426; Public Advertiser, September 30, 1755 (quoted in Davis)
130. Pargellis, 102
131. Dinwiddie, II 221ff
132. Franklin, 268
133. Pargellis, 110; Fitzpatrick, xxix 44; WPaHisMag, xvii 49ff, xviii 118-119
134. ColRec, vi 480ff; GM, xxv 379
135. Pargellis, 110
136. *Ibid.,* 102; St. Clair to Robinson, September 3, 1755, PRO c/o 5/56
137. *Ibid.,* 109
138. *Ibid.,* 108
139. Orme, 357
140. Pargellis, 108
141. Franklin, 268
142. Shirley, ii 321
143. Seamen, 368n.

144. Fitzpatrick, i 151
145. GM, xxv 424; ColRec, vii 342
146. Pargellis, 110
147. *Ibid.*
148. Dinwiddie, II 222
149. Shirley, ii 321; Pargellis, 119; St. Clair to Robinson, September 3, 1755, PRO c/o 5/46
150. WestPaMag, xvii 49ff
151. Sharpe, I 269
152. Pargellis, 110; Cameron, 11ff
153. St. Clair to Robinson, September 3, 1755, PRO c/o 5/46
154. Pargellis, 117
155. Watson, ii 141; ColRec, vi 589
156. Custis, 375
157. Pargellis, 119
158. Dinwiddie, II 222-223; Shirley, ii 388
159. Dinwiddie, II 222
160. Shirley, ii 321; Pargellis, 111
161. Pargellis, 111; Freeman, ii 82
162. PaMag, ii 95
163. Custis, 162n
164. PaMag, xxiii 322-323
165. Custis, 375
166. Pargellis, 101
167. Orme to——(Keppel?) July 18, 1755, PRO c/o 5/46
168. Bland, 135
169. Haas, 112
170. Orme, 357; Pargellis, 120
171. Haas, 112
172. Fitzpatrick, xxix 45; Custis, 162n; Ritenour, 34; *Niles Weekly Register*, May 9, 1818, 179-180

XIV. REQUIEM

1. Sharpe, I 234ff; ColRec, vi 457ff; MdGaz, July 10, 1755
2. VaMag, xxxii 317, "Journal of a Voyage from London to Va., 1754," Nov. 17, 1754–Jan. 19, 1757"
3. *Ibid.;* Sharpe, I 248; ColRec, vi 479
4. VaMag, xxxii 317-318
5. ColRec, vi 478; Sharpe, I 246
6. ColRec, vi 477-478; Sharpe, I 246
7. Dinwiddie, II 98
8. *Ibid.*, 48, 52, 63, 98, 99
9. Fitzgerald, i 148; Dinwiddie, II 116
10. Pargellis, 98ff
11. Dinwiddie, II 116-117, 120
12. Barrington i 113-114; PaMag, ix 489-490, xxiii 310
13. LHW, iii 332
14. *Ibid.*, 334-335
15. *The Public Advertiser*, London, August 27, 1755.
16. GAB, iii, iv 55
17. LHW, iii 336-337
18. "British Newspaper Accounts of Braddock's Defeat," by N. Darnell Davis, PaMag, xxiii 310ff

19. GM, xxv 383, 389
20. *Ibid.*, 383
21. LHW, iii 353
22. "Notations on General Braddock's Will," Principal Probate Registry, London
23. GAB, iii-iv 140
24. Dinwiddie, II 118, 119, 122, 130, 131; ColRec, vi 497ff, 515
25. Sharpe, I 251, 257-258
26. *Ibid.*, 259
27. Dinwiddie, II 142; ColRec, vi 499, 501, 502; Cameron, 14
28. Dinwiddie, II 170
29. *Ibid.*, 143ff; ColRec, 502, 513ff; Sharpe, I 265
30. PaMag, xxiii 323
31. Sargent, 244; Watson, ii 141, 143; PaMag, xxiii 318; *Washington's Expeditions*, James Haddon, 114, 115, 126ff
32. VaMag, xxxii 319
33. Sharpe, I 254; Dinwiddie, II 149
34. Pargellis, 102ff, 109ff, 112ff
35. PaGaz, September 4, 1755
36. Gage to Albemarle, *Op. Cit.*, Chapter XVI
37. PaMag, xxiii 232, 321, 324
38. Fitzpatrick, i 154
39. Hamilton, i 83
40. Franklin, 262-3
41. Fitzpatrick, xxix 45
42. *Niles Weekly Register*, xiv 179, 180
43. *History of Fayette County, Pennsylvania*, ed. Franklin Ellis, 48; Lowdermilk, 189; Ritenour, 234; Haddon, 127.

BIBLIOGRAPHY

LEGEND

ADB—American Dictonary of Biography
Add Mss—Additional Manuscript, British Museum
BM—British Museum, London
BOB—Braddock's Orderly Books
C/O—Colonial Office Papers, Public Records Office, London
ColRec—Colonial Records of Pennsylvania
DNB—Dictionary of National Biography
GAB—An Apology for the Life of George Anne Bellamy
GM—Gentleman's Magazine
HOB—Halkett's Orderly Book
HSP—Harleian Society Publications
JHC—Journals of the House of Commons
LHW—Letters of Horace Walpole
LM—London Magazine
MGaz—Maryland Gazette
MdHistMag—Maryland Historical Magazine
MWDC—Memoirs of William Duke of Cumberland
PaArch—Pennsylvania Archives
PaMag—Pennsylvania Magazine of History and Biography
PGaz—Pennsylvania Gazette
PRO—Public Records Office, London
RS—Register Section
VaMag—Virginia Magazine of History and Biography
VGaz—Virginia Gazette

MANUSCRIPT SOURCES

Public Records Office, London

Colonial Office—Braddock, Edward
Correspondence, instructions, including letters from Orme, Dunbar and St. Clair.
Inquiry into Behavior of Troops at the Monongahela.
Amherst Papers, Vol. lxxi.
Instructions for Edward Braddock, Major-General, etc; Private Instructions; Secret Instructions.
State Papers, Military Expeditions.
Correspondence of Col. Edward Braddock and the Earl of Chesterfield.

British Museum, London

Orme, Robert; Journal, 1755.
Newcastle Papers.
War Office Correspondence.
Additional Manuscript.

Principal Probate Registry, London

Will of Edward Braddock, Esq., late Major General of His Majesty's Forces.
Will of Edward Braddock, of the Parish of St. Margaret's Westminster.
Will of Edward Braddock, Esq., of St. Michael's Parish in the City of Bath.
Will of Dr. John Blow (1648–1708).

Royal Archives, Windsor Castle

Duke of Cumberland Correspondence

British Parish Records

Baptismal Register of St. Margaret's Church, Westminster, London.
The Register of the Abbey Church of SS. Peter and Paul, Bath, England.

Library of Congress, Washington

General Braddock's Orderly Books
Forty-Fourth Regiment Orderly Book, also known as the Halkett Orderly Book.

Other American Depositories

The Clement Library, University of Michigan, Ann Arbor.
Shelburne Papers. Letters from the Earl of Albemarle to Sir Thomas Robinson.
Peabody Institute, Baltimore, Maryland. Journals of John Pendleton Kennedy.

Pennsylvania Historical Society, Philadelphia.
Transcripts of Orme and Seamen's journals.
State Historical Society of Wisconsin, Madison, Wisconsin, Draper
   Manuscript.
Journal of Captain Charles Lewis, 1755.

OFFICIAL AND SEMI-OFFICIAL COLLECTIONS

British Parish Records

A Register of the Christenings, Burials and Weddings within the
   Parish of St. Peters upon Cornhill (HSP, RS I) Edited by G.
   Leveson Gower, London 1877.
The Parish Registers of St. Michael, Cornhill (HSP, RS VIII), Edited
   by J. L. Chester, London 1882.
The Marriage, Baptismal and Burial Registers of the Collegiate
   Church of the Abbey of St. Peter, Westminster (HSP Publication
   X), Edited by J. L. Chester, London 1876.
The Registers of the Abbey Church of SS. Peter and Paul, Bath
   (HSP, RS xxviii), Edited by Arthur J. Jewers, London 1901.
A Register of Baptism, Marriages and Burials, St. Martin-in-the-
   Fields (HSP, RS xxv), Edited by Thomas Mason, London 1898.
The Registers of St. Mary the Virgin, Aldermanbury (HSP, RS lxi),
   Edited by W. Bruce Bannerman, London 1930–32.
The Registers of Christ Church, Newgate (HSP, RS xxi), Edited by
   Willoughby A. Littledall, London 1895.
The Registers of Marriage at St. Mary le Bone, Middlesex (HSP,
   RS xlvii), Edited by W. Bruce Bannerman, London 1917.
The Register of St. Margaret's, Westminster (HSP, RS xliv), Edited
   by Lawrence E. Tanner, London 1935.
The Registers of St. Mary the Virgin, Aldermanbury (HSP, RS
   xlv), Edited by A. W. Hughes Clark, London 1935.
The Register of St. Lawrence Jewry, London (HSP, RS lxx), Edited
   by H. W. Hughes Clarke, London 1940.
The Registers of St. Mary Magdalen, Milk Street and St. Michael
   Bassishaw, London (HSP, RS lxxii), Edited by A. W. Hughes
   Clarke, London 1942.
The Register of St. Lawrence Jewry and St. Mary Magdalen, Milk
   Street, London (HSP, RS lxxi), Edited by A. W. Hughes Clarke,
   London 1941.
Memorials of St. Margaret's Church, Westminster (The Parish Regis-
   ters, 1539–1660), Edited by Arthur Meredyth Burke, London, 1914.

British Marriage License Records

Calendar of Marriage Licenses Issued by the Faculty Office (Index
   Library, British Record Society xxxiii), Edited by George E. Co-
   kayne and Edw. Alexander Fry, London, 1905.

Calendar of Marriage License Allegations in the Registry of the Bishop of London (Index Library, British Record Society lxii, lxvi), Edited by Reginald M. Glencross, London, 1937–1940.

Allegations for Marriage Licenses Issued by The Vicar General of Canterbury (HSP xxxiii), Edited by George J. Armytage, London, 1892.

Allegations for Marriage Licenses Issued by the Dean and Chapter at Westminster (HSP xxiii, xxv, xxvi), Edited by J. L. Chester, London, 1886–7.

Administrations in the Archdeaconry of Northampton (Index British Record Society lxx), Edited by Lucy Drucker, London, 1947.

Visitations

The Visitation of Norfolk (HSP xxxii), Edited by Walter Rye, London, 1891.

Staffordshire Pedigrees (HSP lxiii), Edited by George J. Armytage and W. Harry Rylands, London, 1912.

Calendars

Calendar of State Papers, Domestic Series (of the Reign of Charles II) 1660–1685, Edited by F. H. Blackburne Daniell, London, 1932.

Calendar of State Papers, Domestic Series, of the Reign of William and Mary, 1689–1695, Edited by William John Hardy, London, 1895–1906.

Calendar of State Papers, Domestic Series, of the Reign of Anne, Edited by Robert Pentland Mahaffy, London, 1916–1924.

Calendar of Treasury Books and Papers, Preserved in H. M. Public Record Office, 1729–1745. Prepared by William A. Shaw.

Calendar of Treasury Books, 1660–1713, preserved in the Public Record Office. Prepared by William A. Shaw, London 1904–1955.

Other Sources

List of the General and Field Officers as they rank in the Army, etc., London, 1770.

List of Officers of the First Royal Regiment of Artillery from the Year 1716 to the Present (Revised edition of J. Kane's List of Officers, etc., published in 1815) Woolwich, 1869.

English Army Lists and Commission Register, 1661–1714. Edited by Charles Dalton, London, 1892–1904.

Journals of the House of Commons, London, n.d.

Sharp, Horatio, Correspondence of. (Archives of Maryland), Edited by William Hand Brown, Baltimore, 1888–1911.

Dinwiddie, Robert. The Official Records of. (Virginia Historical Society Collections), Edited by R. A. Brock, Richmond, 1884.

The Colonial Records of North Carolina. Edited by William L. Saunders, Raleigh, 1886–1890.

Sullivan, James. The Papers of Sir William Johnson. Albany, 1921.

Pennsylvania Archives, selected and arranged by Samuel Hazard, Philadelphia, 1852.
Minutes of the Provincial Council of Pennsylvania, Harrisburg, 1851.

Newspapers

Common Sense, or The Englishman's Journal, London 1737–1739.
The Craftsman, London, 1731–1738.
Daily Post, London, 1728–1732.
The Examiner, London, 1710–1714.
The Gazette, London, 1745.
Old English Journal, 1743.
Evening Post, London, 1754.
Philadelphia Evening Bulletin, 1849.
The Maryland Gazette, 1754–1755.
The Pennsylvania Gazette, 1754–1755.
The Public Advertiser, London, 1755.
The Tatler, London, 1709–1711.
The Review of the State of the British Nation, 1710.
The Spectator, London, 1711–1714.
The Times, London, 1949.
The Virginia Gazette, 1754–1755.
Whitehall Evening Post, London, 1754.

Periodicals

The Brethen Evangelist, 1951.
Chamberlayne, Edward. Angliae Notitia: or, The Present State of Great Britain. London, 1684, 1687, 1692, 1694, 1700, 1702.
The Gentlemen's Magazine, 1730–1756.
The London Magazine, 1731–1755.
Maryland Historical Magazine (Baltimore) 1906–.
The Naval Chronicle, 1809.
Niles Weekly Register, 1818.
Notes and Queries (London) First, Second and Eleventh Series, 1852–1915.
Pennsylvania Magazine of History and Biography (Philadelphia) 1879–.
Political State of Great Britain, London, 1711–1740.
Virginia Magazine of History and Biography, (Richmond), 1893–.
The Virginia Gazette, 1754–1755.
Western Pennsylvania Historical Magazine (Pittsburgh) 1918–.
William and Mary College Quarterly (Williamsburg), First Series, 1893–1920; Second Series, 1921–1943.

Maps

Pitt. M. The English Atlas. Oxford 1680–83.
Braddock's Military Road through Pennsylvania, 1755.
Compiled from original surveys remaining in the file of the Department of Internal Affairs of the Commonwealth of Pennsylvania. 1932.

Evans, Lewis. A Map of Pennsylvania, New Jersey, New York, and three Delaware counties, 1749, reproduced in *Lewis Evans* by Henry N. Stevenson.

Lewis, Samuel. Topographical Dictionary of England, London, 1842.

MacKellar, Patrick. No. 1. A Sketch of the Field of Battle on the 9th of July . . . When the Action Began. No. 2. Same . . . Showing disposition of the troops about 2 o'clock. Public Records Office, London.

Plan of the Town of Alexandria, in the District of Columbia, in 1789. Published by I. V. Thomas, New York.

The Route of the Army Under the Command of General Braddock to the Place of their Defeat. Laid Down by Christopher Gist. Henry E. Huntington Library and Art Gallery, San Marino, California.

Six Plans of the Different Positions of the English Army Under the Command of the Late General Braddock. By an Officer. London, 1757. Philadelphia Historical Society.

U. S. Army Map Service (Plastics), Eastern United States, 1,250,000, NJ 17-3 AMS Series V501P (Cumberland) and NK 17-12 AMS V501P (Pittsburgh).

United States Department of Interior Geological Survey, 1:24,000, 1951. Cumberland, Frostburg, Avilton, Grantsville, Accident, Friendsville quadrangles.

United States Department of Interior Geological Survey, 1:62,500, 1949. Pittsburgh, Greensburg, Connellsville, Uniontown, Confluence quadrangles.

GENERAL BIBLIOGRAPHY

Books

Aiken, George A. *The Life of Sir Richard Steele.* New York, 1889.

Alexander, William. *The Conduct of Major General Shirley, Late General and Commander in Chief of His Majesty's Forces in North America.* London, 1758.

Andrews, Alexander. *History of British Journalism.* London, 1859.

Andrews, Matthew Page. *History of Maryland,* New York, 1929; *Tercentenary History of Maryland,* Baltimore, 1925; *Virginia, the Old Dominion,* New York, 1937.

Anonymous. *An Hasty Sketch of a Tour through Part of the Austrian Netherlands, by an English Gentleman.* London, 1788.

Anonymous. *Hirco and Dunno.* London, 1738.

Anonymous. *Historical Memoirs of His Late Royal Highness William Augustus, Duke of Cumberland.* London, 1767.

Anonymous. *Modern Amours.* London, 1733.

Anonymous. *Serious Advice to the Inhabitants of the Northern Colonies.* New York, 1755.

Anonymous. *The Covention.* London, 1739.

Anonymous. *The Expedition of Major General Braddock to Virginia with the Two Regiments of Halkett and Dunbar.* London, 1755.

Anonymous. *The Negotiators.* London, 1738.

Anonymous. *An Authentic Journal of the Remarkable and Bloody Siege of Bergen-op-Zoom, By an English Volunteer.* London, 1747.

Appleton's Cyclopaedia of American Biography. Edited by James Grant Wilson and John Fiske, New York, 1887.

Asgill, —— *The Succession of the House of Hanover Vindicated.* London, 1714.

Ashton, John. *Social Life in the Reign of Queen Anne.* London, 1929.

Ashton, John. *The History of Gambling in England.* London, 1899

Audet, M. Francis-J. *Jean Daniel Dumas.* Montreal, 1920.

Bailey, Kenneth. *The Ohio Company of Virginia.* Glendale, 1939.

——. *Thomas Cresap.* Boston, 1944.

Bakeless, John. *Daniel Boone.* New York, 1939.

Baldwin, Leland D. *Whiskey Rebellion.* Pittsburgh, 1939.

Banker, John. *Oliver Cromwell.* London, 1760.

Barbeau, A. *Life and Letters in Bath.* London, 1904.

Barrington, John Shute. *The Revolution and Anti-Revolution Principles Stated and Compared.* London, 1714.

Basilike, Eikon. *The Works of King Charles the Martyr.* London, 1687.

Bath Guide (The New). 1778.

Beard, Charles A., and Mary R. *A Basic History of The United States.* New York, 1944.

Beaujeu, *Les Heros de la Monongahela.* Montreal, Desalniers &c., 1892.

Bellamy, George Anne. *An Apology for the Life of George Anne Bellamy.* London, 1785.

Belloc, Hillaire. *James the Second.* London, 1928.

Besant, Walter. *London in the Time of the Stuarts,* London, 1903.

——. *London in the Eighteenth Century.*

Bethune, John Drinkwater. *A History of the Siege of Gibraltar.* London, 1786.

Blaikie, Walter Beggar. *Itinerary of Prince Charles Edward Stuart.* Edinburgh, 1897.

Bland, Humphrey. *A Treatise on Military Discipline.* London, 1740.

Bond, Richmond P. *Queen Anne's American Kings.* Oxford, 1952.

Bonner-Smith, D. *The Barrington Papers.* (Publications of the Naval Record Society, Vol. lxxvii) London, 1937.

Boswell, James. *Life of Samuel Johnson.* Boston, 1824.

Bowrey, Thomas. *The Papers of.* London, 1927.

Brackenridge, H. W. *History of the Western Insurrection in Western Pennsylvania.* Pittsburgh, 1859.

Briggs, Maryin S. *Round the Shires.* London, 1946.

Brydall, John. *Camera Regis.* London, 1676.

Brown, John. *John Bunyan.* New York, 1885.

Burk, Solon and Elizabeth. *The Planting of Civilization in Western Pennsylvania*, Pittsburgh, 1939.

Bunyan, John. *Pilgrim's Progress*. London, 1899.

Burnet, Gilbert. *History of My Own Times*. London, N.d.

Burton, John Hill. *A History of the Reign of Queen Anne*. London, 1880.

Cadell, Sir Robert. *Sir John Cope and the Rebellion of 1745*. London, 1898.

Cameron, Duncan. *The Life, Adventures and Surprising Deliverances of Duncan Cameron, Private Soldier in the Regiment of Foot, late Sir Peter Halkett's* (3rd Edition). Philadelphia, 1756.

Cannon, Richard, *The Historical Record of the Fourteenth or Buckingham Regiment of Foot*. London, 1845.

———. *Historical Record of the Nineteenth or the First Yorkshire Riding Regiment of Foot*. London, 1848.

Carlyle, Alexander C. *Autobiography Of* (edited by J. H. Burton). Edinburgh and London, 1860.

Carlyle, Thomas. *Complete Works*. (Crowell Edition). New York, n.d.

Carter, Thomas. *Historical Record of the Forty-Fourth (East Essex) Regiment of Foot*. London, 1864.

Charteris, Evan. *William Augustus, Duke of Cumberland: His Early Life and Times*. London, 1913.

———. *William Augustus, Duke of Cumberland, and the Seven Years War*. London, 1920.

Chancellor, Frank. *Sarah Churchill*. Glasgow, 1932.

Chesterton, Cecil. *The Story of Nell Gwynn*. Boston, N.D.

Churchill, John, first Duke of Marlborough. Letters and Dispatches of. Edited by Sir George Murray, London, 1845.

Cibber Colley. *An Apology for His Life*. (Everyman's Library). London, N.D.

Clode, Charles M. *The Military Forces of the Crown*. London, 1869.

Cobbett's Complete Collection of State Trials. London, 1811.

Cockburn, Lieut.-Gen. G. *A Voyage to Cadiz and Gibraltar*. London, 1815.

Coke, Royal. *A Detection of the Court and the State of England*. London, 1719.

Cooke, George Wingrove. *Memoirs of Lord Bollingbroke*. London, 1835.

Corner, H. G. London, 1932.

Cowan, Samuel. *The Royal House of Stuart*. London, 1908.

Coxe, William. *Memoirs of the Duke of Marlborough*. London, 1872.

Craig, Neville B. *The Olden Times*. Cincinnati, 1876.

Craig, W. H. *The Life of Lord Chesterfield*. London, 1907.

Crawford, Raymond. *The Last Days of Charles II*. Oxford, 1909.

Cromwell, Thomas. *Oliver Cromwell and His Times*. London, 1822.

Cross, Wilbur S. *The History of Henry Fielding*. New York, 1918.

Cunningham, Peter. *The Story of Nell Gwynn*. London, 1903.

Dalton, Charles. *English Army Lists and Commission Registers*. London, 1882. *George the First's Army*, London, 1910.

Davies, G. *The Early History of the Coldstream Guards*. Oxford, 1924.

DeAyala, Don Ignacio Lopez. *The History of Gibraltar*. (Translated from the Spanish by James Bell, London, 1845.)

Defoe, Daniel. *A View of the Real Danger of the Protestant Succession*. London, 1714.

———. *Hanibal at the Gates*. London, 1714.

———. *Plain English*. London, 1712.

Dictionary of American Biography by Allen Johnson. New York, 1928.

Dobson, Austin. *Richard Steele*. New York, 1886.

Dunton, John. *Neck or Nothing*. London, 1713.

Drake, Samuel G. *Tragedies in the Wilderness*. (An Account of the Remarkable Occurrences in the Life and Travels of Col. James Smith.) Boston, 1841.

Earle, John. *A Guide to the Knowledge of Bath*. London, 1864.

Edgemont, Viscount Percival. *Diary of Lord Edgemont*. London, 1920–23.

Edwards, Averyl. *Frederick Louis, Prince of Wales*. London, 1947.

Egan, P. *Walks Through Bath*. London, 1819.

Encyclopedia Britannica. Ninth Edition. New York, N.D.

Encyclopedia Britannica. 1952.

English Poets of the Eighteenth Century. Edited by Ernest Bernbaum. New York, 1918.

Entick, The Rev. John. *The General History of the Late War*. London, 1763.

Evelyn, John, *Memoirs*. London, 1827.

Ewald, Alexander Charles. *Life and Times of Prince Charles Stuart*. London, 1875.

———. *Sir Robert Walpole*. London, 1878.

Farmer, Henry George. *The Rise and Development of Military Music*. London, 1912.

Farquhar, George. *The Comedies of George Farquhar*. London, 1718.

Faure, M. Jean. *Histoire de la Ville de Bergen-op-Zoom*. La Haye, 1759.

Fea, Allen. *King Monmouth*. London, 1902.

———. *James the Second and His Wives*. London, 1908.

Fielding, Henry. *The Covent Garden Tragedy*. London, 1732.

———. *A Full Vindication of the Duchess of Marlborough*. London, 1742.

Firth, Charles Harding. *The Last Years of the Protectorate*. London, 1909.

Fiske, John. *Old Virginia and Her Neighbors*. New York, 1902.

———. *The Dutch and Quaker Colonies in America*. New York, 1902.

Fitzgerald, Percy. *The Life of Lawrence Sterne*. New York, 1904.

Fitzpatrick, John C. *The Writings of George Washington*. Washington, 1931.

Fortescue, J. W. *A History of the British Army*. London, 1899.

Fox Bourne, R. H. *English Newspapers.* London, 1887.
Franklin, Benjamin. *Autobiography.* Edited by Frank Woodworth Pine, New York, 1916.
Genest, The Rev. John. *Some Account of The English Stage.* London, 1832.
Gibbs, Vicary. *The Complete Peerage of England, Scotland, Ireland, Great Britain and United Kingdom.* London, 1913.
Gipson, Lawrence Henry. *The Great War for the Empire: The Years of Defeat. (The British Empire before the American Revolution.)* New York, 1956.
———. *Lewis Evans.* Philadelphia, 1939.
Goldsmith, Oliver. *The Life of Beau Nash.* Bath, 1762.
———. *Works.* New York, 1908.
Green, John Richard. *A Short History of the English People.* New York, N.D.
Green, Mowbray A. *The Eighteenth Century Architecture of Bath.* Bath, 1904.
Greene, Katherine Glass. *Winchester, Virginia, and its Beginnings.* Strasburg, 1926.
Gumble, Thomas. *The Life of General Monk.* London, 1671.
Gwathmey, Edward M. *John Pendleton Kennedy.* New York, 1931.
Hadden, James. *Washington's Expeditions (1753–54) and Braddock's Expedition.* Uniontown, 1910.
Haile, Martin. *Queen Mary of Modena.* London, 1905.
Hamilton, Anthony. *Memoirs of Count Grammont.* Edinburgh, 1908.
Hamilton, F. W. *The Origin and History of the First or Grenadier Guards.* London, 1874.
Hamilton, Stanislaus M. *Letters to Washington.* New York, 1898.
Harper, Charles G. *The Bath Road.* London, 1899.
Hayes, Carlton J. *A Political and Social History of Modern Europe.* New York, 1921.
Hervey, Lord. *Memoirs.* London, 1951.
Historical Record of the Sixth or Royal Warwickshire Regiment of Foot. London, 1839.
Historical Record of the Forty-Fourth Regiment.
History of Fayette County, Pennsylvania. Edited by Franklin Ellis, Philadelphia, 1882.
Hitchcock, Robert. *An Historical View of the Irish Stage.* Dublin, 1787.
Hooke, Nathaniel. *An Account of the Conduct of The Dowager Duchess of Marlborough.* London, 1742.
Hopkins, Mary Alden. *Dr. Johnson's Lichfield.* New York, 1952.
Hughes, Rupert. *George Washington.* New York, 1926.
Hulbert, Archer Butler. *Braddock's Road* ("Historic Highways of America" iv). Cleveland, 1903.
Ibbetson, Laporte and J. Hassell. *A Picturesque Guide to Bath, Bristol, Hot Wells.* London, 1793.
Ilchester, Earl of. *Lord Hervey and His Friends.* London, 1950.

Irving, Washington. *Life of George Washington*. New York, 1883.

Irving, William Henry. *John Gay*. Durham, 1940.

Jackson, Eugene B. *The Romance of Historic Alexandria*. Alexandria, 1923.

James, Charles. *A New and Enlarged Military Dictionary*. London, 1802.

James, Thomas. *History of the Herculean Straits*. London, 1771.

Jerrold, Walter and Clare. *Five Queer Women*. London, 1929.

Jesse, John Heneage. *Continuation of the Memoirs of the Court of England*. Philadelphia, 1840.

———. *Memoirs of the Pretenders and their Adherents*. London, 1845.

———. *England Under the Stuarts*. London, 1857.

Jones, Louis C. *Clubs of the Georgian Rakes*. New York, 1942.

Kane, John. *List of officers of the Royal Regiment of Artillery from 1716 to the year 1899*. London, 1890.

Kelly, Bernard W. *The Conqueror of Culloden*. London, 1903.

Keppel, Thomas. *The Life of August Viscount Keppel*. London, 1842.

Ketton-Cremer, R. W. *Horace Walpole*. London, 1946.

Klose, Charles Louis. *Memoirs of Prince Charles Stuart*. London, 1846.

Knott, Louis. *Robert Dinwiddie*. Glendale, Cal., 1941.

Lang, Andrew. *Prince Charles Edward Stuart*. London, 1903.

Laver, James. *British Military Uniforms*. London, 1948.

Lawrence, Frederick. *The Life of Henry Fielding*, London, 1855.

Livingston, William. *A Review of Military Operations in North America*. London, 1857.

Lockhart, George. *The Lockhart Papers*. London, 1817.

Lopez de Ayala, Ignacio—*The History of Gibraltar from the Earliest Period of Its Occupation by the Saracens*. Translated from the Spanish with a continuation to modern times by James Bell. London, 1845.

Lowdermilk, Will A. *History of Cumberland*. Washington, 1878.

Luard, John. *History of the Dress of the British Soldier*. London, 1852.

Luttrell, Narcissus. *A Brief Relation of States Affairs from September 1687 to April 1714*. Oxford, 1857.

Macaulay, Thomas Babington. *Critical and Historical Essays*. (Everyman Edition.) London, N.D.

———. *The History of England from the Accession of James II*. (Everyman Edition.) New York, N.D.

MacKinnon, Daniel. *Origin and Services of the Coldstream Guards*. London, 1833.

McSherry, James. *History of Maryland*. Baltimore, 1849.

Melville, Lewis (A. P. Benjamin). *Bath Under Beau Nash*. London, 1907. *Nell Gwynn*. New York, 1924.

Mercer, George. *Papers Relating to the Ohio Company of Virginia*. Compiled and Edited by Lois Mulkearn. University of Pittsburgh Press. Pittsburgh, 1954.

Mereness, Newton D. *Travels in the American Colonies.* New York, 1916.

Michael, Wolfgang. *England Under George I: The Beginnings of the Hanoverian Dynasty.* London, 1936.

Microcosm of London, The. London, 1808–11.

Minto, William. *Daniel Defoe.* New York, 1879.

Molloy, J. Fitzgerald. *Court Life Below Stairs.* London, 1882.

———. *Royalty Restored.* London, 1885.

Moreau, Jacob Nicholas. *Memoire Contenant Le Précis des Faits, Avec Leurs Pieces Justificatives.* Paris, 1756.

Morely, John. *Walpole.* London, 1922.

Moreley, Henry. *The Earlier Life and Chief Works of Daniel Defoe.* London, 1889.

Morris, Constance Lily. *Maria Theresa.* New York, 1937.

Morton, Frederic C. *The Story of Winchester, Virginia.* Strasburg, 1925.

Moses, Montrose J. *British Plays from the Restoration to 1820.* Boston, 1929.

Muller, John. *A Treatise of Artillery.* London, 1780.

Murray, John Fisher. *A Picturesque Tour of the River Thomas.* London, 1845.

Needham, Raymond, *Somerset House Past and Present.* London, N.D.

———, and Alexander Webster. *Somerset House, Past and Present.* New York, N.D.

Old Cheque Book of the Chapel Royal from 1561 to 1744. Edited by Edward F. Rimbault. London, 1872.

Otway, Thomas. *Works.* Edited by Thomas Thorton. London, 1815.

Pargellis, Stanley. *Military Affairs in North America 1748–1765.* New York, 1936.

Parkman, Francis. *Montcalm and Wolfe.* (Everyman's Edition.) London, N.D.

Parkin, Charles. *History of Norfolk.* London, 1809.

Parton, James. *Life and Times of Benjamin Franklin.* Boston, 1867.

Pepys, Samuel. *Diary.* London, 1892.

Petrie, Charles. *The Stuarts.* New York, 1937.

Philip, Robert. *The Life, Times and Characteristics of John Bunyan.* London, 1839.

Pope, W. J. Macqueen. *Theatre Royal Drury Lane.* London, 1945.

Powell, Mary G. *History of Old Alexandria, Va.* Richmond, 1928.

Quennell, Peter. *Caroline of England.* New York, 1940.

Richmond, H. W. *Papers Relative to the Loss of Minorca.* Publications of the Navy Record Society, Vol. xlii. London, 1913.

Rider's British Merlin. London, 1755.

Ripley, Thomas. *The Plans, Elevations and Sections, Etc., of Houghton.* London, 1740.

Ritenour, John. *Old Tom Fossit.* Pittsburgh, 1936.

Roberts, Cecil. *And So to Bath.* London, 1940.

Roscoe, E. S. *Robert Harley, Earl of Oxford.* London, 1902.

Sargent, Winthrop. *History of an Expedition to Fort Duquesne.* Philadelphia, 1856.

Sayer, Captain Frederick. *The History of Gibraltar.* London, 1862.

Scott, W. S. *The Georgian Theatre.* London, 1946.

Scott, Walter. *Memoirs of Johnathan Swift* (Swift's Works.) Edinburgh, 1814.

Secret Memoirs and Manners of Several Persons of Quality. London, 1709.

Serious Advice to the Inhabitants of the Northern Colonies on the Present Situation. New York, 1755.

Shadwell, Thomas. *Works.* Edited by Montague Summers. London, 1927.

Shea, Jean Marie. *Relations Diverses sur la Bataille du Malanguele.* New York, 1860.

Shebbeare, John. *A Letter to the People of England.* London, 1755.

Sheppard, Edgar. *Memorials of St. James Palace.* London, 1894.

———. *The Old Royal Palace at Whitehall.*

Sherwin, Oscar. *Mr. Gay.* New York, 1929.

Shirley, William. *Correspondence of.* Edited by Charles Henry Lincoln. New York, 1912.

Sidney, William Connor. *England and the English in the Eighteenth Century.* New York, 1891.

Skrine, Francis Henry. *Fontenoy.* London, 1906.

Smith, W. H. *The Sailor's Word Book.* London, 186 f.

Smollett, Tobias. *The History of England.* London, 1804.

———. Roderick Random. London, 1951.

Southey, Robert. *Journal of a Tour in the Netherlands in the Year 1815.* New York, 1902.

Sparks, Jared. *The Life of George Washington.* Boston, 1849.

Steele, Richard. *Grief A La Mode.* London, 1735.

———. *Mr. Steele's Apology for Himself and His Writings.* London, 1714.

———. *Poetical Miscellanies.* London, 1727.

Sterne, Lawrence. *The Life and Opinions of Tristram Shandy, Gentlemen.* (Modern Library.) New York, 1950.

Stevenson, Henry N. *Lewis Evans.* London, 1920.

Stuart, Dorothy Margaret. *The English Abigail.* London, 1946.

Suffolk, Countess of. *Letters.* London, 1824.

Sullivan, James. *The Papers of Sir William Johnson.* Albany, 1921.

Swift, Jonathan. *Journal to Stella.* Edited by Harold Williams. Oxford, 1948.

———. *The Public Spirit of the Whigs.* London, 1714.

———. *Works.* Edinburgh, 1814.

Thackeray, William Makepiece. *The Virginians.* London, 1884.

Thickness, Philip. *A Year's Journey through the Pais Bas.* London, 1786.

Thomas, James W. (With T. J. C. Williams.) *History of Allegany County Maryland.* Cumberland, 1923.

Thompson, Mrs. K. B. *Memoirs of the Court and Times of George II.* London, 1850.

Toland, John. *The Art of Restoring.* London, 1714.

Toynbee, Mrs. Paget. *The Letters of Horace Walpole.* Oxford, 1903.

Traill, H. D. *Social England.* London, 1909.

Trevelyan, G. M. *English Social History.* London, 1946.

———. *England Under Queen Anne.* New York, 1930–34.

Thwaites, Reuben Gold. *Daniel Boone.* New York, 1903.

Van Doren, Carl. *Benjamin Franklin.* New York, 1938.

Virginia: A Guide to the Old Dominion. (American Guide Series.) New York, 1940.

Walpole, Horatio. *A Catalogue of Royal and Noble Authors of England, Scotland and Wales.* London, 1806.

Walpole Horace. *Letters of.* Edited by Mrs. Paget Toynbee. Oxford, 1903.

———. *Memoirs of George II.* London, 1847.

Waugh, W. T. *James Wolfe, Man and Soldier.* New York, 1928.

Webster, Alexander, and Raymond Needham. *Somerset House, Past and Present.* New York, N.D.

Welch, Joseph. *A List of Scholars at St. Peter's College, Westminster.* London, 1788.

Wheatley, H. B. *Hogarth's London.* New York, 1909.

Wesley, John. *Journals.* Everyman's Library. New York and London, N.D.

West, Willis Mason. *American History and Government.* New York, 1913.

Whitely, J. H. *Wesley's England.* London, 1938.

Whitworth, Charles. *The Succession of Parliaments.* London, 1764.

Williams, T. J. C. *History of Frederick County, Maryland.* Baltimore, 1915.

———. *History of Western Maryland.* Baltimore; (With James W. Thomas) *History of Allegany County, Maryland.* Cumberland, 1923.

Willson, Beckles. *The Life and Letters of James Wolfe.* London, 1909.

Wilkinson, Clennell. *Bonnie Prince Charlie.* Philadelphia, 1940.

Withers, Alexander Scott. *Chronicles of Border Warfare.* Clarksburg, 1831.

Wood, George Arthur. *William Shirley, Governor of Massachusetts.* New York, 1920.

Wood, John. *An Essay Towards a Description of Bath.* London, 1749.

Wyon, Frederick William. *The History of Great Britain During the Reign of Queen Anne.* London, 1876.

Wyndham, H. Saxe. *Annals of Covent Garden Theatre.* London, 1906.

INDEX